Indonesia–Malaysia Relations

Drawing on social media, cinema, cultural heritage and public opinion polls, this book examines Indonesia and Malaysia from a comparative postcolonial perspective. The Indonesia–Malaysia relationship is one of the most important bilateral relationships in Southeast Asia, especially because Indonesia, the world's fourth most populous country and third largest democracy, is the most populous and powerful nation in the region. Both states are committed to the relationship, especially at the highest levels of government, and much has been made of their 'sibling' identity. The relationship is built on years of interaction at all levels of state and society, and both countries draw on their common culture, religion and language in managing political tensions. In recent years, however, several issues have seriously strained the once cordial bilateral relationship. Among these are a strong public reaction to maritime boundary disputes, claims over each country's cultural forms, the treatment of Indonesian workers in Malaysia, and trans-border issues such as Indonesian forest fire haze. Comparing the two nations' engagement with cultural heritage, religion, gender, ethnicity, citizenship, democracy and regionalism, this book highlights the social and historical roots of the tensions between Indonesia and Malaysia, as well as the enduring sense of kinship.

Marshall Clark is Director of the Australian National Internships Program and a Senior Lecturer at the School of Politics and International Relations at the Australian National University. He is the author of *Maskulinitas: Culture, Gender and Politics in Indonesia* (Monash University Press, 2010).

Juliet Pietsch is a Senior Lecturer of Political Science at the School of Politics and International Relations at the Australian National University. Juliet is a Principal Investigator of the Australian Election Study, the World Values Survey and the National Asian Australian Survey.

Media, Culture and Social Change in Asia

Series Editor
Stephanie Hemelryk Donald, University of New South Wales

The aim of this series is to publish original, high-quality work by both new and established scholars in the West and the East, on all aspects of media, culture and social change in Asia.

Indonesia–Malaysia Relations

Cultural heritage, politics and labour migration

Marshall Clark and Juliet Pietsch

Routledge
Taylor & Francis Group

LONDON AND NEW YORK

First published 2014
by Routledge
2 Park Square, Milton Park, Abingdon, Oxfordshire OX14 4RN

and by Routledge
711 Third Avenue, New York, NY 10017

First issued in paperback 2016

Routledge is an imprint of the Taylor & Francis Group, an informa business

British Library Cataloguing in Publication Data
A catalogue record for this book is available from the British Library

Library of Congress Cataloging in Publication Data
Clark, Marshall Alexander, author.
  Indonesia-Malaysia relations : cultural heritage, politics and labour
migration / Marshall Clark and Juliet Pietsch.
    pages cm -- (Media, culture and social change in Asia ; 37)
  Includes bibliographical references and index.
  Summary: "Examines the international relations of Southeast Asia,
focusing on how these are affected by the special Indonesia-Malaysia
bilateral relationship - Malaysia and Indonesia, although separate states,
can be seen as constituting a single Indo-Malay cultural world"-- Provided
by publisher.
  1. Indonesia--Relations--Malaysia. 2. Malaysia--Relations--Indonesia.
3. Malay Archipelago--Civilization. I. Pietsch, Juliet, author. II. Title.
  DS640.M34C55 2014
  303.48'25950598–dc23
    2013033537

ISBN 13: 978-0-415-78801-4 (pbk)
ISBN 13: 978-0-415-68752-2 (hbk)

Typeset in Times New Roman
by Taylor & Francis Books

For Don – 'terima kasih'

Contents

List of Illustrations

Tables

Acknowledgements

It is not often that one can pinpoint the period in which a seed of an idea transforms, chrysalis-like, into a tangible product, such as the present book. In this case, we can. The beating heart of this book took its shape and form during the Spring semester of 2010, when we were based at the Southeast Asia Forum (SEAF) at Stanford University in the United States. Here, under the attentive eye of our affable host, Prof Donald K. Emmerson, best known simply as 'Don', we were able to enjoy the intellectual company of a number of scholars working on Southeast Asia at Stanford. There were six visiting scholars in all – apart from us, there was James B. Hoesterey, Christian von Luebke, Sudarno Sumarto and Thitinan Pongsudhirak. Each of us shared our findings and thoughts on Southeast Asia in talks hosted by SEAF, and we also enjoyed the rare opportunity to read each other's work in progress and share ideas as to how it might be improved in a weekly seminar series. As Don has described it in his annual report of 2009/2010, 'These conversations gave specific, heuristic, and collegial meaning to the abstract notion of "a community of scholars."' For our part, this book is the fruition of this process. It is for this reason why this book is dedicated to Don who – there are no two ways about it – was a superb host at Stanford, nurturing and challenging us intellectually. We are proud to say that we also managed to experience some of the best of what San Francisco and indeed California has to offer, including more baseball matches and Mexican meals than a couple of Australians could have ever predicted or hoped for. We also thank SEAF's Lisa Lee for accommodating our visit and finding us an office at Stanford, which is no mean feat.

An underrated element of Stanford University is its proximity to the University of California, Berkeley. Here, we were able to share our relatively unpolished ideas and arguments with a visiting scholar there, Douglas Webber, and his hosts and colleagues at UC Berkeley's Department of Political Science, including Vinod K. Aggarwal and T.J. Pempel. We thank each of them for their good-natured, yet uncompromising, input. We also warmly thank Neil Fligstein and Sarah Maxim for fruitful discussions there.

It was only after our American sojourn that we were able to make a series of fieldwork trips to Indonesia, Singapore and Malaysia, allowing the research project to pick up momentum. These trips were not our first to the region, of course, as we had both been learning some of the languages employed in maritime Southeast Asia, including Indonesian, Javanese and Chinese, since the mid-1980s. The resulting book has been enhanced by the friendships and insights of a number of Malaysians and Singaporeans, sometimes stretching back several decades. For this reason we thank Rizal Mohamed Ali, Freddy Wong, Mohinder Manocha, Gregore Lopez, Zan Azlee, Elyna Shukri, Mohd Anis Md Nor, Ismail Samsudin, Syed Muhd Khairudin Aljunied, Razif Bahari, Romzi Ationg, and Mhd Nasir Ibrahim. In the few years devoted to writing this book, we have been encouraged by the enthusiasm of a number of Indonesian friends and colleagues, many of whom have displayed a deeply personal interest in our project, gently moulding and improving our arguments and conclusions. In this regard, we owe a special debt of gratitude to Eko Nugroho Mardi Saputro. We also thank Yasmi Adriansyah, Stella Kumala Susilo, Ambo Tuwo, Asbir Tin Biru, Ilham Qadir Palimai, Dafri Agussalim, Lukas Gunawan, Ristian Atriandi Supriyanto, Badrus Sholeh, Cakti Indra Gunawan, Cut Dewi, Erna Wati, Jajang C. Noer and Garin Nugroho.

The School of International and Political Studies, Deakin University, and the College of Arts and Social Sciences, ANU, have provided funds to support the research and travel needed for this book. In this supportive context, we have been inspired by the collegiality and scholarly insights of Sven Schottmann, Daniel Novotny, Amarjit Kaur, Baogang He, Joost Coté, Andy Fuller, Philomena Murray, Harold Crouch, Christine Campbell, Wendy Mukherjee, Dirk Tomsa, Ed Aspinall, John Funston, Anthony Reid, Virginia Matheson Hooker, Timo Kaartinen, Sverre Molland, Tracy Ireland, Ken Taylor, Stephen Foster, David Williams, Caroline Turner, Sharon Peoples, Sally K. May, Sandy Blair, Charlotte Galloway, Melanie Eastburn, Christine Clark, Michelle Antoinette, Takashi Inoguchi, Doh Chull Shin and Amitav Acharya. Harry Aveling, Campbell Macknight, Marcus Meitzner, James B. Hoesterey, Fitrian Ardiansyah, and, especially, Raimy Ché-Ross provided helpful advice on early drafts of a number of the chapters appearing here. Any remaining errors or shortcomings, of course, are entirely our own fault.

We thank those who have given us the opportunity to present some of this material elsewhere: Hatta Azad Khan at Universiti Teknologi Mara (UiTM), Lily Zubaidah Rahim at the University of Sydney, Minako Sakai at the University of New South Wales (ADFA), Julian Millie at Monash University, Douglas Webber and Sarah Maxim at University of California (Berkeley), and Gauri Parimoo Krishnan at the Asian Civilisations Museum, Singapore. Students of the ANU liberal arts course, 'Museums, Art and Society in the Asia-Pacific', are recognised here for their many valuable comments and discussions on the general theme of museums and cultural heritage in Southeast Asia. We especially thank Rachel Salmond, who proof-read the manuscript from beginning to end, providing us with many valuable comments and suggestions.

Sections of this book are revised versions of previously published material. Parts of Chapter 1 and 8 use material from 'Indonesia's postcolonial regional imaginary: from a "neutralist" to an "all-directions" foreign policy', *Japanese Journal of Political Science*, 12(2): 287–304, 2011, and are reprinted with permission. Chapter 2 draws from a previously published chapter, 'The *Ramayana* in Southeast Asia: Fostering Regionalism or the State?', in Gauri Parimoo Krishnan (ed.) *Ramayana in Focus: Visual and Performing Arts of Asia* (Singapore: Asian Civilisations Museum, 2010). A revised version of Chapter 3 appears as 'The politics of heritage: Indonesia-Malaysia cultural contestations', *Indonesia and the Malay World*, 41(121), 2013. An early version of Chapter 4 appears as 'Tangible heritage of the Macassan–Aboriginal encounter in contemporary South Sulawesi' in Marshall Clark and Sally K. May (eds) *Macassan History and Heritage: Journeys, Encounters and Influences* (Canberra: ANU E-Press, 2013). A portion of Chapter 5, co-authored with James B. Hoesterey, appeared in '*Film Islami*: Gender, Piety, and Pop Culture in Post-authoritarian Indonesia', *Asian Studies Review*, 36(2), 2012, and is reprinted with permission.

Introduction

Indonesia's relationship with Malaysia is rarely straightforward, never more so than during the brief period in Indonesia's history dominated by the so-called 'Manodrama'. In June 2009, an Indonesian–American teenage model by the name of Manohara Odelia Pinot caused a bilateral kerfuffle – one of many between neighbouring Indonesia and Malaysia – when she said that her husband, a Malaysian prince, had slashed her with razor blades, locked her up and used her as a sex slave during their year-long marriage. Manohara's husband, Prince Fakhry, the brother of the present Sultan of Kelantan, promptly filed a police report against Manohara. He stated that she was making false allegations. Meanwhile, accompanied by her mother, Daisy Fajarina, Manohara publicly accused her husband of kidnapping, sexual abuse and torture. Adding to the public interest, Manohara was only able to make her statement after a dramatic midnight escape to Jakarta from a luxury hotel in Singapore, where she had been visiting her ill father-in-law who, at the time, was the Sultan of Kelantan. Manohara's desperate bid for freedom, in which she was assisted by local police and officials from the United States embassy, involved a confrontation in the hotel elevator, where royal minders armed with tranquilisers tried to stop her from fleeing. According to media reports, as Manohara was escorted by her bodyguards down from the 13th floor suite of Singapore's Royal Plaza Hotel, she repeatedly pressed the lift's emergency button, summoning Singaporean police, who took her to a room on another floor. In Manohara's words, 'the police told Fakhry that he would be held in jail if he did not let me go. No one could force me against my will in Singapore and I knew I had a chance of escape' (MacKinnon 2009). At one stage, there was even a tug-of-war between the Singaporean police and the royal bodyguards, with the lift door opening and closing against Manohara, who was being dragged in both directions. The Singaporean police eventually won out, managing to pull Manohara free and, as the lift doors slammed shut, the bodyguards were heard angrily thumping the doors from the inside. With further assistance from local authorities, Manohara was met at Singapore's international airport by her mother and her stepsister who accompanied her on a flight back to Jakarta.

Shortly afterwards Manohara appeared at a media conference, dressed in military clothing. The media conference was organised by a paramilitary group called Laskar Merah Putih (Red and White Force). This Jakarta-based organisation has a track record of stirring up anti-Malaysia sentiment and, playing up the 'damsel in distress' narrative, the media story of Manohara and Prince Fakhry was perfect for their latest episode of chauvinistic chest-beating (Fitzpatrick 2009). The fact that Manohara is Indonesian–American added to her appeal in the media; many Indonesian actresses, beauty contestants and celebrities are of mixed ethnic background.[1] Adding to her cultural cachet, Manohara was named by *Harper's Bazaar* magazine as 'one of Indonesia's 100 precious women', and rumour has it that she had been a girlfriend of society heir Adindra Bakrie, the playboy son of an Indonesia entrepreneur and politician, Aburizal Bakrie. It was, however, her underage marriage to a Malaysian prince and the unraveling of the marriage that attracted the considerable interest of the Indonesian popular media.

Manohara first met Fakhry at a function at the Jakarta residence of Malaysia's then Deputy Prime Minister, Najib Razak. According to Manohara's stepsister, Dewi Sari Asih, when they first met the Prince, he seemed like a nice man, 'gentleman, smart, well intention [sic]' (Putra Raja Kelantan Culik 2009). Manohara's mother was also glowing in her early assessments of Fakhry's character, describing him as polite, well mannered and pious (Setiyaji 2009: 123). At the time, December 2006, Manohara was barely 15 years old. In the following months, each time Fakhry visited Jakarta he kept in touch with Manohara and the friendship gradually developed into a romantic relationship. Before her 17th birthday, Manohara married Prince Fakhry in Kelantan in August 2008 and the couple resided in one of the many royal palaces dotted around Kota Baru, the capital of Kelantan. From late 2008 onwards, however, rumours emerged suggesting that all was not well with Manohara's marriage. The rumours were sparked by reports that Manohara had fled from the confines of Kelantan's royal family in December 2008. Reports (for example, Putra Raja Kelantan Culik 2009) suggest that Prince Fakhry repeatedly tried to entice Manohara back to Malaysia, but to no avail. Convinced that all was not well with her daughter's marriage, Daisy Fajarina regularly talked to Indonesia's gossip-hungry media. She too came under fire from some commentators, who felt that she was the fly in the ointment, rather than Fakhry, and was frequently stereotyped in the media as a gold-digger who had auctioned off her daughter to the highest bidder. Despite Daisy's concerns about her daughter's welfare, Manohara returned to Malaysia in early 2009. Soon after, Daisy and Manohara's stepsister were formally invited to accompany Manohara and Fakhry on a pilgrimage to Mecca. According to Daisy Fajarina, 'we were courteously invited by the Tengku [Fakhry]. They said, we should all forgive each other and this issue should be laid to rest properly in front of the Ka'bah. I felt that to reject such a well-intentioned invitation would be sinful'.[2] In Mecca, Fakhry promised to renew his wedding vows in Indonesia, so that Manohara's extended family could attend. But after completing the pilgrimage, Manohara flew back to Malaysia in the royal family's private jet, whereas Daisy Fajarina was literally abandoned on the runway and had to find her own way home on a commercial flight. It was alleged that after her return to Malaysia Manohara was subjected to a long period of sexual violence and torture at the hands of her husband (Fitzpatrick 2009).

In May 2009 a colourful demonstration was held outside the Malaysian embassy in Jakarta. Organised by the aforementioned Laskar Merah Putih paramilitary group, it was intended to publicise Manohara's fate and was addressed by Manohara's mother. According to Daisy Fajarina, Manohara was being held in Malaysia against her will and was no longer allowed to communicate with her family in Indonesia. Manohara's mother eventually met the Malaysian ambassador for an hour and was assured that her desire to meet with Manohara would be conveyed to the Kelantan royal family. Outside the embassy gates, the Laskar Merah Putih throng were less diplomatic. They called for Manohara's return to Indonesia and threatened to conduct sweepings of Malaysian businesses in Indonesia and forcibly repatriate Malaysian citizens if she was prevented from returning. Indeed, the Indonesian media did report that there were sweepings elsewhere in Jakarta. Outside the Malaysian embassy one of the demonstrators held aloft a white chicken in a cage, which was said to represent Manohara. Later, the chicken was unceremoniously thrown up against the Malaysian coat-of-arms on the embassy gates in another symbolic gesture.

Most Indonesian demonstrations are characterised by large, professionally made posters. For this demonstration half a dozen large posters were constructed, including one depicting Prince Fakhry as a blood-sucking vampire. Another poster, which Manohara's mother held at one stage, was inscribed with a somewhat abrasive poem. The poem was entitled 'Puisi Untuk Manohara' (A Poem for Manohara). The English translation is as follows:

> Neighbour, oh neighbour.
> How can you brazenly do this !!!
> You steal all that is mine !!
> Do you not remember our past friendship ?
> Why are you so brazen, my love ?
> I let you steal my Reog Ponorogo !!
> I let you steal my slogans !!
> I let you steal my borders !!
> So then now, why are you stealing my Manohara ?
> Are you not content with everything you stole from me, Malay-burglar-sia ?[3]

Narrated to represent the point of view of the Indonesian nation, the poem was addressed to Malaysia. Mindful of the fact that the two nations are neighbours, the poem starts out reasonably enough. However, as a number of issues leading to recent tensions between the two nations are listed, an accusatory tone soon emerges. The issues include well-worn ones, such as territorial disputes, as well as more recent disputes, such as the unauthorised inclusion of a clip of an East Javanese dance, the Reog Ponorogo, in a Malaysian tourism campaign. The most recent insult mentioned in the poem, the 'stealing' of Manohara, appears to be one provocation too many, which may explain the final line's reference to Malaysia as 'Malingsia', a neologism combining two words: Malaysia and *maling* (burglar). The use of this deliberately provocative term and the undeniably angry tone of the poem are, it must be said, not isolated incidents. In recent years, anti-Malaysia sentiment has been spreading, especially on the Internet, where it is quite evident that Indonesians appear to be losing patience with the cavalier attitude of their nearest and dearest neighbour. Many posts are as creative as they are offensive. The following translation is of a post by Omen in 2008, which is typical of the genre:

> Malayria: *Malayria* is a dangerous strain of contagious disease where less than 22 million people in the region of the Fed-sex-eration[4] of Malaya have been infected, with difficulty in finding a cure, let alone ordering them to repent. *Malayria* is caused by the Protonsaga[5] parasite (the Malay for 'Protozoa'), which is usually found in a muddy location, best known as Kuala Lumpur [translatable as 'muddy river mouth']. Symptoms of this *malayria* disease include the development of an overblown sense of confidence; racism; a desire to torture and rape Indonesian migrant workers; illegal logging; stealing islands; and stealing their neighbour's culture as well as claiming it. This *malayria* disease is usually immune from criticism and also demonstrations, because *malayria* has long muffled press freedom. This disease is terrifying. Be on full alert![6]

In response to the ever-expanding flood of Indonesian cyber-vitriol, some Malaysians have responded in kind, using similarly questionable humour. To take just a few examples at random from Malaysia's largest online community, lowyat.net, comments such as the following are typical: 'Indon'; 'Well then, stop coming our country to find a job'; 'They got nothing better to do, since they can't travel to Europe due to the ban imposed on Garuda Airlines'; 'they have mental problem, nuff said'; 'indon are nothing, they are just bunch of crap that have nothing to do'; 'without malingsia, indon are as good as dead' (again, that Hate Malingsia group in Facebook 2009). Among Malay-speaking Malaysians, '*dasar Indon*' (bloody Indons) is the most popular cyber-put-down.

Another poster at the Manohara rally, also professionally made, is interesting for another reason. It makes an explicit link between Manohara and one of Indonesia's most prominent mythological prototypes, Srikandi. Srikandi is a well-known woman-warrior of the *Mahabharata* cycle of tales, which is regularly performed in the Javanese *wayang* shadow puppet theatre. Manohara is likened to Srikandi. The paramilitary thugs holding the poster appeared serious in their call to the President:

My President SBY !!!
Form a team of state lawyers
Rescue Indonesia's Srikandi
Manohara !!![7]

Manohara's links with another mythological character of Java, Princess Manohara, were to emerge not long afterwards. Popularised by several reliefs on the second level of the western wall of the magnificent Borobudur temple of Central Java, the legendary Manohara is a beautiful maiden, half-woman and half-bird (although the Manohara reliefs at Borobudur picture her as all-woman). The full blow-by-blow details of the Manohara legend were described in several 2009 newspaper articles. The author of Manohara's unauthorised biography (Setiyaji 2009) even went so far as to suggest that 'our' Mano resembles the beautiful Manohara inscribed on the Borobudur reliefs. One particularly thorough tabloid exposé, whose author is not identified, outlined the parallels between the mythological Manohara, who can fly, and the real-life jetsetting Manohara ('Manohara dan Fakhry' 2009). In this report, each Manohara is married to a prince for a time and both marriages encounter trials and tribulations in a foreign land. According to John Miksic (1990: 77), the series of Borobudur reliefs depicting Manohara appear to be based on a text called the *Divyavadana*, in which the mythical Manohara and her prince, Sudhana, return to their home kingdom of Pancala where the prince is enthroned as a king and they live long and happy lives, and are always kind and generous to their subjects (Miksic and Tranchini 1990: 81).

The most prominent banner of the May 2009 demonstration is written, in red lettering on a white background, from Manohara's perspective. It is a jingoistic rallying cry, a call-for-arms: 'Bersatu Bangsaku: Ganyang Malaysia [Be United, My Nation: Crush Malaysia]'. It refers to Sukarno's anti-Malaysia vitriol of the *Konfrontasi* (Confrontation) era (1963–65), epitomised by the ubiquitous '*Ganyang Malaysia*' rallying cry. In the current era the use of a large '*Ganyang Malaysia*' banner might seem excessive, especially in the context of a demonstration calling for a reunion between a mother and her married daughter. Nevertheless, rumblings over Manohara had been brewing for several months before the demonstration and, as mentioned above, Daisy Fajarina had already made several public statements about her daughter's ill treatment. It was also reported that Daisy Fajarina had been blacklisted without explanation from travelling to Malaysia (Budianto 2009). She was denied entry into Kuala Lumpur in March 2009, for instance, and forced to return back to Jakarta the same day.

By the end of June 2009, at the height of what was pejoratively referred to as the 'Manodrama', Manohara and her mother had been interviewed on numerous talk shows and celebrity infotainment programmes. Travelling overland between Denpasar, Yogyakarta, Bandung and Jakarta at the time, it was difficult for us not to notice. We saw many television interviews and press conferences featuring a tearful Manohara. However, during our travels in

Malaysia in the following month, we noticed little media interest in the story. According to Khalid and Yacob (2012: 372), Malaysians were sceptical about Manohara's allegations. In Indonesia the media frenzy had also provoked a great deal of scepticism, as well as cynicism.

Despite cynicism from the general public, journalists and bloggers alike, Manohara's legal team lodged a written report with the Indonesian police detailing the alleged abuse. Malaysian authorities were reluctant to pursue Manohara's claims, as she was no longer residing in Malaysia. The Kelantan palace issued a statement on 3 June 2009, stating that the Manohara issue was a personal matter, which should be resolved according to the law. Fakhry lodged a police report in the Malaysian capital Kuala Lumpur, denying that he had raped and tortured his wife. 'We will be contemplating legal action with regard to the false allegation,' said Fakhry's lawyer, Mohamad Haaziq Pillay (Malaysian Royal Denies Abuse 2009). The police report was, however, referred to the Kelantan police. 'The investigations will be transferred to the Kubang Kerian police station in Kelantan as the incident was alleged to have occurred there and comes under the jurisdiction of the police there', said Kuala Lumpur District Police Chief, Zulkarnain Abdul Rahman (Malaysian Royal Denies Abuse 2009).

In Malaysia, reports emerged presenting Prince Fakhry's side of the story, and almost a year later he won a defamation suit against his teenage wife (Malaysian Prince Wins 2010). During this period Malaysian media reports also highlighted the criminal past of Manohara's mother, who, they alleged, faced a jail sentence in France for her involvement in a sexual assault.[8] Malaysia's Deputy Prime Minister, Muhyiddin Yassin, said that the government would not investigate the matter, adding 'I think this is more of a personal matter' (MacKinnon 2009). Also seeking to downplay the affair, Malaysia's Home Minister, Datuk Seri Hishammuddin Hussein, said that the issue was a personal affair, in which one party, moreover, was not a Malaysian citizen. He expressed the hope that the Manohara issue, 'sensationalised' by the Indonesian media, would not tarnish relations between Malaysia and Indonesia. 'This is where I think (foreign media) should be more responsible' (Hishammuddin Hopes 2009). The Malaysian ambassador to Indonesia at the time, Datu Zainal Abidin Mahama Zain, also criticised the Indonesian news media for their negative coverage of the abuse of Indonesians in Malaysia. 'Violence doesn't only happen in Malaysia, but also in Indonesia, Saudi Arabia and other countries', he said; 'The Malaysian government did not want anyone, including Indonesian workers, to undergo abuse. Please don't portray us as bad people. Fifty percent of prisoners in Malaysia are Indonesians, why do we never hear about this in the news?' (Malaysian Ambassador Asks 2009).

Tit for tat, several Indonesian politicians insisted that the Manohara case was much more than a domestic issue. According to Yusron Ihza Mahendra, a member of the House of Representatives, 'We need to improve our embassies' performance to protect Indonesian citizens abroad. Manohara is only one case. If we look at past records, we see embassies were slow in protecting citizens'

(Hermawan 2009). He was referring to a number of cases in which Indonesians, particularly migrant workers, were physically abused in Malaysia. He added that the House would summon the Foreign Ministry to seek clarification on Manohara's criticisms of the Indonesian embassy in Kuala Lumpur, which, according to the media, turned a blind eye to Manohara's case. 'We're going to ask them about our embassies' performance,' he said (Hermawan 2009).[9] Finally, Indonesian President Susilo Bambang Yudhoyono (SBY) had a few hard-hitting words to say about Manohara and the other simmering bilateral issue at the time, the Ambalat territorial dispute off the coast of Kalimantan. In relation to Ambalat, the President merely echoed the latest eruption of nationalist sentiment in the public and the legislature to restate the government's nationalist position, making it adamantly clear that Indonesia would on no account cede Indonesian territory. On the Manohara case, the President made a public statement expressing his sympathy for Manohara's case, reporting the fact that he had discussed the issue with the Malaysian Ambassador to Indonesia in May 2009 (Aswadi and Osman, 2009). For a brief period, Manohara's 'Manodrama' seemed to preoccupy all levels of Indonesian society, from the gutter press to the presidential palace.

The 'Manodrama' as metaphor

The Manohara affair is deeply revealing and, like any bilateral kerfuffle, should not be viewed in isolation. For one thing, it tells us a great deal about contemporary Indonesian cultural and political mores. It demonstrates the political power of Indonesia's liberalised media, unfettered since the fall of Suharto. It also highlights the fundamental fragility and complexity of Indonesia–Malaysia relations and the differences in how Indonesia and Malaysia approach a very personal yet politicised issue. In our opinion, the Manohara case demonstrates the need to examine how these two countries often share, but also contest, many issues relating to culture, politics and migration. Although the Manohara affair may seem trivial and was heavily sensationalised in the Indonesian media, it perhaps highlights at a political level the latest eruption of Indonesian nationalist sentiment, in a long line of many such eruptions, beginning with Sukarno's *Konfrontasi*-era patriotism. SBY's presidential interjection noted in the paragraph above, which presents a thinly veiled warning to Indonesia's nearest neighbours, supports this particular interpretation. The politicisation of personal scandals involving individuals from Indonesia and Malaysia in domestic political discourse cannot be ignored, especially as SBY's comments were delivered in the middle of an election campaign.

In terms of migration, the Manohara affair highlights broader concerns about the treatment of Indonesian migrants in Malaysia. Indonesian migrant workers are particularly poorly treated in Malaysia. Numerous media headlines tell of Indonesian workers being sacked, deported and even returned deceased in a body bag, often without justice being served. Manohara's experience in

Malaysia may be extreme in some ways, but, in general terms, her fate is not uncommon or unexpected, as many Indonesian workers have fallen foul of Malaysia's local and state authorities. As the number of Indonesian workers seeking employment overseas rapidly increases, the calls for enhanced migrant worker protection in the guise of improved civil and human rights are becoming increasingly strident. Consequently, Manohara's poor treatment is of genuine interest to many Indonesian citizens, particularly to poorer Indonesians who often regard labour migration as a legitimate means of raising themselves out of poverty. The underlying banality of the story was given a 'revolutionary' slant by the fact that Manohara stood up for herself and escaped her unfortunate situation. In addition to this, the creation of a mythological sub-narrative with links to Borobudur – one of the world's finest examples of Hindu–Buddhist architecture and Indonesia's single most visited tourist attraction – provided a mythopoeic layer to the media frenzy. Although the Manohara affair was highly sensationalised as a result of the widespread media attention it attracted in Indonesia, it revealed much about anxieties associated with the ongoing construction of Indonesia's national identity.

With the vague linkages to Indonesia's precolonial history, the emotive nature of the Manohara affair can also be understood in terms of the politics of cultural heritage, especially in the pressure-cooker context of the Indo-Malay world. There is no escaping the cultural history of these two nations, where Manohara is but the latest in a long line of princesses or princesses-to-be ferried across the waters to Malaysian royal families. The long history of human movement from the Indonesian archipelago to the Malay peninsula, which has by no means been limited to royalty, means that many present-day Malaysians have deep personal ties with Indonesians, often through direct blood relations. Among them is Malaysian Prime Minister, Najib Razak, who is proud that he can directly trace his ethnic roots to the Bugis royal family of South Sulawesi. More generally, many present-day Malaysians are naturalised immigrants from Indonesia. Consequently, the Indonesia–Malaysia relationship as a whole is very special to both nations and has a great deal of meaning to both parties. Indonesia–Malaysia bilateral brouhahas, therefore, should be examined as a broad comparative exercise, focusing on the deep cultural overlapping of the Malay world, where the imagined postcolonial nation-states of Indonesia and Malaysia are merely components of a much bigger picture. Viewed in this light, the extended examination of a starlet such as Manohara can evoke a great deal. After all, rogue Malay princes and runaway princesses from the Indonesian archipelago have always been an element of what remains a hybrid cultural narrative.

Theoretical approach

Inspired by postcolonial literary theory, we emphasise in this book the broadly hybrid nature of postcolonial Indonesia's relationship with its region and its closest regional neighbour, Malaysia. We compare and contrast the culture and politics of Indonesia and Malaysia, focusing on the transcultural overlaps and the impact of the colonial encounter. By drawing on post-colonial discourse in reference to the cases of Indonesia and Malaysia, this book can be accused of pushing the boundaries somewhat. This is because a straight-down-the-line postcolonial approach, insofar as one exists, would tend to place emphasis on the 'postcoloniality' of subaltern literary expression. Indeed, there are several excellent studies devoted to a postcolonial analysis of modern Indonesian or Malaysian literature, with a particular focus on the novel (for instance, Bahari 2003, 2007; Day and Foulcher 2002; Foulcher 1995, 2008; Hooker 2000; Maier 2004). Considering that the colonial history of both nations and the growth and development of modern Malaysian literature and Indonesian literature, particularly during the late colonial era, were inseparable, a postcolonial approach to Indonesian and Malay writings seems sensible.

As Malay scholar Ahmad Kamal Abdullah (2006) notes, the close links between Indonesian and Malay literature first began in the 1930s, when young Malay writers such as Harun Aminurrasyid, Muhammad Yasin Makmur and Abdullah Sidek were intensively engaged with the works of the Indonesian Pujangga Baru writers. But, as Budiawan (2012) documents, the links were forged even earlier. Around the mid-1920s, according to Roff (1967), many students of Sultan Idris Training College (SITC) in Tanjung Malim, Perak, were exposed to Balai Pustaka novels and other modern Indonesian literature purchased for college libraries. Individual teachers and students also subscribed to Indonesian periodicals, which they read in conjunction with the new Malay newspapers and journals emerging at the time. This is significant because 'as an educational institution to train teachers for the Malay schools, the SITC was the primary site from which Indonesian influences were spread throughout the Peninsula' (Budiawan 2012: 146). Ironically, this was seen as a positive move because, as Hooker (2003: 172) observes,

> its graduates believed that Malays were not keeping up with the changes of the modern world and needed to work hard to catch up with the progress they believed was happening around them. In touch with anti-colonial and nationalist student movements in Indonesia, they went out into their communities determined to inspire change through teaching and writings.

In this way Indonesia was widely promoted as a source of inspiration for improving Malay schools and, by exposing a generation of students to Indonesian nationalist activism, students were pivotal in forming nationalist organisations such as Belia Malaya (Malayan Youth) in 1930 and Kesatuan Melayu Muda (Union of Malay Youth) in 1938. In addition to this, a significant proportion of the Malay intelligentsia became fascinated with Indonesian literary activism, which exposed them to notions such as 'politics' and the ins and outs of Indonesian political movements. As a source of inspiration for literature and political ideas, Indonesia eventually became a Mecca for the writers of

Malaya, especially the Malay writers (Budiawan 2012: 143). Some activists, such as Ibrahim Yaakub, were even inspired to struggle for Malayan independence as part of the Indonesian independence movement, which would take the form of a broader postcolonial archipelagic nation-state to be known as *Indonesia Raya* (Greater Indonesia) (Budiawan 2012).

The irony of the above account lies in the fact that since independence both nations have suffered from what Budiawan (2012: 144) refers to as a more 'inward-looking' nationalistic tone in their creative processes, with much less in the way of formal interaction. As a result, despite the historical connections and deep cultural influences shared by the two literary systems, Malaysian literature is as foreign to contemporary Indonesians as the literature of England, France or the Netherlands (Mahayana 2001). Although Indonesian literature is by no means unfamiliar to Malaysians, since it has long been considered as a branch of Malay literary expression (Maier 2004), in the post-*Konfrontasi* era in particular a modest effort has been made to differentiate between and separate Indonesian and Malaysian language, literature and learning. This is despite the long historical precedent of links between the literati of the two countries and the heavy cultural traffic between them, especially between independence and *Konfrontasi* (Budiawan 2012). In the current era, there have been few postcolonial analyses that combine the study of Indonesian and Malaysian literature. Perhaps disappointingly for some, this book does not aim to fill this lacuna in scholarship for several pragmatic reasons. Historically, only a small minority of Indonesians or Malaysians have ever read novels and even fewer are prepared to devote their career to serious literary analysis. A key reason for this is that the novel, introduced by the colonial authorities as a means of civilising or, rather, controlling their subaltern subjects, can be regarded as an anachronism in the Malay world, which remains very much a society devoted to oral rather than print literacy (Derks 1996). With the rising popularity of television, cinema, social media, gaming and other forms of electronic entertainment, literature is even more culturally marginal today than it was in the past. Regardless of its historical aura of cultural prestige, *sastra* (writing) no longer plays a central role in the national narrative of either Indonesia or Malaysia. Popular culture, however, is flourishing, ubiquitous and influential. For example, when the Indonesian president attends a screening of a particular film, heads turn, tongues wag and the mass media take notice. Acknowledging the increasingly pervasive nature of popular culture, this book focuses on what could be called the 'familiar unknown', namely the culture of the masses, and in doing so encompasses both popular cultural expression and the real-life experiences and opinions of everyday citizens.

There are a number of reasons why a postcolonial approach is relevant to our study. First, this book seeks to unravel how postcolonialism has shaped the culture and politics of contemporary Indonesia and Malaysia. Besides the few studies mentioned above, the postcolonial template has rarely been used in a comparative politics context. The experience of postcolonialism has undoubtedly shaped ideas of identity and nationhood in Indonesia and

Malaysia. Both countries have experienced colonisation and its associated legacies, such as cultural dislocation, cultural appropriation, and hybridity. European domination took root in Southeast Asia in the 19th century and imperialism reached its height at the beginning of the 20th century. During these centuries Indonesia was colonised by the Dutch, with brief interregnums by the British and the Japanese, and Malaya was colonised by the British, with a brief period of Japanese rule. Many have argued (for example, Jedamski 2009) that postcoloniality and its associated colonial paradigms did not necessarily end at the moment independence was declared or obtained. According to Foulcher (1995: 151), subaltern discourses can be ideologically, not temporally, constituted, and they can 'shadow colonial paradigms at all historical stages of the colonial experience'. This book is premised on the notion that Indonesia and Malaysia have been shadowed by colonial and anticolonial paradigms up until the present day. The dark underside to Indonesia and Malaysia's foreign-policy orientation – characterised by enduring undercurrents of anti-Westernism, anti-Americanism and, in Indonesia's case, anti-Malaysianism – can also be partly considered as a product of the postcolonial experience.

Second, to this day neighbouring Indonesia and Malaysia seek to assert their similarities and differences not only through cultural and political symbols but also through divergent responses to globalisation. Since independence Indonesia and Malaysia have moved in different directions in their social, economic and political development, leading at times to serious bilateral tensions. Malaysian commentator Karim Raslan (2012) describes the extent to which politics and contemporary history have altered both countries:

> In short, there are fundamental socio-political differences beginning with our Dutch and British colonial experiences. Thereafter, this gap has only widened. In essence, Malaysia has been ruled by a quasi-aristocratic Malay elite since 1957. Change, if at all, has always been gradual and evolutionary. But change in Indonesia has generally been revolutionary, dramatic and at times tumultuous. Malaysians can hardly begin to comprehend Indonesian history. The spiral of events is beyond our understanding – beginning with the pro-Marhaen, ultra-nationalist rhetoric of the Sukarno years, followed by the traumatic blood-letting of the mid-60s, Suharto's New Order and then a second period of uncertainty before Yudhoyono's ascendance.

Despite their cultural and political differences, Indonesia and Malaysia share a long history of migration which has resulted in a great deal of cultural overlap, common in a region noted for its 'fluid pluralism' (Reid 2000: 10). This book reveals a wide diversity of experience both between and within Indonesia and Malaysia, where the colonial encounter has proven to be profound and especially influential in terms of constituting conceptions of ethnicity and interracial relations. We aim, therefore, to explore the link between postcolonialism and contemporary ideas of culture, society and politics, as experienced among everyday citizens in the Southeast Asian region.

Third, postcolonialism is eminently useful in approaching the comparative politics of Southeast Asia. Within Indonesia and Malaysia, views about the extent to which postcolonial Indonesia and Malaysia should engage more deeply with globalisation are often structured along ethnic and religious lines. It is in this context that the reverberations of the colonial encounter continue to be felt in the region. To take just one example, it has been argued within the region that the trappings of imperialism are as thoroughly infused in the globalised transnationalism of the postcolonial era as they were in the colonial era. Former Malaysian Prime Minister Mahathir Mohamad argued along these lines in his view of globalisation as an imperial instrument for re-establishing Western colonial control over the developing world:

> [Developing] countries are faced with globalization, a single world in which they know they will have little say, their voices drowned, and their interest ignored in the pursuit of global interests and objectives as defined by others ... History would have turned a full circle within just two generations. Fifty years ago the process of decolonization began and in a space of about 20 years was virtually completed. But even before all the colonies of the West have been liberated, indeed before any had become truly and fully independent, recolonization has begun. And it is recolonization by the same people.
>
> (Mohamad 1996)

The extent to which this view is shared among everyday citizens from different cultural, ethnic and religious backgrounds is yet to be determined. For some, the colonial experience created opportunities and experiences that were taken away by post-independence nationalist and assimilationist policies. For example, the Chinese in Indonesia and Malaysia, who arrived in large numbers in the region at the onset of colonialism, share a history of cultural marginalisation and victimisation in times of political unrest, particularly in the post-independence era. Although colonialism is a shared experience that unites Indonesia and Malaysia, the experience of postcolonialism within Indonesia and Malaysia may vary considerably depending on one's cultural, ethnic and religious background.

Finally, if recent Islamist discourses on globalisation emerging from Indonesia and Malaysia are taken into consideration, it can be argued that the present era is simply the latest stage of the colonial experience. For example, in Muslim Southeast Asia anti-Americanism has grown since the terrorist attacks of 11 September 2001. Many in Indonesia perceived the US-led invasion of Afghanistan as a war against Islam and the Iraq war – a pre-emptive strike against a predominantly Muslim country – was universally condemned in Indonesia and triggered anti-American demonstrations (Murphy 2010: 371–72). Antagonism towards Western-driven globalisation has also led to a surge of activities to counter globalisation or, rather, to promote a form of Islamic alternative globalisation. These activities include the increasingly widespread use of Islamic calendars, the promotion and study of Arabic script in Indonesia and Malaysia, the rise of Islamic popular culture, films and music in Southeast Asia, the prevalence of wearing Islamic head-coverings by Muslim women, greater Islamic solidarity in trade, and the promotion of Islamic banking principles and practice (Riddell 2008). In addition to this, anti-Western and anti-American sentiments are shared by many Islamists in the Southeast Asian region, including radical anti-Western Islamists in hardline groups such as Front Pembela Islam (Islamic Defenders Front), which is ubiquitous in post-Suharto Indonesia. If we want to get to the roots of these types of attitudes, which to some extent have played a role in the ongoing development of a Southeast Asian regional imaginary, we need to explore the nexus between the colonial encounter and its sociopolitical aftermath.

The focus of this book is not theoretical posturing. Our aim is rather to offer a deft combination of empirically based cultural and political analysis, which engages with the contemporary lives and experiences of everyday citizens in Indonesia and Malaysia. We argue that culture is innately political. This is especially the case in Indonesia and Malaysia where, for much of their postcolonial political history, culture has been one of the few domains in which writers, poets, artists, puppeteers, musicians, curators, migrants and everyday citizens have been able to create and redefine politics in their own terms according to their own experience. From the joint authorship of this book emerges a unique blend of cultural and political analysis, underpinned by a postcolonial theme. Our approach is justified because in Indonesia and in Malaysia culture is political, politics is cultural, and the present is postcolonial.

Structure and aims of this book

Chapter 1 of this book outlines what we consider to be the salient issues in Indonesia's relationship with Malaysia. We begin with a historical delineation of the bilateral relationship, which has tended to reflect the dominant political culture of particular historical periods. In chronological order, these periods are the early postcolonial period dominated by Indonesia's first president, Sukarno; the authoritarian strongman era dominated by Suharto and Mahathir; the post-Suharto, post-Mahathir *reformasi* era; and the era of Indonesia's President Susilo Bambang Yudhoyono and Malaysia's Prime Minister Najib Razak. Other leaders, such as Malaysia's second Prime Minister, Hussein Onn, have also played minor roles in this sometimes cantankerous bilateral shadow play. This chapter also introduces some of the sensitivities associated with the deep cultural affinity shared by both nations. We examine two case studies, namely the public spat following media reports of Malaysian claims on a Sumatran folk dance, the Tor-Tor, and the case of the ceremonial Malay dagger, the *keris*, which has long been a cultural emblem of the Indo-Malay world. Examining cultural heritage contestations on a case-by-case basis is important because they demonstrate the inherent fragility of the bilateral relationship between Indonesia and Malaysia.

While post-Suharto Indonesia's foreign diplomacy appears to be gathering momentum in ever-expanding concentric circles, Jakarta remains quick to take offence, nonetheless, especially when Indonesian national pride is perceived to be under attack. As Kassim (2005: 2) observes, in an era when Indonesia appears to be vulnerable to economic and political instability, not to mention a never-ending series of natural disasters, 'the Indonesian elite and public take exception easily, they respond robustly to the most innocent of incidents if these are perceived as affronts to their dignity'. Territorial disputes, poor treatment of Indonesian workers and cultural heritage contestations have all been grist to the mill, creating what Kassim (2005: 2) terms as 'a creeping unease' in Jakarta that others, Malaysians in particular, are not treating Indonesia with sufficient respect. Setting the scene for an in-depth analysis of such sentiments, Chapter 2 outlines the reasons for Jakarta's feeling that it deserves a greater measure of respect in the region, in particular from Kuala Lumpur. It highlights some of the cultural factors that have enabled Indonesia and Malaysia to pull back from the edge of armed conflict, no matter how grave the insult. Essentially, we investigate some of the shared cultural underpinnings of the Indo-Malay world, such as the Malay and Indonesian languages, *wayang* shadow theatre and the Ramayana cycle of tales that, together with an array of other cultural forms, have encouraged a deep sense of kinship between the two countries. Diplomats of both countries have long sought to use these longstanding cultural connections as a means of overcoming bilateral tensions. We conclude, however, that a common language or culture appears to hold little sway in the modern world. By analysing two avant-garde films appropriating the Ramayana mythology, we suggest that the contemporary arts of both countries are focused on domestic sociopolitical concerns rather than transnational bridge building. This parochial perspective emerges as a persistent leitmotif in Indonesia–Malaysia relations.

In Chapter 3 the gloves are off. We examine the various cultural contestations between Indonesia and Malaysia and their corrosive effect on the bilateral relationship. Indonesians are particularly upset by allegations that Malaysia has attempted to patent supposedly 'Indonesian' cultural heritage forms such as *batik* and *wayang*. For their part, Malaysians are increasingly frustrated by Indonesia's rampant anti-Malaysianism, which was clearly evident during the Southeast Asian (SEA) Games in 2011, hosted by Jakarta and Palembang. This chapter examines Indonesia's hosting of the SEA Games, which from Malaysia's perspective was a resounding failure because of Indonesia's poor sportsmanship. We then investigate one of the root causes of Indonesia's anti-Malaysianism, namely Malaysia's alleged claims on Indonesian cultural forms. On the one hand, this chapter argues that Malaysia has never officially laid claim to any of Indonesia's leading heritage forms. On the other hand, it highlights the Malaysian popular opinion that Malaysia is well within its rights to lay claim to Malay heritage forms, regardless of whether they are 'Indonesian' or not. Many of these contested forms of cultural expression are found throughout maritime Southeast Asia and, in terms of the quality of preservation and conservation, probably much better off in Malaysian hands anyway. Chapter 4 examines the veracity of this assertion through a consideration of the funding of museums and other national cultural institutions in Malaysia – pillars of its ongoing nation-building project – which is much better than in Indonesia, where history has little honour. In particular, we compare and contrast the manner in which the maritime cultural heritage of two counterpart port cities, Indonesia's Makassar and Malaysia's Terengganu, has been either willfully ignored or professionally collected and curated. Through a tale of two cities, this chapter tells a tale of two countries.

Chapter 5 initially considers the way that Islam has been promoted as a key element of the inherent cultural connectedness between Indonesia and Malaysia. Like other supposedly cohesive factors in Indonesia–Malaysia relations, such as a common language and culture, however, Islam has promised much more than it has delivered. Even as political Islam and popular Islamic culture become much more entrenched in the politics and societies of contemporary Indonesia and Malaysia, Islam has failed to enhance cooperation between the two countries. Nevertheless, the recent resurgence of Islam tells us a great deal about the dominant sociocultural mores of both nations, as well as about political trends in both nations, which appear to be gradually diverging. By examining representations of Muslim men and women in a sample of contemporary Indonesian and Malaysian films, we present a snapshot of both nations. On the one hand, the so-called 'Islamic' cinema of Indonesian filmmakers such as Hanung Bramantyo reveals much about how Islam acts as a lightning rod for exploring ideas about gender, class and nation. The art-house cinema of Malaysian filmmakers such as Yasmin Ahmad, on the other hand, demonstrates that Islam is almost identical to the Malays and is thus a question of ethnicity. We argue that ethnicity in Malaysia cannot be divorced from the fundamental problem of Malaysia's politics, namely the deep divisions along ethnic lines.

While Yasmin Ahmad and other Malaysian intellectuals like her have sought to reconcile Malaysia's seemingly insurmountable racial divide, Chapter 6 examines the extent to which this issue has become more deeply ingrained in Malaysia's sociopolitical DNA than many assume, beginning with the initial drafting of its constitution. Indonesia has also had its own problems in keeping a lid on ethnic divisions, as we shall examine. In Indonesia, however, ethnic tensions are more often than not closely related to surface or transactional issues in local and regional economics and law enforcement and not as deeply rooted as the ongoing threats they pose to Malaysia's fragile ethnic harmony. Mindful of this book's emphasis on the postcolonial status of Indonesia and Malaysia, we address what we consider to be a fundamental element of the question of ethnicity for both countries, namely the colonial experience, which differed fundamentally in each. Indonesia was colonised by the Dutch and Malaysia by the British, but the impact of colonisation on both nations was far-reaching. During the British colonial era, when Malaysia was known as Malaya, the export of tin, sugar, coffee and rubber in the increasingly connected world economy was only made possible by the colonial authorities promoting the importation of Chinese and Indian labour. But the effects of these policies have been far-reaching.

Chapter 7 examines the complex relationship between economic development and citizenship rights for Malaysia's ethnic minority groups. Although it focuses on how different ethnic groups are structured in Malaysia's differentiated model of citizenship, it also addresses a new underclass in Malaysian society, Indonesian migrant workers. We explore the government's failure to deliver basic rights, concluding that migrant workers suffer disproportionately from Malaysia's unflagging expansion of its political economy, which has tended to come at the cost of upholding human rights.

In Chapter 8, we examine in more depth labour migration, from a regional perspective. Malaysia has a history of accepting migrant labour, including Javanese coolies, dating back to the British colonial era. More recently, post-colonial Malaysia's manufacture of goods for export within an increasingly globalised economy has relied on the importation of migrant labour from Asian countries such as Indonesia. But Malaysia also has a record of mistreatment of Indonesian migrant workers and many Indonesians resent Malaysia's policies towards Indonesian workers. Democratisation in Indonesia has tended to complicate matters. Democracy has brought the liberalisation of Indonesian media, which has enabled unfettered commentary on previously sensitive issues such as migrant workers. With the emergence of public opinion polls, popular opinion now carries more weight than it once did and inevitably influences political decision-making. As it becomes more democratic and broadens its regional foreign policy orientation, the Indonesian government is strengthening its determination to deal with the human rights of Indonesian migrant workers. For Indonesia, the challenge lies in developing regional policies that address human security issues in the region, such as the provision of migrant rights in receiving countries, such as Malaysia. The core problem, we argue, is that Malaysia is not experiencing a similar democratic awakening. Consequently, Malaysia continues to regard the migrant worker issue as a national security issue rather than, as Indonesia regards it, a regional human security issue whose solutions lie in regional decision-making. While Malaysia's politics continue to be dominated by one particular political party, national sovereignty and non-interference remain dominant and deep suspicion about concepts connected to human rights persists. Malaysia's fragile ethnic balance also tends to politicise and constrain debate on either migrant labour or immigration.

Democratisation is often assumed to be the answer to the labour migration dilemma, as well as to many other social and political concerns in the region. But support for democracy is probably just as important as, if not more important than, its mere existence. In Chapter 9 we examine whether democracy actually has the support of different ethnic and religious groups in Indonesia and

Malaysia. Our underlying argument is that democracy in newly democratising countries matters little if citizens do not support their country's democratisation process. As we compare Indonesia and Malaysia one more time, it will become evident that the different level of democracy in the two countries has led to contrasting attitudes towards numerous issues, including models of citizenship and human rights questions such as the treatment of migrant workers. In terms of Southeast Asian regional integration, the findings of this chapter are relevant. Given that the drivers of internal political liberalisation in Southeast Asia are likely to come from within states, and not from external sources such as the Association of Southeast Asian Nations (ASEAN), it is important to understand salient social and political trends in the countries that are the region's movers and shakers, such as Indonesia and Malaysia. As Indonesia consolidates its democracy, question marks remain over Malaysia's commitment to a democratic political system.

Overall, this book questions the notion that Indonesia and Malaysia are supposed to enjoy an inherent closeness because they share many things in common. We argue that on many occasions the two countries have threatened to come to blows over their shared cultural base. In this fraught context, tensions associated with transactional issues such as the Malaysian repatriation of illegal Indonesian workers assume much greater importance than they might ordinarily deserve. Historically, these tensions have tended to escalate quickly into threats of armed conflict and loose talk of war. Nevertheless, in the interests of creating a region of stability and cohesion, the governments of Indonesia and Malaysia have, to their credit, carefully nurtured the bilateral relationship for many years. Their status as foundation members of ASEAN has played a key role in this regard, as armed conflict between ASEAN members has been sternly discouraged from its inception. As foundation members of ASEAN, Indonesia and Malaysia have felt compelled to abide by the so-called 'ASEAN Way' and its operating strictures of non-confrontation and non-interference. Consequently, while Indonesians may be increasingly upset over what they perceive as Malaysian provocations, including alleged threats on Indonesian cultural forms and territorial integrity, another campaign of confrontation between the two nations is unlikely. Instead, it appears that Indonesia has bigger fish to fry, especially since it has embraced democracy, which has emboldened the nation on the world stage. Malaysia may need to prepare itself to look to Indonesia once again as a positive role model.

Notes

1 Manohara's birth father, George Manz, is an American citizen and her mother, Daisy Fajarina, is of Bugis heritage. After a messy divorce, Fajarina married a French citizen, Reiner Pinot Noack. This marriage also ended in divorce.
2 'Kami diundang baik-baik sama Tengku. Mereka bilang, kita harus saling memaafkan, masalah ini harus diluruskan baik-baik di depan Ka'bah. Saya merasa berdosa jika niat baik itu ditolak' (Putra Raja Kelantan Culik 2009).

3 'Tetangga oh tetangga. ... | Tega nian kau !!! | Kau mencuri semua milik-ku !! | Tak ingat kah kau akan pertemanan kita dahulu ? | Mengapa engkau tega, sayang ? | Aku biarkan kau curi Reog Ponorogo-ku !! | Aku biarkan kau curi sloganku!! | Aku biarkan kau curi batas-ku !! | Lalu sekarang, mengapa kau mencuri Manohara-ku ? | Belum puaskah kau akan segala yang kau curi dariku, Malingsia ?'

4 The Indonesian word used by Omen, *persetubuhan* (sexual intercourse), is a play on the word *persekutuan*, Malay for 'federation'.

5 The Proton Saga, a car produced by Malaysian auto manufacturer Proton, is also known as Malaysia's 'national car'.

6 'Malayria: Malayria adalah sejenis penyakit menular berbahaya yang mana kurang lebih dari 22 juta orang di daerah Persetubuhan Tanah Melayu telah terinfeksi dan sulit dicari obat penawarnya, apalagi disuruh bertobat. Malayria disebabkan oleh parasit Protonsaga (bahasa melayunya Protozoa) yang biasa berada di daerah berlumpur, dikenal dengan nama Kuala Lumpur. Gejala dari penyakit malayria biasa ditandai dengan tumbuhnya rasa percaya diri yang tinggi sekali, rasis, ada keinginan untuk menyiksa dan memperkosa TKI, mencuri kayu (illegal logging), mencuri pulau, mencuri kebudayaan dari negara jiran serta mengklaimnya. Penyakit malayria ini biasanya kebal terhadap kritikan dan juga demo, karena malayria sudah menyumbat urat nadi kebebasan pers. Mengerikan sekali penyakit malayria ini. Waspadalah!' (AWAS!!!! Malayria KL, 2008).

7 'Wahai Presiden-ku SBY !!! | Bentuk tim pengacara | Selamatkan Srikandi Indonesia | Manohara !!!'

8 According to Indonesian media reports, Daisy's former husband had an affair in France with a family friend, an Indonesian woman, who lodged a claim for sexual assault after she was asked to leave the Pinot family home.

9 The fact that Manohara had rung the embassy late at night during a weekend and reached only an answering machine was overlooked.

1 Uneasy neighbours

Introduction

The Indonesia–Malaysia relationship is one of the most important bilateral relationships in Southeast Asia, especially because Indonesia, the world's fourth most populous country and third largest democracy, is the most populous and powerful nation in the region. Both states are committed to the relationship, especially at the highest levels of government, and much has been made of their 'sibling' identity. The relationship is built on years of interaction at all levels of state and society. During the first decade of the twenty-first century, however, several issues have seriously strained Indonesia's once cordial relationship with Malaysia. Among these are strong public reaction to maritime boundary disputes, claims over each country's cultural heritage, the cross-border impact of haze from Indonesian forest fires, the poor treatment of Indonesian workers in Malaysia, and the widespread belief that Malaysians regard Indonesians as their poor cousins. Relevant to the last of these, Ali Alatas, Indonesia's Foreign Minister from 1988–99, in 2007 summarised the perception of the relationship thus: 'Malaysians are arrogant, Indonesians are jealous' (Bayuni 2010).

In one of the few extended Malaysian commentaries on the bilateral relationship, Khalid and Yacob (2012) suggest that the unequal pace of democratisation in the two countries over the last decade has made the relationship increasingly problematic. The emergent role in the relationship of variables external to the two governments, such as non-governmental organisations (NGOs) and the mass media, has been crucial in this regard. Yet, in relation to the impact of variables external to the two governments, it is largely a story of Indonesia's democracy, Indonesia's NGOs and Indonesia's mass media rather than Malaysia's democracy, Malaysia's NGOs and Malaysia's mass media. We shall discuss the particular roles of democracy and NGOs later in the book. In terms of the mass media, the heavily controlled Malaysian media has been 'intentionally sober and restrained' in its reporting of sensitive issues involving Indonesia, thus reflecting Kuala Lumpur's diplomatic approach to Jakarta (Khalid and Yacob 2012: 373). On the other hand, Indonesia's liberal mass media, a capstone of its democratic consolidation progress, has played a key role in inflaming the tensions. In addition to numerous anti-Malaysia columns, editorials and blogs, several books discussing the bilateral relationship, often in highly inflammatory language, have been published in Indonesia in recent years. Almost all of them have provocative titles, such as *Indonesia vs Malaysia* (Susilo 2009), *Maumu Apa Malaysia?* (What is it that you Want, Malaysia?) (Lazuardi 2009), *Ancaman Negeri Jiran* (The Threat of a Neighbouring State) (Usman and Din 2009a), *Panas Dingin: Hubungan Indonesia–Malaysia* (Hot and Cold: Indonesia–Malaysia Relations) (Purwanto 2010) and *Ganyang Malaysia* (Crush Malaysia) (Efantino and Arifin 2009).[1] As we mentioned in the Introduction, the rally cry 'Ganyang Malaysia' harks back to Indonesia's *Konfrontasi* (Confrontation) with Malaysia in the period 1963–66, when it was popularised by Indonesia's first president, Sukarno, who viewed the formation of Malaysia as a neo-colonial plot. To this day, it is a frequently used phrase in Indonesia–Malaysia rhetoric.

This chapter begins with an overview of the principal causes and outcomes of the confrontation between Indonesia and Malaysia. We then examine the relatively stable relationship between the two countries under Suharto and Mahathir, before introducing some of the complex cultural tapestry shared by the two nations that has enabled a deep cultural affinity to form, which has greatly influenced bilateral relations in the postcolonial, post-independence eras. We gradually open up the discussion with a few case studies, such as the public spat over the Sumatran Tor-Tor folk dance and the cultural sensitivities associated with shared cultural heritage items such as the ceremonial *keris* dagger, found throughout the Indo-Malay world. We close the chapter by raising the possibility of alternative avenues of investigation, such as employing cultural analysis based on concepts such as the pan-Malay *Nusantara* (The Archipelago), or alternatives such as *Jawa* (Java) and *Melayu* (Malaya). The postcoloniality of Indonesia and Malaysia subtly infuses each of the cases discussed here, ensuring that this is, above all, a discussion of two nation-states. Alternative imaginaries for the Southeast Asian archipelago, such as those based on a shared kinship, race or ethnicity, hold little sway.

Konfrontasi

In his classic book on the Indonesia–Malaysia confrontation, Jamie Mackie (1974) argues that understanding domestic politics is crucial in understanding the period of confrontation between the two countries. More specifically, Mackie views the confrontation essentially as a result of Indonesia's convoluted domestic politics, which were largely determined by Indonesia's post-independence president, Sukarno. Others have chosen to frame *Konfrontasi* against the broader context of the Cold War, where it is interpreted as a diplomatic quandary inspired by external factors (Brackman 1966; Subritzky 1999; Jones 2002). Liow (2005: 98) prefers to consider the internal political dynamics within the Malay world, arguing that *Konfrontasi* 'can also be viewed as the climax of antagonistic diplomacy between two kin states whose understanding of the basis of their relations as sovereign nation-states was evolving along diametrically opposite planes'. Although on the one hand we do not wish to overemphasise the role of external factors, on the other we would argue that the role of Malaysia is perhaps overstated in Liow's account. Malaysia's role was passive, at best. Instead, along the lines of Mackie's perspective (1974), we argue that *Konfrontasi* is best understood in terms of Indonesia's domestic politics, which revolved around the mercurial figure of Sukarno, a nationalist firmly committed to eradicating the last vestiges of European imperialism from Southeast Asia (Subritzky 1999).

By the 1960s, Sukarno had developed a neutralist foreign policy, dominated by his doctrine of New Emerging Forces. In essence, his ideology was one of continuing revolution against neo-colonialism, which was usually represented by the colonisers. After Indonesia had successfully claimed and incorporated West New Guinea in 1962, the last remaining colonial power of any substance in the region was Britain. By early 1963, Sukarno had led his country into direct opposition to British plans regarding Malaysia. Sukarno objected to the idea of a confederation of the former British territories and annexes of Singapore, Sarawak, North Borneo, and Brunei with Malaya in a single political entity to be called the Federation of Malaysia. Yet when Tunku Abdul Rahman floated the Federation proposal on 27 May 1961, Indonesia raised no objections, primarily because Sukarno assumed that it was part of a decolonisation project. By January 1963, however, Sukarno had officially rejected the plan and launched a policy of confrontation (*Konfrontasi*). It appears that soon after his initial reaction to the Tunku's proposal, Sukarno had become convinced that the Malaysia project was not an act of decolonisation but a manifestation of neo-colonialism in its own backyard, and that it was likely that Britain would retain its extensive economic interests in the region, not to mention its naval base in Singapore. The Jakarta elite had long held reservations about the close cooperation between Britain and Kuala Lumpur, suspecting that the latter was susceptible to colonial influence. These suspicions were quite normal in the context of the international politics of the day. Anticolonial sentiment was at its peak, and anticolonial and post-independence movements were often marked by bloody revolution, as was the case in Indonesia. Malaysia's warm postcolonial camaraderie with Britain appeared, therefore, to be a rather peculiar aberration.

For Indonesians, it appears that *Konfrontasi* was a statement against the encroaching neo-imperialism that Malaysia was seen to embody. Sukarno's ideological posturing did little to quell the flames. In addition to the various objections outlined above, Sukarno objected to the Malaysia plan because he did not approve of the continuing power of the Malay sultans in the new federation, which he regarded as 'undemocratic' (Cribb and Brown 1995: 86). Sukarno was also of the opinion that the federation was being imposed in the face of what seemed to be popular opposition in the territories in Borneo, an opinion that was not without some substance, particularly in the case of Brunei (Mackie 1974; Poulgrain 1998; Subritzky 1999). 'Underlying these objections', according to Cribb and Brown (1995: 86), 'was also a sense of pique that Indonesia, the largest country in the region, had not been consulted at all by Britain in its planning'. Sukarno also saw Kuala Lumpur's failure to consult its neighbour with its plans as a sign of disrespect for Indonesia's leaders. This sense of pique, we should point out, was more closely associated with the snub to Indonesia than any residual irredentist sentiments. Although Indonesians had occasionally urged that British Borneo should be liberated from colonial rule, few had suggested publicly that it should be annexed to Indonesia (Mackie 1974). It is unclear what they might have been thinking behind closed doors. As Mackie observes (1974: 5), we know very little about the underlying dispositions and motivations of individual actors involved in the dispute, including to what extent they were motivated by pan-Malay *Indonesia Raya* (Greater Indonesia) chauvinism or anticolonial sentiments, or even by Sukarno's ideological indoctrination.

Although *Konfrontasi* never reached the extremes of a full-scale war, Sukarno vigorously supported an anti-Malaysia insurgency in Borneo, which was characterised by a mix of naval blockades, organised rebellions, subversions and Indonesian paratrooper landings on Malaysian soil (Jones 2002; Mackie 1974). A direct military confrontation was always out of the question because the British, with strong military backing from Australia and New Zealand, had vastly superior forces in the region (Subritzky 1999). As an alternative, Sukarno attempted to use diplomatic pressure to force concessions, including an international campaign to exclude Malaysia from Third World gatherings. When Malaysia became a temporary member of the United Nations Security Council in January 1965, Indonesia withdrew from the United Nations and began moves to organise an alternative body, namely the Conference of the New Emerging Forces (CONEFO). Both the military and diplomatic elements of the confrontation came to nothing. British, Australian and New Zealand forces easily defeated the armed incursions into Malaysia and the Indonesian hostility cemented the Malaysian national identity rather than undermining it. In the diplomatic sphere, none of Indonesia's allies from the Asia–Africa bloc followed Indonesia when it left the United Nations, which meant that Indonesia experienced a long period of diminished influence in the Non-Aligned Movement.

Despite the apparent humiliation, many Indonesians were proud of the increased attention that Indonesia was receiving from around the world. While Indonesia had little power to project beyond its own borders, Sukarno's activist foreign policy-making was designed to give the impression that Indonesia was a great power. For a country that was deeply disappointed with the fruits of independence, Sukarno's foreign policy grandstanding had a powerful appeal. Sukarno's greatest attraction was his ability to unify the nation through embracing a national politics with a national agenda, which he described as a return to the armed revolution against the colonial powers. The confrontation with Malaysia was emblematic of Sukarno's efforts to bring a sense of dynamism and shared purpose back into national political life. A similar argument can be made today in relation to the resurgence of the Sukarno-esque '*Ganyang Malaysia*' rallying-cry. One could argue that the anti-Malaysia grandstanding of the post-Suharto era is in part an expression of the sense of chaos, anti-climax and disappointment of the post-authoritarian era, just as the confrontation of the mid-1960s must have been, to some extent, an outward function of the overall disappointment and intractability of the social and economic problems of the time (Cribb and Brown 1995).

Post-independence ambivalence

Considering Indonesia's colonial background and the anti-Western antagonism displayed by Sukarno, it is ironic that Indonesia's post-independence foreign policy was – and is – generally oriented toward the West. From the outset of independence, Indonesia opted to develop a strong relationship with the West and with the United States in particular. Initially, this was primarily as a means of retaining sovereignty in the face of a possible return of the Dutch (Hadiwinata 2009: 62). Consider the following argument by Prime Minister and Foreign Minister Sutan Sjahrir in 1945, which highlights the importance of a strong and friendly relationship with the United States:

> Indonesia is geographically situated within the sphere of influence of Anglo Saxon capitalism and imperialism. Accordingly, Indonesia's fate ultimately depends on the fate of Anglo Saxon capitalism and imperialism … It is clear that till now Dutch power has simply been a pawn in a political chess game that the British have been playing. But we must recognize that Dutch power here has by no means the same significance for American as it does for British foreign policy. In this fact lie possibilities for us to win a new position for ourselves in harmony with the political ambitions of the Giant of the Pacific, the United States.
>
> (Leifer 1983: 8)

In the following years Indonesia opted for a supposedly 'neutral' position by introducing the concept of *Politik Luar Negeri Bebas Aktif* (independent and active foreign policy), signifying that it would not take sides in the Cold War between the US-led Western bloc and the Soviet-led Eastern bloc. Instead, according to Dewi Fortuna Anwar (2008: 184), Indonesia intended to chart its own course in international relations, based on its own perceptions of its national interests. Throughout the period of multiparty politics (1950–57), however, Indonesia's foreign policy orientation was often contested. On the one hand, ongoing efforts were made to forge a close relationship with the United States, at least until the early 1960s; on the other hand, these efforts were endangered by President Sukarno's growing hostility towards the 'Old Established Forces' in world politics, countries spearheading what he called NEKOLIM (neo-colonialism and imperialism), and advocacy of the NEFOS

(New Emerging Forces). Not surprisingly, this stance caused relations with the West to deteriorate (Hadiwinata 2009: 62).

Tensions between Indonesia and the West worsened after the Bandung Conference of 1955, which signified the desire and confidence of African and Asian countries to play a more autonomous role in international politics, transcending the Cold War ideological divide. According to Herb Feith (1978: 391), '[a]s the U.S. government saw it, Indonesia had moved fast from a friendly neutralism to one which was pregnant with hostility'. Moreover, the United States government had become convinced that Indonesia was moving towards communism when the Indonesian Communist Party (PKI) came fourth with 16.4 per cent of the vote in the parliamentary elections in September 1955, the first ever democratic elections in Indonesia (Anwar 2008: 188). This was seen as a blow to American interests in the region. Throughout the 1950s, the United States had been trying to persuade Indonesia to join in the anti-communist alliance that Washington was trying to forge, which was aimed at containing China and preventing communist forces from gaining political power in newly independent nations such as Indonesia.

Historians have generally agreed that Sukarno was never a communist, but, rather, a nationalist who was strongly opposed to colonialism and imperialism. His flirtation with China and the Soviet Union, as well as his trenchant anti-Western rhetoric, did not necessarily mean that he was leaning towards communism. Rather, according to Anwar (2008: 188), it was most probably an attempt to put pressure on the United States to push the Netherlands towards negotiating the issue of West New Guinea. As far as the Netherlands was concerned, when sovereignty over the Dutch East Indies was formally transferred over to the Republic of Indonesia in 1949, the province of West New Guinea was not included in the transfer. Thus the Netherlands was reluctant to engage further in the dispute, especially as the United Nations had voted on the issue, albeit with an undesirable result from Indonesia's point of view. The United States, who did not wish to alienate the Netherlands, a valuable NATO ally, was unwilling to be involved.

Sukarno's brinkmanship ensured that Indonesia continued to reject United States pressures to align itself with Washington, except for a brief and seemingly aberrant period in the early 1950s. According to Dewi Fortuna Anwar (2008), during the Sukiman cabinet (April 1951–February 1952), dominated by politicians from the Islamic Masyumi Party who were avowedly anti-communist, Indonesian Foreign Minister Subardjo secretly signed an agreement in Washington in January 1952, in which Indonesia would accept United States economic and military assistance under the terms of the 1951 Mutual Security Agreement. Disclosure of this agreement, however, caused controversy that led to the fall of the Sukiman government in the following month. 'From then onward', says Anwar (2008: 185), 'no Indonesian government would take the political risk of formalising a security tie with the United States'. The consequent idea of holding an Asian-African conference, proposed by Prime Minister Ali Sastroamidjojo, was aimed not only at promoting greater autonomy for Asian and African countries in international politics but also to distinguish his administration from the previous pro-American government. Indonesia's general disavowal of the United States, coupled with Sukarno's increasingly strident anticolonial rhetoric, meant that Indonesia's response to the United States-backed Southeast Asian Treaty Organization (SEATO) – a Southeast Asian counterpart of NATO that included Pakistan, New Zealand, Australia, and England, with Thailand and the Philippines as the only Southeast Asian members – was lukewarm. Sukarno also tried to pull out of the United Nations and Indonesian foreign policy veered to the left, becoming closer to communist China. It was in this context that two short-lived regional organisations were established – the Association of Southeast Asia (ASA) in 1961 and MAPHILINDO in 1963. The ASA (1961–66) consisted of Thailand, the Philippines and Malaya; MAPHILINDO (1963–66) consisted of Malaysia, the Philippines and Indonesia.

Both organisations failed for a variety of reasons, but much of the blame for their failure can be placed at Sukarno's feet. ASA, for instance, was undermined from the start by its inability to persuade Indonesia to join. The ASA was the initiative of Malaya's President Tunku Abdul Rahman, a vehement anti-communist. The Philippines President Garcia was also a staunch anti-communist. Southeast Asia's communist states, moreover, were not invited to join, giving rise to the perception within the region that the organisation was less than independent, not unlike like the United States-backed SEATO. To add to this impression, Soviet propaganda presented ASA as an appendage of SEATO, that is, 'a means for enticing Southeast Asian neutral states into SEATO' (Tarling 2006: 114). Indonesia's President Sukarno could not see in ASA anything but 'an Anglo-U.S. plot to subvert the newly independent states of Southeast Asia', and consequently he claimed he would not 'touch ASA with a barge-pole' (Ba 2009: 46). A postcolonial approach to these statements, the attitudes that gave birth to them and the intra-regional consequences, we would argue, can potentially provide us with a fresh insight into the complexity of Indonesia's regional imaginary, particularly in the years preceding the establishment of ASEAN. A postcolonial approach, we believe, can also reveal a great deal about the regional reverberations to Sukarno's antipathy to what he called 'neo-imperialism'. For instance, both ASA and MAPHILINDO were unable to cope with the intra-regional disputes between the Philippines and Malaysia, let alone the subsequent *Konfrontasi*. As mentioned earlier, Sukarno saw the proposed creation of Malaysia as a challenge to Indonesia's regional leadership and his own particular plan for a pan-Malay confederation, describing the federation as a British 'neo-colonial plot', aimed at the 'encirclement of Indonesia' (Ba 2009: 46).

As for the Philippines, who supported Indonesia's 'Crush Malaysia' campaign, their opposition to Malaysia focused on North Borneo, which the Philippines also claimed (Tarling 2006: 112). The Philippines, according to the new President in 1963, Diosdado Macapagal, had 'a valid and historic claim to North Borneo. In addition, the pursuit of the claim itself is vital to our national security' (Tarling 2006: 115). The Philippines, like Indonesia, were also keen to make an anticolonial nationalist stand against Western powers such as the United States, which had given its support for Malaysia's incorporation of the North Borneo territory. It is also worth pointing out that Macapagal's claim to North Borneo was lodged in the context of the proposed Federation of Malaysia project. This claim was to initially involve the Philippines and Malaya, and then involve Indonesia as well. Such a claim, it was felt, 'would boost the Philippines' anti-colonial image, at the same time responding to a longstanding pan-Malayan element in Filipino nationalism' (Tarling 2006: 115). These arguments were at odds with ASA, which was associated with Macapagal's predecessor. Ultimately, the Malaysia plans, besides provoking Indonesia and the Philippines, stood in the way of developing ASA. Consequently, MAPHILINDO, which was doomed because there was no working relationship between Indonesia and Malaysia, suffered the same fate. Nonetheless, both ASA and MAPHILINDO were 'of' and 'by' the region, and these organisations 'provided indigenous foundations, albeit not terribly deep ones, for the establishment of ASEAN in 1967' (Beeson 2009: 19). Ultimately, it can be argued that the shadow of the colonial experience directly shaped the emergence and subsequent failure of the organisational precursors to ASEAN and has, in turn, played a part in the birth of ASEAN.

The birth of ASEAN

Developments between 1965 and 1967 opened a window of opportunity for fresh thinking about regional relations and regional organisations. Sukarno's ouster in Indonesia was the most important element in the equation. According to Ba (2009: 53), because of Sukarno's association with the radicalisation of Indonesian foreign policy toward its neighbours, his removal was essential if there was to be any redirection or sense of change in the overall pattern of Southeast Asia's intra-regional relations. With the new government in Jakarta, reconciliation between Indonesia and Malaysia was eventually achieved under Suharto's leadership. As a consequence, the possibility of Southeast Asian political integration greatly improved. Among other factors bringing fresh possibilities for Southeast Asian regionalism were the election of a new president in the Philippines and consequent reparation of its relationship with Malaysia, a problematic American war in Vietnam, and confirmation of Britain's plans to divest itself of formal empire in Southeast Asia (Subritzky 1999). Each of these factors is important, but the marked improvement in the Indonesia–Malaysia relationship was perhaps the primary factor in the initial establishment and consequent success of ASEAN.

The founding members of ASEAN were Indonesia, the Philippines, Malaysia, Thailand, and Singapore. Beeson (2009: 19) describes its initial statement of purpose as 'remarkably bland, open-ended and non-specific'. This had much to do with the perception within the region that Indonesia, under the charismatic but erratic leadership of Sukarno, was widely regarded as a potentially destabilising regional presence. The *Konfrontasi* with Malaysia and the attempts to undermine the new Malaysian Federation seemed to confirm this. The ASEAN declaration's emphasis on the promotion of 'peace and stability through abiding respect for justice and rule of law' is consequently, in Beeson's words (2009: 20), 'entirely understandable'. Similarly, in investigating why ASEAN made so little tangible progress in its first decade, Beeson (2009: 20) emphasises the need to place ASEAN in its historical context: 'The newly independent states of Southeast Asia were preoccupied with promoting domestic economic development, internal political stability and the complex array of processes associated with nation-building'.

In many ways a large part of the common glue that brought the countries of ASEAN together initially was not a shared history and culture but rather a shared need to govern newly-independent and often fragile countries, many of which were still traumatised by the colonial encounter. This commonality of experience and explicit preoccupation with promoting domestic economic development and internal political stability also insulated countries in the region from external involvement in, and external criticism of, domestic affairs. In these circumstances, any sort of intra-regional engagement or cooperation had the potential to be problematic. In contrast to the deeply integrated political structures and the pooling of sovereignty that had developed in Western Europe under the auspices of the European Union, when the ASEAN countries joined forces they were far more concerned about protecting and reinforcing their often fragile sovereignty than pooling it. In a nutshell, this is what Suharto concentrated on throughout his three decades in power: to step up regional diplomacy, primarily through the non-confrontational ASEAN prism, whilst safeguarding his most basic concerns – the security and integrity of the Indonesian nation (Sebastian and Lanti 2009). The roots of his conservative foreign policy stance, it can be argued, lie in the trauma of Indonesia's colonial experience and the domestic and regional instability associated with the radical anticolonial attitudes that had come to dominate Sukarno's presidency.

Post-*Konfrontasi* rapprochement

When all is said and done, Indonesia–Malaysia relations reached their nadir with *Konfrontasi*. Diplomatic ties greatly improved with regime change in Indonesia, when Suharto ousted President Sukarno. With the changing of the guard in Jakarta, the Malaysian press went to great lengths to portray Suharto as the antithesis in personality of Sukarno. In comparison to Sukarno, who was regarded, above all, as 'erratic', Suharto was described as 'modest, gentle, hard-working, reticent' (Liow 2005: 114). These comments highlight the importance of personalities in what has, for better or worse, largely become a kinship-based relationship. Personal ties have remained paramount in the Indonesia–Malaysia relationship, despite real contributions from an array of institutionalised and routinised formal bilateral structures. As Weiss (2010: 187–88) argues:

This dimension dates back to early days: after the strain and mistrust of *Konfrontasi*, it was personal visits – by the Tunku to Indonesia in March 1968 and by Suharto to Kuala Lumpur two years later – that truly signalled a new phase in the relationship and a return to the kinship framework temporarily lost.

Even during *Konfrontasi*, the future Malaysian Prime Minister Tun Abdul Razak was negotiating 'behind the scenes with less-antagonistic elements of the Indonesian military and government' (Weiss 2010: 188). As with so many politicians of both countries, Razak maintained close personal friendships with his Indonesian counterparts including, ironically, Foreign Minister Subandrio, 'who along with Sukarno was considered as an instigator of *Konfrontasi*' (Liow 2005: 117).

The post-*Konfrontasi* rapprochement was followed by three decades of relatively calm relations between the two countries, with increasingly improved economic and security cooperation. Under Hussein Onn, who succeeded Razak on his death in 1976, extensive mechanisms for military cooperation developed, 'from joint training exercises to training on each other's territory to collaborative arms production and technology exchange' (Weiss 2010: 182). Until the early 1980s, a pattern of informal face-to-face meetings, characterised by a degree of Malaysian deference to Indonesian preferences, ensured a high level of policy congruence and cordiality (Weiss 2010: 183). Throughout this period there was an emphasis on fostering ASEAN and establishing regional security architecture. The stability of Suharto's New Order regime also brought a renewed spirit of 'blood brotherhood' and close affinity, even if the culture of 'calculated deference' under Razak and Hussein was replaced by a more businesslike 'diplomatic nonchalance' under Mahathir, thus substantially eroding the previously high level of amity in the bilateral relationship (Liow 2005: 134). Personal relations between Suharto and his Malaysian counterpart, the fiercely ambitious, vocal, Malay-chauvinist Prime Minister Mahathir Mohamad, were prickly, bringing about a subtle change in the bilateral relationship in which the two countries began to spar for greater regional prestige. But of the two, Indonesia felt somewhat miffed by this turn of events. The reason for this is that Indonesia's expectations of the relationship were historically higher. This extends back to the immediate post-independence period. As George Kahin (1964: 260–61) describes it, 'among Indonesians there has developed a widely-based belief that because of their country's size and armed power, and because it won its independence through revolution, it has a moral right to leadership in Asia'. Yet Malaysia developed comparable expectations, especially under Mahathir Mohamad in the 1980s and 1990s, which were primarily based, in Weiss's words, 'on sheer entitled chutzpah' (Weiss 2010: 187). Because of these underlying tensions, bilateral ties between the two nations remained somewhat 'brittle', despite high-level assurances of the importance of the ties to both countries (Weiss 2010: 187).

Overall, relations between Indonesia and Malaysia were cordial and constructive under Mahathir and Suharto, as they are today. Nevertheless, during this era there were two key areas of contention, which persist today – territorial disputes and issues related to labour migration. Other issues, such as cultural heritage disputes, cross-border environmental issues and the question of Islam, discussed in later chapters, have become more salient in the first decade of the twenty-first century. Of the territorial disputes, the most notable was the dispute over two very small islands, Sipadan and Ligitan, located in the Sulawesi Sea, off the northeast coast of Borneo (Map 1.1).[2] The dispute began in 1969, when Indonesia and Malaysia initiated petroleum exploration off the east coast of Borneo along the continental shelves of their respective territories. The dispute gathered momentum in the 1980s when Malaysia developed Sipadan as a tourist resort for scuba diving, which provoked Indonesia into sending troops to the area (Weiss 2010: 174). From that point, tensions mounted quickly and, after both parties were unable to reach an agreement after a series of bilateral negotiations, the disputants referred the case to the International Court of Justice (ICJ) in 1998 (Liow 2005: 143–46; Weiss 2010: 1974). Malaysia presented a strong case that included evidence that Malaysians had been responsible for the regulation and harvesting of turtles and their eggs on the islands since the early 1900s and that the British North Borneo colonial authorities had established a bird sanctuary on Sipadan in 1933.[3] Malaysia also presented the case that British colonial authorities constructed lighthouses on both islands in the early 1960s, which Malaysian authorities were still maintaining in 2002. In their defence, the Indonesians claimed evidence of patrols in the area by Dutch Royal Navy vessels, as well as Indonesian Navy activity and fishing by Indonesians. But none of the acts they cited were of a legislative or regulatory nature, and nor did they pertain specifically to Sipadan and Ligitan. The measures taken to regulate and control the collecting of turtle eggs and the establishment of a bird reserve, cited by Malaysia as evidence of effective administration over the islands, were viewed by the ICJ as sufficient regulatory and administrative assertions of authority over territory. In December 2002 the court ruled that the islands belonged to Malaysia (Case Concerning Sovereignty 2002).

While this particular dispute may have been relatively amicably resolved, the ICJ did not rule on the issue of maritime boundaries. Consequently, Indonesia has been very proactive in surveying and naming thousands of small islands throughout the Indonesian archipelago, even if some of these islands are little more than reefs or atolls, in order to assert and protect Indonesian sovereignty (Baird 2012). The ICJ ruling has also presaged subsequent, similarly intractable maritime territorial disputes such as the dispute over the Ambalat Block in the Sulawesi Sea (see Map 1.2 and Rüland 2009: 392–94), and demonstrates the extent to which Indonesia–Malaysia relations had deteriorated since the 1970s. By the time the Sipadan-Ligitan decision was handed down, relations had moved well and truly beyond a 'sibling' focus on cultural, historical or kinship ties. Since the 1980s, international norms, rather

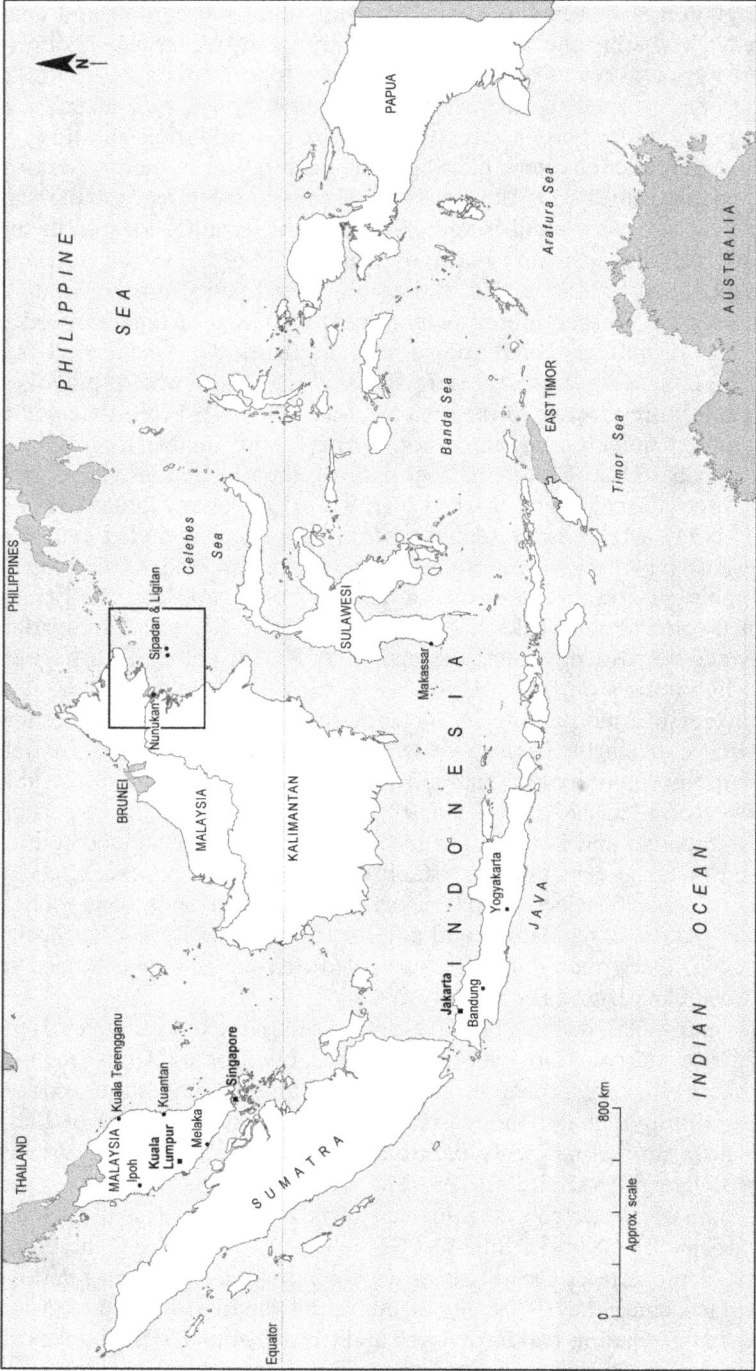

Map 1.1 Map of Indonesia and Malaysia, with Sipadan and Ligitan islands.
Source: Peter Johnson

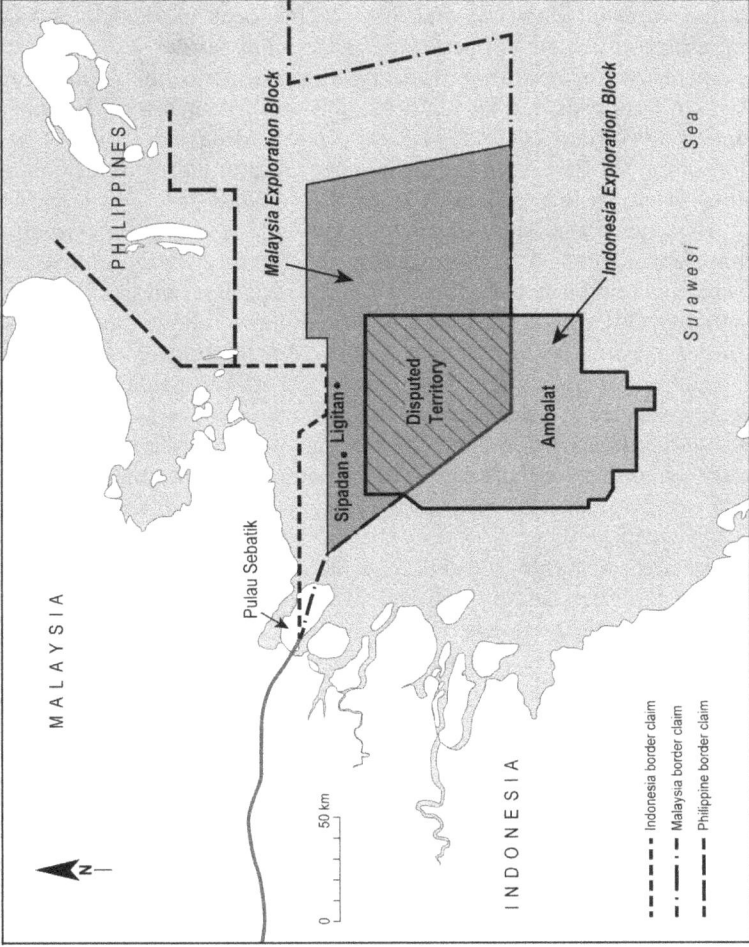

Map 1.2 The disputed Ambalat Block area of the Sulawesi Sea.
Source: Peter Johnson

than mere appeals to brotherhood, have increasingly governed Indonesia–Malaysia relations, although references persist in the relationship to a shared culture and an inevitable degree of what Weiss (2010: 186) refers to as 'symbiosis'.

Bilateral relations after Suharto and Mahathir

The period that has followed the Asian financial crisis of late 1990s and the subsequent departure of Mahathir and Suharto has been marked by a focus on economics and military cooperation, with joint border exercises and shared arrangements for maritime security. Between 2001 and 2005 trade between the two countries doubled and Malaysian investments in Indonesia increased markedly (Weiss 2010: 171). Many more Malaysian tourists have visited Indonesia in the first 14 years of this century, many of whom purchase large amounts of cheap Indonesian goods to sell in Malaysia. This trend has become so pronounced that the influx of Malaysian tourists in cities such as Bandung has been identified as contributing to increased traffic congestion. More frequent direct flights between Kuala Lumpur and Bandung add credence to this claim. Meanwhile, approximately two million Indonesians work in Malaysia, more than in any other destination country (Garcés-Mascareñas 2012: 56). Indonesian migrants are a critical part of the Malaysian labour force, comprising around 70 per cent of all foreign workers in Malaysia (Chin 2008: 290). But as already suggested, the migrant worker issue has become a serious matter of contention between the two countries. Malaysia has a long track record of mistreatment of Indonesian workers and resentment of Malaysia's disdainful policies towards the workers has steadily increased among Indonesians (Arifianto 2009). Consequently maintaining the bilateral relationship has not been smooth sailing and the strengthening of regional and extra-regional connections has been punctuated by sporadic tensions and much overblown chest-beating, even though Susilo Bambang Yudhoyono is not inclined towards grandstanding and is said to have good personal relations with Malaysia's most recent Prime Ministers, Abdullah Badawi and Najib Razak.

As in previous eras, a fundamental problem for Indonesia and Malaysia has been Indonesia's deeply held sense of primacy and entitlement in the region, an attitude that has been particularly pronounced in its relationship with Malaysia. The pecking order within this fraught familial relationship has always been contested, as the relationship is an unequal one. Malaysia is a small country, with a population of fewer than 30 million. Indonesia is the world's most populous Muslim country, with a population of over 240 million, and is one of the G20 major economies. It has long been courted by the United States and Australia. Indonesia is much more democratic than the soft-authoritarian Malaysia, but it is also much poorer. In general, Indonesians feel that Malaysia does not display a suitably deferential attitude towards its bigger and more powerful neighbour. Malaysia, meanwhile, has long been sensitive to Indonesia's tendency to play the role of big brother (*abang*) towards its little brother (*adik*) in the region. The front cover of the 23–29

October, 2007, edition of *Tempo* magazine encapsulates the problematic power dynamic, showing a caricature of Indonesia's President Susilo Bambang Yudhoyono, towering over a caricature of his Malaysian counterpart, Prime Minister Najib Razak. Of course, there are strong historical reasons why Indonesians feel justified in bragging about its superiority over Malaysia, even though Malaysia has a far superior economic track record. Indonesia's sense of regional entitlement derives largely from a Javanese worldview, which can be traced to the pre-colonial era, when Java, as the base of the Majapahit Empire, sought to dominate archipelagic Southeast Asia from the thirteenth to the sixteenth century.

Despite the vast potential for conflict, the most common metaphor for Indonesia–Malaysia relations has been the notion of *rumpun* (or *serumpun* or *satu rumpun*), which emphasises the shared kinship between the two countries. It is now commonplace to hear of phrases such as *saudara serumpun* (brothers of the same stock), and *bangsa serumpun* (nations of the same stock), and even *rumpun Melayu*, which has been introduced in discussing pan-Malay aspirations. According to Milner (2008: 215), who quotes Ismail Hussein, '*rumpun Melayu* conveys the idea of a loose "family" of Malays – "in *rumpun* everything grows spontaneously, autonomously on their own, from the same roots"'. Concomitant with the *serumpun* metaphor, the notion of Indonesia and Malaysia as a family of Malays, straddling a Malay world (*alam Melayu*), has been alluring for many years. In the late colonial period, in particular, pan-archipelagic schemes such as *Indonesia Raya* (Greater Indonesia) or *Melayu Raya* (Greater Malaya) were frequently discussed and debated, as was the enduring pan-Malay imaginary of *Nusantara* (Archipelago).

The pan-Malay discourse reached its peak towards the end of World War II, when the Japanese set up a committee for the preparation of Indonesian independence. The committee featured the future leaders of independent Indonesia, including Sukarno, Hatta and Yamin. According to Holst (2007: 329),

> Although it was not clear from the beginning whether an attempt would be made to include Malaya into the future Indonesian republic, a strong commitment developed during the negotiations in July 1945: in the second session on 11 July 1945, a majority of 45 out of 66 members voted for a territorial definition that would include the Malay Peninsula in the newly formed nation.

Sukarno believed that Indonesia would never be secure if the whole Straits of Malacca were not under the control of Indonesia, and Yamin argued that 'the territory should be determined according to pre-colonial boundaries, for example the kingdom of Majapahit' (Holst 2007: 329). Hatta was more cautious, preferring to see the people of Malaya independent within a Greater East Asia. On the day that Indonesia declared its independence, the Partai Kebangsaan Melayu Muda (PKMM, Malayan Malay National Party), which strove for immediate independence from British rule and a unified independence with Indonesia, was founded. However, with the rise of the conservative-traditionalist United Malays National Organisation (UMNO) in the following year, the radical pan-Malay nationalists of PKMM lost influence and the dream of uniting the pan-Malay peoples faded. As Liow (2005: 68) observes, for the traditional Malay elite of UMNO,

> the concepts of *Melayu Raya* and *Indonesia Raya* were not based on equality of status for Indonesia and Malaysia. Rather, they were viewed as subservience of Malay interests to those of a proclaimed egalitarian Indonesia-inspired nationalism, which they felt was a cover for Javanese hegemony.

UMNO supporters suspected that the pan-archipelagic proposal was more about Indonesia expanding its reach, as Java aimed to do at the height of the Majapahit Empire, than the other way around. Despite promotion by some of the region's finest intellectuals and political leaders, including numerous Malay nationalists, 'the end of the war and UMNO's rise thus dashed all hopes of a pan-Malayan state' (Holst 2007: 330).

On the one hand, the people of archipelagic Southeast Asia have a long and deep common history, underpinned by a shared language, a shared culture and a shared religion; on the other hand, a pan-Malay regional imaginary premised on the inhabitants of *Nusantara* having the same broad racial and cultural identity could never encompass the diverse cultural and religious groups of the region (Holst 2007: 338). Even the obvious cultural affinities are open to conjecture. As Holst (2007: 338–39) observes, most Indonesians and Malaysians have 'a lack of understanding of the common cultural heritage', so much so that 'an Indonesian who claims to be Malay would face a dis-believing raise of eyebrows from his Malaysian counterpart'. There are also serious racial divisions between Malays and non-Malays that even a very broad definition of Malay culture, encompassing all of the different cultural groups of the Archipelago, could not overcome. Malaysia, for example, has sizeable minorities of Indians and Chinese, who could never be conceived as Malays. It is equally inconceivable for indigenous groups, who share many close ties with Malays, to be categorised as Malay.

Ultimately, the deep historical affinities of the Malay world have come under threat from political and economic interests generated by the colonial incursion. Territorial boundaries set by the colonial powers and, subsequently, centuries of economic exploitation, to some extent ruptured previously unfettered migration and trading lines within the archipelago, which had nurtured cultural exchange in the region in pre-colonial times. Although cross-border encounters continue to flourish in some parts of the Indonesia–Malaysia border zone (see, for instance, Eilenberg (2012) and Mee (2010)), hopes for a broader common future after the end of colonial rule came to nothing. The postcolonial emphasis on notions such as *serumpun*, or blood brotherhood, therefore, often rings hollow.

In this regard, the case of the ongoing border dispute over Ambalat, off the eastern coast of Kalimantan, is a particularly vexed one (Map 1.2). Comprising contestations over oil and other natural resources, the dispute over Ambalat has involved a long series of bilateral discussions interspersed by naval blockades, the arrest of fishermen, and various other forms of low-level bilateral brinkmanship (see Usman and Din 2009b). Visser and Adhuri (2010: 93) describe one of many Ambalat-related flashpoints thus: 'An incident occurred when a Malaysian navy ship disturbed the construction of a navigational tower in Karang Unarang in the vicinity of Ambalat and was chased by an Indonesian navy ship'. How did it come to this? According to Kassim (2005: 1–2), the 'current tensions began innocently enough, with [Malaysia's] Petronas awarding contracts for hydrocarbon exploration to its subsidiary, Petronas Carigali, and the Dutch oil giant, Shell'. Indonesia promptly claimed Ambalat as Indonesian territory, which meant that Petronas, therefore, had violated Indonesia's sovereign territory. Malaysia objected to the Indonesian assertion, however, as it insisted that Ambalat was within its jurisdiction. This confidence was no doubt based on the International Court of Justice's ruling in 2002, granting Malaysia ownership over the nearby islands of Sipadan and Ligitan. With Jakarta and Kuala Lumpur using different maps to demarcate maritime boundaries, both countries have had to endure a series of overlapping claims and border-related incidents. Ambalat has been the most explosive of these incidents and, with both countries disinclined to seek the assistance of either ASEAN or the International Court of Justice, there is little hope of resolution. The problem with this is that the issue remains incredibly sensitive. Both countries have come close to the brink of an armed clash on several occasions, with Jakarta deploying warships and jetfighters 'to assert its sovereignty over the disputed waters' (Kassim 2005: 2). Jakarta has also backed other measures, such as urging shrimp trawlers based in the nearby East Kalimantan ports of Tarakan and Nunukan to fish in the Ambalat area 'in an effort to lay a stronger claim to the Ambalat area' (Visser and Adhuri 2010: 93).

Shrimp, oil and natural gas aside, the diplomatic and military skirmishes over Ambalat are not too dissimilar to the confrontation of 1963–65. Not surprisingly, some Indonesian journalists were quick to label the Ambalat dispute, rather ironically, as '*Konfrontasi* Part II' (Kassim 2005: 2; Usman and Din 2009a: 109). As we saw with *Konfrontasi*, the Ambalat dispute did not emerge from within a cultural and political vacuum. It has, in fact, had a complex lead-up period, beginning with Indonesia's unsuccessful claims over Sipadan and Ligitan. Both cases are a manifestation of Indonesian attempts to protect its own strategic interests in the region. We would argue that this urge, in the more recent case, is to some extent an expression of hurt national pride arising from the Sipadan and Ligitan case. It could also be an expression of postcolonial shame, engendered by the very fact that it was the colonial powers that set the boundaries. In Indonesia's case, there are nagging suggestions that it drew the short straw in being colonised by a third-rate colonial power. In comparison with the British colonial officials of Sabah, who were rigorous in establishing sovereignty over the entire region under their command, the Dutch made relatively little effort to establish sovereignty. This uncomfortable fact was evidenced by the Sipadan and Ligitan case in which Malaysia triumphed.

We can elaborate on many other territorial disputes, such as the 2011 case related to allegations that Indonesia had lost 1,490 hectares of land to Malaysia in West Kalimantan because the marker that delineated the border was 'lost' (Malaysia Hits Out 2011). A year later, there was ongoing haggling over the exact location of the shared border along five points between Indonesia's Nunukan district in East Kalimantan and the Malaysian state of Sabah. Media reports suggest that the points of contention include the location of the border across the Sinapad and Sumantipal rivers, as well as across Sebatik Island. The issue with the Sinapad River was that a small section of the river, which flows from west to east, dipped south. Malaysian authorities, however, deem the entire river to fall within their territory, whereas Indonesian authorities assert that the southern section crossed over into Indonesian territory. According to Indonesian authorities, if the Malaysian claim should prevail, Indonesia would lose 4,800 hectares of land (Mattangkilang 2012). The standoff over the Sumantipal River is similar in nature, with Malaysia wanting to declare the entire river as falling within its territory. Indonesian authorities argue that this would result in the commonly agreed-on border being pushed south, farther into Indonesian territory (Mattangkilang 2012). The case of Sebatik Island is not dissimilar. 'On Sebatik Island', Mattangkilang (2012) reports, 'where the border is simply marked by a series of concrete blocks and there are no border posts set up by either country, the border issue has been around for almost a century'.

To counter our consideration of these disputes, we could also describe at length the ways in which the Indonesia–Malaysia border is actually quite porous, as few of the communities living in the Kalimantan–Sarawak border zone regard the border solely as an 'institution of exclusion' (Eilenberg 2012: 11). Along the border, there is a great deal of cross-border trade and travel occurring on a daily basis, and Indonesians and Malaysians alike openly admit this. As Eilenberg (2012: 11) observes,

> working in Malaysia, trading with Malaysians, marrying Malaysians, joining ethnic celebrations in Malaysia, and using Malaysian hospitals when ill are ubiquitous topics when border inhabitants tell their life stories. Many men and (less commonly) women hold both Indonesian and Malaysian identity cards; some even have two passports, which are proudly displayed despite the fact that most have expired.

In order to do justice to the question of territorial disputes and borderland encounters, however, we would need to spend months, if not years, living in a border community or an offshore island, taking part in the daily interactions, not to mention the diplomatic negotiations. But the focus of our study is the cultural, rather than the physical, landscape of Indonesia and Malaysia, in which the number of potential critical case studies grows every year. We will now introduce two case studies briefly that reflect the eclectic nature of this book – the Tor-Tor dance and the *keris* ceremonial dagger. While one or two commentators (for example, Chong (2012) and Mapson (2010)) have examined similar cases, most cases have passed by without scholarly comment. Although the cases of the Tor-Tor and the *keris* have been seldom discussed, they deserve attention, as we shall demonstrate, because they shed a great deal of light on broader issues in the Indonesia–Malaysia relationship.

Tor-Tor

In recent years, the image of Indonesians and Malaysians as sharing the same roots, Malay or otherwise, has been tested by many cases other than the Ambalat dispute, which has received considerable media attention. Under-pinning the political tensions between the two countries are contestations over symbols of national pride and identity. The recently disputed Tor-Tor folk dance is a case in point. In this particular case, which flared up in 2012, some Indonesians expressed outrage over what they regard as Malaysia's illegal claims on this art form. Malaysian politicians have countered these accusations by denying anything untoward and the Malaysian government is quite openly stating that plans to add the Tor-Tor to Malaysia's National Heritage Act are aboveboard and in no way designed to denigrate the distinctly Indonesian origins of cultural heritage forms enjoying popularity in Malaysia. Rais Yatim, the current Malaysian Information, Communications, and Culture Minister, is well aware that the Tor-Tor folk dance originated in Indonesia, but he insists that some Malaysians, who share deep, intimate and enduring cultural roots with Indonesians, feel a sense of ownership of the dance too (Malaysian Official 2012). The Tor-Tor is a dance practised by Malaysia's Mandailing ethnic group, who are native to Indonesia's North Sumatra province. According to some accounts, the Mandailing first began migrating to Malaysia in the 1920s and to this day their descendants still feel a strong sense of kinship with their Mandailing cultural heritage, epitomised by the Tor-Tor dance. The Malaysian government added the dance to Malaysia's national heritage list in 2005 and has used it in promotional tourism materials. But, according to Rais, this had nothing to do with bilateral one-upmanship:

> It is the Mandailing people [in Malaysia] who want the Malaysian gov-
> ernment to recognize and register their arts. We hope Indonesians will
> consider this fact, instead of speculating that Malaysia is trying to swallow
> Indonesian arts … But we really don't mean to snatch away Indonesian
> traditional arts and claim them as our own. The Malaysian government
> only acknowledges the presence of the arts in our country and the need to
> protect them (Malaysian Official 2012).

Malaysia's Deputy Prime Minister Muhyiddin Yassin has also weighed in on the debate, telling journalists that the goal was to preserve the Mandailing heritage and not 'to claim it as our own' (Hassan 2012).

Apparently, the heritage list registration of the Tor-Tor and another ethnic Mandailing art form, Gordang Sambilan drumming, takes into account Indonesia's views and does mention its origins. According to Yassin, 'By registering it under the National Heritage Act, it will also benefit Indonesia in the long-run as it is meant to preserve and conserve, otherwise the culture will disappear with the passage of time' (Hassan 2012). Nonetheless, Malaysia's reported efforts to promote the Sumatran Tor-Tor and the Gordang Sambilan as its own cultural heritage sparked protests in Jakarta in June 2012, when a group torched Malaysia's flag and threw stones at its embassy. The acrimony persisted for much of the latter half of 2012, when Indonesians took to social networking sites in attack mode. On Twitter, they have used the hash tag #TorTorPunyaIndonesia, which can be translated as '#TorTorBelongsToIndonesia'. Some Indonesian commentators have been particularly outspoken. For example, the Partai Demokrat (Democratic Party) politician Ruhut Sitompul, whose family hails from North Sumatra, said Indonesia must use 'hard diplomacy' to defend the country's cultural heritage: 'Once in a while, I think it's necessary that we bomb [Malaysia] as a form of shock therapy. Otherwise they will keep oppressing us. There's no need for diplomacy – they always find excuses' (Malaysia, Indonesia in a Dance-Off 2012). Opposing views were quickly posted on one newspaper's website in response to these comments. According to one online commentator,

> Indonesia does not hold the copyright for any culture. Perhaps it should start leading by example and actually spend some Government money on preserving its own rich heritage instead of being in a perpetual reactive mode whenever a neighbor (benignly, I may add) decides to gazette something in their own national heritage list.
>
> (Wyvern 2012)

The Tor-Tor case is merely the latest in a long line of disputes between Indonesia and Malaysia, whose citizens have often been involved in heated exchanges, especially online, and especially over cultural claims such as the Tor-Tor and, more sensationally, *batik*, *wayang kulit* and the *keris*. This is despite the fact that *batik* is worn throughout maritime Southeast Asia, *keris* appear throughout mainland and maritime Southeast Asia, including Indonesia, Thailand and southern Philippines, and shadow theatre was once just as popular an art form in the northern Malaysian state of Kelantan as in Java and Bali, where it still is popular. As we examine an eclectic array of cultural texts, films and furores, we cannot help but note the recurrence of controversies, stories, motifs, images and ideas from the earliest examples of *Nusantara* culture. Even in cases that carry an air of absolute modernity, such as transnational claims on 'Indonesian' heritage, sometimes involving UNESCO, there is also an element of the ancient. It is for this reason that the first few chapters of this book address discussions of cases, such as the Tor-Tor case, which link the archaic concepts, narratives and forms of the traditional with the ephemeral productions, controversies and contestations of mass culture. Of course, there has always been a fine line between traditional and popular in the region, whose differentiation and provenance can to a large extent be identified as the colonial interjection.

It is important to note at this point that UNESCO's role in elevating one cultural form over another and thus one nation over another is not without precedent in the region. The awarding of UNESCO's stamp of approval to *batik, wayang* and *keris*, art forms closely associated with the high court culture of Central Java, is merely the latest chapter in the West's attempts to come to terms with the complex of identity, language and literature in the maritime Southeast Asia region through processes of categorisation, standardisation, elevation and, concomitant to this, displacement. There have been numerous centres of authority in the study of the cultures of Indonesia and Malaysia, almost all of them located outside Southeast Asia. The encounter between colonial Dutch and British scholars and the Javanese and Malay ruling elites began this process. For instance, there are many accounts of what the colonial authorities regarded as high and low, as *Melayu* (Malay) or *Jawa* (Javanese), as traditional or modern, particularly in regards to language and literature. But terms such as these, which emerged out of the colonial context, have tended to displace all other forms, thus denying difference. In colonial Java, for instance, Dutch scholarship elevated the language and culture of the Central Javanese courts to be the epitome of Javaneseness. To this day, this has meant that regional variants of Javanese language and culture have remained marginal. As part of the ongoing postcolonial project of creating a national cultural identity, the New Order regime, with its deep Javanese underlay, actively promoted the peaks of Indonesian culture (Hooker and Dick 1995), which just so happened to be the very same Central Javanese cultural forms appropriated and promoted by the Dutch colonial scholars, including *wayang kulit* and *batik*. Ironically, these are the very same cultural heritage products deemed sufficiently worthy of a UNESCO listing. We shall discuss the case of *batik* in more depth later in this book, but briefly examine here another form of intangible cultural heritage recognised (and confirmed by UNESCO) as distinctly Indonesian, as opposed to Malaysian, namely the renowned traditional weapon of the Malay world, the *keris*.

Keris

In focusing on the manner in which the *keris* has evolved over the centuries, we aim here to demonstrate that the Malay world before independence was not one of clearly demarcated boundaries of either space or influence, as patterns of cultural overlap can be traced throughout the region. Adrian Vickers (1997) highlighted cultural overlap in an essay in which he describes the way in which in Palembang and Jambi the courts produced literature in both Malay and Javanese, with styles of textiles such as *batik* and *songket* that can be related to both those of Java and the Malay Peninsula. Vickers also noted the regional similarities of the elaborate hilts and sheaths of ceremonial *keris* daggers, describing the stylistic similarities among the *keris* daggers of South Sulawesi, Java, Sumatra and the Malay Peninsula. On this particular theme Vickers is not a lone voice. Malaysian scholar Farish Noor impressively delineates both the ubiquity and the pan-Malay character of the *keris* in a more recent essay:

> Its use was widespread throughout the archipelago, as it made itself known in practically all arenas of life. It was seen in the istanas and kratons, as well as the kampong and on the fleets of Malay war prahus. Krises were even made especially for women and children.
>
> (Noor 2000: 239–40)

Noor argues that in the development of the *keris* we can also trace the civilisational development of the Malays. For example, *keris* production reached its peak during the Hindu-Buddhist era, primarily in the court centres of Java, Bali and South Sumatra. In particular, the Majapahit era was marked by the first recorded example of a damascened *keris* (*keris berpamor*), produced at Pajajaran under the rule of the second prince of Majapahit. Known as the 'Majapahit *keris*', it is renowned for its unique hilt, sculpted in the form of a squatting or sitting human figure. At the time, *keris* were highly esteemed and worshipped as sacred objects imbued with spiritual power, and *keris*-makers were regarded as among the elite of Javanese-Hindu society, along with the nobility and priests. In this era *keris* production and usage had reached their highest level of sophistication. *Keris* produced in the courts were luxurious items of the highest quality and workmanship, and according to Noor (2000: 251),

> some of the krises of the courts had become excessively decorated affairs, bedecked with goldleaf, diamonds, rubies, and other trinkets and ornaments. Spoiled and pampered in their ritual perfumed-oil baths, these krises seldom, if ever, performed the duties the state demanded of them.

With the arrival and consolidation of Islam, and especially between the fifteenth and seventeenth centuries, *keris*-making became more commonplace and eventually occurred outside the confines of the courts and temples. What had once been a sacred symbol and object of luxury and status was gradually reduced to the level of a profane weapon of deadly seriousness:

> As the Malay archipelago came into the orbit of the Muslim world, new technologies, including armaments, ballistics and armour were introduced into the region from India and the Arab world. The kris had no choice but to compete with the weapons brought by both the Arab and Indian Muslims as well as their enemies, the Ferenggi. Such innovations and

modifications (for example the longer Kris Sundang of the Moros from the southern Philippines, and the rapier-like Kris Bahari from Sumatra) were the order of the day.

(Noor 2000: 258–59)

In general, Islam's influence was most discernible in the attempts to curb and condemn the cultural excesses in courtly literature, art, architecture and lifestyle. This in turn had a profound effect on *keris* naming and design. In terms of the design of *keris* hilts, the sculpted figures of the ancients gods and demons deriving from the Hindu-Buddhist past 'were gradually submerged under a carpet of arabesques, floral tapestries and geometric patterns that anticipated the "greening" of the Malay archipelago under Islam in the centuries to come' (Noor 2000: 260). It is interesting to note, however, that while during the Hindu–Buddhist era *keris* production was heavily influenced by elements of the religious and the occult, *keris*-makers during the Islamic period introduced a wide array of new talismanic codes, utterances, incantations and taboos. Noor (2000: 260) argues,

Contrary to the claims of contemporary Islamists, who state categorically that the arrival of Islam eradicated the myths and superstitions of the pre-Islamic era, there is ample evidence that Islam's arrival in the Malay world simply contributed another layer of belief to the already crowded and overdetermined cosmos of the Malays.

As the arrival of Muslim traders and Islam had in the earlier centuries, Western colonial rule played a key role in the transformation of the Malay worldview. The British and the Dutch, the latest in a series of colonial powers to come to the region, also forced on the Malays an agenda for change. This had an impact on the development of the *keris*, as the arrival of Islam had, and it was eventually marginalised as an element of native culture, beliefs and religion. Because only the sepoys of the British colonial forces were allowed to bear arms, any Malays who had the temerity to bear one of the weapons of their ancestors were regarded with suspicion and regarded as 'pirates, religious fanatics, or murderers' (Noor 2000: 269). Eventually the use of *keris,* and the circulation of arms in general, was heavily policed along ethnic and cultural lines, leading to the eventual displacement of the *keris.* But the Malays themselves played a part in this displacement. By the nineteenth century, partly in reaction to the colonial encounter, the Malay world was in closer contact with the rest of the Islamic world than ever before. The closer contact inspired the new Muslim revivalists in the region to direct their polemical broadsides at the twin evils of modern colonialism on the one hand and pagan traditions still evident in Malay–Muslim culture on the other. In dealing with the second of these two evils, calls were made to purify Islam in the Malay world of any pre-Islamic elements. The fervour for purification eventually contributed to the rejection and marginalisation of the *keris* in Malay society. Other traditional Malay cultural forms, such as *wayang kulit*, have suffered similarly, particularly in present-day Malaysia, where an emphasis on Muslim piety and religiosity has encouraged its people to turn their backs on pagan pre-Islamic traditions.

For the *keris*, the end result of the twin processes of colonial interference and Malay-Muslim modernism was that 'the keris of the gods now found itself locked up in the museums of the new colonial masters' (Noor 2000: 270). The large *keris* collections now in the leading museums in the region, such as the National Museum in Kuala Lumpur and the Asian Civilisations Museum in Singapore, magnanimously demonstrate regional leitmotifs, thus recognising appropriately the many local stylistic variations in their design and production. Of course, there are many examples of modern *keris* hilts, sheaths and blades that are completely divorced from the history and the traditional styles of the region. As Noor (2000: 276) observes, 'Today more and more unorthodox and non-traditional hilt forms are being produced by local craftsmen to suit local tastes. Older blade styles and hilt forms that bear traces of the pre-Islamic past are increasingly frowned upon'. But the key element of the *keris* case study outlined above is that the *keris* cannot be relegated to the vaults of one or other national museum and claimed as an immutable form of intangible cultural heritage belonging to one or other nation, or one locality. Unfortunately, the UNESCO listing of *keris* as a distinctively Indonesian intangible cultural heritage form has heightened Indonesians claims to cultural superiority over their Malaysian brothers and sisters. Yet, somewhat ironically, many Indonesians claim the reverse – that Malaysians feel culturally superior. For their part, Malaysians are equally frustrated. In a letter to *The Jakarta Post*, one Malaysian asserts: 'The fact, which is clear to everyone else outside Indonesia, is that nobody is "claiming cultural superiority" over Indonesians. Rather, Malaysia is just claiming what is ours, which is as much as yours, too, anyway' (Me 2011).

Melayu and *Jawa* in the postcolonial era

As in the pre-colonial and colonial eras, clearly demarcated borders between Indonesian and Malaysian cultural spheres cannot be drawn in the post-independence era either. As Zulhasril Nasir (2009) observes, similarities between the traditional songs and dances of Indonesia and Malaysia are not uncommon, especially in regions such as the Malaysian state of Negeri Sembilan, where many Malays can trace their ancestry back to West Sumatra. The traditional architecture of Negeri Sembilan also has much in common with the Minangkabau architectural style of West Sumatra. Throughout Malaysia, performances of supposedly Indonesian songs such as 'Burung Kakatua' and 'Rasa Sayang' are commonplace. Together with *wayang kulit* shadow puppet theatre, the use of supposedly Indonesian musical instruments such as *gamelan* and *angklung* are also common in some parts of Malaysia. This is because their artists and audiences, like so many Malays, can often trace their ancestry directly to the Indonesian archipelago. They widely acknowledge that their ancestors brought their cultural heritage across maritime Southeast Asia, from as far afield as Maluku and from as close as Sumatra and the Riau archipelago. More recent examples include the case of so-called 'Malaysian' *batik*, which is now usually produced by immigrant artisans from Java who, attracted by higher wages, are routinely recruited by Malaysian *batik* producers (see Chapter 3). But there is no dispute about the inherent Javaneseness of the Malaysian *batik* industry. The most obvious clue to the distinctly Javanese provenance of *batik* is Javanese etymological origin of the word '*batik*', which is widely known to be from the Javanese word '*ambatik*', consisting of two Javanese words – '*amba*' which means 'to write' and '*titik*' for 'dots'. '*Ambatik*' has become '*batik*' in both Malay and Indonesian.

Inspired by the historical evidence and the present-day tangle of social, cultural and economic ties, in approaching the Indonesia–Malaysia relationship we are keen to reintroduce the key element of difference to the analysis of the Malay world. In doing so, we seek to highlight hybridity and cultural and political overlap, as well as the role of European and other outside elements in the genealogy of Malay writing, language, culture and heritage. Part of this project, therefore, involves highlighting the alternatives to Benedict Anderson's now classic assumption that the nation is *the* unit of study and is, therefore, seen as describing the limits of the cultures of modernity (Anderson 1991). Anderson's approach reinforces parameters such as 'modernity' and its antithesis because in his view the modernity of nationalism was a radical break from the hitherto 'un-modern' past. Thus, from Anderson's perspective, the colonial encounter determines everything, including the rise of nationalism. But perhaps more emphasis needs to be placed on demonstrating first that there was no clean break between the pre-colonial and the postcolonial and, second, that there might be alternatives to nationalism.

As opposed to the cut and dried concepts of 'Indonesia' and 'Malaysia', are labels such as *Melayu* and *Jawa* useful as alternative terms of reference in the contemporary era? The problem with *Melayu* and *Jawa* is that they were never exclusive or separable terms – they covered a multitude of possible identities, they were constantly interacting – and in some cases the differences between them were not differences in their essential nature, but were differences designated by an invented tradition (Vickers 1997). *Melayu* and *Jawa*, therefore, are as invented as 'Indonesia' and 'Malaysia'. In one sense, the UNESCO *batik* listing, with the Indonesian President's subsequent call for a national *batik*-wearing day, is merely an extension of a history of invented tradition and thus of invented difference. Ultimately, despite their designated geographical demarcations, postcolonial Indonesia and Malaysia continue to share and produce patterns of cultural overlap. Instead of relying on relatively neat dichotomous labels such as *Melayu* and *Jawa*, perhaps we need to highlight the shifting identities of the Malay world, the cultural interactions, and shared cultural patterns. As Vickers (1997: 196) observes:

These patterns go along with patterns of physical movement, movement of texts from one area to another, movement of wandering princes throughout the area of the Malay Peninsula, Sumatra, Kalimantan and further afield, movement of Bugis and Makassarese throughout Southeast Asia, movements of 'pirates' and 'mercenaries' (who were often the same people as princes), marriages across the waters, movements of the nomadic *bajau* or 'sea gypsies', and the numerous exchanges involved in the slave trade.

Vickers concludes that for both Indonesia and Malaysia there is no history of a fixed, essential or immutable national culture. Likewise, we suggest that we do not need to limit ourselves to the forms of texts, literary or otherwise, normally associated with the invented traditions of Indonesia and Malaysia. For this reason this book opened with a lengthy examination of the lowbrow case of Manohara, the runaway bride briefly married to a Malaysian prince. This case, we believe, embodies the potential of a counter-hegemonic approach. This book aims to examine a number of other 'counter-hegemonic' cases in a similar vein.

Conclusion

This chapter has delineated the key elements to consider when approaching not only the Indonesia–Malaysia relationship but also the two countries as discrete entities existing in a discrete region, Southeast Asia. We have demonstrated that alternative conceptions of the terrain shared by the two countries, such as those based on a shared kinship, race or ethnicity, have proved unconvincing. The postcolonial experience, however, seems to be a persistent cultural unifier, for better or worse. But emphasising postcoloniality has not been a dominant theme in in the modest amount of scholarship on the Indonesia–Malaysia bilateral relationship (for example, that of Liow (2005) and Weiss (2010)). Despite the many compelling reasons for weaving a postcolonial perspective with disciplines such as political science or international relations, there has been a reluctance to conceptualise or envisage postcoloniality in the field of comparative politics. This has been a lost opportunity – particularly so given the popularity of books such as Hardt and Negri's *Empire* (2000) which highlight the manner in which globalisation has transformed the world in ways not unlike the colonial encounter between the First, Second, and Third World. As Pelizzo (2010: 248) notes, 'in the course of the so-called War on Terror, which involved, among other things, military attacks on or, if one takes a more benevolent view, military intervention in Afghanistan and Iraq, the word "empire" emerged from oblivion'. Consequently, given widespread discontent with the United States administration both within and outside the United States, it is not surprising that 'empire' quickly became associated with the United States and in many respects represented a banner of anti-Americanism. Nevertheless, at least one of the authors of *Empire* has taken pains to argue that the United States is not the 'empire' they had in mind; they were applying the word to the combination of globalisation and global capital, which is quite different from the old, state-based forms of imperial domination (Negri 2008). Instead, it is a de-territorialised and non-state based concept, operating through global instruments of collective capital. As we have discussed, Malaysia's former Prime Minister, Mahathir Mohamad, has presented similar arguments for several decades.

Neither this chapter, nor the book as a whole, argues that the United States is imperialist. Nor do we suggest that the United States has played a colonial, or neo-colonial, role in postcolonial Southeast Asia. Instead, what we have intended in this chapter is to make a preliminary attempt to reconsider the historical vectors of Indonesia's love–hate relationship with the neo-colonial 'Old Established Forces' of Britain and the United States. To some extent, Indonesia's troubles with these powers can be considered as a product of Indonesia's colonial past. The troubled Indonesia–Malaysia relationship also, to some extent, is imbued by the colonial pasts of both countries. An approach emphasising the postcoloniality of Indonesia and Malaysia in their relations with each other, therefore, is increasingly important, because, as time goes by, the United States is becoming more closely associated with the global instruments of collective capital such as the International Monetary Fund (IMF), the World Trade Organization (WTO) and the World Bank, each of which has played a crucial role in the domestic politics of Southeast Asia. The ongoing influence of the United States in Southeast Asia, as well as the negative regional impact of its aggression in Iraq and Afghanistan, suggest that the role of American primacy must be incorporated into contemporary studies of the comparative politics and of postcoloniality of Southeast Asia. At the very least, the United States was instrumental in laying the groundwork for the establishment of ASEAN's precursors, such as SEATO. Yet ASEAN, which emerged from the ashes of SEATO, ASA and MAPHILINDO, has proven to be much more effective than America in achieving a modest degree of regional cooperation in Southeast Asia. This chapter suggested that the shared colonial experience and the resulting drive to decolonise the region were crucial instigators of ASEAN's establishment. It has also argued that the formation of ASEAN was in large part a consequence of a regional desire to resolve the destabilising tensions generated by the *Konfrontasi* between Indonesia and Malaysia as well as an effort to foster collective strength against external threats. As well as considering these particular historical circumstances, however, it must be restated that the ASEAN grouping was established in the light of a common need – to build internal security in order to domestically reinforce the governments of fragile, newly independent postcolonial states. Thus, the establishment of ASEAN was a consequence of both external and internal circumstances, with the colonial experience the common link.

Finally, we argue that Southeast Asia's postcolonial condition – as much a product of globalisation and the crisis (or 'hybridity', to borrow postcolonial parlance) of the nation-state as it is a product of the traumas of European colonialism – is also an impulse to be reckoned with. Although indigenous concepts and practices have been used to conceptualise and describe regional relations in the region, such as the concept of Indonesia and Malaysia being part of a pan-Malay *Nusantara*, or Archipelago, the immediate post-independence period was dominated by discourses such as nationalism, decolonisation and the anti-Westernism of Indonesia's first president, Sukarno. The New Order foreign policy orientation was focused on endorsing the formation of ASEAN in 1967, in a new policy initiative explicitly based on the lessons drawn from Indonesia's anti-imperialist confrontational behaviour under Sukarno. Just as Indonesia under Suharto sought to establish domestic stability after the social and political chaos of the immediate postcolonial period, both Indonesia and Malaysia sought to turn ASEAN into a regional presence to promote regional stability, thus minimising potential threats to national security. The following chapter will expand on this argument, demonstrating the ways in which shared cultural memory and cultural affinity have been championed in asserting a sense of both national and regional cultural identity. The effect of this transnational cultural posturing, however, has been negligible.

Notes

1 A rare Malaysian perspective is presented in Raslan (2010).
2 The two islands are about 15.5 nautical miles apart. Ligitan is an uninhabited sandy island, with low vegetation and some trees. Sipadan (approximately 0.13 square kilometres) is larger than Ligitan, and was not inhabited on a permanent basis until the 1980s. It is densely wooded and is the peak of a submerged volcano around which a coral atoll has formed (Case Concerning Sovereignty 2002).
3 Unless otherwise noted, the account of the ICJ hearing is derived from the summary of the judgment (Case Concerning Sovereignty 2002).

2 Language and mythology

Seemingly indigenous concepts and practices have been borrowed from time to time as a means of conceptualising regional relations in maritime Southeast Asia. One such concept was of Indonesia and Malaysia being part of a pan-Malay *Nusantara*, or archipelago, a concept that enjoyed some popularity in the late colonial era in particular. For some nationalist leaders, pan-Malayism under the umbrella of terms such as '*Nusantara*' or '*Melayu*' appeared to be an eminently sensible suggestion, notwithstanding the fact that such notions were unimaginable in the pre-colonial era. 'In days of yore', as Maier (2004: 7) observes, '*Melayu* did not bear the burden of being an exclusive or comprehensive term leading to restrictions and constraints; it did not become prominent until 'others' made their presence more intensely felt and forced the people living on the shores of the Strait of Malacca and the South China Sea and beyond to become aware of the possibility that they were closely related, formed a 'nation', and should feel part of a community in a shared 'language' and a shared set of behaviours and ideas, in a 'Malay Archipelago''. Over time, however, these very same 'others' actively encouraged the local populations to map themselves not in terms of cultural unity but rather in terms of culturally different peoples, tribes, and nations. According to Maier (2004: 7):

> In their desire for stability and money, European merchants, missionaries, administrators, and scholars were unable to appreciate this vast fluidity from the very start of their involvement with the local population in this part of the world. They felt the need to construct sets of norms that could be used to make distinctions between various heterogeneous yet familial communities on the Islands (by which I mean what is now Indonesia) and the Peninsula (now known as Malaysia). They wanted to distinguish, say, the 'Javanese' from the 'Buginese', the 'Acehnese' from the 'Bataks'; and then judge 'Javanese', 'Buginese', Acehnese', and 'Batak' behaviour and discourse in terms of good and bad, correct and incorrect, whereas the local people tended to think in terms of relevant and irrelevant, appropriate and inappropriate.

Maier (2004: 7) also makes the pertinent observation that by way of print, education and administration, in the nineteenth century the colonial powers were able to sway local men and women to appreciate the utility of these invisible boundaries, and assist the colonial powers in asserting them. It is perhaps not surprising, therefore, that despite the popularity of pan-Malay imaginings, the immediate post-independence period, the fate of which was in the hands of a colonial-trained elite, was dominated by discourses of nationalism, decolonisation and the anti-Westernism of Indonesia's first president, Sukarno. In this manner, the postcolonial political elite merely replicated the colonial masters as they strove to implement invisible borders, which would somehow characterise 'Indonesians' and 'Malaysians' and then place them within clear boundaries. Ironically, post-independence Malaysia enjoyed a warm relationship with its former colonial power (Poulgrain 1998; Subritzky 1999), a handy by-product of which was ready access to the armed forces of Britain and its allies, Australia and New Zealand. This proved to be particularly useful in averting full-blown warfare between Malaysia and Indonesia during the period of confrontation. Nevertheless, despite the differing colonial experiences of the two nations, their national awakening and their competing visions of how a postcolonial society should take shape, the cultural affinity shared by the two postcolonial nations was often promoted as a means of enhancing cross-straits diplomacy. A key pillar of this notion was the belief that the two countries shared a similar linguistic heritage.

Most neutral observers would agree that the Indonesian language is closely related to Malay. Both languages can be understood by those who speak either, and there is much historical and linguistic evidence to support the assertion that they are closely related. Malay was originally spoken as a mother tongue in the areas around the Strait of Malacca, and more, precisely, in the Riau-Johor area, which has come to be labelled as the 'cradle of Malay' (Maier 2004: 17). When Melaka became the centre of trade in archipelagic Southeast Asia in the late fifteenth century, Malay experienced incredible growth. According to Liow (2005: 33):

> many of the various ethnic groups in the Indo-Malay Archipelago adopted one essential lingua franca to facilitate their integration into the regional network built around Melaka, giving rise to the spread of the Malayo-Polynesian language and its cognate derivatives from the Austronesian language family throughout the peninsula and archipelago with trade.

To this day, Malay, whether it is understood as *Bahasa Melayu* (the Malay language) or *Bahasa Indonesia* (the language of Indonesia), remains a lingua franca in the region. As fluent speakers of Indonesian, therefore, we rarely encountered any difficulties communicating in Malaysia during our fieldwork. Perhaps this was because, early on in our work, we were given very useful, if politically incorrect, advice – 'to speak Malay rather than Indonesian, simply speak Indonesian slowly'. We cannot vouch that this was the advice exactly, or even remember its source, but in general, our deliberately decelerated Indonesian has always served us well in Malaysia. Of course, we have tended to speak in textbook Indonesian, using slightly old-fashioned Malay Indonesian words and phrases such as *bercakap-cakap* or *bincang-bincang* (to chat) instead of the more colloquial Indonesian *ngobrol* or *ngomong*. Among other examples are our use of the Malay *boleh* ('can' or 'able to') instead of the Indonesian *bisa* ('can' in Indonesian and 'poison' in Malay), and the colloquial Malay *macam mana* (how) instead of its Indonesian equivalent, *bagaimana*. The Malaysians we encountered – whether they be Malay, Chinese, Indian or Iban – would respond either in English or standard Malay. But, regardless of accent or choice of vocabulary, as we prepared for this book, we rarely encountered either difficulty or prejudice when we spoke Indonesian in Malaysia. This was the case whether we were conversing with Chinese taxi drivers in Kuala Lumpur and Miri, bus drivers in Kuantan, Iban villagers in the jungles of Sarawak, Malay labourers in Terengganu, or academics in Shah Alam.

For many years the post-independence governments of both nations have attempted to minimise the linguistic divide between Malay and Indonesian, the latter of which is, in effect, Indonesian Malay. For example, serious efforts were made to implement a shared spelling system between Malay and Indonesian, with an emphasis on bridging alternative versions resulting from different transliterations of the Malay script dating from the colonial era (Liow 2005: 34). Majlis Bahasa Brunei, Indonesia dan Malaysia (MABBIM) (Brunei-Indonesia-Malaysia Language Council), established in 1972 as part of a resurgence of cultural exchange in the aftermath of *Konfrontasi*, has continued to pursue the unity of the two languages. As an example of cultural diplomacy, MABBIM has played a commendable role in fostering the cultural similarities between the two societies.

Despite the centripetal efforts of Malaysian organisations such as MABBIM, the extreme plurality of Malaysian society, with its multiethnic, religiously diverse peoples who speak a variety of languages, must be emphasised. Ethnic Malays make up less than two-thirds of the Malaysian population and, as the popularity of English increases and regional dialects such as Kelantanese persist, we have no real sense of certainty that Malay is the major language of communication in the country. Another factor that undermines MABBIM's efforts is the knowledge that the history of the Indonesian language cannot be divorced from Indonesian nationalism. In 1928, *Bahasa Melayu* was renamed and replaced with *Bahasa Indonesia*, which meant 'the language of Indonesia' as opposed to 'the Malay language'. As Lindsay (2012: 50) observes: 'Naming Malay "Indonesian" was a nationalist statement and an act of appropriation, marking distinction and national boundaries. "This language is ours," it said, "and we will mark ourselves as a nation by using it in our own way."' Consequently, Indonesian has grown within the national boundaries of Indonesia and has, therefore, inevitably grown apart from Malay. Differing media and education systems in both nations have fostered significant differences between the standard Malay of Indonesia and that of Malaysia. Today, many

Indonesians think of Malaysian Malay as a different language, and many Malay speakers in Malaysia think of Indonesian Malay as a different language too. The irony is that, today, national boundaries, and thus national languages, are becoming increasingly fluid. As Lindsay (2012: 51) argues, 'Technology, the media, and mobility all help to reveal that national boundaries are quite arbitrary, and in the case of Indonesian/Malay, they are a relatively recent imposition on a shared language spoken with huge variation over a very large area'. Besides the clear, broad differences between standard Malay and standard Indonesian, variations in the language spoken in different regions and by different generations are increasing in both Malaysia and Indonesia.

The construction of a sense of cultural affinity along ethnic or linguistic lines has long been tenuous from an anthropological perspective and, as suggested in the previous paragraph, increasingly irrelevant in a functional sense. In the late 1980s, Jusuf Wanandi poured cold water on the notion of a sense of fraternity based on ethnicity: 'generally both Malaysia and Indonesia may be Malay nations ... but they should not expect too much from Indonesia based on the "Malay stock" factor ... The vast majority of Indonesians are Javanese, who do not regard themselves as Malay' (quoted in Liow 2005: 156). Although it is the national language, Indonesian Malay is not the mother tongue of the majority of the Indonesian population, despite the fact that more people now speak only Indonesian, that is, only Indonesian and no other regional language of Indonesia. Likewise, as we have hinted at above, Malay is not the mother tongue of Malaysia's substantial ethnic minorities, namely the Indians, Chinese and the indigenous peoples of Sabah and Sarawak.

It is significant that in recent years diplomatic meetings between Malaysia and Indonesia have been conducted in English, purportedly in recognition of the significant differences between the two languages, which go beyond differences in accent. Given that English has become the default language of ASEAN diplomacy, diplomats claim that to revert to Indonesian and Malay in either bilateral or multilateral settings would seem inappropriately parochial. It would certainly require a lot of unnecessary translation and duplication of material; indeed, we have heard anecdotal accounts of how bilateral meetings between the two countries are characterised by confusion over which language to use. In the broader context, although Malay remains the trading lingua franca of the citizens of Indonesia and Malaysia, it appears that, as both nations become more global in orientation and multicultural in ethnic makeup, any historical linguistic affinity between them is slowly but surely being overwhelmed by what is increasingly identified as the 'world language', English. A similar process has occurred in relation to the once-shared cultural heritage of the two countries, which has now become less an expression of *rumpun*-based fraternity and more a pawn in an ever-escalating game of cultural chauvinism. In relation to contestations over cultural heritage, UNESCO is having an effect that is not unlike the linguistic encroachment of English, although it appears to be playing more of a divisive role than a unifying one. We will return to this debate in the next chapter.

The growing cultural distance between Indonesia and Malaysia in recent decades has not diminished efforts by regional organisations to either enhance or create a sense of shared cultural identity within the region. With the emergence of ASEAN as a regional organisation in Southeast Asia in the 1960s, a great deal of effort was expended in inculcating a sense of community and shared cultural identity. Not surprisingly, the question of culture has become an important factor in the study of regionalism, especially so now, as more evidence emerges to suggest that feelings of community tend to arise from the 'bottom up', independently of regional institutions (Katzenstein and Checkel 2009: xi). Nevertheless, most studies of regional integration have tended to focus on political institutions rather than on identity construction, although constructions of community and collective identity are now gaining importance in the study of comparative politics. Nowhere are such constructions more important than in the context of Southeast Asia, particularly in relation to the bilateral relationship of the major nations here, Indonesia and Malaysia.

A shared sense of cultural and historical affinity has always been important in mainland and maritime Southeast Asia, where cultural, or soft, diplomacy has long held sway. The sense of linguistic affinity between Indonesia and Malaysia has been a significant element of this discourse, even as Malay and Indonesian appear to be gradually drifting apart. A somewhat dogmatic collective sense of shared cultural identity has added over time significant ballast to the Indonesia–Malaysia bilateral relationship, as it has to other relationships, primarily under the ASEAN regional umbrella. Cultural identity holds an important place in regionalism because, to some extent, states are often guided by what is considered culturally appropriate behaviour, determined according to a collective identity. The degree to which collective identity determines appropriate behaviour depends on the impact of symbols, myths and other markers of cultural identity on political actors and their audiences (Jetschke and Rüland 2009: 187). The shared norms, ideas and worldviews that form collective identity, sometimes referred to as 'cultural memory', can be inculcated by art, media, education, historiography, public commemoration and other means. As Jetschke and Rüland (2009: 187) observe, 'although the rhetoric in which these ideas are couched may change, propagated by the elites and adopted by the population to varying degrees, they form a deeper stratum of the cultural memory, which is nevertheless constantly activated to gauge and interpret current events and social interactions against the backdrop of previous experience'. In the postcolonial context, cultural memory is used to recreate a shared past and reconstruct a shared cultural identity. Myths, in particular, can support political integration by providing a common identity. In Europe, a sense of identity, among other things, has emerged from common historical Christian myths. In contrast, the diversity of Southeast Asia has meant that there is very little in the way of shared political or legal histories, and no shared philosophical tradition. But there is a shared mythology – the ancient Sanskrit epic of the Ramayana – and some have believed that it might have the potential to significantly shape the Southeast Asian cultural identity.

There is much to suggest that the Ramayana can be regarded as a shared mythology of Southeast Asia. It is common to many nations in the region and especially well known in Indonesia and Malaysia. Throughout Southeast Asia, the Ramayana has a long history in performance, literature and visual arts. Moreover, either the Ramayana or variations on the tale, such as the Malay *Hikayat Seri Rama* and the Javanese *Serat Rama*, have been profoundly influential in the evolution of Southeast Asian political systems. Nowadays, the Ramayana epic is widespread throughout Southeast Asia and has become an important performance emblem in the region (Lindsay 2003). But, has the Ramayana played a role in the development of a shared Southeast Asian cultural identity? The answer to this must be in the negative, despite the fact that there were hints in the 1970s that a convergence of the collective mythological narrative – the Ramayana – with the collective political imperative would be a natural and sensible process. Resink (1975: 230), for example, has observed that the availability of a single great myth enjoying popularity throughout Southeast Asia, acting as a source of inspiration for literature, ballet and theatre, 'is a uniting force of the first order'. Throughout the 1990s, ASEAN attempted to develop the Ramayana's potential to enhance Southeast Asia's regional relations. Despite the modest rise of Southeast Asian regional cooperation over the past 40 years, it is still unclear to what extent cultural forces such as the Ramayana epic have fulfilled their potential as a means of fostering the collective political will and, more specifically, the bilateral will of Indonesia and Malaysia. This chapter will examine the extent to which a shared cultural affinity, epitomised by similar languages, myths and legends, has provided a historical–cultural foundation for broader and deeper regional and bilateral dialogue.

ASEAN and the Ramayana

Although the tales of the Mahabharata cycle are more regularly performed in Indonesian shadow (*wayang kulit*) and doll puppet (*wayang golek*) theatre, most other Southeast Asian countries, where the Mahabharata is not as well known, share the Ramayana tradition. As already noted, Resink (1975) has suggested that the popularity of the Ramayana throughout Southeast Asia can be regarded as an important cultural unifier, making the claim in the mid-1970s, when Southeast Asian states were engaged in a concerted effort to integrate regional cooperation, including in the cultural sphere. Attempts at regional integration in the 1950s and 1960s, such as the formation of SEATO, ASA and MAPHILINDO, had not met with the hoped-for success. As discussed in the previous chapter, each of these regional groupings failed because their respective political leaders and policymakers could not agree on the common threat they faced or on the goals of the institutions. More importantly, there was no consensus with regard to the rules and norms of intra-regional political behaviour.

The creation of ASEAN in 1967 was widely regarded as a fresh start for regional integration in Southeast Asia. In contrast with the previous failures in institutional collaboration, ASEAN prided itself on establishing co-operative norms and prohibiting the use of force in solving intra-regional disputes and has subsequently grown and prospered to the extent that it is now considered one of the world's most important regional organisations (Ba 2009). Among factors leading to its success are: the ability of ASEAN members to turn good fortune into strong economic development; the ability of ASEAN to provide benefits to its members that they would not have otherwise received; and the way in which ASEAN's principles and norms with regard to the conduct of regional and international relations resonated with member governments and indeed with other governments in East Asia (Stubbs 2009: 237–41). With the early success of ASEAN and its counterpart regional organisations, such as the European Union (EU), the need to develop political integration and a common heritage has become even more important in recent years. The rise of constructivist approaches to regional relations, which emphasise the role of culture, identity and a sense of community, has also influenced the scholarship on Southeast Asia's regional relations. According to Acharya and Stubbs (2006: 127):

> Going beyond traditionalist perspectives that regarded material forces such as military balances and great power alliances as the critical determinants of regional stability, constructivists argued that ideational forces, including norms and identity, are very much a part of the regional environment or 'structure' that shapes Southeast Asia's regional order. Moreover, the agency of local actors and their regional institutions matter and should not be viewed (as some realist accounts of regional order maintain) as a mere adjunct to the great power balancing.

Although it was a common fear of externally backed communism that initially pushed ASEAN countries to embrace regionalism, ASEAN's ability to 'hang together' and avoid intra-regional conflict has in many ways depended on ideational factors, such as regionalist norms and culture and identity-building processes (Acharya 2009: 173).

There are a number of cultural and historical legacies underpinning the success of ASEAN and the ASEAN Way. They include indigenous forms of collective action, as embodied in the village traditions of the Malay world, such as *gotong royong*, and dispute mediation procedures based on local custom (*adat*), such as *musyawarah* and *muafakat*, often referred to as *mufakat*. Hindu-Brahmanic elite constructions of power, based on the assumption that a ruler is surrounded by concentric circles (*mandalas*) of foes and allies, have also been historically influential. The Hindu-Brahmanic *mandala* worldview perhaps explains why Southeast Asian nations are so 'amenable to notions of pragmatic Realpolitik with its predisposition towards state survival, national sovereignty and foreign policy autonomy' (Jetschke and Rüland 2009: 188). The Indian epics of the Mahabharata and the Ramayana have long conveyed Hindu-Brahmanic concepts of kingship and rule. Although knowledge of the

Hindu-Brahmanic concepts of politics and leadership may have been limited to the cultural and political elites, according to Jetschke and Rüland (2009: 188) the broader Southeast Asian population is reasonably familiar with the general political lessons. As mentioned earlier, the Mahabharata and Ramayana epics have played a key role in the dissemination of Hindu-Brahmanic political theory, if it can be termed as such. As Jetschke and Rüland (2009: 188) observe in relation to the Mahabharata and Ramayana epics:

> Widely known in much of Southeast Asia and popularized through translation, the school curriculum, shadow plays (*wayang*), architecture, songs, radio broadcasts, comics and Internet blogs (Charnvit Kasetsiri 1976: 133; Thongthep 1993: 5; Weinstein 2004), they convey the message that even the good and the virtuous are persistently challenged by villains and evil demons. Warfare, violence, intrigue, insecurity and tragedy are thus depicted as unavoidable facts of life.

Although the political worldviews exhibited in the ancient Indian epics have frequently been recognised in local-language writings by Southeast Asian security commentators up to the present day (see, for instance, Kusnanto 2005), on the whole, international relations specialists tend to ignore the deeper cultural strata underpinning Southeast Asian regionalism.

Within Southeast Asia, there is a general understanding that shared norms, values and mythologies have played an important part in developing and enhancing Southeast Asia's regional integration. This was both acknowledged and demonstrated in 1997 when the ASEAN Committee on Culture and Information (COCI) decided to undertake a 'high-impact' dance project that would reflect shared ASEAN cultural values. The intention was to transcend the usual ASEAN exercise of performing an anthology of dances originating in each of the ten member countries. Instead, in a desire for a creative collaboration among leading writers, choreographers, composers and dancers of each of the countries, the Ramayana was chosen as a binding theme. A similar exercise had been undertaken in 1992 in an ASEAN joint theatre production, also based on the Ramayana epic.

The dance drama that emerged from the ASEAN collaboration, *Realizing Rama,* directed by Nestor O. Jardin from the Philippines, was billed as 'Ramayana, An Asian Cultural Confluence'. As Lindsay (2003: 143) observes, 'other than vocal music as dance accompaniment, the performance uses no language' – no doubt, as a means of dealing with the tricky problem of which language to use. Premiering at the sixth ASEAN Summit in Vietnam in 1998, the production toured extensively in Asia and Europe. Ultimately, *Realizing Rama* was deemed so successful that since 1998 it has been official COCI policy to mount pan-ASEAN flagship productions that display the 'culture of ASEAN' (Lindsay 2003: 143). *Realizing Rama* reinterpreted the Ramayana as an enquiry into the theme of selfless leadership. According to Saran and Khanna (2004: 211), 'In the production Sita is projected as Rama's heart and

Lakshmana as his mind. Accompanied by them he transcends ego and self, realizing his true nature as a leader endowed with wisdom and compassion'.

Niconor G. Tiongson, the Filipino librettist of the production, gave a similar perspective: 'The libretto compounds the notion that Rama becomes a true leader of the people only after going through the exile of self-purification, where he confronts and conquers the temptations of Wealth, Lust and Power' (Saran and Khanna 2004: 211). Not surprisingly, these themes, as do the general themes of the Ramayana, share some similarities with the basic organising principles of ASEAN, such as a balance-of-power approach aimed at preventing the domination of the region by any single outside power, the preservation of regional order by reducing the likelihood of intra-regional conflict and, most importantly, the enhancement of domestic stability by not interfering in the internal affairs of ASEAN members. Like the inward-looking Rama of *Realizing Rama*, ASEAN's cardinal principle of non-interference has allowed ASEAN members to focus on domestic political authoritarianism. In terms of leadership, by focusing on cohesion, ASEAN has become the hub of Asian regionalism and plays a prominent leadership role in most East Asian regional institutions.

It is hard to determine the degree to which the Ramayana has been incorporated as a cultural unifier into the context of Southeast Asian relations, especially because it has has little social or political relevance in contemporary Vietnam, Brunei and Laos, not to mention Myanmar, Singapore and the Philippines. Even in Indonesia and Malaysia its relevance is easily and frequently overstated. It is, indeed, difficult to demonstrate the political efficacy of cultural expression anywhere in the world, or even its social or cultural impact. Nevertheless, it can be argued that the ideas and episodes of the Ramayana still resonate in the deeper strata of the collective or cultural memory of Southeast Asians, particularly in certain groups in Indonesia and Malaysia, where *wayang kulit* still enjoys a modest amount of popularity. The production referred to above also suggests that the Ramayana has proven useful in cultivating ideational ties among all of the ASEAN countries, not just between Indonesia and Malaysia. The regionalising potential of the Ramayana has not dimmed with the passage of time. The urge to present cultural commonality as an ASEAN reality has led to other efforts to translate that commonality to the stage. In 1994, for example, the Japan Foundation hosted an ASEAN performing arts festival in Japan, which has developed into a regular event and expanded into a broader Asian arts festival, often resulting in pan-Asian productions (Lindsay 2003: 144).

Despite the success of the region-building projects mentioned above, it can be argued that, overall, the Ramayana's potential regional role has been simultaneously overrated and underplayed. This is primarily due to the fact that ASEAN has been an inward-looking organisation, concerned principally with regime survival and state-building objectives. Southeast Asian governments, having achieved their hard-won independence from the colonial powers, were understandably reluctant to embrace supranational European-style integration schemes when they preferred a model of regional cooperation focused on strengthening national capabilities. The state-centredness of the ASEAN Way, which has drawn on regional cultural worldviews, played a fundamental role in creating a pleasant and friendly atmosphere in order to avoid conflict. According to Jetschke and Rüland (2009: 192), 'The ASEAN Way performs precisely this function in inter-state relations: cultivating stable and predictable relationships through friendship, harmony, restraint, non-intervention into the internal affairs of neighbours and peaceful dispute settlement'. In this context, where the ASEAN Way facilitated peaceful interaction and a measure of cooperation among ASEAN members, there has been little need for an alternative regional master-narrative along the lines of Resink's Ramayana proposal. Instead, narratives with a 'regionalising' potential were adopted for alternative means, namely state-building. Indonesia's authoritarian President Suharto, for instance, appropriated Ramayana characters and episodes as a means of enhancing his own domestic political authoritarianism; enhancing regional integration was of secondary importance.

The Ramayana as propagated by Indonesian cultural and political elites

The popularity of the Ramayana elsewhere in Southeast Asia has led to a revival of sorts of the Ramayana in Java. In 1960, on a visit to Cambodia, Indonesia's then Minister of Communications, Telecommunications and Tourism, Major General G.P.H. Djatikusumo, witnessed a Ramayana-inspired performance of the Ballet Royal du Cambodge at Angkor Wat (Moehkardi 1983: 3). He was so impressed that he commissioned a similar kind of performance in Java. As Lindsay (2003: 138) observes, this commissioning 'shows there was already a sense of developing art form for both nation *and* region'. Since then, during the dry season the Ramayana Ballet has continued almost nightly at the Prambanan Temple on the outskirts of Yogyakarta. Catering almost entirely to domestic and foreign tourists, the ballet incorporates Javanese dance movements in its presentation of episodes of the Ramayana, accompanied by a traditional *gamelan* orchestra.

In Yogyakarta, the popularity of the Ramayana Ballet performances has in turn led to nightly tourist-oriented *wayang* shadow theatre performances, also accompanied by *gamelan*. Held in walking distance from the Sultan of Yogyakarta's palace, the *wayang* performances attract a dozen or more foreign tourists each night. These truncated performances, about two hours in duration, are usually based on episodes of the Ramayana epic, because, we have been told on several occasions, it is assumed that foreigners are more interested in and knowledgeable of the characters and plot of the Ramayana than of the Mahabharata. Although the puppeteers and *gamelan* musicians involved, like most Javanese, are much more interested in the tales of the Mahabharata, they are nonetheless quite happy to cater to the lucrative tourist market. The fact that each performer is paid a modest amount for their efforts is, no doubt, an important factor in the enduring success of this initiative. Financial factors also underpin the reasons for Indonesian writers to draw upon the tales of the Ramayana in their published short stories, novels or poems. An impressive honorarium is paid to a writer or poet for publishing their work in Indonesia's leading newspapers, including *Kompas, Republika*, and *Media Indonesia*. One of Indonesia's best-selling novels, Sindhunata's *Anak Bajang Menggiring Angin* (1983), which is based on the Ramayana, was first published in *Kompas* in serial form. It is quite natural for Indonesian writers, particularly of Javanese, Sundanese or Balinese origin, to draw inspiration from the myths of their childhood. Indeed, the Indian epics and their localised interpretations have proven to be a fertile source of literary inspiration ever since the rise of print-literacy in the late nineteenth century. This natural tendency to mine indigenous myths and legends is heightened at times of extreme social, political and economic turmoil, such as the last years of President Suharto's New Order regime. According to Saran and Khanna (2004: 209), 'during the period leading up to the overthrow of Suharto, well-known Ramayana characters and episodes were used by his allies to defend his rule and by his opponents to present sharp social and political satire'. Clark (2001) has also commented on this tendency in the context of the New Order.

In the highly-politicised context of the late New Order, some of Indonesia's leading writers may have drawn on the Ramayana precisely because they knew that this literary strategy would guarantee presidential attention. The language and ethos of the *wayang*, after all, was second nature to Suharto. Ethnically Javanese, Suharto was well known for his appreciation of the Javanese *wayang* shadow theatre, and the Ramayana, in particular, held a deep attraction for the President. According to Suharto's Minister for Tourism, Post and Telecommunication, Joop Ave, an important episode in the Ramayana cycle of tales, *Rama Tambak*, was performed especially for President Suharto whenever he faced serious problems in the early years of his presidency (Lubis, Ramelan and Syahban 1998). In a semi-official biography of Suharto, there is a photo of him posing in his presidential office in front of a large painting depicting Hanoman fighting on the side of good against the evil King Rahwana, also spelled as 'Rawana' (Roeder 1969: ii). At the height of the 1997–98 Asian economic crisis, which devastated the Indonesian economy and led to massive street demonstrations, Suharto allowed his government ministers to further emphasise his links with Hanoman. Consequently Suharto's Minister for Tourism endorsed a series of lavish Ramayana *wayang kulit* and *wayang golek* performances to be performed and televised throughout the major cities of East, Central and West Java, as well as in the capital, Jakarta.

The government-funded – and thus pro-Suharto – Ramayana performances were roundly criticised. First of all, journalists, academics and commentators attacked their exorbitant cost at a time of grave national crisis. Second, the performances, which were claimed to be a form of *ruwatan* (exorcism) aimed at cleansing the nation from its social and economic woes, did not lead to any discernible upturn in the nation's fortunes. Third, very few felt that Suharto, who was politically on his last legs, could be regarded as a Hanoman-like saviour. Suharto's efforts to align himself with Hanoman and his monkey army were in stark contrast to the impression conveyed in subsequent publications such as Soebadio Sastrosatomo's *Politik Dosomuko Rezim Orde Baru* (The Politics of Dosomuko's New Order Regime) (Sastrosatomo 1998). This book, like many short stories, poems and essays appearing at the time, represents Suharto as the evil Dosomuko (Rahwana). Hanoman and the monkey army in the service of Rama are a crude representation of the increasingly impoverished and frustrated populace. Perlman (1999) has observed that Soebadio's 'blistering' comparison between Dosomuko and Suharto's regime would do many a *dalang* (shadow puppeteer) proud. It is useful to note that *Politik Dosomuko* was published in February 1998 and was banned and withdrawn from sale on 22 April of the same year, in the month before Suharto's resignation (Clark 2001: 170). The speedy banning of the book is an indication of how seriously and personally the President took such writing.

Thus it appears that when interpreting the role of the Ramayana in Southeast Asia, national interests tend to dominate, at the expense of a regional focus. The following section will compare and contrast two Southeast Asian films inspired by the Ramayana epic – Indonesia's *Opera Jawa* (Javanese Opera) (2006) and Malaysia's *Wayang* (2008). It will become evident that the two films provide cinematic windows onto domestic social and political issues in Indonesia and Malaysia, respectively.

Contemporary reinterpretations of the Ramayana

Garin Nugroho's Javanese-language film, *Opera Jawa* (2006), is a particularly striking example of how the Ramayana worldview has the capacity to gauge and interpret current events such as the sociopolitical tensions of post-authoritarian Indonesia. However, the analysis in this section will also suggest that the broad thematic scope of *Opera Jawa* extends beyond the national context. It encompasses themes of international relations and regional order, as well as reflecting broader Indonesian attitudes towards regional relations. Before beginning this analysis, we will briefly discuss the background, plot, style and key artistic features of the film.

Garin Nugroho was born in the Central Javanese city of Yogyakarta and, like the vast majority of the Javanese, he grew up steeped in the tradition of the *wayang* and the Hindu-Javanese epics. In *Opera Jawa* the Ramayana love triangle is re-imagined as a conflict between married village artisans Setio (Martinus Miroto) and Siti (Artika Sari Devi) and a village heavy, Ludiro (Eko Supriyanto). When Setio embarks on a business trip, Ludiro tests Siti's fidelity. The romantic intrigue is envisioned through a soundtrack of haunting *gamelan* melodies, as well as acrobatic dance choreography. The film is also interspersed with sculpture, installation art, shadow puppetry and traditional artistic images of the master-narrative underpinning the film, the Ramayana.

If we consider the production of *Opera Jawa* as empirical evidence of the ongoing popularity of the Ramayana and the general social and political lessons it conveys, by analysing just one of the many installation artworks (contributed by Nindityo Adipurnomo, Entang Wiharso, Sunaryo, Agus Suwage, Tita Rubi, S. Teddy D. and Hendro Suseno) incorporated in the film, we can highlight the ways in which the Ramayana is representative of broader social and political themes in Indonesia. Garin invited Bandung-based artist Sunaryo to create an installation around the Plaosan temple, Central Java, which was related to the scene in the Ramayana in which Sukesi, the mother of Rahwana (Ludiro in the film), sews a piece of red cloth to help her son seduce Sinta (Siti in the film). Sunaryo's installation consisted of more than 2,000 bamboo poles as masts for red flags, a backdrop to thousands of metres of red fabric, spread over the temple and nearby tobacco fields, village roads and rice paddies. A number of fish traps, alluding to Siti's eventual entrapment, were placed on the temple walls and in a nearby river. It took more than two months, in late 2006, to prepare and construct the installation, entitled *Semedi Ning Jenar* (Meditation in Red), which filled a large physical space. Beyond the immediate vicinity of the Plaosan temple, Sunaryo placed red cloth along streets, clearings and riverbanks in the village of Kasongan, not far from the temple. In the Kasongan scene, the red of the cloth, 'a symbol of the temptation of desire upon Sinta' (Susanto 2007: 43), is used as a lure. Driven by desire, Siti follows the red cloth until it leads to Ludiro, who is entangled, also by red cloth. The seduction is completed symbolically when, in the middle of a river, the red fabric and several fish traps are set alight.

Sunaryo's installation can be interpreted in several ways, as can *Opera Jawa* as a whole. The red fabric can be unproblematically regarded as a symbol of Siti's temptation. Art critic Mikke Susanto (2007: 118) has, however, referred to Sunaryo's belief that the colour red is also a symbol of bravery and a sign of power and war. This suggests that Sunaryo's artistic intention was as much to comment on international politics as it was to address the psychological dynamics of the Ramayana love triangle. Along similar lines, Garin Nugroho suggested in an interview that *Opera Jawa* is a comment on the power inequities of contemporary geopolitics:

> The character of Rahwana is similar to big, rich countries that always want money and have a stable economy but then use their power to intimidate small, weak countries. Rama is like those small countries who finally get angry and declare a war. Both the strong and the weak characters are violent. Siti is a symbol of a land that is fought over by the strong and the weak character. This symbolizes what is happening in the world now.
>
> (Kurnia 2007)

In an interview with Lisa Williams (2007), he made a similar point:

> The film is about disaster and violence. The three main characters are symbolic in the main way as classical Javanese puppets are. Siti means 'land'. She represents what has happened to the people as a result of natural disaster, conflict and the fight for holy land. She goes through three months of conflict when people fight for her body for these different reasons. She says in the film, 'I'm not a holy land, I'm a human being'. The character Ludiro represents people who have power in the economy and military and who abuse this power. Setio represents the people who are disempowered and so become violent. That is the way of the world.

Garin's choice of the Plaosan temple complex as a backdrop to his film, rather than the nearby and much better known Prambanan temple which depicts the stories of the Ramayana epic on the temple reliefs, is also indicative of social and political themes, such as the cultural and religious diversity of the Southeast Asian region. Prambanan was built by Rakai Pikatan, a Shivaite (Hindu) who held power in the ninth century. He also built Plaosan, in collaboration with his wife Pramodhawardani, who was a Buddhist. Unlike Prambanan, Plaosan has no link with the Ramayana. Its purpose was twofold: as an act of devotion to Buddha and as a display of quality workmanship. According to Susanto (2007: 101):

> Garin's choice was based on his thoughts about the existence of different religions. Garin is apparently fascinated by ideas about the order and balance of nature, and the harmonious mingling of cultures and religions. If we observe his work so far, it is evident that Garin often creates works with multicultural themes, talking about matters related to the differences in life, including in terms of religions. Indonesia is indeed rife with such differences – and this, for Garin, is a fertile ground he can unceasingly explore.

By emphasising the choice of filming location, Susanto points to an alternative angle – the dialectic nature of both *Meditation in Red* and *Opera Jawa*:

> In breezy Plaosan, a cool atmosphere embraces us, clearing our mind. We are far away from the cacophony of the city, in harmony with nature and the locals. Sunaryo (equipped as he was with his aesthetic ideas that enjoyed conflicting matters) employed the coolness of the place, contrasting it with the redness of the fabric, hinting at some hot conditions. *Meditation in Red*, in this sense, was like a stage of struggle and perhaps a meeting room displaying two profoundly different matters. It seemed that there were two desires, there were complexities, there were struggles (perhaps there was Sinta's desire and sanctity, there was possessive Rama

and aggressive Rahwana, there was goodness and evil, and perhaps there was also Garin and Sunaryo being "in competition").

(Susanto 2007: 117)

Ultimately, anyone who has viewed *Opera Jawa* will agree that attempting to pin down a higher 'meaning', or a number of possible 'meanings', is a daunting task, given the beguiling barrage of colour, costume, music and movement. As Garin himself says:

> the important thing about the film is that some of it is chaotic ... we tell the story of living in a chaotic place where the future is unpredictable. In Asia there is so much unpredictability, but that is the beauty of it.

(Williams 2007)

We could also argue that the chaos and, indeed, the power conflict described above is a comment on the social, economic and political instability concomitant with Indonesia's relatively recent embrace of democratisation.

Hatta Azad Khan's *Wayang* (2008) is by no means a response to Garin's *Opera Jawa*, but it is another example of the way in which the Ramayana can provide a commentary on national sociopolitical trends and it provides us with an opportunity to make a few preliminary comparisons between Indonesia and Malaysia. The film revolves around a traditional *wayang kulit* puppeteer in the Malaysian state of Kelantan, Awang Lah (Eman Manan). He teaches puppeteering skills to two semi-orphaned children, a blind boy called Awi (Zul Huzaimy) and a girl with a speech impediment, Melor (Mas Muharni). Because he is blind, Awi focuses on learning how to narrate, sing songs and deliver the puppet's dialogue with the correct voice timbre, pronunciation and intonation. Much to his teacher's dismay, he also successfully incorporates modern innovations into his performances. For instance, in combination with the traditional *gamelan* orchestra, Awi sings up-tempo love songs accompanied by a guitar. Because of her speech impediment, Melor focuses on the manipulation of the puppets. Eventually Awi and Melor perform as a team and fall in love. Inspired by the Ramayana episodes they have been learning, practising and performing for over a decade, they secretly regard each other as Rama and Sita Dewi (Sinta). When Awi eventually summons the courage to reveal his romantic attraction, he asks Melor if Sita could ever fall in love with a 'blind Rama'. After a sleepless night, she answers in the affirmative.

In many ways the developing love story between Awi and Melor resembles the narrative arc of the Ramayana, with several contemporary twists. Not unlike the Ramayana's evil Rahwana, Jusoh (Wan Kenari), a fundamentalist Muslim who covets Melor as a second wife, constantly harasses the Rama-Sinta-like couple of Melor and Awi. Ironically, Jusoh, who is also Awang Lah's cousin, has no fondness for *wayang kulit*, as he believes it is blasphemous. At an early point in the film Jusoh asserts that '[t]he *wayang kulit* is *haram*. Idolising puppets, giving humans attributes to puppets'. Jusoh, who is also jealous of Awang Lah's modest financial success as a puppeteer, eventually attacks his cousin's *wayang* screen, setting it alight. Mirroring the conflict between Rahwana and Rama, Jusoh attacks Awi on several occasions, but is thwarted each time. Echoing the questions regarding the identity of Sinta's father in the Indian and Javanese versions of the Ramayana, it is revealed late in the film that Awang Lah is actually Melor's real father.

Ostensibly using the Ramayana as a narrative frame for the love story of Awi and Melor, *Wayang* can also be regarded as a commentary on broader themes in contemporary Malaysian society. In one sense, the fundamentalism of Jusoh can be broadly understood to represent the rising *ketuanan Islam* (Islamic supremacy) ideology in Malaysia, which is closely associated with the recent rigorous implementation of Islamic law and values and with ongoing attempts to transform radically the concept of the 'Malay'. Riddell interprets more precisely the conflict between Awang Lah and Jusoh as a reflection of the tensions in Malaysian politics 'between a modernising approach to Islam, as represented by the national government dominated by the United Malays National Organisation (UMNO) and its supporters, and a conservative literalist approach to Islam, as represented by PAS [Parti Islam Se-Malaysia (the Pan-Malaysian Islamic Party)]' (Riddell 2009: 398). Riddell argues that UMNO sees the role of Islam in Malaysia's political life as being to promote inclusivist values that accommodate Malaysia's rich heritage of culture and tradition. Perhaps this is superficially the case, but it could be argued that UMNO is as chauvinistic about maintaining the 'purity' of Islam as PAS is, if not more so. Nevertheless, for PAS, all facets of state and society should revolve around Islam, which leaves little room for sympathy for traditional pre-Islamic cultural forms such as *wayang*, which are heavily dependent on the narratives and characters of Hindu-Buddhist epics such as the Ramayana. This was demonstrated in 1990 when the PAS gained power in Kelantan and banned *wayang kulit* and various other traditional Malay art forms, accusing them of being 'un-Islamic'. The prohibition was only lifted after the puppeteers of Kelantan abandoned the Ramayana epic in their performances, drawing on local folk tales instead.

In *Wayang*, the conflict between UMNO's promotion of Islamic values and PAS's conservative insistence on strict Islamic literalism is played out on various levels. On the one hand, Jusoh's denigration of the *wayang* follows the PAS party line. On the other hand, Awang Lah's love for the *wayang* as a mode of entertainment reflects UMNO's relative respect for traditional culture, albeit as long as it brings in the tourism dollar. Meanwhile, Jusoh often wears white robes and a white skullcap or white headdress in classical Islamic mode, perhaps in imitation of what is perceived to be Middle Eastern Islamic garb. In contrast, Awang wears traditional Malay *batik* and no headdress. Riddell (2009) observes that the varying dress codes extend to the two antagonists' children; Jusoh's twin sons wear white *kopiah* or skullcaps, whereas Awang Lah allows Awi not to wear any headdress and Melor to have her hair free, without an Islamic headscarf. There are other important examples of the conflict of values, such as when Awang's wife rebukes her husband for bringing two orphans into their home, saying that their house is not a shelter for the homeless. Awang responds that she lacks a sense of pity and compassion, expressing the view of moderate Muslims in Malaysia who seek to stress the Islamic values of compassion, especially to orphans. In contrast, Jusoh is seen to be rather legalistic in insisting that his two sons wear Islamic *kopiah*, even though their teachers at the *pondok* are critical of this preoccupation with form (Riddell 2009). Not unlike the bitter divide between UMNO and PAS, the conflict between Awang Lah and Jusoh gradually escalates throughout the course of the film, especially after Jusoh destroys Awang Lah's *wayang* screen.

In another sense, the tension between the traditionalist puppeteering master, Awang Lah, and his innovative and increasingly successful protégé, Awi, can be regarded as a reflection of the tensions of modernity in Malaysian culture and society as a whole. As Milner (2008) observes, much of what was important in past centuries is less relevant for contemporary Malaysian society, especially such things as the tales of the *wayang kulit*. As Maier has suggested, in the Malay world the ancient stories are now treated not as knowledge but as beliefs and superstitions, even if so-called 'traditional' tales are apparently still being recited in public (Maier 2004: 28). Nonetheless, the *wayang kulit*, based on the ancient stories of the Ramayana, simply does not have the same meaning in today's society that it once possessed. In Malaysia's urban milieu, despite government support for traditional Malay culture, the *wayang kulit* is regarded as an antiquated art form, very much a relic of the rural world of traditional beliefs, superstitions and conservative cultural values. Younger Malaysians are now much more interested in digital and visual media, such as television, the Internet and cinema. Moreover, cinemagoers tend to flock to films that appeal to populist tastes. Social realism set in Kelantan, with most of the dialogue in the Kelantanese dialect of Malay, is not exactly flavour of the month, as reflected in *Wayang*'s lacklustre box-office takings. Garin Nugroho speaks of a similar process in Indonesia, where banal consumerist politics are dominant: 'Now, in the post-Suharto era, Indonesian film-makers face a massive, fast-growing consumerism that is without ethics and which gives no space to marginal cultural forms' (Kurnia 2007: 63).

Wayang's muted response from the Malaysian public was attributed on an entertainment website to 'among other things perhaps because the title of the film wasn't sensational enough'.[1] Hatta Azad Khan, its director, has indicated that he places little importance on box-office receipts and thus he was not particularly disappointed by *Wayang*'s poor box-office takings (Hamid 2008). Instead, he points to the need to preserve Malaysia's traditional arts, although at the same time he highlights the importance of updating tradition to suit contemporary tastes. He argues that the film deals with important and enduring themes, such as love, modernity and religious intolerance. His film also points to the inexorability of change, particularly in the cultural sphere. For example, Hatta's decision to present the Rama-esque Awi as blind was a deliberate departure from the Ramayana epic:

The reality is that life demands change, and change is experienced by everything, and so for this very reason I created the blind character of Awi in order to bring about change in *wayang kulit* performances. If I had created the character as a young man who is able to see, then it would be very difficult for him to bring about change as he would be able to see the immediate reactions of those around, besides being accustomed to seeing what has always been before his eyes.[2]

Likewise, Hatta himself displays the traditionalist outlook of Awang Lah whilst demonstrating, to some extent, the blindness of Awi. Perhaps this is precisely the approach needed to make a film that seems so far removed from the banal consumerist tastes of modern society?

The interpretation of *Wayang* in this chapter has been dominated by the immediate concerns of Malaysia's domestic social and political context, in particular by the conflict between UMNO and PAS. There is little evidence that *Wayang* is intended to discuss broader themes that transcend Malaysia's borders. Indeed, the most obvious narrative link to Malaysia's largest neighbour, the *wayang kulit* performed and discussed throughout the film, is under-developed. The fact that the *wayang kulit* tales studied and performed in Kelantan are based on the Ramayana is incidental. No mention is made of the similarities among the *wayang kulit* of Kelantan and Java and Bali. It would be stretching the point to suggest that *Wayang* is representative of the broader corpus of Malaysian films, especially since the film was in many ways a one-off campus project, directed, filmed and produced by staff and students of the Universiti Teknologi Mara (UiTM), where at the time Hatta was Dean of the Faculty of Artistic and Creative Technology. Perbadanan Kemajuan Filem Nasional (FINAS), Malaysia's national film development corporation, provided assistance and support. Although *Wayang* was very much a boutique project, it provides us with a revealing snapshot of Malaysia's Malay-centric society and politics. Inspired by this preliminary discussion, we will examine the social engagement of recent Indonesian and Malaysian cinema in more depth later in the book. But, even with a lengthier discussion, cinema can only provide us with a snapshot of the everyday reality of contemporary Malaysia. Consequently, our focus on cinema and other forms of cultural expression will be complemented by in-depth analyses of several other elements pertaining to the Indonesia–Malaysia equation.

Conclusion

In this chapter, deliberately preliminary in its scope, we have examined the role of culture in Southeast Asian regionalism by tracing contemporary rein-terpretations of a fundamental element of Southeast Asia's collective identity, the Ramayana. By tracing the manner in which the Ramayana has been promoted by ASEAN for region-building purposes and by Indonesia's New Order regime in the pursuit of national interests, this chapter has demonstrated that the Ramayana has generally not been used as a force for collective culture and identity-building processes. In fact, in Southeast Asia, and in Malaysia and New Order Indonesia in particular, the Ramayana has been used principally as a means of representing social and political interests. Hatta Azad Khan's *Wayang*, for example, which is set in the conservative Malaysian state of Kelantan, can be easily understood as a reflection on the tensions in Malaysia's politics between the national government, UMNO, and the Islamic political party, PAS. The film's depiction of traditional *wayang* shadow puppet theatre as a threatened art form in Kelantan is very much a political statement, drawing attention to the conservative literalist approach to Islam championed by PAS. Apparently, at the time the Malaysian government was attempting to get Malaysian *wayang kulit* nominated for UNESCO heritage listing, so it could also have been just an UMNO public relations exercise, while also taking a swipe at PAS' more extreme views. As Riddell (2009: 398) observes, 'For PAS, Islam should rather underpin the whole structure of state and society, through the establishment of an Islamic state which adheres to a literalist interpretation of sharia law, with little room for traditional pre-Islamic cultural forms such as wayang'.

Although it draws attention to a general sense of bilateral ambivalence between Indonesia and Malaysia, this chapter has shown that there are occasional examples of cultural agents in post-New Order Indonesia utilising the Ramayana myth to represent their interests. Thus domestic concerns are not necessarily the *raison d'être* of high-brow cinema such as Garin Nugroho's *Opera Jawa*, especially when films like this are far more likely to get better audiences internationally than in Indonesia, where art-house cinema is generally poorly received. Nevertheless, the impact of films like this in neighbouring countries such as Malaysia is minimal, even though the two countries share a mythopoeic imaginary, epitomised by the Ramayana and the performative genres in which it organically occurs, including the *wayang kulit* and its *gamelan* musical accompaniment. The reverse scenario is equally depressing, as Hatta Azad Khan's *Wayang* was never screened in Indonesia for the simple reason that Malaysian films are never released there, despite the shared language, myths and legends. This might seem a bit unfair, given that blockbuster films from Indonesia are often released in Malaysia and usually are commercially successful, even though they may not win critical acclaim. Indonesian music is also popular in Malaysia, with many of Indonesian best-known rock bands and performers, such as Slank, Dewa 19 and Peterpan regularly touring, with large audiences and strong album sales. The Malaysian public's love affair with Indonesian musicians has a long history. According to Heryanto (2008: 1), 'It dates back several decades, with the success of artists such as Titik Puspa, Lilies Suryani, the Titik Sandhora-Muchsin duet, Koes Plus, D'Lloyds, Broery Marantika, Bob Tutupoly, Harvey Malaihollo, and Vina Panduwinata'. Similarly, some Malaysian performers enjoy great commercial success in Indonesia. The female Malaysian singer Dato' Siti Nurhaliza, for instance, is 'much adored in Indonesia' (Heryanto 2008: 2), and she has collaborated frequently with Indonesian pop singers. We should not be surprised by a 2005 anti-Malaysia demonstration, which was distinguished by an ironic poster: '*Ganyang Malaysia – Selamatkan Siti Nurhaliza!*' (Crush Malaysia – Save Siti Nurhaliza!). Siti Nurhaliza's success in the 2000s – which occurred despite the political tension associated with the initial phase of the Ambalat dispute and the recurrent Indonesian forest fires resulting in haze blanketing the Malay peninsula – has inspired other Malaysian artists. Moreover, in order to tap into the lucrative Indonesian market, some Malaysian singers, such as Anuar Zain, have engaged well-known Indonesian songwriters and composers to help them create an authentic 'Indonesian' sensibility in their music (Malaysian Singer Opts 2007).

The next chapter will demonstrate that, despite a deep cultural and historical affinity, the differences between the two countries seem to outweigh the similarities. Indeed, the similarities only tend to highlight the differences. For example, when a neutral observer points out the similarities between Indonesian and Malay, citizens of both nations will be very quick to point out the differences, even if the differences are merely cosmetic. We will also address the uncomfortable reality that not all Indonesians are glowing in their assessment of their Malaysian brothers and sisters. A noisy minority of Indonesians loves nothing more than to belittle and denigrate their arch rivals.

Notes

1 'Mungkin judul filem itu yang tidak sensasi antara penyebabnya' (Judul filem 2009).
2 'Hakikatnya kehidupan ini menuntut perubahan dan semua perkara akan mengalaminya, justeru saya mewujudkan watak Awi yang buta untuk membuat perubahan dalam persembahan wayang kulit. Jika saya mencipta watak pemuda celik, perubahan pasti sukar dilakukan kerana dia dapat melihat reaksi mereka yang berada di sekelilingnya selain sudah terbiasa dengan apa ada di depan matanya selama ini' (Hamid 2008).

3 Cultural contestations

High-level discussions among government officials and political leaders of Indonesia and Malaysia occur regularly. More often than not they go straight to the business in hand, with little need for public statements or diplomatic fanfare. When joint press briefings are held, however, they are often framed by diplomatic niceties – repeated declarations of fondness, blood brotherhood and friendship pointing to shared values, a special relationship and common cultural traditions, all of which are purportedly anchored by the same racial and ethnic stock (*serumpun*). Malaysian politicians and media, in particular, often mention the familial bond between the two countries (*persaudaraan*). Historically, apart from a relatively frosty period in their relationship when Mahathir was Malaysia's leader and Suharto Indonesia's, both countries have tended to draw on a common cultural heritage in managing political tensions effectively. Nevertheless, despite the diplomatic pleasantries and the many warm and constructive meetings at the government-to-government or minister-to-minister level, bilateral ties over the last decade have generally been marked by rivalry, acrimony and conflict (Chong 2012; Khadijah and Shakila 2012; Liow 2005; Rüland 2009; Weiss 2010).

2009 was a particularly bad year for Indonesia and Malaysia in terms of their relationship. As we have outlined in previous chapters, in addition to the Manohara affair, both nations had to deal with the latest twists and turns in the long-running Ambalat dispute. There was also a public outcry in Indonesia after Malaysia allegedly nominated for inclusion on UNESCO's Representative List of Intangible Cultural Heritage several supposedly Indonesian cultural forms, including *batik*, *wayang* shadow puppetry, *gamelan* and *angklung*.[1] Allegedly, traditional Indonesian songs had also been claimed, such as Maluku's 'Rasa Sayang' and 'Kakatua', Jambi's 'Injit-injit Semut', West Sumatra's 'Musik Indang Sungai', Riau's 'Soleram', Jakarta's 'Jali-jali' and Nusa Tenggara's 'Anak Kambing Saya'. Most extraordinarily, it was alleged that the famous West Sumatran beef curry dish, known as *rendang*, had also been claimed as Malaysian. This is a source of some irony for West Sumatrans, many of whom live in Padang, the provincial capital of West Sumatra. Acclaimed actress Jajang C. Noer humorously describes the true nature of the problem as follows: 'This is all very strange. Indonesians claim *rendang*. Malaysians claim *rendang*. But to tell you the truth, *rendang* is not from Indonesia or Malaysia – it's from Padang'.[2] It cannot be denied that Indonesians and Malaysians have a good sense of humour, and indeed the ongoing cultural contestations are a source of much mirth.

But it has not all been fun and games. In 2009, inflaming the general atmosphere of contestation, it was alleged that the melody of the Malaysian national anthem, 'Negaraku' (My Nation) was plagiarised from an old Indonesian *keroncong*[3] ballad (Rizal and Rafiq 2009). This case is complicated. Apparently, according to Chong (2012: 12) it has been 'confirmed' that 'Negaraku' is 'an adaptation of a nineteenth century French composition'. The French tune in question is called 'La Rosalie' (The Rosalie), and it was composed in the 19th century by Pierre-Jean de Beranger. It enjoyed some popularity in the former French colony of the Seychelles before arriving, via the exiled Sultan of Perak Abdullah Jaafar Moratham, in the Malay archipelago at the turn of the 20th century. Here, the lyrics were rewritten as the state anthem of Perak, and eventually used as the basis for Malaysia's national anthem. There are suggestions, however, that the melody originated from a *stamboel* tune, 'Stambul 1', composed by the Surabaya-based Auguste 'Guus' Constantijn Pierre Mahieu (Cohen 2006: 59), who largely drew on Indonesian *keroncong* ballads for inspiration (Cohen 2001, 2006). Along these lines, some have argued that the melody of a particular *keroncong* ballad, 'Terang Bulan' (Moonlight), is the inspiration for the Malaysian national anthem (Rizal and Rafiq 2009). Dousing cold water on these claims, respected Indonesian author and musician Remy Sylado asserts that the melody of 'Terang Bulan' was actually an adaption of 'La Rosalie' (Malik 2009), which is quite probable. So, in summary, claims that 'Negaraku' has Indonesian provenance have little scholarly consensus, while provoking bemusement among Malaysians. As one Malaysian online commentator observes:

> The Bahasa Indonesia newspapers sell newspapers that have anti-Malaysia thing. Good for sales circulations. By the way, we Malaysians are amused. We really like our Negara Ku. It really doesn't matter where it comes from. This is a trivial issue – to us.
>
> (Malik 2009)

Also in 2009, Discovery Channel featured a series of advertising clips and documentaries on Malaysia produced by a Singaporean production company, a few seconds of which featured a sacred Balinese temple dance, the Pendet, being performed by a Balinese dancer. As Chong (2012: 2) observes, this was widely regarded as yet another attempt by Malaysia to 'steal' elements of Indonesian culture, causing a national 'uproar' in the process. Demonstrations were held in Denpasar in protest against the alleged appropriation (Prathivi and Wardany 2009). In the following weeks the Indonesian media ran numerous reports highlighting Malaysia's alleged cultural affronts (Chong 2012: 2). The Malaysian government went into damage control. According to

Chong (2012: 2), 'Put on the defensive, the Malaysian Minister of Culture and Tourism sent an apology to the Indonesian Culture and Tourism Minister, claiming that the clip was not an official production of the Malaysian Government and did not constitute part of the Visit Malaysia 2009 Tourism Campaign'. Unfortunately, Malaysia has a track record in this regard – the Pendet case was not the first time that an Indonesian art form had been appropriated to advertise Malaysia, albeit in error. In November 2007 images of the East Javanese Reog Ponorogo dance made headlines across Indonesia 'when it featured in a Malaysian tourism commercial as a part of the 2007 Malaysia Truly Asia campaign' (Mapson 2010). For the people of Ponorogo, who felt that the Reog Ponorogo was a mask-dance unique to their local area, this was particularly galling. According to Mapson (2010), 'the use of Reog in this commercial without acknowledgement of its origins was enough to cause an uproar in Ponorogo. But the Malaysians made things even worse by emblazoning the word 'Malaysia' on the mask in the place usually reserved for the words 'Reog Ponorogo''.

The cultural heritage claims outlined above are by no means settled. For some Indonesians, Malaysia's cavalier behaviour still rankles. Malaysians, on the other hand, are becoming increasingly impatient with Indonesia's strident anti-Malaysianism. Many Malaysians are questioning, publicly and privately, why Indonesians should make such a fuss about what is, after all, a shared culture, with shared art forms, and, more importantly, why Indonesians dislike them so much. In this chapter we aim to shed light on a selection of the heritage cases, and to attempt a response to the questions the Malaysians are asking, which seem not to have satisfactory answers. Our discussion is underpinned by this book's central theme, which is that each bilateral brouhaha is a postcolonial symptom of the prickliness of the Indonesia–Malaysia relationship in general – a relationship determined by the fluidity of ongoing transnational flows and, further back in time, by the colonial encounter. As we shall continue to argue, the colonial experience in maritime Southeast Asia has been crucial – as the distinct nation-states have emerged – in determining the manner and extent to which friends in the *Nusantara* region have now become strangers, or worse.

This chapter will examine two particular flashpoints: the 2011 SEA (Southeast Asian) Games and UNESCO's world heritage listing of *batik*, a wax-resistant dyeing technique, as a distinctly Indonesian form of intangible cultural heritage. The latter has been chosen as a case study because it brought the claiming of one country's culture by the other to a head. UNESCO's decision was widely perceived in Indonesia as a snub towards Malaysia. Indonesian media allegations that Malaysia had lodged an unsuccessful UNESCO claim for *batik*, despite the lack of evidence to support such claims, added to the sense of parochialism. The cultural contestations simmered for several years before suddenly bubbling to the surface during the SEA Games held in Jakarta and Palembang in November 2011. These games were marked by rampant anti-Malaysianism, which was broadcast live and without restriction to Malaysian lounge rooms, bars and *mamak* stalls.[4]

This chapter will first explore the anti-Malaysianism of the 2011 SEA Games, with an emphasis on the increasing exasperation amongst Malaysians and the Malaysian media towards their neighbour's apparently discourteous behaviour. It will then seek to explore the roots of this anti-Malaysianism, which is a relatively under-researched, and thus little known, phenomenon. The body of this chapter discusses what many regard as the spark igniting Indonesia's post-2009 anti-Malaysian sentiment, namely UNESCO's listing of *batik*, which was preceded and followed by the listing of several other shared Indo-Malay cultural heritage items. In this regard, this chapter examines the respective *batik* industries of both nations, which have been overshadowed by the bilateral tension instigated by the UNESCO listing.

The 2011 SEA Games fiasco

For many Malaysians, the SEA Games 2011 in Jakarta and Palembang were memorable for two things: the strident anti-Malaysianism demonstrated by the crowds and by officials; and Malaysia winning the gold medal in the football final against Indonesia in front of a partisan crowd of at least 100,000 at the Gelora Bung Karno Stadium, Jakarta. Malaysian correspondents based in Jakarta and Palembang had many other highlights and lowlights, of course, which will be addressed shortly. There was also a minor scandal involving the Malaysian 4 x 400 metres running team that missed their medal ceremony because, to save money, the cash-strapped Malaysian Amateur Athletics Union (MAAU) officials had booked them on an early flight home. But, by and large, it was Indonesia's generally discourteous reception of the Malaysian sportspeople and their entourage that attracted the most attention; it added spice to the Malaysian national euphoria in response to the victory of Malaysia's under-23 football team, the *Harimau Muda* (Young Tigers), who were pitted twice against the host nation's *Garuda Muda* (Young Eagles).

Malaysia's victory was made much sweeter by the parochial crowd dynamics in the cauldron-like Soviet-style Gelora Bung Karno Stadium, built in 1958 with the help of the Soviet Union under Nikita Khrushchev who had a close personal relationship with the late President Sukarno. Before the grand final match the rendition of the Malaysian nation anthem was drowned out by the hisses, boos, cat-calls, heckling, shouting and horns of a large proportion of the parochial crowd, which have been well publicised in YouTube videos and much discussed in Internet chat forums. It is telling that the crowd chanted one word in particular – '*Maling!*' (Burglar!) – a word choice that we will return to shortly. The Malaysian players and officials were obviously uncomfortable, and most probably extremely intimidated, but they continued to sing the anthem nonetheless. One cannot help but feel sorry for the 22 children, presumably of Indonesian nationality, who were the mascots accompanying the players onto the field. Several of the children looked quite ill at ease with such an intimidating experience. Moreover, the official sell-out crowd figure of approximately 100,000 may have been quite conservative, as many of the tens of thousands of fans without tickets milling around outside the stadium were granted entry to avoid a potentially dangerous crush. Even so, groups of supporters set a ticket booth on fire and attacked offices at the stadium, and at least two fans died in a stampede on the day of the match (Two Die 2011). This was not the first time in the Games that the stadium was filled to capacity, either, as Indonesia had already played Malaysia before in the group stage of the tournament.

The earlier match between the two countries had also been marked by the drowning out of the Malaysian national anthem. The Malaysian commentator for sports TV channel Astro Arena had difficulty hiding his disgust and questioned whether a nation could be considered 'developed' (*sudah berkembang*) if it was unable and unwilling to respect the national anthem of its not dissimilar opponent (*satu sama lain*). As the jeers of the crowd died down when the Indonesian national anthem began, he expressed his confidence that the Malaysians in the crowd would be respectful. Of course, there were no Malaysians in the crowd, apart from the 27 Malaysian players and officials, who were heavily guarded. Malaysian citizens were strongly warned not to attend the stadium, for their own safety.[5] Before the match TV cameras had spotted one apparently very brave fan in the packed stadium wearing the yellow and black Malaysian jersey, but as the camera zoomed in it was revealed that he was wearing the shirt back-to-front and that 'MALING' had been screen-printed on it instead of the usual 'MALAYSIA'. The use of the word *maling* is an important element of the story.

Before expanding upon the *maling* sentiment, however, several other points about the SEA Games in general and Malaysia's gold-medal football team in particular are worth noting. First of all, the Malaysian media seemed unusually interested in Indonesia's anti-Malaysia histrionics. Photographs appeared in several Malaysian newspapers depicting the Malaysian football squad being ferried to and from their matches in Indonesian army Barracudas (armoured vehicles with bulletproof windows) (Figure 3.1). Consider the following sports editorial in *The Star* (2011):

INDONESIA VS MALAYSIA. Whether its football, badminton or even the origins of the 'pendet' dance, satay, rendang or batik, it doesn't take much to provoke all sorts of emotions. Simply put, spats are common between the two testy neighbours and this innate animosity is often externalised in the sports arena. Tonight's SEA Games football match will be no different although nothing more than topping Group A may be at stake. Security has been tightened at the Gelora Bung Karno Main Stadium in Senayan and the national team's training session there was called off. Malaysia may, once again, need a Barracuda ride into the stadium.

Much was made of the fact that the Malaysian coach refused to let his team practise on an outdoor pitch, either at Senayan or elsewhere, because of the

Figure 3.1 Malaysian U23 players returning to their hotel in a 'Barracuda' armoured vehicle after defeating Indonesia in a 4-3 penalty shoot-out in the 26th SEA Games football final. Image permission: *The New Straits Times* Press (Malaysia).

expectation of a hostile reception from local Indonesians. At an earlier outdoor training session the Malaysian team had been unhappy about the booing of the local Indonesian crowd (Armoured vehicles escort 2011). So the Malaysians trained behind closed doors in the hotel compound. 'The indoor sessions on the tennis courts have worked well. It's important the boys train in a good environment', said the Malaysian coach, Ong Kim Swee (Defenders Doing a Good Job 2011). By hunkering down the team was certainly able to limit outside distractions and no doubt benefited from the strong and immeasurably valuable team spirit that the circumstances engendered.

The Malaysian media made the most of the tense atmosphere. According to another column in *The Star*, written before the first encounter between the two teams:

> This is going to be a grudge match – a real smackdown – where Indonesia are concerned at least ... this is Indonesia versus Malaysia, a no-holds barred explosive contest between two bitter rivals. Where national pride takes precedence over everything else and sporting spirit takes a backseat, especially at the menacing Gelora Bung Karno Stadium ... the fans who will pack the stadium [are] wanting to see only the Indonesian bull gore the Malaysian matador. This is the moment that all of Indonesia has been waiting for – the time to avenge their defeat by Malaysia in the Suzuki Cup Asean Football Federation Championship here 11 months

ago. And Malaysia are bracing themselves for a torrid night in front of the intimidating Senayan crowd.

(No-holds barred encounter 2011)

The article also mentioned the important fact that the outcome of the match was virtually irrelevant, as both teams were already through to the next round. What was at stake, however, was national pride and the relatively minor matter of final position in the group – the winner of Group A would play the runner-up of Group B (Myanmar), and the runner-up would play the winner of Group B (Vietnam). The article pointed out that neither side was prepared to take their foot off the pedal and rest their key players: 'the stakes – pride, revenge and bragging rights – are too high' (No-holds barred encounter 2011).

The *New Straits Times* resident cartoonist, Samsudin Ismail, produced several cartoons on the glorious feats of the Malaysian 'Young Tigers', including one, titled 'GRRR!', depicting a skinny-looking *garuda* eagle, looking suspiciously like a bush turkey or an *ayam kampung* (village chicken) being swiped aside by a massive tiger paw (Figure 3.2).[6] As Samsudin reflected on his cartoon in the *New Straits Times'* office in Kuala Lumpur, he chuckled, suggesting that it was social satire with a 'very soft touch'. Good-natured humour was the key aim, rather than sharp sociopolitical commentary. He had no particular opinion about the Indonesia question and was merely responding artistically to the key issue of the day, as he does every day of his working week. Another example of this gentle humour was an emotive image and a pithy caption on the back page of *The Star* for 18 November 2011. It was an image of a 'Ganyang Malaysia' (Crush Malaysia) banner at the first match between the *Harimau Muda* and *Garuda Muda*, followed by *The Star*'s response: 'Yes, we can'. The joke underpinning this image and caption, a Malaysian informant explained, lies in the fact that 'Ganyang Malaysia', expressed with the correct intonation and a comma between 'Ganyang' and 'Malaysia', can be also be understood as an imperative, as in 'Crush them, Malaysia'.

A second point worth noting is that, even though it had easily topped the gold medal count at the Games, Indonesia wanted to win the football gold medal more than any other. The Malaysian media made the most of the Indonesian obsession with the football medal. One example of their focus on it was an image in the *New Straits Times* of a grave-looking reader of the 22 November 2011 edition of Indonesia's leading newspaper, *Kompas*, whose front page was emblazoned with a partisan headline: 'Garuda Muda Berjuang hingga Tuntas' (The Young Garudas Fight to the Bitter End). As suggested by the front page, there could be no doubt about how much this match mattered to Indonesians, who had waited for so long to win a major tournament on home soil. Moreover, it was widely trumpeted that Indonesians would have loved nothing more than to beat Malaysia, their greatest rival, in the grand final. Rivalry between the Malaysian and Indonesian football teams is such

Figure 3.2 'We are the Champion' by Samsudin Ismail. Image permission: *The New Straits Times* Press (Malaysia).

that any match between them, at any age level, is historically guaranteed to attract a sell-out crowd.

Thirdly, the Malaysian media correspondents based in Jakarta and Palembang, who seemed increasingly irascible as the Games wore on, made it quite clear that the anti-Malaysia sentiment was pervasive. The Malaysian karate team was booed throughout their three-day tournament, the entire badminton team was not spared, and even Malaysian pole vaulters had to contend with an openly hostile crowd. What was the atmosphere like on the ground? According to the *Sunday Star*'s Wong Chun Wai (2011):

> [Malaysian] athletes, officials and media are facing antagonism daily, whipped up by just about anyone at every venue where Malaysians are competing ... the Indonesian crowd would openly show their contempt and disrespect to our national anthem by refusing to stand up when it played. But it's gone beyond that – whenever the *Negaraku* is played, the crowd would blare horns, shout and jeer. There have been instances where Indonesian fans held up their middle fingers, in a symbolic 'up-yours' protest, to photographers whenever Malaysians compete.

None of the hostility was directed at the other nations competing. As the Malaysian chef-de-mission Datuk Naim Mohamad observed, the Indonesian fans directed almost all of their invective and jeers at the Malaysian competitors:

> Their fans have shown no respect to Malaysians and to our national anthem. This is because of their unsporting culture and because they see Malaysia as a threat to them in sports ... They are not behaving like gracious hosts. They still have a grudge against Malaysia because our football team beat Indonesia in the final of the AFF Suzuki Cup here last year.
>
> (Home fans not sporting 2011)

Much has been said and written about the 2010 ASEAN Football Federation (AFF) Suzuki Cup finals between Malaysia and Indonesia, which consisted of a controversial first-leg game in Kuala Lumpur and a second-leg in Jakarta. The two games were memorable for accusations of foul play and poor sportsmanship, including the shining of laser beams at the Indonesian goalkeeper during the Kuala Lumpur match. Somewhat sensationally, referee Masaaki Toma halted the first game of the 2010 AFF Cup finals series, held in Kuala Lumpur on 26 December, for five minutes soon after halftime when Indonesian goalkeeper Markus Haris Maulana complained that Malaysian fans were using laser pens to shine laser beams into his eyes to distract him. Other Indonesian players also complained of being distracted by the lasers. After long negotiations between the referees, coaching staff and match officials, play resumed. In the heated lead-up to the second game in the series, held in Jakarta on 29 December, Indonesia's President Susilo Bambang Yudhoyono stated that he hoped Indonesian fans attending would support fair play and 'not be like Malaysia' (Yoong 2010). For their part, Malaysian players said the atmosphere in the build-up to the second leg in Jakarta 'was like going to war' (Malaysia Celebrates Cup Success 2010). When Malaysia won the series tie on goal difference, Prime Minister Najib Razak declared 31 December 2010 a public holiday. Despite the fanfare, the Suzuki Cup fiasco was just another episode in a long-running rivalry between the two football teams and thus cannot be seen as the primary reason for the rampant anti-Malaysianism at the 2011 SEA Games. As we shall see, many other factors were at play.

Outside the sporting arenas, there were clashes between Indonesian and Malaysian journalists and officials. The Malaysian football coach, for instance, was clearly aggrieved when Indonesian officials insisted on testing the Malaysian footballers for drugs straight after their gold-medal winning triumph. This triggered many accusations in the Malaysian media, such as the suggestion that the over-eager drug officials were hoping to have Malaysia's victory annulled so that Indonesia could win by default. Later, Malaysian reporters were banned from covering the last day of the swimming competition. An official at Palembang's aquatic centre was caught on camera yelling at a small group of Malaysian journalists thus: 'Ini semua orang Malaysia! Tak ada otak semua' (These are all Malaysians! None of them have any brains). He then told the journalists 'This is our country! If you don't like it, you can get out!' (Wong 2011). There is little doubt that many of the Malaysian media contingent would have preferred to go home, if they could. Consider the following column by the *Star*'s Lim Teik Huat:

> I have been in Palembang for almost a week, and boy I've struggled to think of something good to say about how the SEA Games have been managed. It has been anything but easy for the media here as the organisers have their own peculiar way of doing things and are not well versed in what it takes to set up a proper functioning working area … And don't get me started on the ridiculous ruling requiring one to take off your shoes when going to the main toilet on the ground floor. It's the first time I've encountered this going into my seventh SEA Games and it has made me start counting down the days to the end of this assignment. It can't come fast enough.
>
> (Lim 2011)

The *New Straits Times*, meanwhile, reported on the way in which the Indonesian hosts used 'every trick in the book' to gain advantage for their own competitors, so that they could be overall champions: 'The 26th Sea Games in Indonesia will be remembered for the hosts' blatant gamesmanship more than anything else' (Ungracious hosts 2011).

When the dust settled, the Malaysian backslapping and soul-searching began. In terms of the backslapping, it appeared that as well as boasting about the prized gold medal in football, Malaysians could proudly reflect on the fact that they would neither bow to intimidation nor ever be ungracious hosts. As 'evidence' for this, in the week after their triumph in Jakarta, the *Harimau Muda* played an Olympics qualifier against Syria in the Bukit Jalil National Stadium in Kuala Lumpur. The manner in which the crowd conducted itself was worthy of a mention in the eagle-eyed *Sinar Harian*: 'Malaysian supporters have learned a lesson from what happened during the SEA Games in Indonesia recently. The proof is, when the Syrian national anthem was played everyone in attendance stood to respect the opposing team'.[7]

The fact that the exhausted Malaysians lost 2–0 was of little concern. Still basking in the Jakarta victory, media commentators congratulated Malaysians on appearing to overcome, at least momentarily, the barely suppressed socio-political divisions that still seem to threaten the national fabric at its most fundamental levels. For example, very little was made of the Chinese ethnicity of the coach of the under-23 team, Ong Kim Swee, although some commentators remarked, somewhat patronisingly, on his surprisingly good command of Malay. Chok Suat Ling of the *New Straits Times* felt that the *Harimau Muda*'s gold-medal winning performance was one of the rare occasions in Malaysia's history that the nation had been truly united:

> On [the night of the *Harimau Muda*'s victory], an aircraft might have detonated in mid-air and no one would have noticed as almost every single Malaysian – including those who don't know what 'offside' means – was glued to the television. Only sports can bring everyone – whether tall, short, thin, horizontally challenged, rich, poor, a Barisan National or opposition supporter, Malay, Indian, Chinese, and 'dan lain lain [and others]' – together. Indeed, sport is a unifier like no other. Every time we won the Thomas Cup right up to 1992, Malaysians slapped each other on the backs, and cheered as one nation. Nobody bothered about the racial background of the players, or thought twice about hugging the sweaty person next to them at the stadium or mamak stall. What else can do that? Some claim open house buffets can, but that's another story.
>
> (Chok 2011)

Unfortunately, the all-encompassing glow of the *Harimau Muda*'s glorious efforts diminished as the nation returned to everyday reality, and other concerns – some of them old concerns, such as Malaysia's deep-rooted institutional racism – took over the national conversation.

In terms of the bilateral tensions, some commentators happily fanned the flames while others preferred to play everything down. In one of the last front-page reports on the SEA Games fiasco, Malaysia's Youth and Sports Minister Datuk Ahmad Shabery Cheek called for a sense of perspective. He insisted that there was no 'bad blood' with Indonesians. If there were any isolated expressions of hostility, he claimed, it was just among 'some people' and certainly not a reflection of the close relationship shared between the two governments:

I believe the love-hate relationship between Indonesia exists because we are so close. It is a tendency among neighbours to have more than a few squabbles ... I don't think there was discrimination against any country by the Indonesian government or event organisers.

(Murty 2011)

Shabery also highlighted the little-known fact that there were announcements at each stadium urging Indonesians to stand up when the 'Negaraku' was played. The article, unlike so many others, paused to consider the underlying causes of the hostility, beyond the notion that Indonesia was seeking revenge for losing the 2010 Suzuki Cup final in acrimonious circumstances, and drew attention to social media sites where claims such as 'Malaysia stole the copyrights of Indonesian traditional textiles' and 'Malaysians are known for abusing housewives and maids' are made. We will now turn our attention to the first of these claims and return to the second later in the book.

UNESCO and the Malaysian *Batik* industry

It is not difficult to connect the anti-Malaysianism of the SEA Games with the Indonesia-Malaysia cultural contestations. The cultural tensions had undermined the relationship between the two countries long before the Games. Indonesians have felt aggrieved since about 2006 or 2007 by what they have perceived as Malaysian attempts to steal, or claim (*mengklaim*), Indonesian cultural heritage. During the same period the neologism *Malingsia* has been coined as a pejorative term for Malaysia. (*Maling*, as mentioned earlier, is an Indonesian word for burglar.) Anecdotal evidence suggests that the neologism derives from the combination of three words: *maling asal Asia* (Asia's burglar), which is a play on words in response to the Malaysian government's Malaysia, Truly Asia tourism advertising campaign. Most Malay-speaking Malaysians seem to be unaware of the meaning of the Indonesian word *maling*, however, as its origins are Javanese rather than Malay, although perhaps many Malaysians are simply turning a blind eye to the insult implied by the neologism. Nevertheless, online commentators, who claim to be Malaysian, have not restrained themselves from coining equally imaginative and abusive terms for their Indonesian cousins, such as *Indonesial* (damn Indonesia), *Indonesialan* (damned Indonesia) and, perhaps most disturbingly or most creatively, depending on which side of the fence you are on, *Indogs sial* (damned Indo-dogs). The term *Indon* for Indonesians has been widely used by many groups in the region for decades, including Australian soldiers in the years following the Second World War,[8] but it is now considered as a derogatory term when used by Malaysians.

Outside cyberspace, which seems to be hardwired for confrontation, the average Malaysian citizen or politician has shown little interest in responding to Indonesian hostility on the cultural front. Bureaucrats at Kuala Lumpur's UNESCO outpost have conveyed to us their disappointment and frustration with the Indonesian media, which have continued to peddle the myth that Malaysia has lodged claims for *batik* and many other forms of supposedly Indonesian cultural heritage. However, Malaysia has never formally lodged any claims for *batik*. Furthermore, it at no point contested or disputed UNESCO's ratification of *batik* as an Indonesian form of intangible cultural heritage. Nor did Malaysia contest UNESCO's listing of other forms of Indonesian intangible heritage, such as the *keris, wayang kulit* puppet theatre and, most recently, *angklung*. In addition to this, as far as we are aware, UNESCO has no record of any unsuccessful nominations by Malaysia for any form of cultural heritage to be listed.

UNESCO officials in Kuala Lumpur were anxious to assert to us that Malaysia had not lodged claims for any disputed forms of Indo-Malay heritage, either tangible or intangible. For Malaysia to lodge an official claim with UNESCO for *batik* to be listed as a distinctively Malaysian intangible heritage item would not only require an army of bureaucrats and a mountain of paperwork but also trigger the serious possibility of provoking its much larger, more powerful and often cantankerous neighbour – a risk, Kuala Lumpur officials suggest, that would never be worth taking. It would take a brave government official or parliamentarian indeed to approve such a potentially inflammatory initiative. Nevertheless, Malaysia has successfully proposed for listing by UNESCO cultural property that is, according to some, shared with Indonesia. For instance, in 2005 UNESCO declared the *mak yong* dance drama a 'Masterpiece of the Oral and Intangible Heritage of Humanity', identifying it as the heritage of Malaysia. But because *mak yong* was brought to Indonesia's Riau archipelago in the late 1800s, it is incorrectly claimed by some as an Indonesian heritage form. We shall return to this anomaly in the next chapter.

Meanwhile, UNESCO's listing of *batik* as a distinctly Indonesian intangible cultural heritage has barely registered among Malaysians. The *batik* industry in Malaysia is threatened neither by the UNESCO decision nor by the Indonesian *batik* industry. In fact, despite UNESCO's ruling, the *batik* industry in Malaysia continues to experience a prolonged resurgence, to the extent that the industry contributes considerably to the national GDP. It could be argued that the large number of Malay women wearing *batik* every day demonstrates its robust popularity. Datin Seri Endon Mahmood, the late wife of the former Malaysian Prime Minister Tun Abdullah Ahmad Badawi, initially inspired this practice. As the patron of Malaysia's *batik* industry, in 2004 Endon Mahmood called for Malaysians, and not just public servants, to wear *batik* at least once or twice a month. This call was embraced by Malaysian government departments, which required their employees to wear *batik* on every first and 15th day of the month. Since 2008 the required frequency has become once a week, leading to what has become known as '*Batik Khamis*' (*Batik* Thursday). According to a report in the *Star*, the decision to increase the frequency to once a week was made not only to boost the Malaysian *batik* industry by getting civil servants to wear it more often but also 'to make it easy for them to remember as to when they should put on their batik shirts' (Anis and Krishnamoorthy 2008). Just in case the decree might lead to an unlikely surge in popularity for Indonesian-made *batik*, Chief Secretary to the Government Tan Sri Mohd Sidek Hassan added that 'it will have to be Malaysian batik, of course' (Anis and Krishnamoorthy 2008). The requirement that it be Malaysian seems to be the wrinkle in the ointment of the directive. This is because Indonesian *batik* is usually made of cotton and is, therefore, more practical in a humid climate than Malaysia's *batik*, which is made of '*kain fuji*', a cotton-based fabric made to imitate silk, but having the texture of satin, which can cling to one's skin, and is somewhat sticky in tropical heat. Nevertheless, *Batik* Thursday has achieved such popularity that many Malaysians, particularly women, have chosen to wear *batik* not only on Thursdays, but on every other day of the working week as well. Given the ubiquity of the *batik*-patterned dresses, sarongs and *kebaya* blouses among Malay women (approximately 30% of the nation's population), a very large amount of it is regularly produced, sold and worn (see Figure 3.3).

The thriving nature of Malaysia's *batik* industry is further demonstrated in many ways, including the publication of numerous high-quality coffee-table books and magazines on *batik*, and Malaysian *batik* in particular. A recent coffee-table book is *Malaysian Batik: Reinventing a Tradition* (Yunus 2011). Written by Nur Azlina Yunus with the support of Yayasan Budi Penyayang Malaysia (PENYAYANG), a charitable foundation founded by Endon Mahmood, the book is glossy, colourful and informative. It includes a particularly useful and comprehensive list of Malaysia's best-known *batik* designers, entrepreneurs and schools. Equally useful are the attractive *batik* magazines such as *myBatik* and *Batik Guild Magazine*, which is published by PENYAYANG,

Figure 3.3 *Batik* fashion, Kuala Lumpur.
Photo: Marshall Clark

supporter of the Galeri Seri Endon and the Malaysian Batik Association. The magazines keep their predominantly female readers informed of the ins-and-outs of the Malaysian *batik* industry and of Malaysia's many *batik* industry-related events. They often include essays by guest columnists and interviews with *batik*-loving politicians, designers or entrepreneurs.

On one of our fieldwork trips to Malaysia, we could not help but be impressed by the number of museums, exhibitions, galleries, fashion shows and even charity walks devoted to showcasing *batik* art, design and fashion. For example, the Muzium Tekstil Negara (National Textiles Museum), located in the heart of central Kuala Lumpur's tourism district, has an impressive collection of *batik*. It regularly holds textile demonstrations and public lectures, as well as weekly, if not daily, *batik*-making classes. Other museums cum galleries include the Kompleks Budaya Kraftangan (Handicrafts Complex) in Kuala Lumpur, with resident artisans, as well as the Galeri Seri Endon (Seri Endon Gallery) and the Galeri Petronas (Petronas Gallery) located in the mall at the base of the Petronas Twin Towers. From late 2011 to early 2012 an exhibition, 'Irresistible Wear', showcased creative fashion attire, much of which was *batik*. Many of the Malaysian designers exhibited used local textiles such as *batik* and *songket* to transform clothing into works of art. Similar exhibitions regularly occur elsewhere.

In the *batik* production heartlands of the state of Terengganu, there are numerous factories and large *batik* shopping complexes such as Noor Arfa Batik, which has expanded from its origins in Kuala Terengganu to have out-lets in Kuala Lumpur and Melaka as well. Almost every shopping centre throughout Terengganu, no matter how rural or remote, seems to have one or two *batik* fashion shops. The pattern of the spread of *batik* outlets extends to the north along the coast to Kelantan and, to a lesser extent, south to Pahang.

There is some evidence to suggest that a number of the artisans working in the *batik* factories of Terengganu and Kelantan are Indonesians, a good pro-portion of whom are now naturalised Malaysian citizens. As reported, rather sensationally, in Indonesia's *Tempo* magazine, it is not unusual to meet middle-aged and older women throughout Kelantan and Terengganu who are working as *batik* artisans and who originate from renowned Indonesian *batik* centres such as Laweyan, Solo, Pekalongan and Yogyakarta (Suditomo, Pudjiarti, and Dimyathi 2009). The fascinating story of one such artisan, Mbah Sum, was told in detail in *Tempo*'s infamous exposé of the 'Indonesianness' of the Malaysian *batik* industry. Mbah Sum is now based in Terengganu, to which she was invited by a Malaysian businessman in the late 1990s to work in his *batik* business. Now Mbah Sum's whole family has settled there and she speaks of her experience thus:

> This is enjoyable work. Even though I'm working in a foreign country, I feel as though I'm in my home town … I am very thankful, as now myself, my children and my grandchildren live comfortably.[9]

This is in stark contrast to her previous life in Laweyan, Solo, where she was forced to work long hours for very little financial compensation:

> Before living in Kuala Terengganu, she lived for decades with her family in the *batik* city [Solo], where she was born. From one generation to the next she has been a *batik* artisan, but she has never been able to make ends meet. As an artisan, she had an obligation to supply her *batik* wholesaler with her own hand-made *batik* productions. Yet, her life was always one of deprivation. 'Even though I produced large amounts, the prices were permanently cheap. Any profit was only enough to cover food, clothes and schooling costs', she said.[10]

Since her move to Malaysia, her whole life has been turned around:

> Now she is pleased. 'During my time here, every year my children and grandchildren have been offered the opportunity to carry on their schooling wherever they want. I've also been given the opportunity to go on holidays to wherever I've wanted to go', she says happily.[11]

Sum's story of Indonesian rags to Malaysian riches is by no means isolated. The *Tempo* report also presents the account of Ratmini, another former Indonesian citizen:

> Ratmini, a *batik* artisan from Yogya who works for Fine Batik Malaysia, explains that it is not that she doesn't love her own country, it's just that while she has lived in Malaysia she has felt better understood and better appreciated. She has not needed to worry about problems such as schooling, health, or recreation. 'Honestly, our duty is just to do our best possible effort at making *batik*'.[12]

There is certainly heavy demand for experienced artisans such as Ratmini, who are offered decent wages. Noor Arfa's *batik* factory in Kuala Terengganu, for example, regularly displays a large banner advertising vacancies (see Figure 3.4). The fact that Noor Arfa's factory is located within walking distance of other factories with Indonesian workers on the payroll suggests that banners such as these and word of mouth are the only advertising it needs to do to attract workers.

Meanwhile, at the other end of the scale, *batik* fashion shows are regularly held in Malaysia, especially in Terengganu and Kuala Lumpur. The trend of holding *batik* fashion shows was perhaps inspired by the previously discussed Endon Mahmood, who established the annual Minggu Batik Malaysia (Malaysian *Batik* Week) as well as other innovations such as the Piala Seri Endon (Seri Endon Cup), an annual *batik* design competition for *batik* designers, with categories for fashion, soft furnishings and handicrafts. It is not uncommon in Malaysia, of course, to see *batik* simply *everywhere* – not just in the

Figure 3.4 Advertisement for workers, Noor Arfa *batik* factory, Kuala Terengganu.
    Photo: Marshall Clark

form of shirts, *kebaya* blouses, dresses, sarongs, shawls and headscarves, but also in paintings, pyjamas, chair coverings, tablecloths, headrests, handkerchiefs, footwear and even ties. *Batik* is also ubiquitous in Malaysian cinema and television, which is probably a fair representation of reality, particularly that of the Malay majority.

In contrast to Indonesia, Malaysia has many *batik* innovators, including *batik* artists such as Fatimah Chik and Datin Sharifah Kirana, and truly interesting *batik* 'modernisers', such as Datuk Radzuan Radziwill, who has been collaborating with a group of prisoners at the Kajang Women's Prison (see Galeri Petronas 2011). All of these artists regard themselves as 'artists', first and foremost, rather than mere *batik* designers or artisans. Fatimah Chik, for instance, goes out of her way to welcome art-loving visitors to her studio and she regularly conducts *batik*-making courses in Kuala Lumpur. Like many of Malaysia's leading *batik* artists, Fatimah has lived and studied in Indonesia, including in *batik* centres such as Yogyakarta. Fatimah learned a great deal in Indonesia, but she has long appreciated the freedom of living in Malaysia, far away from the traditional centres of Java and their somewhat conservative attitude towards *batik* design. Malaysia's much higher standard of living, of course, allows an artist such as Fatimah to enjoy modest financial rewards for her art. In Indonesia, meanwhile, *batik* is less an art, and more a craft and a commodity, oftentimes appropriated for nationalistic purposes. *Batik* in Malaysia is a business too, of course, but a sense of aesthetic experimentation, common to works of art, is more evident there than in Indonesia. As Noor Azlina Yunus (2011: 10) observes, lengths of *batik* are no longer simply converted into sarongs in Malaysia: 'More often they are creations that display all the characteristics of works of art – originality of composition and design, effective use of colour, a high level of technical expertise and, above all, a flair for working in the medium of batik ... the old system of anonymous artisans is giving way before a new style and organization of the batik industry that encourages individual talent and promotes recognized batik designers and artists'.

UNESCO's listing of *Batik*: what does it mean for Indonesia?

UNESCO's 2009 decision to add the Indonesian traditional dyeing technique of *batik* to its Representative List of the Intangible Cultural Heritage of Humanity was greeted with some fanfare in Jakarta. To acknowledge the listing, President SBY asked all Indonesians to wear *batik* on 2 October 2009, after it had been confirmed. The listing itself, which many welcomed, as it would give the age-old *batik* tradition a degree of protection under the UNESCO charter, was made official at a meeting of UNESCO's Intergovernmental Committee in the United Arab Emirates, between 28 September and 2 October 2009. According to Aburizal Bakrie, the then Coordinating Minister for People's Welfare:

> Batik is regarded as a cultural icon with its own uniqueness. It contains symbols and a deep philosophy of the human life cycle – and it was submitted by Indonesia as a non-material element of cultural heritage ... We've been told that batik has been recognized as an element of global cultural heritage produced by Indonesians.
>
> (Maulia 2009)

As in Malaysia, in Indonesia *batik* is a generic term referring to a process of decorating fabric by making use of a wax-resistant dyeing technique. But, with modern advances in the textile industry, the term is also used for fabrics incorporating traditional *batik* patterns that are not necessarily produced using traditional *batik* techniques. Until recently, *batik* had a reputation for being worn mostly by middle-aged or older Indonesians, and, even then, only at formal events. It is now becoming increasingly popular, even among the younger generations apparently, as *batik* factories have begun to manufacture more comfortable, practical and fashionable *batik* outfits. As in Malaysia, many professionals, office workers and public servants now wear *batik* every day, and local designers compete to produce more attractive designs.

Aburizal explained the UNESCO decision-making process, noting that the UNESCO evaluators of the nomination for the List had inquired about the origins of Indonesian *batik*, about government protection of it, and about the extent to which it was a part of local community life (Maulia 2009). Indeed, all of these aspects are included in the official application, which also gives an outline of several projects that will be conducted to help revitalise and maintain the status of *batik* and the industry. The inscription in the UNESCO List gives details:

> The techniques, symbolism and culture surrounding hand-dyed cotton and silk garments known as Indonesian Batik permeate the lives of

Indonesians from beginning to end: infants are carried in batik slings decorated with symbols designed to bring the child luck, and the dead are shrouded in funerary batik. Clothes with everyday designs are worn regularly in business and academic settings, while special varieties are incorporated into celebrations of marriage and pregnancy and into puppet theatre and other art forms. The garments even play the central role in certain rituals, such as the ceremonial casting of royal batik into a volcano. Batik is dyed by proud craftspeople who draw designs on fabric using dots and lines of hot wax, which resists vegetable and other dyes and therefore allows the artisan to colour selectively by soaking the cloth in one colour, removing the wax with boiling water and repeating if multiple colours are desired. The wide diversity of patterns reflects a variety of influences, ranging from Arabic calligraphy, European bouquets and Chinese phoenixes to Japanese cherry blossoms and Indian or Persian peacocks. Often handed down within families for generations, the craft of batik is intertwined with the cultural identity of the Indonesian people and, through the symbolic meanings of its colours and designs, expresses their creativity and spirituality.

(Indonesian Batik 2009)

Put this way, it is not difficult to understand why *batik* was awarded a UNESCO listing. The nomination form and supporting images and video clips, which can be viewed with the inscription in the List online (Indonesian Batik 2009) are impressive and are an indication of the effort that was put into the application. Obviously the right people were involved in the process, including some of the same people who prepared the successful UNESCO *wayang* puppet theatre nomination.

Culture and Tourism Minister Jero Wacik weighed in on the celebratory atmosphere, boasting that *batik* was Indonesia's third tradition to secure UNESCO's recognition, after *wayang kulit* and *keris*. 'We will keep fighting for our heritage one tradition at a time,' Jero said (Maulia 2009). Further good news came for Indonesia in November 2010 when 'Indonesian' *angklung* – supposedly identified by Malaysia for listing as a part of its cultural heritage – was listed by UNESCO (Indonesian Angklung 2010; Unesco Recognizes 'Angklung' 2011).

The UNESCO listing of *batik* has had a very positive impact in Indonesia, particularly for the *batik* industry. Demand for this unique product has increased since 2009, throughout Indonesia and particularly in Indonesia's fashion capital, Jakarta. Moreover, according to Ika Krismantari (2010), 'with Jakarta's growing love of batik, on every corner of the city – in malls, on sidewalks and in bus stations – it seems there are people selling clothes with traditional printed motifs'. Apparently, not unlike Malaysia, new policies in local and national government departments and private companies oblige employees to wear *batik* every Friday. By all accounts, Indonesians are happy with Friday being *hari batik* (*batik* day) and there are few complaints.

Obligatory *batik*-wearing has been embraced in the last few years, mainly because it is seen both as a way of recognising and promoting the UNESCO listing and as a means of ensuring that Malaysia cannot pursue its supposed claims on *batik*, which many believe it still wants to do.

Understandably, the obligation to wear *batik* every Friday has contributed to a massive increase in demand for *batik* products. Lala Gozali, whose Gianti Creation produces clothes that combine modern designs and traditional motifs, told *The Jakarta Post*:

> since this batik craze began my business has continued to grow ... Lala said she collected woven fabrics and *batik* cloth from across Indonesia and made clothes from them, earning profits of up to Rp 40 million (US $4,400) a month – a big increase compared to what she had earned in 2003, when she first started out.
>
> (Krismantari 2010)

Many other business people have found their own niche in the new *batik*-boom, some of whom avoid traditional processes, choosing to sell mass-produced *batik* instead. With the cheaper fabrics, textile sellers are able to cater to a different, mall-based market rather than to the up-market, high-end *batik* designers such as Gozali. Mass-produced *batik*, for instance, can be found in most shopping malls at prices starting at around Rp20,000 (US$2) a piece, whereas traditional hand-made *batik* can be found in the fabric and fashion stalls in Yogyakarta at prices ranging from Rp200,000 (US$20) to Rp500,000 (US$50) and above for a piece. In the exclusive fashion boutiques of Jakarta's luxury malls, Rp500,000 would be at the low end of the scale, although the prices in Jakarta's malls are still much lower than the average prices of *batik* designer fashion in Kuala Lumpur or Singapore. Of course, much of the 'tourism' between Malaysia and Indonesia is conducted by Malaysian wholesalers purchasing *batik* and other textiles in Indonesia to be imported and sold in Malaysia at a considerably higher price.

Conclusion

Malaysian designers and artists have long been willing to adopt the motifs and textures of *batik* textiles into their latest designs, which are then exhibited in art galleries, fashion boutiques and malls and sold at international prices. They continue to produce *batik* designs, albeit without any UNESCO recognition of *batik* as a distinctly Malaysian form of intangible cultural heritage. Given the ongoing bilateral ill-will generated from allegations that Malaysia is intent on claiming *batik* as its cultural heritage, as expressed in the rampant anti-Malaysianism at the 2011 SEA Games, it appears that Malaysia has little hope of ever securing UNESCO acknowledgement of its own distinct Malaysian *batik* tradition. The same can be said for other forms of intangible heritage occurring in Malaysia, including *wayang kulit*, *keris*, *gamelan* and *angklung*. Indonesia has jealously guarded these forms of intangible cultural heritage by systematically and professionally lodging claims with UNESCO, which have met with success. Not surprisingly, besides the case of *mak yong* folk drama, Malaysia's UNESCO office has generally shied away from nominating contested or even shared Indo-Malay heritage items. Thus Kuala Lumpur has turned its attention elsewhere, to literary manuscripts such as the *Syair Almarhum Baginda Sultan Abu Bakar di Negeri Johor* (The Poem of the late Sultan Abu Bakar of Johor), for instance, which has been nominated, most recently in 2012, for the UNESCO's Memory of the World Register of documentary heritage. Unfortunately, while the *Syair Almarhum Baginda Sultan Abu Bakar di Negeri Johor* nomination is relatively uncontroversial, on the whole it lacks conviction. This is especially so when it is virtually impossible to locate the original manuscript of this work and there are already three extant copies, each of which is well preserved. Given these factors, it is difficult to fathom the motivation for such a listing. In the particular case of the *Syair Almarhum Baginda Sultan Abu Bakar di Negeri Johor*, it could well be nothing more than a public relations exercise in the lead-up to the 2014 coronation ceremony for the Sultan of Johor Sultan Ibrahim Sultan Iskandar.

Meanwhile, despite UNESCO's listing of Indonesian *batik*, many Indonesians fear that Malaysia will again attempt to claim one form of Indonesian cultural expression or another, including, belatedly, *batik*. Other critics, cognisant of Kuala Lumpur's successful marketing of *batik* abroad to the United States, France, England and other countries, have criticised Jakarta for its poor ability to market forms of Indonesian cultural heritage (Chong 2012). Thus *batik* and other cultural forms in Indonesia have become a bit like the ball used in the SEA Games football final, mere pawns in a much larger game of transnational one-upmanship. Malaysia, meanwhile, has problems of its own, most obviously the struggle to ensure ongoing economic prosperity in a society and political scene riven by ethnic tensions. This has tended to divert government attention and resources from contesting or disputing nominations for UNESCO listings. One could also argue that for the Malaysian government the politics of cultural heritage is more of an internal issue, involving domestic contestation among the nation's different ethnic groups, each of which seeks to assert its own forms of cultural heritage. Few would argue that Malay cultural heritage forms have long been promoted over the art, culture and heritage of ethnic minorities such as the Chinese. Although difficult to quantify, a cursory examination of Malaysia's leading art galleries, exhibitions and museums would indicate an overwhelming emphasis on Malay cultural forms and the post-independence period, which has been dominated by Malay-centric policies.

As this chapter has shown, Indonesian *batik* sellers seem to have few qualms about selling Indonesian *batik* to their arch-rival. Similarly, Indonesian *batik* artisans living and working in Malaysia seem unperturbed about the purely commercial appropriation of a distinctly Indonesian heritage occurring every day in Kelantan and Terengganu, the heartland of Malaysia's *batik* industry. As we shall reiterate in the next chapter, Indonesia, at both a national and a regional level, has little motivation to maintain and revive much of its cultural heritage; the nationalistic *causes célèbres* of *batik* and *wayang* are exceptions to the rule.[13] Generally, as long as Indonesia's economy is still developing, questions of economic growth and the alleviation of poverty are of a much higher priority. State-run galleries or museums, therefore, endure a chronic lack of financial support. Although entrance to museums in Indonesia is either inexpensive or free of charge, most Indonesians other than groups of schoolchildren avoid them. This is because Indonesian museums are generally unattractive, poorly curated and, most importantly, still closely associated with Suharto-era indoctrination, as Adams (2003), for example, notes. Ironically, as demonstrated by its recent and ongoing *batik* 'buzz', it is Malaysia that is far more determined to ensure that history and heritage play leading roles in the national cultural narrative. In contrast to Indonesia, many of Malaysia's state museums and galleries are well funded, employing state-of-the-art curation practices and technologies and often attracting modest numbers of visitors and corporate sponsorship. If we move beyond the nationalistic grandstanding epitomised by Indonesia–Malaysia football matches and the cultural nationalism epitomised by the successful nomination of Indonesian *batik* for UNESCO's cultural heritage listing, in terms of systematically maintaining and promoting cultural heritage, Indonesia still has some way to go. In relation to the advocacy and efficacy of museums, cultural theme parks and cultural heritage tours and trails, of the Southeast Asian nations, Malaysia is among the front-runners.

Notes

1 *Angklung* is a traditional bamboo musical instrument consisting of two to four bamboo tubes suspended in a bamboo frame, bound with rattan cords. It is popular in West Java and Banten, Indonesia.
2 Personal communication with Jajang C. Noer, Berkeley, 14 April 2010.
3 *Keroncong* is an Indonesian musical style that typically makes use of the *kroncong*, a ukulele-like instrument, usually performed in an ensemble consisting of a flute, a violin, a guitar, a cello, a string bass, and a female or male singer.
4 The term *mamak* refers to Malaysian Tamil Muslims, and a *mamak* stall is a type of restaurant that serves *mamak* food. These food establishments are generally owned and operated by Tamils.
5 Towards the end of the SEA Games it was reported in the Malaysian media that a Malaysian businessman visiting Jakarta had disappeared after one of the Malaysia–Indonesia matches. There was much fear for his safety and his name and image were widely broadcast. It turned out to be a false alarm.
6 Reading between the lines – as one must when reading Malaysian newspapers, given their continuing practice of self-censorship – we can perhaps detect a subtext relating to Malaysia's identification, in November 2011, as having the highest level of obesity in Southeast Asia (Obesity 2011). Our observations are that as a nation Malaysians do not exercise enough to counterbalance a high-fat three-meals-a-day diet of dishes, such as *nasi lemak, nasi campur, char kway teow, nasi kandar, roti*

canai, curry laksa, satay ayam, and *goreng pisang*, interspersed with junk food from Western franchises, such as KFC, McDonalds and Burger King, all of which is often accompanied by the ubiquitous *teh tarik*, iced teas and soft drinks with a high sugar content. As a Terengganu taxi driver mentioned, Malaysians not only eat these foods every day but also eat at all hours of the day and well into the night. Of course, Samsudin's cartoon may indeed simply refer to the competition between the *Harimau* and *Garuda*, and not support any other interpretation such as that we have given here.

7 'Penyokong Malaysia mengambil iktibar di atas kejadian yang berlaku sepanjang temasya Sukan Sea di Indonesia baru-baru ini. Buktinya, ketika lagu kebangsaan Syria dimainkan semua berdiri bagi menghormati pasukan lawan' (Tabik Penyokong 2011).

8 We would like to convey our warm thanks to Harold Crouch for this observation.

9 'Ini pekerjaan yang mengasyikkan. Meski sekarang bekerja di negeri orang, Mbah merasa seperti di kampung sendiri ... Matur nuwun sanget, sekarang Mbah, anak-anak, dan para cucu hidup berkecukupan' (Suditomo, Pudjiarti and Dimyathi 2009: 100).

10 'Sebelum tinggal di Kuala Terengganu, ia lahir dan puluhan tahun tinggal bersama keluarga besarnya di kota batik itu. Turun-temurun ia membatik, tapi tak pernah berkecukupan. Sebagai perajin, ia punya kewajiban menyetor kain batik buatannya ke rumah para juragan batik. Toh, hidupnya selalu kekurangan. "Walaupun jumlahnya banyak, tetap saja harganya selalu murah. Hasilnya hanya cukup untuk makan, pakaian, dan sekolah", ia bercerita' (Suditomo, Pudjiarti and Dimyathi 2009: 100).

11 'Kini ia bersukacita. "Selama di sini, setiap tahun anak dan cucu Mbah sudah disodori daftar mau meneruskan sekolah ke mana saja. Mbah juga diberi kesempatan pelesir ke mana pun yang Mbah suka", ucapnya sumringah' (Suditomo, Pudjiarti and Dimyathi 2009: 100).

12 'Ratmini, pembatik asal Yogya yang bergabung dengan Fine Batik Malaysia, menuturkan, bukannya tak saying kepada negeri sendiri, selama tinggal di Malaysia ia justru merasa lebih dipahami dan dihargai. Ia tak pernah pusing dengan masalah sekolah, kesehatan, atau rekreasi. "Jujur, tugas kami hanya membatik sebaik mungkin"' (Suditomo, Pudjiarti and Dimyathi 2009: 101).

13 Despite its UNESCO status and global prestige, the *wayang* of Java, Sunda and Bali does not quite yet enjoy untouchable status in contemporary Indonesia. Mirroring the fate of *wayang kulit* in Malaysia's northern states, *wayang* has been threatened by Islamist groups. For example, in September 2011, in Purwakarta, West Java, several statues depicting characters from the *wayang* shadow theatre were vandalised and destroyed by a mob emerging from a prayer session in the city's largest mosque. According to a *Jakarta Globe* report, ropes were tied from a van to a statue of puppet character Gatotkaca to pull it from its foundation. The crowd then turned its attention to a statue of Semar and, after throwing rocks and pulling it to the ground, hit it with sticks and metal rods before setting it on fire. A statue of the *wayang*'s Bima was also targeted and set on fire, before the mob moved on statues depicting the twin brothers of the *Mahabharata*, Nakula and Sadewa (Krisna 2011). Fortunately, hundreds of police and army officers were already on hand, guarding the Nakula and Sadewa and when it started raining the mob dispersed. Although it was never determined which Islamic group was responsible for the damage, the hardline Islamic People's Forum (FUI) had opposed the statues when the project was announced by the Purwakarta city administration in 2010. FUI argued that the statues were 'against the Islamic identity of the city' and claimed the statues would encourage people to have 'superstitious beliefs' (Krisna 2011).

4 Museums

Although it is claimed that both Indonesia and Malaysia prefer to celebrate and exalt in their shared cultural, linguistic and religious bonds (Raslan 2012), as the previous chapter has demonstrated, Indonesia will take extraordinary steps to ensure that Malaysia does not claim any of Indonesia's distinctive heritage forms as its own. Indonesia's pre-emptive jingoism, which demonstrates the politically shallow nature of the grand-sounding but hollow *serumpun* notion, may have its roots in the history of rivalry between the two countries. Its intra-regional manoeuvring may also stem from Indonesia's slightly more aspirational foreign policy stance during the transition to democracy in the late 1990s. Since the fall of Suharto in 1998, Indonesia has become much less insular and much more concerned about its global positioning. This concern is handsomely epitomised by its newfound enthusiasm for taking on a leadership role in ASEAN, joining the G20 and lodging a series of claims with global heritage bodies such as UNESCO.

Post-Mahathir Malaysia, meanwhile, which appears to have weathered the abrasive provocations of its neighbour with some fortitude, has been forced to find satisfaction of a sort with a solitary UNESCO intangible heritage listing – for the *mak yong* dance drama, added to UNESCO's intangible heritage list in 2005. *Mak yong* combines ritual, theatre, music and spontaneous dialogue and is performed predominantly by female troupes, accompanied by an all-male ensemble of musicians playing traditional instruments such as the *rebab* (fiddle), *serunai* (reed wind instrument), *tetawak* (gongs) and *gendang* (elongated barrel drums) (Malaysian National Commission for UNESCO 2008). According to both UNESCO and Malaysia's UNESCO office, *mak yong* originates in Kelantan, northern Malaysia. We can add that it is as much a Terengganu tradition as it is Kelantan's. More importantly, the supposed 'Malaysianness' of *mak yong* may be subject to debate, which is of little surprise given the centuries of cultural and textual flow among the courts, sultanates and states in the region. As Andaya (2010: 13) puts it, 'pre-colonial Southeast Asia was not subject to international conventions confining individuals within a fixed space, imposing on them a specific ethnic or national identity'. A similar argument can be made for art forms. Just as ethnic identity was a fluid concept, cultural identity was also fluid and the decision to practise or transmit particular cultural forms elsewhere in the region was the privilege of the individual. Thus it is not surprising that the *mak yong* folk theatre is found not only in northern Malaysia, but also in Indonesia's Riau archipelago, off the eastern coast of Sumatra, where it was introduced in the late nineteenth century as a result of the strong links between the Terengganu royal family and the rulers of Riau. Fortunately, the Indonesian government has not considered contesting the UNESCO listing of *mak yong* as a distinctively Malaysian cultural heritage form.[1]

As we determined during our conversations with representatives of Malaysia's UNESCO office in Kuala Lumpur, the Malaysian government is sympathetic to the advice that shared Indo-Malay heritage not be contested. Consequently, the less said about the supposed – and incorrect – Indonesian provenance of *mak yong*, the better. Even officials at regional government level are aware of the transnational sensitivities involved, as demonstrated in 2012 when a member of the Selangor State Legislative Assembly, Shafie Abu Bakar, led a delegation to Palembang in southern Sumatra to seek permission to adopt *songket* as the official dress of Selangor, Malaysia's most populous state. After studying the provenance of the *songket* motif, Abu Bakar's office had found that its origins could be traced directly to Palembang. Although the Indonesian House Speaker consented to the Selangor delegation's request, the Malaysians showed caution in pursuing it further with the Palembang government. According to the *Jakarta Globe*, the Palembang government might seek to patent the motif 'in order to solidify Indonesia's claim over it' before granting its approval (Indonesian House Speaker OK 2012).

Malaysia's federal government heritage officials have judiciously focused their energies on forging closer ties with UNESCO in general and on maintaining Malaysian sites already registered on UNESCO's World Heritage List, including Melaka and George Town, recognised in 2008 as 'Historic Cities of the States of Malacca' (Melaka and George Town 2011). Ironically, Malaysia's heritage success stories could serve as good models for Indonesian urban planning officials. Take the attractive, if dilapidated, historic neighbourhoods of Jakarta, Surabaya and Semarang, for example, 'all of which', according to Raslan (2013), 'have failed to "take off" in terms of restoration or redevelopment'. Raslan's advice for Indonesian officialdom is apt, albeit a bitter pill for most Indonesians to swallow: 'As local policy makers try to figure out what to do to revitalize these iconic quarters, they could do worse than to visit the Malaysian city of Georgetown on the island of Penang'.

With the exception of UNESCO-listed *batik*, *wayang* and Borobudur, cultural heritage, whether tangible or intangible, in Indonesia is given little recognition or support by individuals, communities, or the state. The process of nominating cultural heritage for UNESCO listing is extremely complex and fraught with conflict at many different levels. Of the nomination of the highland Toraja village of Ke'te' Kesu' on the island of Sulawesi as a UNESCO World Heritage Site, Adams observes that 'the emergence of heritage sites is not a "natural" process, but rather one born out of complex exchanges, competitions, and collaborations between local groups, as well as national and international entities' (Adams 2010: 103). While indigenous ideas about heritage need to be considered, many heritage sites in the Indonesian context are very much a product of the Dutch colonial past. Thus processes and institutions that stretch far beyond the local shape heritage sites and intangible heritage forms. Although local actors and rivalries between local elites are salient to understanding the processes behind any UNESCO nomination, what is being nominated must be exposed to a more informed analysis that situates it into a larger national and global context (Adams 2010: 103). The ambivalence of the *songket* case, coupled with the jingoistic Indonesian media ccoverage, demonstrates the importance of situating contested heritage disputes in a transnational context. But if we take away the grandstanding of transnational cultural contestations, the discrete comparative examination of the heritage of each nation is revealing. By comparing the maritime heritage of two major port cities – Makassar in eastern Indonesia and Kuala Terengganu in eastern peninsular Malaysia – this chapter will highlight the contrast between cultural heritage management in Indonesia and Malaysia. As we shall see, in regional Indonesia, cultural heritage is a marginal phenomenon. In regional Malaysia, however, cultural heritage is very much a fundamental element of the national conversation.

In its broadest sense, the contrasting attitudes towards cultural heritage are representative of the differing politics of the two nations. Indonesia's democratic progress has been encouraging, but also long, messy and painful. Indonesia has also, to some extent, projected its democratic transformation onto the region, with mixed results. For example, Indonesian calls for political reform within ASEAN, epitomised by its efforts to promote democratisation in Burma and broker peace between Thailand and Cambodia, have only been half-heartedly supported. Demonstrations of regional one-upmanship, as in the repeated transnational cultural contestations with Malaysia, have also added tensions. Riding the crest of a democratic wave, Indonesia is testing the acceptance of democracy in the region, while domestically much has stayed the same. Corruption, for instance, is still rampant, and much has fallen by the wayside including developing a more widespread sense of respect for the nation's history and heritage. As one commentator posted in response to the *Jakarta Globe*'s article on the *songket* drama, 'So be it, if the Malaysian [sic] were happy to wear it we have no qualms since most Indonesian today never appreciated it anyway so it is an honor for Palembang *songket*' (Indonesian House Speaker OK 2012). The Malaysian government, on the other hand, has enough to concern itself, without monitoring Indonesia's each and every move, especially in regards to scoping, designing and lodging heritage claims. The Malaysian government's primary concern is, we argue, the ongoing struggle to maintain economic prosperity in the context of a society and mildly authoritarian political milieu internally riven by ethnic tensions. As we shall see, the Malaysian government's promotion of museums, cultural theme parks, and tangible and intangible cultural heritage is very much a manifestation of its rather parochial political preoccupations.

As in previous chapters, this chapter uses case studies to support and explain our argument. In this chapter, however, we will present two discrete case studies and compare the findings of each, rather than emphasise the flows between the two nations. Transnational cultural flows remain an element of our argument, of course, and they will receive some attention, but they will be tangential, as our principal objective in this chapter is to compare the maritime cultural heritage of the port city of Makassar in South Sulawesi with the maritime history of Kuala Terengganu, a major port on the east coast of peninsular Malaysia. Our starting point will be just one element of Makassar's broader maritime heritage: the 'Macassan' trepang industry.

Macassans and museums

The Macassans[2] were trepang fishermen originating from the Sulawesi port of Makassar who voyaged to the coastal waters of northern Australia to fish for trepang, also known as sea cucumbers, from at least 1720 to 1906. The Macassans were ethnically diverse. Besides the ethnic Makassarese, who are predominantly located on the western coast of the South Sulawesi peninsula, the next largest group from Sulawesi-based populations involved in trepang gathering were the Bugis (or Buginese) and the Bajau (or Sama-Bajau or Bajau Laut, also known as sea gypsies). By all accounts, the fleets of Macassan *perahu* (wooden fishing vessels) ranged from 30 to 60 each year, carrying possibly as many as 1,000 trepangers, who had deep and often enduring interactions with the indigenous communities of the Kimberley and Arnhem Land (Macknight, 1976: 29). The significance of this number lies in the fact that the total adult male population of Makassar in 1730 is said to have been no more than about 2,500 (Knaap 2001: 96). For a time, trepang was a major item of import and export from Makassar, where its trade boomed in the 1780s when it was Makassar's main export, especially to China.

Considering the length and breadth of the historical encounter between Makassar and Australia's Arnhem Land, which was known as Marege', one could be forgiven for assuming that Makassar's museums would incline towards showcasing the Macassan history. This has not occurred, for many reasons, including the fact that contemporary Indonesian understandings of the past have failed to throw light on the Macassan heritage question. There is also some ambiguity surrounding the term 'Macassan heritage', which needs explication. In previous decades, we could safely understand 'Macassan heritage' as encompassing authentic monuments and historic sites with distinctive connections to the Bugis-Makassarese, or 'Macassan', fishermen and entrepreneurs of centuries past. But it will soon become evident that tangible Macassan heritage is now practically non-existent, both in Makassar and across South Sulawesi. But this should not mean that there is no Macassan heritage in Indonesia, especially if one defines the Macassan heritage of Sulawesi not simply in terms of a selection of tangible cultural products but rather as an ongoing cultural process with associated intangible values. To do this, Macassan heritage needs to be understood as an element of a continuous and dynamic process through which a variety of identities are formed.

If Makassar's Macassan heritage is viewed as an embodiment of everyday life, or as living history, it can be argued first of all that Macassan heritage is far from dead and buried. From this perspective, it can be argued that both the marginal and ongoing nature of Makassar's Macassan heritage ensures that it has largely escaped the objectifying processes of 'museumising' and 'heritagisation', which are generally frowned upon in Southeast Asia, especially in postcolonial Indonesia and Malaysia. The resistance to these processes stems mainly from a perception throughout the Malay world of museums – or rather, the restoration of archaeological monuments – as a fundamental element of the colonial civilising project.

As Anderson (1991) argues, from the early nineteenth century onwards, the colonial rulers exhibited a great deal of interest in the antique monuments of the civilisations they had subjected. Thomas Stamford Raffles, British Lieutenant-Governor of Java from 1811 to 1816, was the first of the colonial officials who not only amassed a large personal collection of local *objets d'art* but also studied their history systematically. 'Thereafter', in Anderson's words, 'with increasing speed, the grandeurs of Borobudur, of Angkor, of Pagan, and of other ancient sites were successively disinterred, unjungled, measured, photographed, reconstructed, fenced off, analysed, and displayed' (Anderson 1991: 179). Consequently, sacred sites were transformed into museums and were able to be incorporated, both literally and figuratively, into the map of the colony. Monumental archaeology, which was soon linked to tourism, allowed the colonial governments to appear as guardians of a generalised, but also local, tradition. After 'discovering' the monuments, the colonisers documented and photographed them, eventually publishing books with images that illustrated the 'discovery' process. Through surveillance and reproduction, the colonial government ensured that long-abandoned historical traditions became secular and thus available for tourism. The museumising process also served to perpetuate the colonial order, as the reconstruction process always placed the builders of the monuments and the colonial natives in a certain hierarchy: in colonial Southeast Asia, there was a widespread argument that the builders of these monuments were long gone and that contemporary colonial natives were no longer capable of achieving what their predecessors had. Viewed from this perspective, the reconstructed monuments, jutting out in the midst of rural poverty, said to the colonised natives: 'Our very presence shows that you have always been, or have long become, incapable of either greatness or self-rule' (Anderson 1991: 181). In this context, museums and museumising were profoundly political. Has much changed in the contemporary era?

Physically, Indonesia's state museums are very much relics of the Dutch colonial era, which was when they were first established.[3] Their functions and methods of cultural representation have barely changed since the colonial era. Echoing Anderson, Kneps (2003) observes that museums in the Indies were established to further the political, economic and cultural interests of the colonists. Despite government claims that the role of the museum in independent Indonesia would differ from the role of the museum in the Dutch East Indies, the underlying political purpose is the same, namely, to further develop and modernise, but this time serving the political interests of the postcolonial state (Kneps 2003). Museums are by no means the only resources mobilised for such purposes. For example, in the Suharto era, the state's impulse towards museumising traditional cultural forms was closely associated with the New Order regime's authoritarian aims, that is, to incorporate and subsume the local or traditional as a means of establishing a national cultural hegemony (Pemberton 1994). The regional museum of South Sulawesi, Makassar's City Museum, established in 1916, does little to promote either the indigenous cultures or histories of the South Sulawesi region. In its reluctance to promote the local or regional, it can be classed as a New Order museum *par excellence*, which, as we have suggested, owes much to its colonial beginnings. The museum is a dark and dusty place, with little in the way of labeling, interpretation and interactive displays. Apart from the obligatory mannequins garbed in traditional Bugis wedding costume, there is little recognition of the distinct local traditions and histories of Makassar's Islamic, Bugis, Makassarese and other identities. At worst, it could be argued that these histories, as well as other histories, such as the 'Macassan' history, have been ignored. At best, it could be argued that these histories have yet to be domesticated by the neo-colonial museumising imagination. Either way, besides the colonial overtones described above, state museums have long been seen as instruments of New Order indoctrination and are, consequently, poorly patronised in the post-authoritarian era.

In the more economically advanced postcolonial nation-states in the Malay world such as Malaysia and Singapore, the museumising impulse has taken a much more pervasive hold than in developing Indonesia, where day-to-day economic survival appears to be a much more pressing concern (Adams 2003). In reference to open-air museums and cultural theme parks in particular, Hoffstaedter (2008) suggests that they inevitably spring up, as they have done in Malaysia and Singapore, as the drive towards industrialisation and modernisation replaces an everyday focus on rural heritage and the past. The aim of museums and theme parks, it appears, is to preserve rural and traditional arts, crafts and lifestyles in the face of industrialisation. But politics can also play a key role in this process. In Malaysia, for instance, the promotion of museums, traditional craft fairs and cultural theme parks, with the associated museumising of the material culture of both the modern and the past, is closely related to government initiatives to instil national pride among Malaysian citizens (Hoffstaedter 2008). The Malaysian government has a proclaimed aim of becoming a fully industrialised country by the year 2020 and iconic modern elements of this project, such as Kuala Lumpur's Petronas Twin Towers, the tallest twin towers in the world, are given equal weighting with traditional elements of the nation's narrative, such as the Sultan's palace with its wood-crafted dwellings and the many material cultural artifacts found in museums and theme parks (Hoffstaedter 2008: 142). The postcolonial state's reification, which Nor (2011: 53) calls 'heritagization', of traditional Malay court and folk dances is another expression of this pattern. Kuala Lumpur's Kompleks Budaya Kraf (Handicraft Complex), with its colony of artists and artisans employed to give daily performances of *batik*-making, jewelry-making, dancing, and so on, is a similar expression of this museumising impulse.[4] A parallel process is occurring in Singapore, where several excellent museums, including the National Museum and the Asian Civilisations Museum, play a large part in government efforts to instil a greater sense of a distinctly Singaporean national cultural identity among its people. Although the museums focus on different aspects of Singaporean history, their exhibitions emphasise the broader cultural heritage of contemporary Singaporean citizens, most of whom can trace their ancestry to other countries in Asia, such as China, India and Malaysia (Adams 2003; Henderson 2005).

In fairness, it should be noted that, despite the obvious economic differences, Indonesia has not been completely left behind by its wealthier neighbours. For instance, there is a modest amount of museumising in Indonesia, such as the well-established Taman Mini Indah Indonesia theme park in Jakarta and the Sultan of Yogyakarta's Palace in Central Java, which has a number of ceremonial and historical artefacts. Moreover, as mentioned earlier, there appears to be modest growth in the establishment of new museums and cultural heritage tours and trails, particularly in regional cities and towns such as Magelang, Jepara, Banten and Demak. With rising incomes, the regions appear to be seeking to claim and highlight their specific and unique heritage and culture. On the whole, however, these efforts, which attempt to replicate the now *passé* Western concept of heritage as tangible, material, authentic and old, are still poorly funded, ad-hoc in nature, and poorly patronised. As we described earlier, the government-funded Makassar City Museum, for example, is unkempt and dusty, with depressingly inadequate lighting and labelling. The museum is free of charge and is manned by student volunteers with little understanding of the historical significance of any of the museum's artefacts, which are seldom rotated or enhanced by new acquisitions. Fortunately, it can be argued that in Makassar, as in Indonesia generally, 'living history', as opposed to anachronistic 'museumified history', is a better source for gaining an understanding of the culture of the region.

Offering a point of comparison between 'living history' and 'museumified history', the penultimate section of this chapter will discuss the seafaring and fisheries galleries in the Terengganu State Museum in the port city of Kuala Terengganu, Malaysia. The discussion is intended to serve as an illustration of how a tangible Macassan or seafaring cultural heritage might be embodied or interpreted. Beforehand, however, we need to state the fact that using Malaysia as a point of comparison has its flaws, particularly in relation to museums. As Karim Raslan observed in the mid-1990s, Malaysia is a middle-class nation with middle-class preoccupations (Raslan 1996: 128) and Malaysia's middle-class preoccupations have deepened since then. Among the preoccupations is the preservation and promotion of history and heritage. Indonesia differs from Malaysia in many ways. In terms of economic progress and democratic consolidation, developing Indonesia still has a very long way to go. In terms of print literacy, despite rising educational levels and a sharp decline in the level of illiteracy, Indonesia's oral cultural and literary traditions still predominate (Derks 1996, 2002). Consequently, any serious examination of the history and heritage of contemporary Indonesia must move beyond a negative comparison with Malaysia, which is an entirely different kettle of fish. Instead, it should be premised on the understanding that the cultural landscape of South Sulawesi is an ongoing cultural process, an intangible 'living history', rather than an objective cultural product, an argument that will be elaborated on in the final section of this chapter.

Makassar and a proposal for Macassan Heritage

Makassar is now one of the largest cities in Indonesia and, after Jakarta and Surabaya, the third largest port city. The city, which was known in the New Order period as Ujung Pandang, is the capital city of the province of South Sulawesi. Makassar is also southern Sulawesi's primary port and has many domestic and international shipping connections, which means that it is the major maritime trading centre of the eastern part of the Indonesian archipelago. Makassar has a modest international airport, with direct and regular flights to and from Singapore, Jakarta, Denpasar, and many other domestic destinations, including all the major centres in Sulawesi. Makassar has been described, somewhat romantically, in the following way:

> Bugis schooners, the ancient walls of the city and the minarets and domes of mosques impart a medieval look to South Sulawesi's bustling port and capital, Ujung Pandang. Indeed, the city still exhibits many vestiges of the 16th century when it was known the world over as Macassar, maritime center of the Dutch East Indies.
>
> (Behr 1990: 204)

Two decades later much of this description holds true. Among many other types of vessels, in Makassar's Paotere harbour there certainly are the odd *pinisi* (Bugis schooner) or two, distinguished by their spectacular masts and spinnakers. The minarets and domes of Makassar's mosques are still in abundance. The imposing walls of Fort Rotterdam are a stark reminder of Makassar's Indies past. During the early mornings and evenings, when the *adzan*, or Muslim call for prayers, over numerous loudspeaker systems seems particularly pronounced, Makassar's Muslim heritage is obvious. These days, however, the Makassar skyline is dominated by a string of five-star luxury hotels along the Losari beachfront thoroughfare, not to mention the many large container cranes at Makassar's main wharf. As the region's major trading hub, Makassar is the self-proclaimed gateway to the many provinces and islands of eastern Indonesia and to the idyllic heritage tourism area of Tanah Toraja in the highlands of South Sulawesi. Much has been written about the rich Torajan cultural heritage, with an emphasis on the role of heritage tourism and its impact on traditional Torajan society and culture (for example, the books by Adams (2006) and Waterson (2011)). There have also been ongoing calls for the Toraja region, as we alluded to earlier, to be proposed as a site for the UNESCO World Heritage List (Adams 2010). Ironically, the local and national authorities working on the Toraja claim would be well served by collaboration with their Malaysian colleagues, who have overseen the listing of several World Heritage Sites, including Kinabalu National Park in Sabah, the Gunung Mulu National Park in Sarawak and the historic cities of George Town and Melaka mentioned earlier.

Despite the push for Tanah Toraja to be listed by UNESCO as a World Heritage site, there has so far been little interest in listing tangible or intangible evidence of South Sulawesi's major role in the Macassan trepang industry, which is a significant feature of the history of the region. As Macknight (1976) and many others have observed, the regular arrival of the Macassan fleets along the coastline of northern Australia resulted in frequent social, cultural and economic interaction between the trepangers and the peoples of the Australian coastline, which included the movement of Australian Aboriginal people to live, work and die in Makassar. The Macassan heritage is therefore imbued with cultural and historic significance for the indigenous people of northern Australia and for the people of South Sulawesi, which, most neutral observers agree, needs to be rediscovered, preserved and conserved. As Indonesia's vibrant democratic consolidation begins to attract more international investment and tourists, and allows for the growth of a truly globalised middle class, it may now be timely for Macassan heritage sites to be nominated for UNESCO listing as world heritage, perhaps in a joint proposal by Australia and Indonesia. More precisely, the Makassar–Marege' maritime trade route might be appropriate for nomination in the category of cultural routes, introduced by UNESCO's World Heritage Committee in the mid 1990s. There is also the possibility of documenting and assessing Australian components of the Macassan trepangers' heritage for inclusion on Australia's National Heritage List in recognition of their relevance in Australian history. At present, although none of the Macassan sites along the northern coastline have been inscribed on Australia's National Heritage List, they are protected as archaeological sites under the Northern Territory's Heritage Act 2012.

The preparation of a joint Australia–Indonesia nomination for listing a series of transnational Macassan heritage sites as part of a cultural route, each sector of which is in some way outstanding, authentic and complementary, would be a difficult undertaking. As we have seen in the previous chapter, Indonesia has shown little interest in developing transnational claims for shared intangible heritage. At its most fundamental level the nomination proposed here would need to transcend not just Australian state and territory borders but also the national borders of both Australia and Indonesia. Challenges would also arise from the inevitable complexity of conveying an authentic sense of Macassan history and heritage through a series of separate sites, each of which has a variety of elements. Many important questions would demand answers: Are there any heritage sites in South Sulawesi that could possibly fulfill UNESCO's strict criteria? Can any of the sites in Sulawesi be considered as truly out-standing examples of heritage sites displaying an important aspect of human history? Can any of the sites demonstrate satisfactory levels of general protection and management of the property? Can any of the sites demonstrate that there is no major threat to the site and its surrounding property? Can any of the sites demonstrate proper visitor reception and interpretative facilities? Measuring what might be considered as Macassan cultural heritage sites against the UNESCO criteria behind these questions might result in the assessment of some as partly eligible, but most will fall short.

The case of Unusu Daeng Remba's house in Jalan Maipa

The best-known Macassan heritage site, a house (see Figure 4.1), is in fact one that would fall short of UNESCO's requirements for World Heritage listing.

Figure 4.1 Unusu Daeng Remba's house in Jalan Maipa, Makassar, shortly before its demolition, 3 November 2011.
Photo: Marshall Clark

The house is described by Macknight (1976: Plate 18) as 'the building said to have been Unusu Daeng Remba's house in Kampong Basi, Macassar'. Unusu Daeng Remba was captain of the *Lakarinlong* on its voyages to Arnhem Land between 1882–83 and 1889–90 and of the *Kampong Basi* in 1897–98, and also sailed on several other boats, including the *Mannongkoki*. One of the most prominent captains as the trepang industry declined, he was known to have hosted Aboriginal people in his house in Makassar (Macknight 1976: 86). According to Ibu Saribinong Nganne (born 1904), the daughter of another well-known captain in the last years of the Macassan trepang industry, Using Daeng Rangka, at least two of the Aboriginals were men who lived and worked in Remba's house and died there in the 1930s (Stephenson 2007: 31). Cooke (1987: 45) gives their names as Lahurru and Lakkoy, while Stephenson (2007: 31) names them Lahurruk and Lido. They were 'responsible for guarding the *empang* or fishponds at the back of the house, cleaning the *mushollah* [small Muslim prayer house] … and pump[ing] water up bamboo ducts to the house and *mushollah*' (Ganter 2006: 36). The Kampung Basi locale is around Jalan Maipa, a street that is now in central Makassar, in walking distance from Makassar's palm-fringed Losari Beach and several of Makassar's best-known luxury hotels. The main roof beams, posts and structural foundations of the house are said to have been constructed of ironwood brought back from Arnhem Land more than 100 years ago.

At this point it should be noted that Unusu Daeng Remba's house no longer exists. The house, which in its final form consisted of an impressive two-storey house and a row of boarding rooms and classrooms, set in a courtyard extending 50 metres to the south, was demolished on 3 November 2011. This fact alone will ensure that it will never meet UNESCO's protection and management criteria. It was demolished so that the nearby up-market Kenari Towers Hotel could construct a new wing. A sign in the front yard of the house, prominent on the day of the demolition and in the following weeks, read: 'Mohon Doa Restu: Lokasi Ini Akan Dibangun Kenari Tower Hotel Unit 2 [Please Offer Your Prayers of Blessing: This Location will be used to Build Unit 2 of the Kenari Tower Hotel]'. The house was reportedly sold for Rp10 billion (US$1 million), which by Indonesian standards is a fortune. There is little doubt that the neighbourhood around Jalan Maipa, which runs from the picture-postcard beach into an area of schools and luxury hotels, holds some of Makassar's most sought-after real estate.

The previous owner of the property, KH Darwis Zakaria, was well aware of the heritage value of the house's timber. Before its demolition, in conversation with us the visibly upset Darwis, who grew up in the house, claimed that it would be carefully collected and used in the construction of a new house on the rural outskirts of Makassar. Nevertheless, much of this historically precious timber was destroyed in the demolition and large chunks of it lay strewn amongst the ruins (see Figure 4.2). When we asked a neighbour why the leftover timber was not being collected – or indeed stolen, considering the very high cost of ironwood – the response was prescient: 'No-one would be

Figure 4.2 The remains of the Daeng Remba house, Makassar, mid-November 2011.
Photo: Marshall Clark

brave enough to steal that wood, as it is sacred (*keramat*)'. Carbon testing
would probably confirm that the wood was well over 100 years old and,
therefore, would be considered, as the neighbours suggested, far too '*lapuk*'
(dilapidated) for further use.

It was widely understood in the Jalan Maipa neighbourhood that the timber
used in constructing Unusu Daeng Remba's house was transported from Arnhem
Land in a boat captained by Daeng Remba over 100 years ago. Some believed,
perhaps mistakenly, that the house was built by a team of Aboriginal people. As
noted earlier, Aboriginal Australians were known to have lived in the house,
perhaps as slaves, from time to time. It is possible that an Aboriginal woman
may also have lived at the Jalan Maipu house. Aboriginal people in Arnhem
Land knew of an Aboriginal woman, Garngarr, who lived out her life in
Makassar. Garngarr was taken as a teenage girl from Arnhem Bay, northeast
Arnhem Land, to live in Makassar where she married a Macassan man and
had a number of children. At the age of 99, Garngarr was reunited in 1986
with a number of her family from northern Australia, including Yolngu elder,
Lak Lak Burarrwanga, who may be her great-great-granddaughter.

Although the Garngarr story is shrouded in uncertainty, it is fascinating.
According to Mattjuwi's account in Ganter (2006: 36), an Aboriginal woman
from Elcho Island, not far from Arnhem Bay, named Garnggar, was abducted
by someone known as Captain Maliwa. Cooke (1987: 45) suggests that this

person may be Daeng Mallewa, a trepanger from the Spermonde island of Barrang Lompo. Ganter observes that Garnggar had a daughter, Gunano, who was born in Makassar. There are differing versions of Gunano's story, however, with varying accounts of how long she may have lived in Makassar, if at all. For instance, Macknight (1976: 87) reports that Using Daeng Rangka is said to have fathered about ten children by three mothers in eastern Arnhem Land and one of his daughters there, Kunanu, later visited Makassar, but is unlikely that she spent the rest of her life there. According to Mangngellai Daeng Maro, the son of Unusu Daeng Remba, 'a woman named "Kunano" went to Makassar and was later returned home before the end of the trepang industry with all the other Aborigines who were in Makassar at the time' (Cooke 1987: 43). Putting aside the question of how long Gunano/Kunano lived in Makassar, we can discount the notion that Gunano/Kunano is the same person as Garngarr/Garnggar, as their names have not been linked by any sources. It remains difficult to determine precisely how Lak Lak is related to Garngarr/Garnggar and it is likely to remain difficult to do so. As noted by Cooke (1987: 39), 'most Aboriginal kinship terms simply do not have an English equivalent, and must be expressed in a roundabout way and with plenty of explanation'. Lak Lak's account of the reunion in Makassar in 1986 reads:

> When we got there she jumped from the chair and walked towards us saying this is the family from Arnhem Land. She was still thinking of when she left many years before. So we grieved. She was crying for me and we were crying for her.
>
> (Lloyd *et al.* 2010: 710)

After the initial reunion, stories were shared:

> So we talked about what happened to her. She told stories. She was really old – about 99 – but she was very strong. She told the story for the great grandsons. So we stayed there, made her company. Her husband had now died. We stayed for one night with her, me and my cousin Djalinda. The next day we went back and she called us up so that we should go to the museum where her nephew worked. His name was Hussein and we went to see. When she was young she was beautiful. We saw all the things she wore and her husband. We could see the sword. He was a prince, her husband. We see clothes. Everything was kept in the museum.
>
> (Burarrwanga 2012)

Garngarr has now passed away and, according to residents of Jalan Maipa, is purportedly buried with her husband somewhere in West Sumatra. Unusu Daeng Remba's great-great-grandchildren and other Jalan Maipa residents vividly recall a large group of Aboriginals (presumably Lak Lak's group of six) touring the house several decades ago (in 1986, to be precise). Lak Lak has also recounted a few other Makassar-related stories, most notably that

Garngarr worked at a church where she used to sweep and mop the wooden floor, which was apparently made of ironwood from northeast Arnhem Land. There is a Catholic school in the Kampung Basi locale, so perhaps this is an avenue of future investigation.

One further point about the Jalan Maipa house is that neighbours were certain that it was haunted. Haunted houses are not a phenomenon unique to Makassar, of course, as belief in ghosts and other supernatural activity is widespread and deeply rooted throughout maritime Southeast Asia. The stories of ghosts inhabiting the Japan Maipa house may explain the general reluctance to tamper with the abandoned timber. One middle-aged man told us of how he had slept overnight in the house a few times when he was a boy. He distinctly remembers being disturbed in the early hours of the morning by dark-skinned Marege' (Aboriginal) ghosts. Although the ghosts were not threatening, the experience was unsettling and not easily forgotten. It might be useful to establish whether the new house on the outskirts of Makassar, which will purportedly utilise the remaining Arnhem Land ironwood, is haunted as well. Given that intangible heritage such as ghosts and other paranormal activity are often associated with objects of tangible heritage, particularly in relation to objects of historical or spiritual significance to Aboriginals, it would not be surprising if there were reports of the new house being haunted.

Museums, tombs and graveyards

Makassar's other Macassan heritage sites can be summarised in a few paragraphs. The Makassar City Museum, for example, occasionally mounts a display on the Macassan trepang industry, such as that referred to by Macknight (2008: 141). At present, the City Museum holds mounted photographs relating to the Macassan voyages to Arnhem Land, as well as of joint theatre productions between Australian and Makassar-based performing arts groups. One of the mounted images is an intriguing map of the indigenous state of Gowa, which was a dominant local power around the city of Makassar by the end of the sixteenth century. According to this map, which has been observed in other locations in present-day Makassar (Cooke 1987: 45), Gowa's authority is shown by the map to have stretched throughout eastern Indonesia and to the Northern Territory in the first half of the seventeenth century. According to Macknight (2008: 141), who has seen two editions of the map, 'the Top End of the Northern Territory is included with a date of ± 1640 in the first edition of the work in 1967, and ± is removed in the second edition of 1983'. Although most scholars would suggest that a map such as this one is unreliable (see Macknight 2008: 141), it is generally understood that Gowa's influence was felt on the east coast of Kalimantan, in Lombok, and eastwards to the Aru-Kei island group (Ricklefs *et al.* 2010: 160–61). Gowa's role as the main spice-trading state of eastern Indonesia attracted Asian and European communities, including the Dutch Vereenigde Oost-Indische Compagnie (VOC), whose attentions resulted in hostilities between Gowa and the VOC in 1615. In the wake of this warfare, the peace treaty of Bungaya eventually brought Gowa's dominance of trade to an end. This information is not documented in the Makassar City Museum and the mounted photographs referred to above are currently locked in a dusty cabinet in one of the museum's ground-floor galleries.

Similarly difficult to locate is the tombstone of Puddu Daeng Tompo, who died about 1912. The tombstone is in a laneway off Jalan Somba Opu, behind Mesjid Ansar, the main mosque of Kampung Maloku, central Makassar (see Figure 4.3). Daeng Tompo was the main financier or entrepreneur (*punggawa*) of the Macassan trepang industry in its final stages. According to Macknight (1976: Plate 16), he probably devoted some of his profits to building the mosque, which might explain why his tombstone has remained reasonably well maintained to this day. Several prominent figures in the neighbourhood, including the Kampung Maloku district head and direct descendants of Daeng Tompo, informed us that Daeng Tompo owned much of the property in the area around the mosque, at the southern end of what is now Makassar's modest Chinatown.

The final location of Macassan heritage that is worth highlighting is quite possibly in fact a series of sites. On the larger islands in the Spermonde Archipelago out from the Makassar coastline are a number of cemeteries said to contain the graves of fishermen who voyaged to Arnhem Land. It is extremely difficult to ascertain simply by looking at the graves which are

Figure 4.3 The tombstone of Puddu Daeng Tompo in Kampung Maloku, Makassar. Photo: Marshall Clark

those of trepangers from the time of the Macassan trepang industry; local people are unable to identify them either. The oldest graves are very dilapidated and many of them are unmarked, but it is very likely some of those buried beneath them were islanders involved in trepang fishing. According to Meereboer (1998: 257), 'some sea cucumber species were named after one of the islands, that is Kodingaring (Lompo), the southern-most island in this archipelago'. In 1823, at the height of the Macassan trepang industry, the *kodingaring trepang* were the most valuable and the *pasir kodingaring* (sand *kodingaring*) was the most expensive of them all (Sutherland 2000: 88). As noted earlier, it was a trepanger from one of the Spermonde islands who was said to have kidnapped an Aboriginal woman. There is a strong possibility, therefore, that the Spermonde cemeteries contain the graves of trepangers from the Macassan era, thus making them potentially sites of Macassan historical significance.

One of the largest of these supposedly Macassan cemeteries can be found on Kodingareng Lompo, which is most probably the island Lak Lak Burarrrwanga referred to in her account of her trip to Sulawesi:

> Then the next day we crossed in a Makassan boat to an island called Gunyaŋgarri, a small island about 1000 people staying there and it was also very difficult. There was an outside shower with the water hole. We saw the grave for the people who had been there, to Arnhem Land. It held people from Sulawesi who had been to Arnhem Land. They take them to that island to get away from the city when they got old and they died there. All the poles and flags were there. It's similar to here. One man took us to the wishing stone where they used to wish for the NE wind. It's a rock there.
>
> (Burarrwanga 2012)

The island of Kodingareng Lompo, popularly known as Kodingareng, has a population of least 1,000 people and life there could indeed be described as 'very difficult' because of such inconveniences such as outdoor showers located near wells. The 'wishing stone' mentioned in Lak Lak's account is not immediately identifiable in Kodingareng, but there are a number of very large boulders near the cemetery. There are also a number of Chinese tombstones that might be of marginal relevance. The calligraphy on the headstones of these imposing tombstones identifies them as marking the graves of Chinese entrepreneurs. From our conversations with local residents, we learned that many of the Chinese who lived and died in the Spermonde islands were traders and *trepang* collectors. On Barrang Lompo, in particular, there are several very prominent Chinese tombstones, as well as the tombs of prominent Muslim traders or aristocrats, one of which is at the base of a 50-foot high banyan tree – the roots of the tree literally grow in and around the tombstone, which is now part of the tree itself. Of course, none of this tangible Macassan history and heritage is documented or advertised and only mosque officials and the very oldest people in the community are able to give any account of the significance of these sites. In present-day Makassar and its environs there is little tangible evidence of a distinct Macassan cultural heritage. So, if there were to be such a thing as a Macassan heritage, what form would we like it to take? More precisely, in order to fulfil UNESCO's criteria for World Heritage listing, what shape or form might an appropriately managed Macassan heritage site or interpretative facility take? As we have done so often in this book, we can look to Malaysia for some answers.

Terengganu State Museum

A good example of what could have been labeled a seemingly ideal Macassan interpretative facility is the Fisheries Gallery at Kuala Terengganu's Terengganu State Museum, Malaysia. In one sense using a Malaysian example to support an argument for the identification of heritage sights in Indonesia is a little unfair as it is, after all, Malaysian, rather than Indonesian. Yet, as anyone who has stepped inside a museum in Indonesia, Malaysia or Singapore can attest, the archipelagic and peninsular Malay world shares a great deal, especially in terms of history and heritage. Indeed, museums in each nation – above the protestations of Indonesian football fans and online commentators – magnanimously showcase many of the same cultural traditions, such as *batik*, *wayang*, *gamelan* and *keris*. The origins of many of these heritage items, be they the Bugis of South Sulawesi, the Minangkabau of West Sumatra or the Javanese of Central and East Java, are also publicly acknowledged. This theme of cultural affinity is a common thread uniting the Indo-Malay region, which as mentioned earlier, was once known as *Nusantara*. Moreover, Kuala Terengganu, like Makassar, is a port city with a long and proud history as a coastal hub, connecting the trading vessels of the eastern Malay Peninsula with the Bugis traders of southern Sulawesi and vessels from China, Thailand, Vietnam, and elsewhere in the Malay world. So, in an important sense, Makassar and Kuala Terengganu have more similarities than differences.

In terms of physical structure, the Terengganu State Museum is the largest museum in Malaysia (see Figure 4.4). Several displays in the Museum highlight the close historical links between Terengganu and Sulawesi. In the fashion gallery, for instance, the *batik* styles of Terengganu are placed alongside the silk *batik* styles of the ethnic Bugis of South Sulawesi. To this day, the Bugis 'boxed', or quadrate, silk *batik* motif is very popular in Terengganu, if not all of Malaysia, and can be seen in many items, including *sarong*, blinds, tablecloths and seat furnishings.

Outside the Terengganu State Museum building, two schooners are housed in the museum grounds – a *perahu besar* (big boat) and a *pinis dogol* (dogol schooner). The semantic link between the Malay *pinis* and the Bugis *pinisi* is evident in the two words and supports claims that for many centuries there were strong trade links between the coastal kingdoms of peninsular Malaysia and the seafaring Bugis of South Sulawesi, who were distinguished by the

Figure 4.4 Terengganu State Museum, Kuala Terengganu.
    Photo: Marshall Clark

majestic *pinisi* schooners they sailed (Ricklefs *et al.* 2010). The value of each of the *pinisi* vessels at the Terengganu Museum is such that security guards are camped nearby and the boats appear to be closed for on-board tours while renovations occur. Although there may be conservation and preservation concerns with the present set-up, the location of both boats – barely 20 metres from the banks of the Terengganu River, which is often swollen by heavy rains, especially during the monsoon season – is in one sense perfect. Each boat has appropriate interpretive signs, in English, Malay and Chinese, giving full and helpful details of its style, provenance and sailing history, and of historical links with the Bugis *pinisi*.

   The Bugis, like the Indians and Chinese, have had an important and widely influential role in the history of the Malay Peninsula. Not long after the rise of a Bugis dynasty in Aceh in 1727, Bugis power was established in the kingdom of Johor in 1728. According to various accounts, a branch of the Bugis royal family was transferred to the Johor line after a particularly brutal regicide. The Bugis domiciled in Riau and Johor took pains to demonstrate their support of the Malays and their traditional institutions (Andaya 2010: 139). Inter-marriage with Malay royalty and nobility enabled the Bugis to identify with and become increasingly *Melayu*, and their influence spread throughout the peninsula. In 1766, for instance, Raja Lumu, son of the powerful Bugis Raja Muda of Johor, was installed as the first Sultan of Selangor (Andaya 2010: 228–29). Although the Bugis are relatively recent settlers and, therefore, associated with a home area outside Malaysia (Andaya 2010: 13), in the postcolonial era the links between the Bugis and the Malays have proven to be a cause of great pride for both peoples. For example, Makassar has a street named Jalan Tun Abdul Razak, which recognises the much-publicised fact

Figure 4.5 Open-air *perahu* display, Terengganu State Museum.
Photo: Marshall Clark

that Malaysia's first prime minister and the prime minister at the time of writing this book can trace their lineage back directly to the sixteenth-century Bugis royal line of the Bugis-Makassarese Kingdom of Gowa. The present-day royal family of Johor is equally proud to share these ties with Bugis royalty. Occasionally Malaysian government delegations tour Makassar, where they are met with great fanfare.[5]

Returning to our discussion of the Terengganu State Museum, not far from the large *pinisi* schooners is another area where several full-sized trading *perahu* (see Figure 4.5) are displayed. These vessels are included in in the Museum because they are used in the Terengganu area, both up its rivers as well as in the open seas. Each replica has an accompanying interpretative sign in English and Malay, discretely located to respect the great care taken both in the preservation of the boats and in the landscape of the site. Indeed, in the *perahu* exhibition precinct one is likely to encounter half-a-dozen gardeners, such is the care being taken to maintain a site that is beautified with ornamental flowers and trees and with water features around each display island, on which the boats are raised above the ground. Visitors can take any number of routes through the display islands to the Fisheries Gallery, which in many ways is exactly what Makassar needs to display its fishing heritage.

Inside the Fisheries Gallery, Terengganu's maritime history is revealed, with an emphasis on local history, through the use of dioramas. Displays

Figure 4.6 Decorated *perahu* prows, Terengganu State Museum.
Photo: Marshall Clark

Figure 4.7 Traditional fishing traps, Terengganu State Museum.
Photo: Marshall Clark

focus on such things as the types of vessels used in the Terengganu region, traditional nets and fish traps together with modern trawler nets, hooks, sinkers and fishing lines of all shapes and sizes, the clothing of traditional Malay fishermen, and decorated *perahu* prows, some of which represent characters from the traditional *wayang kulit* shadow theatre (see Figures 4.6 and 4.7). About 100 yards from this gallery, along the riverbank, a small footbridge passes halfway across the Terengganu River to a small island, Pulau Sekati. Inhabitants of this island, ethnic Malays, collect coconuts from the island's many coconut trees to sell to the Museum's cafeteria. Although Pulau Sekati is not officially part of the Museum, the detour certainly enhances the maritime ambience of the seafaring and fishing section of the Museum.

What if there were to be a similar museum, in similar marine environs, in Makassar? After all, Makassar's maritime heritage is no less impressive than that of Terengganu.[6] But, it is unrealistic to assume that the experience of setting up a museum in Malaysia has any relevance to preserving maritime heritage in Indonesia. Compare, for instance, the Terengganu museum's army of security guards and gardeners with the army of highly skilled boatbuilders and trepang fishermen one encounters anywhere along the southern Sulawesi coastline. It is no secret that foreign workers, including many Indonesian fishermen, are the mainstay of Malaysia's fishing industry, not to mention its very limited boatbuilding industry. In a more general sense, it could be argued that the comparison neatly highlights the difference between middle-class Malaysia's thoroughly museumised cultural heritage and developing Indonesia's living history continuum. In Indonesia, especially in South Sulawesi, trepang fisheries and trade and traditional *perahu* building are still big business.

South Sulawesi's living maritime heritage

If we expand our understanding of Macassan history and heritage to include post-Macassan trepang fisheries and trade, it soon becomes evident that Makassar's Macassan heritage is alive and well. It is convincingly demonstrated in a number of locations and contexts: Makassar's proud maritime culture; Makassar's Paotere harbour, where many traditional *perahu* wooden sailing vessels come and go; the traditional wooden boatbuilding industry of Bulukumba in southern Sulawesi; and the contemporary trepang fishery, in which Bugis-Makassarese trepangers from the Spermonde islands and from Makassar participate.

Makassar's much-vaunted maritime culture, based on centuries of demonstrated seafaring prowess by the Bugis and the Makassarese, is acknowledged still in many ways, most obviously in the many statues and images displaying traditional Bugis *pinisi*. The masthead of the Makassar edition of the *Tempo* newspaper is distinguished by an image of a *pinisi*, and the architectural façade on the top storey of the building housing the local newspaper, *Fajar*, replicates the style of a billowing *pinisi* sail. Makassar's inexpensive seafood cuisine is well known throughout the region and one of Indonesian President

Figure 4.8 Moored *perahu* at the Paotere boat harbour, Makassar.
Photo: Marshall Clark

Susilo Bambang Yudhoyono's favourite restaurants is said to be a seafood grill not far from Makassar's Paotere boat harbour. At Paotere, echoes of the Macassan trepang industry can be seen every day, as trepang specimens are sometimes sold at the open-air fish market. Many wooden sailing vessels line the harbour (see Figure 4.8). They are still known as *perahu*, as they were in the Macassan industry era (Macknight 1976). The *perahu* moored at Paotere are intra-regional fishing boats, inter-island goods transportation boats and local ferries, many of which connect the populations of the nearby Spermonde islands with the major businesses and educational institutions of the region in Makassar. Indeed, many schoolchildren travel from the Spermonde islands each morning to attend school in Makassar. Apart from their motors, these *perahu* have very little in the way of modern fishery and maritime technological accoutrements, such as sonar, radar, GPS and satellite beacons. As in the Macassan era, many of the contemporary fishermen and traders making their way to and from Makassar rely on traditional navigation methods, such as the position of the stars and a deep and intimate knowledge of all the islands, ports, reefs, straits and other major landmarks passed down through generations.

As noted above, most of the many sailing vessels frequenting Makassar's harbours and ports are *perahu*, made almost entirely of wood. Although some boats are built in the offshore islands of the Spermonde archipelago, the region of Bulukumba, on the southernmost shores of South Sulawesi's peninsula about three-and-a-half hours southeast of Makassar, remains Indonesia's best-known hub for wooden boatbuilding. Here, the sandy shores are lined with stalls devoted to the construction of *perahu* of all shapes and sizes (see Figure 4.9). After we had spoken to many boatbuilders along these shores, it

Figure 4.9 Perahu boatbuilding at Tanah Beru, Bulukumba, South Sulawesi. Photo: Marshall Clark

Figure 4.10 A *perahu padewakang* used for trepang fishing, Spermonde Archipelago. Photo: Marshall Clark

became evident to us that many of these *perahu*, particularly *perahu padewakang* (trading *perahu*), end up in the Spermonde islands, where fishermen continue to fish for trepang (see Figure 4.10). In many ways, these present-day trepangers, mostly of Bugis-Makassarese ethnicity, are the contemporary embodiments of the Macassans of centuries past. Although the supply of trepang in the Makassar area, and indeed throughout the Indonesian archipelago, is greatly diminished (Choo 2008), large quantities continue to be collected and processed in Makassar and its environs for export to China, Singapore, South Korea and Malaysia. It is the consistently high prices that the trepangers get for their trepang that drive the industry, which, according to members of the fishing community of South Sulawesi, is still centred in Makassar, with the Javanese port of Surabaya also playing a significant role.

It should be emphasised that most of the present-day Bugis-Makassarese trepangers are based offshore in the Spermonde islands, where the trepang (see Figure 4.11) are initially processed and cured by *pengumpul teripang local* (local *trepang* collectors). After this initial minimal processing on the *perahu* or in the Spermonde, the trepang are then delivered directly to *pengumpul*

Figure 4.11 A trepanger with cured *teripang susu* (white teatfish), Barrang Lompo Island, Spermonde Archipelago.
Photo: Marshall Clark

teripang (trepang collectors), most of whom are located in Makassar. These *pengumpul teripang* procure and then process the trepang to meet the particular requests and demands of the overseas markets. Thus, as in the heyday of the Macassan trepang industry in the mid-1800s (Meereboer 1998; Sutherland 2000), Makassar remains a vital hub for the fishing, processing and exporting of trepang. Makassar-based middlemen continue to play just as an important role in the industry as the trepang fishers do. Makassar is, however, not the only centre of the trepang trade, and diasporic communities of Bugis-Makassarese trepang fishermen are to be found throughout the Indonesian archipelago.

Conclusion

This chapter has drawn attention to examples of what could be regarded as Makassar's sites that can be viewed as displaying important aspects of a Macassan tangible cultural heritage. Almost all of them provide fresh insights into the little-known local impact of the centuries of interaction between the trepangers of the Indonesian archipelago and Aboriginal communities of northern Australia. However, at none of the sites can satisfactory levels of general protection and management be demonstrated. One site in particular – the two-storey house said to have been made of ironwood from Arnhem Land in Jalan Maipa – has very recently been demolished to make way for the expansion of a nearby luxury hotel. None of the sites have proper visitor reception and interpretative facilities, unless one takes into account the ubiquitous groups of interested neighbours and onlookers who are able to recount or embellish well-known oral history narratives.

Through an examination of the maritime and fisheries displays of the Terengganu State Museum in the Malaysian port city of Kuala Terengganu, this chapter has outlined what might be achieved in Makassar should a concerted effort be made to create a museumified or static form of cultural expression to showcase Makassar's rich maritime heritage. However, a negative comparison with a Malaysian institution does little to help explain Makassar's deeply layered Macassan history and heritage. Unlike the economically advanced Malaysia, Indonesia might not yet be ready for its rich and continuous cultural heritage to be mothballed and museumised, for the simple reason that much of Indonesia's traditional heritage, such as *perahu* fishing vessels, is still in use. This is particularly the case in South Sulawesi, whose coastal communities are among Indonesia's poorest, where many fishing folk eke out a meagre existence on small fishing boats in primarily artisanal fisheries. In present-day Sulawesi, Makassar's maritime history is very much an ongoing cultural process that is still being lived on a daily basis.

If we move beyond the previously hegemonic Western understanding of cultural heritage conservation, in which 'cultural heritage resided mainly in great monuments and sites' (Taylor 2009: 14), it becomes evident that South Sulawesi's Macassan history is far from non-existent, especially if we consider Makassar's contemporary maritime culture and trepang fisheries. If we regard the contemporary trepang fishermen, trepang collectors and wooden boat-builders of southern Sulawesi as participants in Makassar's living history continuum, then we can argue that Makassar's Macassan past has clearly not yet ended, just as the Makassar-based trepang fishers did not entirely cease their trepang collecting along the northern coast of Australia in 1906, when the industry was effectively closed by the South Australian authorities. The previous chapter ended with critical comments, which questioned Indonesia's commitment to preserving its culture, heritage, and traditions; this chapter, however, has suggested that much of Indonesia's intangible cultural heritage is still in use, which adds layers of complexity to our discussion of Indonesia's heritage, especially when we compare it to the heritage of Malaysia and its preservation and management.

The next chapter will examine what some regard as Indonesia and Malaysia's most likely cultural unifier – Islam. In many ways the story resembles our earlier examinations of the Ramayana and the *wayang kulit* in Indonesia and Malaysia. That is, the more one explores the similarities between the two countries, the more the differences emerge, which brings to mind the old joke about England and the United States – the one thing separating them is their common language. Similarly, nothing seems to separate Indonesia and Malaysia more than the religion they have in common. As we shall see, Islam is represented in different ways in the two countries. Representations of Islam reveal, on the one hand, a great deal about how the practice of Islam differs in each country and, on the other, how attitudes towards Islam, gender and race have developed on parallel paths over time.

Notes

1 Ironically, when PAS came to power in Kelantan in 1990, it banned *mak yong* (as well as *wayang kulit*), on the grounds that such traditional performances allow men and women to perform together on stage, which is not condoned in Islam. Kelantan's Chief Minister Nik Aziz also wanted to eradicate 'alien elements' – such as the Hindu content of many of the stories and epics performed in the *wayang kulit* and the animistic elements in *mak yong* performances – from theatre practised in Kelantan (Hoeffstaedter 2011: 120). Since the art form was awarded UNESCO World Heritage status, however, the federal government pressured the Kelantanese state government to allow PAS-sanctioned versions of *mak yong* to be performed at the *Gelanggang Seni* cultural centre in the state capital, Kota Bahru, for domestic and international tourists. As Hoeffstaedter (2011: 124) observes, this was a good compromise: 'This performance space is contained and controllable and thus presents no threat to the state; indeed, as the performances are scripted and approved by state officials, they represent an Islamicised performance of traditional arts'.

2 No-one from Makassar, either now or in the past, would identify themselves as 'Macassan'. As Macknight (2011: 129) observes, 'the term "Macassan" (or "Makassan") has no currency in an Indonesian context'. Nonetheless, most of the trepangers voyaging to Australia's north regarded Makassar as their home port and because the trade in trepang was centred in Makassar, for better or worse, scholars, including Macknight in his earlier publications, have embraced the term.

3 In recent years there has been some modest evidence of a burgeoning growth in regional heritage interest throughout Indonesia, including the emergence of local cultural heritage tours. But these commercially oriented operations are marginal phenomena at best and rarely persist, because of the lack of an audience or state funding. On a more optimistic note, international dialogue on potential heritage ventures offers a great deal of hope. For example, in October 2012 an international workshop entitled 'Ikat Weaving (*Tenun Ikat*) as Heritage for Sustainable Development in East Nusa Tenggara, Indonesia', funded by the International Institute for Asian Studies (IIAS) in the Netherlands, was held in Indonesia. It aimed to bring together scholars, government representatives and local stakeholders in order to establish 'a policy framework integrating research, conservation, production and marketing activities to help sustain the tradition of *Tenun Ikat* in Eastern Indonesia' (Peycam 2012: 3). Events such as these are extremely important in eliciting the attention of both state governments and, more importantly, international institutions such as UNESCO and the World Bank.

4 Given its undeniable lack of authenticity, not to mention its blatant exploitation of rural artisans, India's national handicrafts museum in New Delhi has been harshly criticised (see Greenough 1993; Bharucha 2000). Similar criticisms can be levelled at the Kuala Lumpur Handicraft Complex.

5 Our thanks to Raimy Ché-Ross for this observation.

6 In Makassar, the maritime display in the La Galigo Museum in Fort Rotterdam is the closest one can get to Terengganu's impressive maritime and fisheries display. It must be said that it is not in any sense a very good display, in which the boats are miniature models rather than life-size replicas.

5 Islam

Alongside language and culture, Islam has long been promoted as a pillar of the cultural connection between Indonesia and Malaysia. Given the increasing prominence of Islam in both nations, can it be considered as the potential glue to hold these two rival nations steadfastly together? As Liow (2005: 151) observes, 'it is the recent resurgence of political Islam in both countries that draws attention to the instrumentality of religion as a cohesive factor for bilateral relations in future'. If we go back to the pre-colonial and colonial eras, it becomes clear that Islam has played a cohesive role in the region. For instance, in the sixteenth and seventeenth centuries, Aceh, a sultanate with a strong Islamic orientation, became a productive centre of Malay-Islamic literary activity and offered itself as an Islamic model of administration and behaviour for Malay courts such as Melaka (see Andaya 2010: 129). But this process was not necessarily seamless and by no means was it a two-way affair. While Aceh shared many features with Malay Melaka, Aceh was much more influenced by the ideas and models offered by other Islamic civilisations, such as the Ottoman Empire. As Andaya (2010: 129) observes, 'Malayu culture as represented by Melaka and later Johor was an amalgam of indigenous, Hindu-Buddhist, and Islamic ideas, whereas Islam formed the underpinnings of society in Aceh'. Over time, many Malays from the Malay Peninsula came to serve the Aceh rulers, establishing connections that helped transmit Islamic ideas back to the Peninsula and throughout the region. Similar sharing and transmission of Islamic ideas, teachings and literary texts occurred in the colonial era (see Budiawan 2012; Liow 2005; Milner 2008). In recent years, there has been frequent discussion among scholars and policy-makers and in the mass media of purported links between Indonesian and Malaysian Islamic terror cells, especially between Indonesia's Jemaah Islamiyah and Al Qaeda (Hadiz and Khoo 2011). This discourse was exacerbated by the apparent radicalisation of many Indonesian Islamists after a sojourn in Malaysia. The involvement of a number of Malaysian citizens in high-profile bombings in Indonesia, most recently in July 2009, has also exacerbated matters (Hadiz and Khoo 2011). The news media, however, and the security-oriented discourse they feed off, are often accused of being misleadingly alarmist, and Islamic dissent in Indonesia and Malaysia overwhelmingly abides by the rules of secular state authority. There are many more examples of positive interactions between networks of Islamic institutions, schools and societies than negative ones. Nevertheless, until now, Islam has not been used in the postcolonial era as a channel for enhancing bilateral co-operation or policy coherence. As Weiss (2010: 181) posits, 'Islam has never been a major premise for bilateral co-operation in the past, and Islam takes on a different political timbre in each state'.

Although Islam has always played a modest role in the popular politics of Indonesia and Malaysia, the governments of both countries have consistently downplayed that role. There are several reasons for this, including the secular basis of both governments and, in previous eras, the fear of Islam providing a rallying point for separatist sentiment. Importantly, Hadiz and Khoo (2011: 464) argue that, from their colonial beginnings, the trajectories of Islam in Indonesian and Malaysia diverged at important points, with significant consequences for the character and role of Islamic politics in both nations:

> A key divergence appeared when Islamic politics in Indonesia was expressed through parties and parliaments soon after independence, amidst a tumultuous process of post-colonial state-building that included insurgencies. In contrast, the comparatively smooth establishment of the post-colonial state in Malaysia more easily incorporated Islamic politics. With subsequent capitalist transformation and integration due to processes of globalization, Islamic politics provided an ideological resource for articulating social and political discontent. Yet Indonesia's authoritarian state brutally 'demobilized' any such discontent until Soeharto's New Order was overthrown in 1998, while the state's official Islamization in Malaysia managed and constrained Islamic dissent.

Under Suharto's dictatorship in particular Islamic dissent was brutally repressed. Over the last decade, concerns about lending credence to or uncovering evidence of Islamist terrorist ties have had a dampening effect on the domination of Islam in the government of both countries. The Malaysian government has been keen to demonstrate that Malaysia is a moderate Muslim nation that does not support militant Islamism. Likewise, in an effort to be a good global citizen, the Indonesian government has gone out of its way to eradicate terrorist groups operating within its territory and has continued to do so as hardline Islamist groups have become increasingly visible in recent years.

Although it has never had a driving role in the politics of the region, Islam has not always been as contained to the margins of government as it is at present. In the pre-independence era, for instance, the Islamic links between the peninsula and the archipelago were strong, particularly in the context of Islamic resurgence and anti-colonial struggle. The belief that followers of Islam are considered part of the *Ummah*, or Muslim brotherhood, has long encouraged a sense of religious affinity. More specific to the Indo-Malay world, however, 'was the fact that Islam provided a cultural avenue through which affiliation could be built, whereby the Indo-Malay Archipelago can be broadly viewed as a single religious entity' (Liow 2005: 34).

Around the thirteenth century Islam was brought to what is now known as the Malay Peninsula and the Indonesian Archipelago, primarily, it seems, by Muslim traders from Gujerat and Bengal (Andaya and Andaya 2001: 54). In his account of his visit to Sumatra in 1292, Marco Polo referred to a new Muslim community founded by Moorish traders in Perlak, and by the early thirteenth century the spice traders of Aden, in Yemen, were aware of Muslims inhabiting a place they called Jawa, which is now present-day Java (Laffan 2011: 4). In the following centuries, Islam attracted not only the ruling elites but also those participating in the international trade networks flowing from Southeast Asia to the Mediterranean and European markets through the heartlands of Islam (Hooker 2003: 61). Significantly, language was closely related to the spread of Islam, which perhaps underpins the quiet emphasis on the role of language as a means of forging connectedness within the region. According to Liow (2005: 34),

> It was with the aid of the Malay language that Islam spread throughout this region, and in so doing consolidated the Muslim worldview through the medium of Islamic philosophical literature published in the Malay language. In that sense, the fact that an archipelago-wide lingua franca already existed facilitated the spread of Islam throughout the Indo-Malay world.

In an interesting historical reversal, the increasing marginalisation of the Malay language in the Indonesia–Malaysia relationship is occurring at a time when Islam can no longer offer ideological cohesion, just as the shared history and heritage of the two countries appears to offer little to bring them together. Each of the potential cultural unifiers has proven to be increasingly complex, problematic, and even divisive. Nonetheless, as this book argues throughout, it is important to understand the contours and trajectories of Indonesia's troubled relationship with its closest neighbour, even if there appears to be no ready solution in sight.

In one important sense, Islam is now more relevant to the peoples of both nations than ever before, even if it has little impact on the dynamics of the relationship between those peoples. Because of its increasing relevance, representations of Islam can reveal much about the societies and politics of present-day Indonesia and Malaysia. The rising importance of Islam in both countries is closely related to two sets of trends – global trends in the Muslim world and trends in domestic politics. Neither of these can be delineated by referring only to Islam or Islamic politics; they must be considered in the context of the social contestation through which Islamic identities and agendas are forged, which includes the discourses of gender and popular culture. Given that popular culture can be viewed as an important point of intersection between these global and domestic trends, most of this chapter will focus on cinema, one of the most popular cultural forms in Indonesia and Malaysia, as a means of exploring one site of social contestation. This chapter will tend to take the form of a comparative exercise, mainly because 'Indonesian Islam' and 'Malaysian Islam' are intrinsically different, just as the cinema of each country is intrinsically different. As such, representations of Islam in both countries are reflective of a distinctive national and religious culture. The contrast is even more marked if we combine the study of popular Islamic culture in both countries with an examination of gender, as this chapter aims to do.

In terms of global trends in Islam, Indonesia and Malaysia have much in common. Over the last few decades, new media throughout the Muslim world, including Indonesia and Malaysia, have paved the way for new Muslim publics, new articulations of Islam, and new figures of authority (see Eickelman and Anderson 2003; Eickelman and Piscatori 1996). Muslim intellectuals, novelists, televangelists, artists, musicians and film-makers have become pop-culture prophets who claim to speak on behalf of both Islam and nation. In the context of Indonesia, Hasan (2009: 231) has observed: 'The development of an Islamic pop culture has taken place in Indonesia where Islam has become part of an extensive consumer culture and served as much as an important identity marker as a sign of social status and political affilia-tion'. Likewise, Heryanto (2008: 34) has argued that popular culture can at times be 'at the very heart of Indonesian national politics'. Weintraub (2011) gives an example of Malaysian media participation in placing Islam at the fore-front of popular culture in his description of the success of Malaysian television producers in integrating Islamic themes into television programming, epitomised by popular contestant shows such as *Imam Muda* (Young Teacher of Islam). In this show, in which the prize is an all-expenses-paid trip to Mecca, 'ten young men display their integrity, compassion, lecturing skills, and knowledge of Islam as they vie to become Malaysia's next "young Imam"' (Weintraub 2011: 7). Many other Malaysian media forms are also popularising Islam. In contrast to Indonesia, however, Islam in the Malaysian context is first and foremost an ethnic or racial marker. It is for this reason that popular culture in Malaysia, especially popular culture depicting Muslims, shines a penetrat-ing light on contemporary Malaysian political culture, which has long been dominated by ethnic Malays who, according to law, must be Muslim. In examining Islam in Indonesia and Malaysia, therefore, we cannot avoid addressing broader social issues, including the question of race and ethnicity in the national politics of the two multicultural countries.

The following discussion will examine the expression of Islamic values in the popular culture of Indonesia and Malaysia. Focusing on a selection of *film Islami* (Islamic cinema) of post-New Order Indonesia and Malaysian inde-pendent cinema, we will reveal the ways in which Islam acts as a conduit for exploring ideas about gender, ethnicity and nation. In particular, we delineate representations of Muslim gender relations, which arguably reveal quite distinctive differences in the aesthetics of morality and spirituality of the two nations. This chapter also argues that, in Indonesian and Malaysian cinema, gender – encom-passing femininities and masculinities – can also be regarded as a platform for discussion of the broader 'state of the nation' of both countries.

Pop Islam and the 'Thorny Rose' in contemporary Indonesia

Since the onset of the *reformasi* era, popular Islamic cultures have become a part of daily Muslim life in Indonesia. They have also become embedded in daily life in Malaysia, especially since the end of the Mahathir era in 2003. As Weintraub (2011: 1) observes of both countries, 'Sermon-filled soap operas, veils on rock stars, Muslim magazines, newspapers and portals, consumption of special Ramadan foods at McDonald's, Facebook "Hadiths of the day," and the rippling effects of Prophet cartoons saturate the mediascape of the contemporary Malay world'. The *reformasi* era boom in popular Islamic culture is remarkable for a number of reasons, and we begin by outlining, rather simplistically, some of the boom's possible causes and effects. In terms of causes, among the key structural, social and political transformations that facilitated the rise of popular Islamic cultures are the expansion of the Indonesian middle classes in the 1980s, and, since the 1990s, Islam's increased political clout and the privatisation of state media. With the lax freedom of expression laws in the *reformasi* period, popular culture has been fertile ground for aesthetic experimentation. Products with an Islamic slant are increasingly popular among Muslim middle classes and, as well as a surge in religious commodities such as the digital Qur'an, Islamic fashion and cassette sermons, there was a remarkable rise, during the 1990s and early 2000s in particular, in the Islamic publishing industry, especially in the Islamic self-help market segment (Hoesterey 2008; Widodo 2008). The subsequent boom of popular Islamic cultures, or 'pop Islam', has given rise to genres such as *sastra Islami* (Islamic literature), *film Islami* (Islamic film) and *sinetron Islami* (Islamic electronic cinema, or soap operas).

In this context, determining what makes art forms particularly Islamic is coloured by assumptions about what constitutes both art and religion. Defining the popular Islamic literature genre, for instance, has been difficult, even though the recent growth in magazines, books and novels with a focus on Islam actually preceded the fall of the New Order more than a decade ago. Although a universally accepted definition of the genre in not in place, leading Indonesian bookstores, such as Gramedia, dedicate a stand in their literature sections for bestselling Islamic novels and short story collections under the rubric of *sastra Islami* (or, more prosaically, *sastra Islam*). While the concepts 'popular' and 'Islamic' have been defined in a variety of ways and are the subject of ongoing debate (Weintraub 2011), identifying examples of popular Islamic culture is not difficult. Indonesian television stations, for instance, are peppered with programmes with Islamic content, most obviously in popular genres such as *sinetron Islami* (Islamic soap operas) and *sinetron dakwah* (proselytising soap operas). These programmes are easily recognised by the abundance of Arab vocabulary and Islamic titles and phrases, their widespread depiction of *jilbab*, Muslim headscarves and other Muslim attire, their locations in rural *pesantren* (Islamic boarding schools), and their Islamic-sounding soundtracks, among other things. Together with early-morning

Muslim devotional programmes, these sermon-filled soap operas are now part of the mainstream media. Similarly, films of the Islamic cinema genre are easily recognisable and have been given various Indonesian labels, such as *film religi* (religious films), *film kearab-araban* (Arabised films) or *film Islami* (Islamic films).

In general, the films of the afore-mentioned *film Islami* genre, much like their aesthetic equivalents in calligraphic artworks, religious novels and pop music, are said to be inspired by or 'breathing Islam' (*bernafaskan Islam*) (Hoesterey and Clark 2012). Contemporary Islamic film, like Islamic literature, is especially remarkable for its capacity to articulate forms of aspirational piety that resonate with the anxieties, desires and frustrations of middle-class Muslims in Indonesia. This is particularly important, given the long suppression of Islam and Islamic representations under Suharto's dictatorship, and leads us to the second key aspect of the recent boom in popular Islamic cultures – its effects, including dominant aesthetic styles and the critical reception from mainstream and alternative media.

Understanding the aesthetics and reception of cinematic and literary representations of Islam and Muslim men and women is important, mainly because it allows us to take a cultural snapshot of the current attitudes and motivations of a significant proportion of the contemporary Indonesian population (see, for example, Heryanto (2011), Imanjaya, (2009a) and Weintraub (2011)). One under-examined element of the aesthetics of Islamic popular cultures is the representation of gender relations and Islamic sexual behaviour in particular. Given that many Islamic novels and films seem obsessed with the polygamous marriage, which has not been squarely addressed by scholars or critics alike, we will focus on examining representations of polygamous sexual behaviour. In so doing we will shed light on the broader question of representing gender in post-New Order Indonesia, which differs somewhat to Malaysia where the open representation of sexuality continues to be suppressed.

Some background is necessary, however, before we proceed with our discussion. Until very recently, sex and Islam have been uneasy bed-partners in Indonesia, and their relationship continues to be complex. Putting Islam to one side for the moment, manifestation of the erotic has often been regarded in Indonesian literature and cinema as, to use Aveling's apt phrase, 'the thorny rose' (Aveling 1969). Writers have studiously avoided the full expression of strong sexual desire. In the New Order era in particular, representations of sexual behaviour were closely aligned with the New Order's patriarchal gender regime, which was to some extent premised on the belief that the feminine – feminine sexuality in particular – was a threat to male dominance and thus, by extension, to the state's dominance. As has been well documented, the New Order state's conservative, family-centred gender ideology was built on long-standing cultural forms (Clark 2010; Hatley 2002). Some cultural practitioners were able to escape these cultural lifejackets, however, but they were in a minority. Avant-garde literary texts that unashamedly represented sexual behaviour, such as Y.B. Mangunwijaya's *Durga Umayi* (1991), were more likely to escape censure than the much more heavily policed cinema genre. Other marginal texts such as Linus Suryadi's poetry-novel, *Pengakuan Pariyem* (Pariyem's Confession) (1981), well known for its explicit depictions of carnality, also escaped the New Order's censorial gaze. But in general, for a whole generation of postcolonial writers, full-blooded artistic representations of sex and sexuality were few and far between.

In the *reformasi* era, there has been a boom in fiction by young women writers, many of whom have been keen to redress enduring myths relating to women's sexuality. But as Blackburn (2004: 30) argues, the women's movement still has a long way to go to influence political process, and the feminine continues to be perceived as a threat to male dominance. The fear of the feminine has been evident in the cultural and literary sphere, particularly in the extremely negative reception of cultural texts by women authors who directly broach the 'thorny rose'. The emergence of Ayu Utami's celebration of feminine sexual desire in *Saman* (1998) and Herlinatiens' literary representation of lesbian sexuality (2003), in particular, allowed a number of previously unleashed societal energies to bubble to the surface. After the publication of *Saman*, heated questions were raised for much of 1998 about the authorship of Ayu Utami's novel. According to Hatley (1999: 450), there were allegations that the text was 'in fact the work of a well-known *male* author'. The publication of *Garis Tepi Seorang Lesbian* (The Margins of a Lesbian) (Herlinatiens 2003) incited controversy because of the novel's representations of lesbianism. The main problem was that Herlinatiens was from a strict Muslim background (Marching 2008) and lesbianism, it was argued, is immoral in Islam. Of equal concern to critics, the works of Herlinatiens and Ayu Utami featured unabashed representations of female sexuality. Ironically, it seems that such representation has become a standard feature of the works of almost all young women writers of note in the *reformasi* period. Western critics have been particularly enthusiastic in documenting this trend, claiming that it signifies a significant disruption of Indonesia's patriarchal gender regime (see, for instance, Bodden and Hellwig (2007)). Besides Ayu and Herlinatiens, other writers, including Djenar Maesa Ayu and Dewi Lestari, have embraced the representation of the full gamut of female sexuality, often in explicit detail, to the extent that this stream of writing has even gained its own pejorative label, *sastra wangi* (perfumed literature). Yet some critics, most of them male, have commented that the theme of female sexuality is little more than a marketing ploy (Marching 2008). In general, the disdainful response to the *sastra wangi* genre has demonstrated that Indonesia, whether or not it is in a democratic transition, is still a thoroughly patriarchal society where the old restrictions, taboos and myths of womanhood persist.

The surprisingly heated debates about the fiction of young *reformasi*-era women writers have arisen in the shadow of the increasing frustrations of the predominantly male Islamist-inclined elements of Indonesian society. Early manifestations of these Muslim frustrations include mass Islamist anti-Western protests in 2006, led by the hardline Front Pembela Islam and provoked by the publication of Danish cartoons of the Prophet Mohammad and the launch of an Indonesian *Playboy* magazine. The development of and debate surrounding anti-pornography legislation in 2006 and 2008, which was less about restricting freedom of expression and more about public morality and behaviour (Lindsay 2010), gave rise to popular fears about the return of censorship, self-censorship and the increasing manifestation of Islam. For better or worse, 'Islamisation' has been mentioned often in the Indonesian media since then, and the extent to which Indonesia's new freedom of expression is free of political or religious threat has been questioned. On the one hand, the Indonesian mass media have experienced an unprecedented boom since the fall of Suharto and have become increasingly open, with only modest curbs on the freedom of expression. On the other hand, the political imperatives of post-Suharto politics have often turned out to be contradictory and chaotic, and there is often a considerable lag between political implementation and social acceptance. For example, even though publication permits are no longer required and top-down censorship is no longer applied, a new kind of censorship, sometimes by private individuals and religious organisations, is alive and well. A strain of symbolic censorship had earlier also been clearly evident in the furores surrounding the authors of *Saman* and *The Margins of a Lesbian*. Judgement was passed not by the government but rather by the court of public opinion, where the judge and jury were male critics, many of whom are Muslim.

Representations of polygamy in popular Islamic films

Parallel to the emergence of the heavily criticised *sastra wangi* literary stream, not long after the fall of Suharto enduring historical debate about sexuality, polygamy and the position of women re-emerged in Indonesia's public discourse. There was nothing completely new about the debate, as state and Islamic discourses have long worked together in Indonesia. It can be argued that, in the *reformasi* era, the Islamic emphasis on the sanctity of the family and the valorisation of female domesticity have served to reinforce the patriarchal perspective on gender and sexuality which was firmly entrenched in the New Order era (Blackburn 2004; Blackwood 2005; Robinson 2008). It should not be surprising, therefore, that the deeply conservative line on gender held by many Islamic leaders and publications has caused polygamy to emerge as a hot topic for debate in the post-Suharto public sphere.

In spite of its acceptance among Malaysia's Muslim majority, especially in conservative states such as Kelantan, polygamy is seldom discussed in Malaysia, where the conversation appears to be limited to formal pieces in online publications (for example, Ding 2010; Malaysia to Reward 2011; Othman 2012). This might have something to do with the fact that Islam in Malaysia is generally perceived as more conservative than in Indonesia, which has given rise to a more widespread tradition of polygamy, or more specifically polygyny. Malaysia's relatively superior economic standing has also allowed greater opportunity for some Malaysian men to take more than one wife. As

Khoo (2010) observes, after several decades of Muslim proselytising under the banner of the conservative *dakwah* movement, a public discourse on polygyny emerged at the height of the 1990s, when the economy was thriving and more wealthy Muslim men could consequently afford a polygamous lifestyle.

When considering the rise of a polygamy discourse in Indonesia, we also need to consider the reality of unprecedented growth in the Indonesian economy in recent years. Is it the case that, quite apart from the liberalisation of the mass media and political discourse nowadays, Indonesian men also now have greater financial capacity to support a polygamous lifestyle? It is difficult to quantify exactly how widely polygamy is practised in Indonesia. We can say with some confidence, however, that in the decade following the fall of Suharto the simmering discourse relating to polygamy and the related question of the position of women in Islam bubbled to the surface after several high-profile cases. Yet, even though the discourse surfaced in the public sphere, it appears to have failed Indonesian women, many of whom are as eager for change as the students leading the protest movement were in 1998. The double discourse on polygamy and women in Islam seems to have simply reinforced Indonesia's long-standing patriarchal gender hegemony. According to Sonja van Wichelen, in her observations of pro-polygamy campaigns in Indonesia, the pro-polygamy discourse 'does not seek less patriarchal or less conservative definitions of Indonesian manhood. Instead, discourses of hypermasculinity and (Javanese) paternalism are reaffirmed – albeit enveloped in an Islamic framework' (van Wichelen 2009: 181–82). In this sense the polygamy discourse is little more than a post-authoritarian extension of the New Order's patriarchal gender regime. Several high-profile cases have spec-tacularly demonstrated the ambiguous attitude of most Indonesians towards polygamy, which in recent times has tended towards an attitude of outright distaste.

The first case was the launch of the so-called Polygamy Awards in May 2003, organised by the Muslim Journalists' Forum (MJF). The lavish awards ceremony was held in July 2003 at a luxury hotel in Jakarta and awards were handed out to several dozen men who, in the view of the awards' committee, 'had upheld the high religious and moral standards needed to be a successful polygamist' (Brenner 2007: 28). However, the ceremony was gatecrashed by a large number of protesters, estimated by one source to be approximately 850 people who were all outraged by the event. The protesters were members of Indonesian women's rights organisations, including some with an Islamic orientation. The awards were not held again in subsequent years. The second case was the remarkable public backlash against the charismatic television preacher Aa Gym (Abdullah Gymnastiar) after he took a second wife in 2006 (Hoesterey 2008). His career soon went into a downward spiral and in 2011 his first wife divorced him. The third case was the impressive box-office and critical success of a satirical film depicting polygamy, Nia Dinata's *Berbagi Suami* (Love for Share, 2006). Nia Dinata professes that, in making the film, she did not intend to convey any moral judgement on the issue of polygamy, claiming: 'I just want to communicate with an audience, with people, and give them a slice of life. I don't want to make propaganda for or against polygamy' (Imanjaya 2009a). Despite uncertainty surrounding the aims of the film, it was a success at the box office and well received by the critics. More importantly, it paved the way for the subsequent flood of Islamic films, many of which have unapologetically addressed the practice of polygamy.

The public reactions to the representation of polygamy in popular Islamic films, which range from praise to protest, shed light on how 'pop Islam' has become an arena for public debate and political manoeuvring. To explore this further, we now turn to three films – *Kehormatan di Balik Kerudung* (Honour Beneath the Headscarf), *Ayat-Ayat Cinta* (Verses of Love) and *Perempuan Berkalung Sorban* (Woman Wearing a Turban) – which reflect these threads of the post-1998 Islamic discourse. The first of these films, the truly dreadful *Kehormatan di Balik Kerudung* (2011), was savagely denounced by film critics and bloggers as an extremely mawkish soap opera that, inexplicably, had made its way to the silver screen. Based on an Indonesian novel of the same name by Mamun Affani, it was directed by Tya Subiyakto Satrio and produced by Chand Parwez Servia. Commentators felt that the Islamic aspect to the film was merely a shallow veneer designed to inflate box-office returns. Indeed, the midday screening we attended in Makassar was quite full, mostly with people who were no doubt the target audience of films of that genre – Muslim females, many of whom were wearing headscarfs.

Like many films in this genre, *Kehormatan di Balik Kerudung* is a melodramatic tear-jerker, in which the main protagonist, Ifan (played by Andhika Pratama), marries a pious Muslim woman, Syahdu (played by Donita), after his first love, Sofia (played by Ussy Sulistiawati), is forced to marry a family benefactor. After revealing to her husband on her wedding night that she is still in love with Ifan, Sofia is promptly divorced. Later, when she discovers that the heartbroken Ifan has married Syahdu, she breaks down and succumbs to a lengthy and life-threatening illness. In order to save Sofia's life, the kind-hearted Syahdu suggests that Ifan take Sofia as a second wife. Syahdu's unselfish desire to stop Sofia from dying of a broken heart is commendable, but tensions emerge once the two women are under the same roof. Sofia soon becomes jealous of Syahdu, and Ifan too is unhappy about the situation, as he was perfectly content with Syahdu alone. Fortunately, Sofia, who abandons the apparently unconsummated marriage almost as soon as she has recovered from her mysterious illness, saves his blushes. In a strange twist at the end of the film, Sofia dies, but not before having a child – Ifan's son – which the childless Ifan and Syahdu happily take in as their own. In the small number of reviews of the film (for example, Donita 2011; Siregar 2011), the miracle of this seemingly immaculate conception is not mentioned, just as the film's dramatic, panoramic backdrop of Mount Bromo in East Java barely registers.

Thus, in late 2011, cinematic representations of polygamy appeared not to raise eyebrows in contemporary Indonesia, perhaps because Indonesian audiences are no longer unfamiliar with this particular narrative device, which has become a staple of *film Islami*. An alternative explanation may be that the way in which polygamy and polygamous sexual behaviour, in particular, are presented in films such as *Kehormatan di Balik Kerudung* has been toned down since the release of earlier films in the genre. The film that began the trend in 2008, *Ayat-Ayat Cinta*, is worth briefly discussing in this regard. Based on the bestselling novel by Habiburrahman El Shirazy, *Ayat-Ayat Cinta* depicts the trials and tribulations of Fahri Abdullah (played by Fedi Nuril), an Indonesian student living in Cairo. Fahri is depicted as a model Indonesian citizen, an ideal Muslim 'everyman'. His penchant for wearing T-shirts, jeans, sunglasses and sandals suggests that he is relaxed, casual and easygoing. He is also a good Muslim and refrains from touching any woman other than his mother or his wife. He prays regularly, recites the Qur'an and attends lectures in Islamic theology. He is comfortable mixing with Islamic scholars, preachers and lecturers, is diligent in his studies, and is fluent in Arabic, English, Indonesian and Javanese. He has a small library of Arabic-language texts in his room, as well as posters in Arabic hanging on the walls. In one sense he is almost too good to be true, as he also leads a local Indonesian student association, he helps neighbours with their shopping, he rescues a woman being physically attacked and he defends a pair of international tourists under verbal attack. Fahri is, however, also a polygamist, but even this is presented in a favourable light, as he becomes a polygamist for compassionate reasons. Although he is already happily married, he takes a second wife, Maria (played by Rianti Cartwright), a Coptic Christian who is in love with him. He did so to save Maria from dying of a broken heart, as she was heartbroken when Fahri got married the first time, before she was able to express her deep love for him.

In terms of representations of polygamous sexual behaviour, *Ayat-Ayat Cinta* promises more than it delivers. Nevertheless, the film does not shy away from depicting the awkward reality. The film reveals that when Fahri is married and living with his two wives under the one roof, both wives expect a night-time visit from their husband. But rather than upsetting one of them by sleeping with the other, he decides to sleep on his own, in the lounge room, and there are no signs of sexual activity in later scenes either. Like Ifan in *Kehormatan di Balik Kerudung,* Fahri is saved from embarrassment by the unexpected death of his second wife, who had never really recovered from the shock of his first marriage. It is worth noting that Hanung Bramantyo, the film-maker responsible for *Ayat-Ayat Cinta*, says the aim of this film was to present Islam's true face and to portray Muslims as modern people who practise tolerance, sincerity and honesty: 'Muslims don't just talk about heaven and hell, or about life in the hereafter. They can also talk about love' (Indonesia's Verses of Love 2008). Love, and polygamous love in particular, was what garnered the many headlines associated with this film. The representation of polygamy in *Ayat-Ayat Cinta* was much commented on and much criticised. Bramantyo's fresh take on polygamous romance was a commercial success, making a gross revenue of US$3.5 million by attracting

2.6 million viewers within 2 weeks of its opening and eventually making twice this amount with over 4 million viewers (Haryadi and Pamungkas 2008).

After the box-office success of *Ayat-Ayat Cinta*, copycat films such as *Perempuan Berkalung Sorban* (2009) were released. The explicit representations of marital rape in a polygamous marriage have ensured that *Perempuan Berkalung Sorban* has earned a reputation as one of the more infamous examples of the genre. In this film, Annisa (played by Revalina S. Temat), who as a child was fond of wearing a headscarf, lives in a very conservative *pesantren* in East Java. When she comes of age, she is forced to enter into a marriage of convenience with Samsudin (played by Reza Rahadian), the son of a *kyai* (Muslim leader) who heads a neighbouring *pesantren*, which is equally traditionalist. This means that Annisa must abandon her relationship with her childhood sweetheart, Khudori (played by Oka Antara), who left Java as a teenager to study theology in Cairo. It soon becomes apparent that Samsudin is lazy, abusive and a sex addict. During their brief marriage, Annisa suffers frequently from domestic abuse and marital rape. To make matters worse, she is confronted with the indignity of her philandering husband taking a second wife, Kalsum (played by Francine Roosenda). Once married, Kalsum is also abused and raped, despite being pregnant. Later, when Kalsum's baby is born, Annisa becomes little more than a babysitter and is even forced to nurse the baby while her husband beds Kalsum and makes no effort to conceal the sounds of their lovemaking. Eventually, Khudori returns from Egypt and Annisa takes the necessary steps to annul her marriage. After fleeing to the nearby city of Yogyakarta, eventually she marries Khudori. Like Fahri in *Ayat-Ayat Cinta*, Khudori is intelligent, pious, sensitive and patient. Furthermore, given Annisa's past traumas, he is willing to consent to sexual abstinence for weeks and, if needed, months on end. Khudori's abstinence and Annisa's eventual willingness to consummate her marriage are depicted in a surprisingly frank manner, just as the earlier rape scenes are remarkably explicit and confronting. Muslims have generally responded to this film and its content with distaste (Hellwig 2011).

In the wake of criticisms of the excessively commercial and sensationalist nature of films like *Ayat-Ayat Cinta* and *Perempuan Berkalung Sorban*, a somewhat reactionary response has emerged – the blanket Islamisation of film production. For instance, the filming and production in 2009 of *Ketika Cinta Bertasbih* (When Love Glorifies God) and its sequel was marked by the heavy involvement of the author of the novels the films were based on. Habiburrahman El Shirazy, popularly known as Kang Abik, insisted that a pious Muslim direct the films and it was also mandatory for all producers, actors and cameramen to be pious Muslims. Actors auditioning for the films were subject to stringent character checks, with a focus on their Islamic credentials. In another film adaptation of a Habiburrahman novel, *Dalam Mihrab Cinta* (In the Pulpit of Love) (2010), Habiburrahman took an even more hands-on role and promoted himself as chief director and casting agent.

Habiburrahman El Shirazy's conservative approach has had interesting results, one of which is the increasingly conservative representation of polygamous sexual behaviour in *film Islami*, apparent in the 2011 film *Kehormatan di Balik Kerudung*. Another result of the conservative approach of Habiburrahman's 2009 films is a greater focus on the relationship between Islam and the self-help industry. In *Ketika Cinta Bertasbih* and its sequel the cultural ideal of Muslim masculinity is not that of an erudite religious scholar, or of a polygamist or womaniser. Rather, the ideal masculine model is that of the entrepreneurial and self-actualised Muslim man. The ideal feminine model is based on a similar blend of piety and Islamic self-help principles. The emphasis on the role of the individual in achieving one's spiritual pursuits is part of a broad trend in Indonesia where the Islamisation of consumer culture indicates a shift from a conservative and anti-Western form of Islam to one that is compatible with conspicuous consumption, capitalism and global cultural trends (Heryanto 2011).

In the next section, we turn to study a Malaysian middle class comfortable with its Islamic lifestyle, but find few models of ideal masculinity and femininity. In Yasmin Ahmad's independent films, the social construction of gender is only of tangential interest. Interracial relationships, which bridge religious divides, are of far greater concern. Her primary aim is the interrogation of race relations in contemporary Malaysian society, which is increasingly characterised by a resurgence of Islam in culture and politics.

The Malays, Islam and independent film-makers in Malaysia

The films of Yasmin Ahmad, one of a new wave of Malaysian film-makers, have been received with much critical acclaim in Malaysia and abroad. *Sepet* (Chinese Eyes) (2004), for example, won the Best Asian Film Award at the 18th Tokyo International Film Festival in 2005. When *Mukhsin* (2006) was screened at the Berlin International film Festival in 2007, a full house of about 1,000 people responded positively to the film and applauded for more than five minutes (Muhammad 2006: 109–10). Yasmin's films have featured prominently at successive Australian Malaysian Film Festivals, including her first film, *Rabun* (My Failing Eyesight) (2003), which opened the 2010 festival. The 2009 festival featured all her major films and was dedicated to her, following her sudden death on 25 July 2009. Several actors featuring in Yasmin's films, including Sharifah Amani and Pamela Chong, attended the festival and were noticeably touched by the large and enthusiastic audiences. In San Francisco we happened to attend the Islam Today Film Festival in 2010, at which several of Yasmin's films were well received, as was a panel discussion on Malaysian cinema featuring Elyna Shukri, producer of three of Yasmin's films.

In Malaysia, meanwhile, Yasmin's films, which tend to address issues relating to inter-ethnic relations, have been criticised and subjected to public attack by Malay cultural elites. Another of the independent Malay film-makers who have been targeted is Amir Muhammad. Amir's documentary *Lelaki Komunis*

Terakhir (The Last Communist) (2006), for example, was banned by the Ministry of Home Affairs, even after it had been passed by the national censors, the Malaysian Film Censorship Board (LPF) (McKay 2010). A Malay daily newspaper, *Berita Harian*, ran a series of articles that criticised the LPF's decision to approve the documentary and suggested that the film glamorises communists. Under mounting pressure, the Ministry of Home Affairs finally retracted the LPF's approval (Muhammad 2006). It appears that objections to Yasmin's films arose from their portrayal of taboo issues such as:

> the interracial relationship between a Malay-Muslim girl and a non-Chinese boy in *Sepet* (without any indication of the boy wanting to convert to Islam) … [and] sinful acts in Islam such as prostitution (with the representation of a noble prostitute in *Gubra*) and extramarital affairs (e.g., the wife in *Gubra*, who retaliates against her husband's extramarital affair by having one herself).
>
> (Omar 2011: 158)

Yasmin's representation of Islam, interracial intimacy and sexual relations has, on the one hand, won critical acclaim and, on the other, met with resistance, particularly from Muslim Malays. Gaik Cheng Khoo (2009: 107) argues that Yasmin's outlook, 'which strives for a cosmopolitan Malay subjectivity', is most offensive to Malay critics as it 'does not eschew inter-racial affiliations' and 'advocates a liberal Sufi Muslim perspective to challenge hegemonic Islam in Malaysia'. Yasmin's liberal *sufi* perspective is captured in the words of *sufi* poet, Jalaluddin Rumi, at the very end of her 2006 film *Gubra* (Anxiety): 'The lamps are different, but the light is the same'. This *sufi* equivalent of the pluralist assertion that all religious paths lead to God is illustrated in *Gubra* by a final montage of the film's protagonists either worshipping in a Christian church, submitting prayers and offerings to a Buddhist shrine or reciting the Qu'ran. But upholding a pluralist *sufi* or mystical Islam is in direct opposition to the more scripturalist Wahhabist Islam that is dominant in Malaysia. The fear is that these films undermine not only hegemonic Islam but also, by default, Malay hegemony.

What do we mean when we speak of 'hegemonic Islam' in Malaysia and why would Yasmin's films threaten a hegemonic Malay identity? Perhaps the best way to answer this, at least initially, is to reveal the identities of the Malay critics who attacked Yasmin and her films. As Khoo (2009) and Omar (2011) document, Yasmin's two early films addressing Islam, sexuality and inter-ethnic relations, *Sepet* and *Gubra*, both released in 2006, were publicly attacked on a weekly television forum called *Fenomena Seni* (Arts Phenomenon) on the state-owned public broadcaster, Radio Televisyun Malaysia 1 (RTM1). The forum was entitled '*Sepet* and *Gubra* – Corruptors of Malay Culture' and two invited guests, Akmal Abdullah, assistant entertainment editor of *Berita Harian*, and Raja Azmi Raja Suleiman, a Malay film producer and writer, made hostile comments about the films. According to Khoo (2009: 108), both guests expressed 'highly critical and conservative views' as they argued that certain scenes in the films were unrealistic, unnecessary and potentially corrupting of Malay culture:

> Akmal, the newspaper editor, thought it was impossible for Orked, the heroine of both of Yasmin's films, with her strong religious background, to fall in love with a 'Chinese criminal', the illegal video disc seller Jason, and that Yasmin's film *Sepet* was unrepresentative of the reality of most Malay Muslim lives. Akmal argued that the *bilal* (muezzin) in *Gubra* should have reported the two sex workers in his neighbourhood to the religious authorities rather than showing them compassion and under-standing. He read the fictional world in *Gubra* as expressing Yasmin's 'fantasies', which, he said, promoted 'dangerous' and 'manipulative' values that would 'confuse the religious and moral sensibilities of its [Malay Muslim] audience'.

The two guests were opposed to other on-screen images in *Gubra*, including the *bilal* (Muezzin) cooking in his wife's kitchen and patting a stray dog on his way to morning prayers (McKay 2012).[1] It was, however, the representation on screen of a Malay girl, Orked (played by Sharifah Amani), in love with a Chinese Malaysian boy, Jason (played by Ng Choo Seong), that caused the most consternation. As McKay (2012: 110) observes, one of the closing comments from a participant in the forum summed up the tone of the programme: 'Malaysia belongs to the Malays. That's why it was called Tanah Melayu before'. This statement is interesting because it draws attention to the close relationship of the discourse of Islamic morality to the two dominant discourses in Malaysia – the discourse of race and of the preservation of Malay ethnicity (Khoo 2009). The close relationship among the discourses did not suddenly emerge with the success of *Gubra*. Well in advance of the RTM1 programme, *Berita Harian* – described by Muhammad (2006) as 'a conservative newspaper whose cultural politics verges on the ethnocentric and semi-fascist' – ran a daily campaign for weeks to discredit Yasmin's *Sepet*, especially after it won the Best Film Award at the 18th Malaysian Film Festival in 2005. *Berita Harian*, according to Muhammad (2006), was the only newspaper to take such exception to the interracial romance portrayed in *Sepet* as 'insulting to Malay culture'. Yasmin herself insists that the film's negative reception was not broad-based, but rather created by 'two or three journalists that I know of who got paid by a very big time producer' who claims to speak for all Malays (Khoo 2009). Nonetheless, following the release of *Gubra* in 2006, bloggers used similar arguments castigat-ing Yasmin for her representation of Islam in that film, which was said to be so liberal that it bordered on secularism (Khoo 2009). In addition to this, panellists at an academic forum held at Universiti Malaya on 1 September 2006, which examined whether *Gubra* deserved to win the award for the best film at the 19th Malaysian Film Festival, asserted that the film demeaned the Malay race and the Islamic religion.

How do we explain the rationale of such critics? Khoo (2009) argues that the serial attacks on Malay film-makers such as Amir Muhammad and Yasmin Ahmad articulate, collectively, a deep 'psychic investment' in the 'operations of racialisation' on the one hand and 'the belief in Malay supremacy' on the other. In using the term 'racialisation' Khoo is referring to the manner in which the ethnic ideology of Malayness is just as likely to be defined in negative terms, such as 'who you are not' as opposed to 'who you are' (Nagata (1975: 3) cited in Khoo 2009: 110). In Malaysia, this ideological paradigm ensures that Malayness is most clearly defined against Chineseness. Malaysians of Tamil and other Indian origins, it seems, barely get a look in. In this Malay–Muslim-dominated nation, the Indian diaspora is even more marginalised than the Chinese, who experience significant social, cultural and religious marginalisation. Stereotyping along ethnic lines is a significant aspect of the negative projection of Malaysians who are not Malay. The Chinese are chiefly characterised by their economic prowess, which is boosted by other stereotypical signifiers such as their being industrious, hard-working, thrifty, urban, modern, successful and wealthy. If Malays want to be as successful as the Chinese, they are told that they must emulate them. Yet, as Khoo (2009) observes, Yasmin's films work against the stereotyping by focussing on working-class Chinese characters that lead ordinary lives.

In Yasmin's *Sepet* and *Gubra* the Chinese are neither industrious nor wealthy businesspeople. They lead ordinary lives, working, studying, loving and fighting like any working- or middle-class Malaysian citizen regardless of race or ethnicity. To make this point abundantly clear, Yasmin depicts the extended Chinese family in her film as quite dysfunctional. More subversively, she toys with the racialised clichés relating to Malayness. For example, in *Sepet*, the Malay Orked expresses surprise that Jason, her Chinese romantic interest, can write poetry and his best friend, Keong (played by Linus Chung), can play the piano. In reply, Keong says 'Don't stereotype people. Not every Chinaman is a cheat, and not every Malay is lazy'. Orked responds, in a scene that was partially cut and never heard by local audiences, 'Ah, but that's where you're wrong. Every Malay *is* lazy. There are lazy Chinese, too'. Despite the jocular nature of the conversation, the censor's scissors have inexpertly butchered this scene, which is left with subtitles that have no matching audio or visual cues. The purpose of this censorship is unclear, especially in the light of Amir Muhammad's observation (2009: 67): 'Where on earth would Malaysia be without ethnic humour, anyway?' In this case, the heavy-handed application of the censor's gaze appears to defeat the purpose of such humour, which can be regarded a coping mechanism in what many regard as a deeply racist society.

Although international audiences may find it refreshing to see such racial stereotypes highlighted and mocked, it is not hard to understand that the Malay–Muslim cultural elites, accustomed to their unquestioned cultural dominance in Malaysia, might have been less impressed by having stereotyping turned against them. The Malay 'operations of racialisation' referred to above were only ever meant to revolve around determining Malayness in negative terms – that is, not by defining who the Malays are, but rather who they are not. In *Sepet*, to add insult to possible injury, Orked's Malay parents are relatively unperturbed about her relationship with a Chinese man. Early in the film they are seen dancing to Chinese music, and it is not until the film's denouement that Orked's father (played by Harith Iskandar) expresses his misgivings regarding Jason, who he had heard was involved with gangsters and had got a Chinese girl pregnant. Orked's parents, who are much more progressive than the average Malay *mak* and *ayah*, are perhaps caricatures, but they are clearly part of an effort by Yasmin Ahmad to present, or even construct, liberal Malays who are prepared to accept interracial relationships, especially among the next generation of Malaysia's youth.[2] Film critics, especially Malay critics, were not convinced by the film's unlikely scenario. Both *Sepet* and *Gubra* are much more convincing in their depiction of the ongoing cultural and social alienation of the Chinese. This is demonstrated in *Gubra* when Jason's brother, Alan, plaintively describes being a Malaysian of Chinese descent: 'I don't know whether you guys [Malays] know how hard it is for the rest of us to stay here. Sometimes it feels like loving someone who doesn't love you back.'

Just as Jason was attracted to a Malay woman and wanted to embrace that attraction, the Malaysian racial divide is such that bridging it can sometimes be a serious challenge. In *Sepet*, both Jason and Orked spark all sorts of racist attitudes among their friends and family which might otherwise have remained unspoken. Both protagonists encounter sustained abuse for their willingness to even consider bridging the divide. Ultimately, Jason is forced to break off the relationship, as a Chinese girl, the sister of a violent gangster, claims she is pregnant by him. Jason then dies in a motorbike accident. The heartbroken Orked, however, lives to fight another day and to star in the sequel, *Gubra*. It could be argued that her Malayness guarantees survival of sorts, whereas Jason pays the ultimate price for his Chineseness, or rather lack of Malayness. In Yasmin's series of films focusing on Orked and her family the Malay–Muslim hegemony is challenged, but ultimately not disrupted.

The other element underpinning the Malay critics' attacks on the films of independent Malay film-makers is the belief in Malay supremacy or Malay political primacy, sometimes referred to as '*ketuanan Melayu*'. The Malaysian government contends that *ketuanan Melayu* was mentioned as one of the concepts of nation-building after the Second World War, but fell out of fashion until it began re-emerging in school history textbooks in the early 2000s (Ting 2009). This occurred not long after the controversial declaration in September 2001 by Prime Minister Mahathir Mohamad that Malaysia was 'an Islamic state'. *Ketuanan Melayu* was seen as a reiteration of the ideology of Malayism, which asserted that the interests of the *bangsa Melayu* must be upheld over all else. Upholding Malayism has long dominated the political contests between the ruling party in Malaysia, the United Malays National Organization (UMNO) and the Islamic opposition party, Parti Islam Semalaysia (Pan-Malaysian Islamic Party, PAS). The ongoing contestation between the two parties has been a complicated process. For example, in the 1980s, in addition to its Malay-centred rhetoric and appeals to a more multiethnic approach, Mahathir's UMNO began to be more zealously committed to the Islamicisation of government policies and institutions. One of the reasons for Mahathir's vigorous promotion of Islam was to beat the PAS at its own game. Another reason for promoting state-centred Islam was to provide legitimacy for UMNO and the state in its quest for economic development and modernisation, inspired not by the example of the West but rather by Asian values. Islam, in Mahathir's opinion, was the key to achieving this goal. According to Freedman (2009: 106):

> Mahathir's government spearheaded the creation of a network of Islamic banks, the Malaysian International Islamic University, Islamic Insurance schemes, and the creation of the Hajj Pilgrim Fund … The regime also supported the creation of the Islamic think-tank Institut Kefahaman Islam Malaysia (IKIM), to promote 'progressive' Islamic views, and the government helped restructure and boost the role of many Islamic institutions; the Islamic courts, Shari' a, the building of mosques, religious schools, and the increased request for *zakat* collection, and there was a huge increase in the number of religious officials and *ulama* working in the Prime Minister's Office.

Some have argued that the Islamic discourse, dubbed '*ketuanan Islam*', did not always integrate well with *ketuanan Melayu* (Ting 2009). For example, the Islamic discourse of PAS was often intended to be a rebuttal of the Malayism of UMNO, who at times have been criticised as 'un-Islamic'. Nonetheless, considering that by law Malaysian Malays must be Muslims, in practice the two discourses and the basic logic inherent in both strands are arguably much the same thing. Both discourses are 'about the symbolic domination of one ethnic group over the identity of the nation, disregarding the fact that a significant proportion of the population is non-Muslim, even among those designated as 'indigenous''' (Ting 2009: 39). In effect, whether it is labelled '*ketuanan Melayu*' or '*ketuanan Islam*', Malayism has permeated the outlook of the Malay community. The Malay critics of *Berita Harian* and the like, who took offence at the films of Yasmin Ahmad and other similarly progressive independent film-makers, appeared to have been among those permeated by Malayism. It is not surprising that some critics also took offence at Yasmin's later films, namely *Muallaf* (The Convert) (2008) and *Talentime* (2009).

Islam and gender in Yasmin Ahmad's *Muallaf* and *Talentime*

Besides challenging the elite construction of Malay subjectivity, Yasmin Ahmad's films present a cosmopolitan version of Islam that crosses ethnic and religious boundaries (Khoo 2009). The analysis of her movie trilogy, *Sepet*, *Gubra* and *Mukhsin*, by scholars such as McKay (2012), Omar (2011) and Khoo (2009) has focused mostly on their challenging of the construction of Malay subjectivity. Less attention has been afforded to the strain of cosmopolitanism inscribed in her later films, *Muallaf* and *Talentime*. Before we embark on redressing this, we need to note that Yasmin was not enthusiastic about academic analyses of her films. According to Muhammad (2009: 24):

> Yasmin didn't want her films to be pedantically over-analysed. A lot of killjoy academics, in particular, like to go on about semiotics and *mis-en-scène*, making cinema seem distinctly unsexy.

Muhammad observes, however, that occasionally it is necessary to read into things: 'there's a lot of cultural symbolism going on in Malaysia' and that Yasmin herself was not immune to tapping into this 'cultural symbolism', especially in her parallel and more renowned career as a director of TV commercials, 'most of which were fable-like narratives rather than the hard-sell variety' (Muhammad 2006: 9). As we know, cultural expression has the capacity to not only reflect reality but also to shape it; if it did not, there would be no such thing as advertising. It is not difficult to imagine that, as a former advertiser, Yasmin would seek to use her films to shape the nation's cultural identity to some degree.

Both *Muallaf* and *Talentime* reflect Malaysian society as it is today, drawing on real-life examples of racial tension. More importantly, both films point to a potential future for Malaysian society, as envisioned by Yasmin Ahmad and other independent film-makers of her generation. It is no coincidence that the only book-length study of Yasmin's films, entitled *Yasmin Ahmad's Films* (Muhammad 2009), is by a fellow independent film-maker, Amir Muhammad. Muhammad's monograph contains one of the few scholarly discussions of *Muallaf* and *Talentime*. As Muhammad and many other critics have observed, each of Yasmin's films begins with the Islamic *Bismillah* verse: 'In The Name of God, The Most Compassionate, Most Merciful'. In *Muallaf* the phrase appears in Mandarin and in *Talentime* it occurs in Tamil, the main language of Malaysia's ethnic Indian minority. In each of Yasmin's films, the language in which the *Bismillah* is given encodes the ethnic minority that is to be predominantly represented. *Muallaf* and *Talentime* both depict interracial relationships. *Muallaf* focuses on the relationship between a Chinese man, Brian (played by Brian Yap), and a Malay woman, Rohani (played by Sharifah Amani). *Talentime* depicts a budding romance between an Indian boy, Mahesh (played by Mahesh Jugal Kishor), and a Malay girl, Melur (played by Pamela Chong). Although both films depict many other issues as well, the interracial relationship is the dominant leitmotif of each, which connects the films with parallel events occurring in real-life Malaysia, namely the Lina Joy case (*Muallaf*) and the Kampung Medan incident (*Talentime*).

The similarities between the events depicted in *Muallaf* and the real-life Lina Joy case are difficult to ignore. Lina Joy, born Azlina Jailani, was a Malaysian citizen who converted from Islam to Christianity. Although she managed to change her name on her Malaysian identity card (MyKad), her religion was still listed as Islam on the card, even though she had converted. She made several unsuccessful applications between 1998 and 2000 to have the word 'Islam' removed from her identity card and eventually, in 2006, the matter came to the Federal Court which also ruled against her and stated that it was a faith-based matter which should be settled by an Islamic *syariah* court. The Kafkaesque twists and turns of the process were well covered by the national media and Lina Joy's case is well known in Malaysia (Kortteinen 2008). There have been many other similar cases in Malaysia, although they have not attracted so much public attention.

Although no one in *Muallaf* actually converts from one religion to another, the film's title, which can be translated as *The Convert*, is provocative in its allusion to the real-world events of Lina Joy's case. In the movie, however, the actual conversion in *Muallaf* is deliberately downplayed and reversed in terms of both gender and religion; a Chinese Christian man working in a missionary school, Brian, experiences a religious revival, of sorts, after spending time with a Malay woman and her sister, who inspire him to read the Qur'an and reacquaint himself with his own faith. The sisters are also shown reading the Qur'an to a young Chinese girl in a coma, which is also a deliberate reversal of the Lina Joy conversion.[3] Some erroneously felt that *Muallaf*'s provocative storyline and subject matter had caused it to be 'banned' for some time. To this day the Wikipedia entry on *Muallaf* claims that the film 'was first denied screening in Malaysian cinemas due to the Malaysian censorship authorities request of key scenes to be cut, thus rendering the story meaningless'. Yasmin exacerbated matters by inviting journalists to a photo shoot on the day that Rohana has her head shaved by her abusive father. The attention-grabbing photos were featured in the next day's papers, which led some Islamic leaders to criticise what they regarded as extreme conduct (Muhammad 2009: 146). The film was not released in Malaysia in the 12 months following its Singapore release on 27 November 2008. According to Muhammad (2009: 147), 'the banal truth is that distributors thought the film wasn't commercial enough: too talky, too much English, no romance'. Eventually, the film was released in Malaysia on 24 December 2009, several months after Yasmin's death; a DVD version with subtitles is now available throughout Malaysia. Although it contained too much English for it to be entered into the annual Malaysian Film Festival, it received Special Mention in the Best Asian-Middle Eastern Film category at the 21st Tokyo International Film Festival in 2008.

As with *Muallaf*, there are parallels between characters appearing in *Talentime* and real-life events, which are important because prominent cases such as the Lina Joy case have 'enabled many Malaysian grass roots movements, often representing liberal strands of the Islamist movement, to bring issues such as human rights, rights of women, freedom of religion, etc., into public debate' (Kortteinen 2008: 229). Yasmin's films add to this growing public debate, even if their fictional outcomes mirror the real-life outcomes, especially the victory of the more conservative elements of Islam and the state, which seek to preserve the *status quo* between the races.

The parallels in *Talentime* appear to have been reversed to fit the storyline, as they were in *Muallaf*. At the centre of the plot of *Talentime* is a group of high-school students who take part in an annual talent contest. A deaf Indian boy, Mahesh, is given the task of chauffeuring one of the contestants, a Malay girl named Melur (played by Pamela Chong). The young couple are soon attracted to each other, but when Mahesh's uncle Ganesh (played by Redzuan Adamshah) is killed by his Muslim neighbours, Mahesh's mother's animosity towards Malays strains the relationship. Other side-plots allude to Malaysia's ethno-religious tensions; for example there is a fractious relationship between two other contestants, a Chinese boy named Kahoe (played by Howard Hon Kahoe) and a Malay boy named Hafiz (played by Mohammad Syafie Naswip), who is also caring for his terminally ill mother. Kahoe is resentful of Hafiz's modest academic accomplishments and alludes to the fact that, as a Malay, Hafiz will 'get help' in getting a scholarship for university studies. Thus the film makes reference to Malaysia's *bumiputera* affirmative-action policies such as the New Economic Policy (NEP) and the New Development Policy (NDP), designed to narrow the gap between the poor Malay majority and the more prosperous other races – in effect the Chinese. In practice, the policies have meant that Malays such as Hafiz get preferential treatment when it comes to the awarding of government scholarships. Chinese students, like Kahoe, might get higher marks than their Malay counterparts, but without scholarships and entry to state universities they are often forced to study overseas.

The primary relationship in the film, between Mahesh and Melur, is undermined by Mahesh's mother's distrust of the Malays, which is exacerbated by Mahesh's uncle's untimely death. In this is encoded a tragic real-world parallel with the interethnic violence at Kampung Medan in Selangor in 2001. *Talentime* describes Ganesh's death as occurring during a party to celebrate his wedding while his Muslim neighbours were conducting a funeral. In the real-world incident, a Malay wedding was taking place alongside an Indian funeral and the riots lasted for five days, spreading out to neighbouring villages. Some have argued that the subsequent violence which erupted between working-class Malay and Indian youths was more closely related to spreading urban poverty and deprivation in the midst of rising prosperity, rather than to a national-scale ethnic showdown (Fenton 2003: 141–42). Despite its localised nature, the Kampung Medan violence, and its fictional representation, highlight the fact that many Indian Malaysians have long felt socially and politically marginalised.

In 2007 this sense of disquiet gave rise to the Hindraf (Hindu Rights Action Force), a coalition of Hindu non-government organisations committed to the preservation of Hindu community rights in Malaysia. Hindraf was established in order to organise a demonstration in Kuala Lumpur in which tens of thousands of Malaysian Indians participated. The group aimed to sue the British government for importing tens of thousands of Indian workers to the rubber estates of British Malaya in the nineteenth and early twentieth centuries, which, according to Hindraf, has led to discrimination that has persisted from one generation to the next up to the present day.

The show of force at the Hindraf rally at the Petronas Twin Towers in November 2007 was not without its consequences. Two hundred and forty were detained and later released, but, more significantly, three prominent Hindraf members were arrested the day before the rally and charged with sedition, and others were detained without trial under the Internal Security Act. Nevertheless, the formation of Hindraf and the 2007 rally has publicised the sense of Indian marginalisation widely and drawn attention to ongoing tensions between Indians and Malays, from the Kampung Medan incident of 2001 to more recent grievances, such as the Shah Alam dispute over the demolition and relocation of a Hindu temple in 2009. In Shah Alam dozens of Muslims protested against the proposed relocation of a Hindu temple in their neighbourhood, which they asserted was a predominantly Muslim area. The demonstrators marched from a mosque in the neighbourhood after Friday prayers and provocatively desecrated a cow's head outside the gates of the state government headquarters.[4]

Such overt displays of religious intolerance were formerly almost unheard of in Malaysia, where, despite ongoing tensions, racial harmony among its three main ethnic groups has been nurtured since the race riots of 1969. The Shah Alam temple dispute, which was subsequently resolved with the arrest and charging of demonstrators and the relocation of the temple to another location in the same vicinity, is part of a broader pattern of demolition of Hindu temples (*kuil*) to make way for development projects, such as highways and industrial zones. Temples have been demolished in several different parts of the country, especially since 2000. Hindraf protesters, joined by Hindu leaders, continue to assert that the destruction of their temples and deities curtails their freedom to practise their religion as guaranteed by the Constitution of Malaysia. In general, the demolition of Hindi temples appears to be having a profound effect in awakening Malaysia's long silent Indian minority and there is some evidence that Indians have now become important political contenders. Nevertheless, Indians in Malaysia continue to experience political marginalisation and opposition leaders continue to call for an end to the discrimination against them. In *Talentime*, the fact that Mahesh is a deaf-mute is an emphatic expression of the subaltern position of Indians in contemporary Malaysia.

Given the political and social context outlined above, a romance between an Indian boy and a Malay girl is unlikely. The relationship between Mahesh and Melur in the film is not undermined by difficulties in communication with a deaf-mute, but rather by generations of interracial prejudice. *Talentime* draws attention to the plight of one of Malaysia's smallest, but most politically active ethnic minorities, the Indians. As in *Muallaf*, Malay identity is rendered identical with Muslim identity, thus reinforcing the resurgence of the Islamic movement as strengthening majority Malay rule. Muslim–Malay dominance, therefore, continues unabated, in spite of liberal Malay thinkers and film-makers such as Yasmin Ahmad who question the pro-Malay ethnicisation of the Malaysian state. Tensions among the major Malaysian ethnic groups – Malays, Chinese and Indians – are by all accounts 'higher than they have been in a long while' (Kortteinen 2008: 229). They are evident in the acrimonious nature of public discourse in the country, which is to some extent captured in Yasmin's films.

Conclusion

Yasmin Ahmad will be remembered as a leading independent film-maker. Her background in advertising should not, however, be ignored, as it helped create the 'brand' that has since been associated with her films: 'sentimental and heart-tugging, and frequently foregrounding the melting pot of cultures that we are' (Muhammad 2009: 13). It is important to note that the scripts for Yasmin's films were, more often than not, written in Bali. Yasmin enjoyed her Balinese sojourns, had many good Indonesian friends and was a fan of Indonesian films. We could argue that Yasmin wrote her film scripts in Bali simply because of Bali's renowned creative atmosphere. Muhammad (2009: 112) suggests an alternative argument, which is that Yasmin was somehow unconsciously acknowledging Malaysia's creative debt to Indonesia. 'After all', Muhammad observes (2009: 111), 'our very national language, Malay, was not developed in Malaysia but across the sea border in Sumatra'. While in a technical sense Malay developed in the Johor-Riau region, rather than in Sumatra, as we have emphasised throughout this book, until the advent of colonialism, *Nusantara* was an archipelago in which mobility and transcultural flows were the norm rather than the exception. While Yasmin's film are set in Malaysia – mainly in the predominantly Chinese city of Ipoh – and speak directly to the Malaysian experience, they also reflect the deep cultural ties between Malaysia and its Asian neighbours, including China, India, Singapore and, last but not least, Indonesia. Yasmin was determined to create films that speak beyond the narrow confines of the Malaysian context. In an interview published in a booklet accompanying the DVD of *Mukhsin*, Yasmin says of herself:

> I just see myself as someone who holds up a mirror to Mankind. I'm not so socio-centric; I just want to examine the human condition and nothing pleases me more than to hear that some people from another part of the world laughed and cried when they saw my film. I don't care about national and political borders so much, but only insofar as they create interesting differences in culture and tradition. The fact that Malaysia is multi-racial is really not such a big deal to me. The world is multi-racial.

Yasmin's cosmopolitan perspective probably explains why, uncommonly for Malay films, her film soundtracks are eclectic, featuring Bach, Beethoven,

Debussy, Dvorak, Mozart, and Schumann alongside traditional folk songs and music from India, Malaysia and Indonesia, and Hong Kong and Thai pop songs from the 1970s. Yasmin's films also refer to the poetry of Rabindranath Tagore, Hong Kong soap opera and Chinese *kung fu* movies. In *Sepet*, it is no coincidence that, as a peace offering, a Malay family offers a serving of *rendang*, a West Sumatran dish, to a Chinese *Peranakan* couple (see Chapter 6). They all point to the ongoing cultural heritage shared by all peoples of the Indo-Malay world, established in the region long before the invention of words such as 'globalisation' and 'cosmopolitanism'.

While Yasmin Ahmad and other independent film-makers of her generation may be open to cultures other than their own, they are nonetheless critical of them. The interethnic relations depicted in Yasmin's films are by no means intended as an uncritical celebration of Malaysia's cultural pluralism. A distinctly political agenda is discernible. As Khoo (2009, 2010) observes, inscribing cosmopolitanism in Malay films implies the transgression of racial boundaries, which are policed by state authorities and ordinary people through years of institutionalised racialisation, officially called 'pluralism' and promoted by the government in campaigns such as the recent 1Malaysia programme. The operations of racialisation rely on each ethnic group representing and defending only its own communal interests. Yasmin Ahmad's films, however, because they focus on interracial relationships, give a fictional voice to Malaysia's ethnic minorities, thereby ensuring that her films were labelled 'culturally polluting' by Malay ethno-nationalists. Although we could say that films such as *Muallaf* and *Talentime* broadly address the question of Islam and gender relations in Malaysia, it would be a somewhat simplistic interpretation. This chapter has instead demonstrated that Yasmin's films reveal both the personal and national politics of Islam and gender in a Malay–Muslim-dominated nation.

Representations of Islam, as we have argued in this chapter, reveal more about Indonesia and Malaysia as discrete entities than about the transactional specifics of the bilateral relationship. Independent Malay films tell us much about contemporary Malaysian society; Indonesian Islamic films tell us much about contemporary debates on Islam and associated discourses such as polygamy, changing gender paradigms and the rise of political Islam and hardline Islamist groups. But, as we have discovered, by analysing representations of everyday Muslim men and women in contemporary Indonesian and Malaysian cinema, we can also learn a great deal about present-day similarities and differences between the two countries, as well as about the deep historical affinity between the two countries, not to mention about many unexpected cultural crossovers. The fact that Malaysia has similarly powerful deep cultural connections with India, China and Singapore in no way diminishes its special relationship with post-independence Indonesia, even though the relationship appears on the surface to be hamstrung by possessiveness on Indonesia's part, defensiveness on Malaysia's part and antagonism on both parts. The next few chapters will examine some of the structural reasons why

Indonesia and Malaysia appear to be more inclined towards divergence than to convergence. In particular, we examine contrasting attitudes and policies towards such things as ethnic relations, citizenship, migration and democracy.

Notes

1 Yasmin has stated that the *bilal* is based on an actual Indonesian Muslim cleric who gave free lessons to the many prostitutes in his area (Muhammad 2009: 83).
2 Orked's parents may not represent the ideal Malay parents in the eyes of the broader Malay community, but they are not entirely fictional. In the notes accompanying the DVD of *Mukhsin*, Yasmin states: 'Orked's parents are totally based on my own parents. In fact, as my siblings and I often remark, our parents are even crazier than Orked's'. In the coda to *Mukhsin*, Yasmin's real-life parents perform a duet.
3 *Talentime* presents another version that is similarly a reversal of the Lina Joy case. In this film the Chinese maid of a Malay family, Mei Ling (played by Tan Mei Ling) is revealed as a practising Muslim, much to the surprise and discomfort of a Muslim–Malay family friend, Datin Kalsom (played by Ida Nerina). Datin is critical of Mei Ling's presence; as a Chinese maid, it was felt that she could not be trusted to observe *halal* strictures in a Malay–Muslim home.
4 The demonstrators were a mixture of ethnic Malays and Malay-speaking Muslims of Indian descent.

6   Ethnicity

As we have revealed in the previous chapter, ethnic relations are deeply embedded in the politics, society and economy of Indonesia and even more so in Malaysia in particular. While Indonesia is not typically viewed as having interethnic problems on the same scale as Malaysia, it has experienced significant outbreaks of ethnic and religious violence. Malaysia, on the other hand, is typically viewed as an ethnically divided society but has not seen the same level of violence and unrest seen in neighbouring Indonesia. Tensions in Malaysia tend to be incremental rather than erupt suddenly, as they did at Kampung Medan and Shah Alam (see Chapter 5) in incidents that are exceptions to the rule. Some have argued that the reason Malaysia has not experienced the same level of ethnic tension lies in the politically beneficial effects of the government's affirmative action programmes, the New Development Policy (NDP) and its predecessor, the New Economic Policy (NEP) (Khoo 2004: 2). However, a closer look at Indonesia's history of ethnic tension shows that flare-ups are not always related to economic disparities between different ethnic groups. In Indonesia, political ideology, religion and experience of migration have each played a significant role in contributing to tension and conflict between different ethnic groups.

This chapter focuses particularly on ethnic relations between the ethnic Chinese – sometimes referred to as '*peranakan*', which in Indonesian and Malay means 'descendant' – and the non-Chinese Indonesians of Indonesia and Malays of Malaysia, respectively. Despite the different reasons for ethnic tension and conflict in Indonesia and Malaysia, which will be explored throughout this chapter, there are some parallels between the Malay–Chinese divide in Malaysia and the divide between the ethnic Chinese and non-Chinese in Indonesia. In particular, widespread resentment towards the ethnic Chinese among the non-Chinese population because of their accumulated wealth and capacity to wield influence through close contact between business elites and those in power is a shared theme in Indonesia and Malaysia. To unravel some of the similarities and differences in ethnic relations we examine how the politics of ethnicity is understood and experienced in Indonesia and Malaysia among ethnic Chinese minorities in times of significant political change.

In Malaysia the ethnic Chinese, comprising nearly a quarter of the population, have long been viewed as a political threat to the *bumiputera*, encompassing the ethnic Malays and other indigenous groups (Department of Statistics 2010a). In Indonesia, the percentage of ethnic Chinese as a proportion of the total population is much smaller: only 3.7 per cent of the population identified themselves as ethnic Chinese in Indonesia's 2010 census (Minnesota Population Center 2012). Even though they are a smaller proportion of the population, the Chinese in Indonesia have had a significant influence in economic affairs, which has led to widespread resentment towards the Chinese. In both countries, the degree to which the Chinese can exert influence has varied considerably over the years. Their power and influence have depended not only on their collective wealth but also on the elite status they were afforded under former colonial governments and on whether or not they were born in Malaysia or Indonesia. To trace some of these developments we first look at the experience of ethnic Chinese during the colonial period when they were collectively known as *peranakan*. The second part of this chapter looks at the experience of ethnic tension in the late 1960s and 1990s when ethnic relations between the so-called 'indigenous' populations and the Chinese resulted in outbreaks of violence.

The *Peranakan* in the colonial era

The *peranakan* Chinese and their unique culture has been a topic of interest in Indonesia and Malaysia for some time. Questions remain whether the term is archaic or whether it still has meaning in contemporary society, especially when Chinese migration is more fluid than in previous decades. Other questions have also emerged, including: who are the *peranakan* Chinese? Is there such a thing as a common *peranakan* heritage and identity? Do they share common characteristics throughout the Indo-Malay Archipelago? The term *peranakan* is commonly used to refer to the descendants of the Chinese who migrated to the Indonesian archipelago in the late fifteenth and sixteenth centuries and to the British Straits Settlements during the colonial era. During the nineteenth century, the word *peranakan*, without 'Chinese' following it, was used to refer indiscriminately to Chinese, Indian, Dutch and Arab immigrants, as well as to descendants of intermarriage between Indian Muslims and Malay women. In Indonesia the term originally referred to those who had converted to Islam. However, in general, the term is most commonly associated with the Chinese community (Suryadinata 2002, 2010). Nowadays, the term is used in Singapore, Malaysia and Indonesia. What is distinctive about the *peranakan* is that they tend to adopt a hybrid identity that is neither fully Chinese nor fully Malay or Indonesian. Like Mah (played by Tan Mei Ling) in Yasmin Ahmad's film, *Gubra*, Malaysian *peranakan* tend to dress in Malay clothes such as a *batik sarong* and *kebaya* (traditional blouse), often with their own distinct *batik* patterns incorporating symbols referring to China. *Peranakan* tend to speak in Malay, as Mah does in *Gubra*. A unique *nyonya* cuisine has developed among the *peranakan*, which combines Chinese dishes with local Malay spices and flavours. While many *peranakan* Chinese grow up having never learnt a Chinese dialect, many continue to participate in Chinese customs and ceremonies. For example, at the controversial conclusion to *Gubra*, Mah and her husband are pictured offering incense and praying at a Buddhist temple, which is a way of life for many *peranakan* in Malaysia. These communities are most populous in Singapore and predominantly Chinese cities in Malaysia, such as Melaka (Malacca) and Ipoh. However, given this book's overall theme, in this chapter our attention is focused on the experience of *peranakan* Chinese in Indonesia as well as Malaysia.

In Indonesia, the *peranakan* have a long history. Chinese traders and seafarers have been travelling to Indonesia for thousands of years, since before the Palembang-based Malay kingdom of Srivijaya, the region's first large maritime polity, which existed from the seventh to the thirteenth centuries (Mackie and Coppel 1976: 4). By the early fifteenth century, large Chinese communities had established themselves in different parts of the Indonesian archipelago. Concentrations of Chinese immigrants began in West Kalimantan and the tin mining islands of Bangka and Belitung islands off southern Sumatra. These concentrations were followed by sudden increases in North Sumatra and, later, with the arrival of thousands of Chinese labourers, a second influx on Bangka and Belitung between 1860 and 1890 (Kaur and Diehl 1996). Further large-scale increases occurred after the Dutch government relaxed earlier restrictions on Chinese entry into and settlement in the colony after 1900 (Mackie 1976).

Dutch legislation of 1854 relegated the Chinese, along with the natives, to a level below the Europeans in matters of law and administration. The Dutch colonists referred to the Indies Chinese as 'foreigners' and later 'foreign orientals' (Mackie and Coppel 1976: 9). Even though the long history of Chinese migration to the Indonesian archipelago has resulted in a great diversity of ethnic Chinese experience, the ethnic Chinese have been traditionally categorised into two main groups: the older *peranakan* communities, who have distinctive cultural traits that are neither Chinese nor Indonesian; and the *totok* who were not born in Indonesia but have recently migrated there (Liu 2011: 156). After 1900, the *totok* tended to be more involved in the politics of the Chinese mainland. By contrast, the *peranakan* were discouraged from sending their children to Chinese schools and instead sent their children to Dutch schools especially for ethnic Chinese (Somers 1964: 5). The distinction between the *peranakan* and the *totok* has at different stages in Indonesia's political history been a divisive issue, especially in the 1960s when Willmott (1960: 15) observed that 'the Chinese population is socially divided into two major groups, Totoks and Peranakans, each of which might be called a separate community'. The separate identities are not only formed as a result of birthplace but also because of colonial legacies, which favoured one group over the other. For instance, the Dutch-educated *peranakan* Chinese occupied higher positions in political affairs than the *totok* (Suryadinata 2010), partly because the Dutch authorities were originally wary of the *totok*'s strong ties with Chinese nationalism leading up to the 1911 revolution.

In a similar pattern to Indonesia, the *peranakan* Chinese also have a long history in Malaysia. However, the term *peranakan* has had a slightly different meaning in Malaysia. In contrast to Indonesia, the *peranakan* Chinese were not defined by whether or not they had converted to Islam in the nineteenth century. Instead, if a person was born in the Malay world and spoke a variant of Malay, he or she was considered as *peranakan* Chinese (Suryadinata 2010). Where there is considerable overlap in Indonesia and Malaysia is in the making of a clear distinction between new communities and the more established Chinese communities that have a colonial heritage.

When the British colonised peninsular Malaysia and Singapore the *peranakan* Chinese became known as the 'Straits Chinese'. While the Malay-speaking population used the term *peranakan*, those who were English-educated preferred the term 'Straits Chinese'. The term is still used today, although it is more appropriate to use it when referring to the Chinese in the Straits Settlements, formed when the British placed Penang, Singapore, Dinding and Melaka under one administration (Suryadinata 2010: 72–73). Newcomers who were not born in the Straits were called '*sinkhek*' (new arrivals), which is similar to the usage of *totok* in Indonesian. Historically the Straits Chinese only included those who were born in the Straits Settlements, and did not include Chinese in other states bordering the Straits of Malacca (Khoo 1996: 24). Further terms used to refer to the ethnic Chinese in Malaysia include '*baba*' and '*nyonya*'. The word *baba* originated in India and arrived in Malaysia when the British East India Company extended its trade to the Straits of Malacca. In general it is considered to be a respectful appellation (Khoo 1996: 24). '*Nyonya*', and its variants such as '*nyonyah*', '*nonya*' and '*nona*' are traditional Malay words to address non-Malay married older women (Khoo 1996). The terms '*baba*' or '*nyonya*' and '*peranakan*' are popular in everyday use even among the Chinese. For example, in Chinese-speaking communities in Malaysia, the Chinese refer to the Malay-speaking and partially assimilated Chinese as *baba*. There are two types of *baba* – the Melaka *baba* and the Penang *baba*. The Melaka *baba* are the Malay-speaking *baba*, although the Malay they speak still has evidence of Hokkien influence (Suryadinata 2002); the Penang *baba* are Hokkien-speaking. The Melaka *baba* are considered as the most 'Malayised' and the Penang *baba* tend to be the least Malayised (Suryadinata 2002). Overall, the *baba* of Melaka and Penang are distinct groups within the Chinese culture, which vary in the extent to which they have assimilated with the local Malays (Khoo 1996).

In colonial times, many of the *baba* belonged to white-collar elites. As allies of the British government, they sent their children to elite British schools where they would learn English. As a result the *baba* tended to adopt Western habits and business practices that enabled them to become the trading elite (Khoo 1996: 25). It was during the mid-eighteenth to the mid-nineteenth centuries that the *baba* became quite wealthy because of their more Western education and cultivation of Western business practices. In contrast, the *sinkhek* had a less elite lifestyle. In the nineteenth century, the majority of *sinkhek* would bind themselves to an employer and work in an exploited labour force in the tin mines. Eventually, the influx of new immigrants in the late nineteenth century led to the resinicisation of the long-established Chinese *baba* community. Resinicisation began around the time of the 1911 revolution in China, when many *baba* families began to learn Chinese. In 1926, a *baba* statesman from Melaka, Tan Cheng Lock, pushed for more Chinese participation in government (Khoo 1996). He rallied the Chinese into a political party and began to hold talks with the Indians and Malays. However, when the Federation of Malaya was established in 1948, the ethnic Chinese became increasingly powerless against the rise of Malay nationalism. Even before this, during the Second World War and the Japanese occupation of Malaya, the *baba* suffered greatly because of the resulting economic depression. After the Second World War they went through an even more severe period of deprivation and many sank into poverty. As a consequence, the identity of the *baba* community, who traditionally were a part of the upper social classes, became less distinct from the newcomers. As more and more *baba* Chinese married newcomers, the distinction between *baba* and the *sinkhek* became less clear-cut. Nowadays, the terms *baba* and *sinkhek* are becoming less and less appropriate in defining a single Chinese identity across the Indo-Malay Archipelago. This is partly because the historic definition of *peranakan* has become more complex over time, as new Chinese communities encourage older communities to become more Chinese and as assimilation policies have encouraged ethnic Chinese to abandon their cultural heritage.

Historically, the *peranakan* Chinese in Indonesia and Malaysia achieved a special status, as they were able to provide a bridge between the colonial authorities and newcomers who came to work and do business with them (Wang 2010). In fact, according to Wang Gungwu, their status as Chinese in the colonial context provided them with something akin to a distinct 'national identity' in the eyes of the Dutch and British (Wang 2010: 15). However, this gradually changed in the period of decolonisation when the Chinese were forced to re-examine their identity as *peranakan*. In relation to this, there was a great deal of diversity of opinion over whether the *peranakan* Chinese should be allowed to maintain their distinctive cultural heritage, assimilate or adopt a distinctly Chinese identity through a process of resinicisation. The contemporary period, involving considerable ethnic tension, can in part be traced to some of these historical developments and shifts in political identity, power and resources. In the next section, we will look at how state policies of assimilation have been pivotal in shaping both the identity and status of *peranakan* Chinese in Indonesia and Malaysia at different points in time, but particularly in the postcolonial period.

Assimilating *Peranakan* Chinese in the postcolonial period

The *peranakan* Chinese have enjoyed a modest political presence in Indonesia. This was most evident in the early twentieth century with the rise of Chinese political nationalism and the establishment of the *peranakan* newspaper, *Sin Po*, first published in Jakarta in 1910. Wanting to remain as Chinese nationalists, the *Sin Po* contributors initially lobbied to repudiate their Dutch nationality, which was based on the law that all Indonesian-born Chinese were Dutch subjects (Suryadinata 1999). In response to the challenges of the Indonesian-born Chinese, the Dutch authorities introduced a number of pluralist policies aimed at including the *peranakan* Chinese in local political institutions. The Dutch policy of creating a plural society in which each ethnic group could maintain its own identity began to unravel after the Second World War and the rise of the Indonesian nationalist struggle. When Indonesia gained its independence and the Dutch departed in 1949, identification with the Indonesian nation was encouraged through the establishment in March 1954 of BAPERKI (Badan Permusjawaratan Kewarganegaraan Indonesia (Indonesian Citizenship Consultative Body)), a Chinese–Indonesian political body (Somers 1964: 8). It was an initiative of mainly young Western-educated *peranakan* Chinese interested in consensus politics, who tended to favour integration and cultural pluralism rather than assimilation. For instance, many *peranakan* Chinese went to Baperki University (1958–62), now Trisakti University, and chose to learn English rather than Chinese or Indonesian, showing a preference for Western education (Somers 1964: 5).

In the years immediately after independence, Indonesians generally admired mainland Chinese and praised them for their discipline and hard work. They had less admiration for the ethnic Chinese living in Indonesia, mainly because they resented their local economic dominance. The generally positive sentiments towards the mainland Chinese were widespread at a time of political and economic instability in Indonesia, when Indonesian political elites were also drawn to China's nationalism. For instance, Sukarno was particularly fond of China's unity and strong leadership. The negative views held among indigenous Indonesians, known as *pribumi*, towards the local ethnic Chinese, however, were perpetuated by economic competition, cultural distrust and religious confrontations (Liu 2011: 143, 175). By 1956, a 'pro-Indonesia' or rather 'pro-*pribumi*' movement had emerged, called the 'Asaat movement'. It was named after Asaat Datuk Mudo, who made an important speech arguing that the Chinese had become monopolistic in their business practices by closing all possible entry routes for Indonesian nationals to join the trade market. While blaming Dutch colonial policies for making indigenous Indonesians 'economically weak' (Somers 1964: 16), Asaat pressed for indigenous Indonesians to be given preferential treatment over the larger category of persons possessing Indonesian citizenship in economic affairs (Asaat 1970). During this time Indonesian businesses perceived the Chinese as resisting the entry of non-Chinese into the business world and as monopolistic. In fact, in the 1950s, almost all retail stores in Indonesia were owned by Chinese or Chinese-Indonesians, including grocery stores, hardware stores and even restaurants. Because of their strong economic position the Chinese became the targets of resentment and hostility. In his opening speech for the Indonesian

National Importer Congress (Kongres Importir Nasional Indonesia) in Surabaya on 19 March 1956, Asaat argued that the power of the 'exclusive' Chinese group in the economic field was hindering the progress of Indonesian business in all sectors of economic life. He also asserted that it was impossible to differentiate in the business world between foreign Chinese and Chinese-Indonesian citizens of Indonesia, at least according to citizenship regulations at the time. In response to Asaat's propositions, which were based on broadly held opinions, a law was introduced and approved by President Sukarno in 1959 that banned Chinese businesses from operating outside urban areas. Foreign nationals – in other words the Chinese – were required to either move to urban areas or transfer their businesses to Indonesian operators by 1960. Indonesian Bureau of Statistics data reveals that just over 100,000 Chinese left Indonesia in 1960, including many displaced business owners and their families (Somers 1964: 26). Most of those forced to leave were *totok* Chinese who at the time did not have Indonesian citizenship or documentary evidence of Indonesian status. Arguably, the overall aim of these discriminatory policies was to establish an indigenous middle and upper class.

Ironically, even among the Chinese there was growing support for assimilation policies, which discriminated against those Chinese without citizenship. Bringing contrast to the ideas of BAPERKI, a new assimilationist group among the Chinese, LPKB (Lembaga Pengkajian Kesatuan Bangsa (Institute for the Promotion of National Unity)), was established in the 1960s during the Sukarno era. This military-supported political organisation, led by Sindhunata, a former navy major, argued that it was the Chinese who were responsible for the deteriorating relations between the Chinese and the Indonesians. The new group thought that the Chinese should participate more actively in Indonesian social and political life and disassociate themselves from the *totok* Chinese who were not Indonesian citizens. It proposed that the Chinese should adopt Indonesian sounding names and lower the barriers against Indonesian–Chinese marriage (see Somers 1964). In the early 1960s the superior economic status of the Chinese and the perceived failure to assimilate continued to cause resentment among Indonesians. A newspaper article published in 1960, entitled 'Assimilation and the Political Manifesto', made the case for a policy on the assimilation of Indonesians of Chinese descent (Onghoklam 1970). Soon after, the Assimilation Charter of 1961 was signed by a group of Indonesians, consisting mainly of *peranakan* Chinese, favouring complete assimilation (Suryadinata 1999: 159). The Chinese themselves held a diverse range of views on assimilation. Some political groups, including many *peranakan* Chinese, held the view that total assimilation, involving the merging of all ethnic groups, was necessary. However, the movement for total assimilation was not in line with Sukarno's ultra-nationalist vision for the nation, so the movement soon dissipated.

In contrast to Indonesia, Malaysian nationalism was rooted in challenging the construction of ethnic relations that had been established under colonial rule. An example of the challenge was the struggle to reclaim political status and resources for the Malays, which resulted in a wide array of exclusionary policies that had a direct impact on the political status of non-Malays, especially of *peranakan* Chinese. According to Nair (2009: 87), under colonial rule, policies on education, the economy and the structure of administration shaped ethnic divisions and the construction of an indigenous self in opposition to the immigrant non-Malays, usually referring to the Chinese. This pattern persisted until after the end of the Second World War in 1945, when the war-torn British realised they could no longer hold onto Malaya. In early negotiations, the Malays were concerned about the position of the Malay rulers, whose responsibilities had been reduced to Islamic matters and customs. On 1 February 1948 the Federation of Malaya Agreement was signed, restoring the status of Malay rulers and their subjects. Consequently, between 1948 and 1955 the British had to be extremely sensitive to the interests of the Malay rulers and their subjects and to the fact that their needs had to be protected (see Wong 2007). The Agreement meant that the Federal Legislative Council could have a Malay majority, which alleviated fears among the Malays that they would be overpowered by the economically dominant *peranakan* Chinese. The Malays were given 22 seats, the Chinese 14 seats, the Indians seven, the Europeans five, and the Ceylonese and Eurasians one each (Wong 2007: 166). At a constitutional conference held several years later in London in 1956, the British and the newly formed Alliance government, comprising the United Malays National Organisation (UMNO), Malayan Chinese Association (MCA), and the Malayan Indian Congress (MIC), came together and agreed on independence for Malaya by August 1957. At this conference significant negotiations took place between the interethnic organisations. The Alliance government accepted a constitution that would give special rights to the Malays and the Sultans, establish Malay as the national language and Islam as the national religion. In return, all those born within the Federation on or after independence were to be considered citizens (Voon 2007). Independence was finally achieved in 1957, bringing together the Malay states and the previously separate political entities of Penang and Melaka. Six years later in 1963, the Borneo states of Sabah and Sarawak, as well as Singapore, joined with the Federation of Malaya to form Malaysia. The incorporation of the two British colonies in Borneo into the new nation was a response to fear of the potential political threat posed by the Chinese majority of the other newcomer, Singapore. That threat dissipated two years later when Singapore broke away from Malaysia on 9 August 1965. The assembling of so many former British colonies in Malaysia in 1963 was the culmination of 180 years of colonial and postcolonial negotiation which began with the British occupation of Penang in 1786.

With Independence in 1957 Malays gained considerable political power, even though they still lacked economic power (Wong 2007). The achievement of independence and the special status given to Malays did little to address the widespread poverty among the Malays who were mainly involved in subsistence production. Under the capitalist economic system that emerged, the interests of Malay peasants were largely sidelined and the widespread economic disparity between the Malays and the Chinese persisted. Simmering ethnic tensions erupted in major riots on 13 May 1969 and continued over three months, resulting in the deaths of a large number of people, mainly Chinese. The rioting began when a group of Malays ran amok and, in a series of atrocities carried out that night, overturned and burned a taxi. When the Chinese driver of the taxi attempted to flee, he was thrown back into the burning vehicle (Slimming 1969: 25). Of the incident Malaysian Prime Minister Tunku Abdul Rahman (1969: 7) stated: 'The whole nation suffered a profound shock, shaken to its very core … May 13th, 1969 was a social and political eruption of the first magnitude'.

The 1969 riots brought to the fore simmering tensions underpinning Malaysia's political system, in which greater Malay political power was viewed as necessary to prevent further Chinese encroachment and as a positive instrument for advancing Malay economic and cultural interests. Chinese leaders, however, feared that Malay political power would be used to interfere with the economic opportunities of the Chinese and would lead to the erosion of their culture (Gagliano 1971). By 1969, most Chinese had already begun to experience discrimination in their careers, in not being appointed in the public service, in not receiving scholarships, and in suddenly being required to produce business permits and professional licences. They blamed Article 153 of the Malaysian Constitution, which safeguards the special position of the Malays. Both the Malays and the Chinese in Malaysia perceived some form of 'relative deprivation', mainly in terms of economic power for the Malays and in terms of political power for the Chinese (Gagliano 1971: 4).

The 1969 riots revealed that ethnic leaders under the existing consociational model were not always able to adequately represent their particular ethnic group. Consociationalism was meant to minimise ethnic mobilisation by allowing for consensus and compromise among the different ethnic groups, mainly the Malays, Chinese and Indians represented by UMNO, MCA and MIC, which had earlier formed the Alliance. The Alliance formula for accommodating ethnic interests through consociationalism soon came under criticism, however, as the Chinese became less confident that Alliance could serve their interests. The Chinese were becoming less confident in the elite style of bargaining, which invariably involved the exchange of Chinese cooperation in improving the Malay economic position in return for Malay cooperation in improving the Chinese political position. Overall, the bargain made amongst the elites within the Alliance depended on non-Malay (mainly Chinese and Indian) acceptance of UMNO-led Malay political paramountcy within the political system. According to Ho Khai Leong, the coalition between UMNO, MCA and MIC only ever existed at an elite level; the members of the elites were mainly Western-educated, conservative, strongly nationalistic and committed to communal interests (Ho 2002: 141). The MCA, in particular, consistently failed to satisfy the Chinese, which led to deep political divisions within the electorate. Chinese-based opposition parties began to emerge, the first being the Democratic Action Party (DAP), which emerged from the

Malaysian branch of the Singapore People's Action Party (PAP) in 1965 and, thereafter, criticised the MCA persistently and championed non-Malay rights in terms of education, language and culture (Ho 2002: 143). Just before the 1969 riots, a significant proportion of Malaysian Chinese moved away from the Alliance and voted for opposition parties. The outcome of the 1969 general elections represented a loss of support among the Chinese for the MCA and for the political system as a whole. Whereas the ruling coalition had won about 60 per cent of the vote for the first ten years of independence, in the general elections of 1969 the Alliance only won 48 per cent of the vote (Freedman 2000: 57). While UMNO and MIC suffered minor losses, MCA was roundly defeated, losing 14 seats and clearly losing widespread support among the Chinese in the constituencies it contested (Gagliano 1971).

One of the main reasons for the shift in votes was growing resentment among the Chinese of MCA's inability to meet their demands, one of which was the protection of Chinese language in the school curriculum. In 1966 the Alliance government introduced legislation to make Malay the official language of Malaysia from September 1967. Consequently, Chinese schools were required to change the language of instruction to Malay if they were to get government financial assistance equivalent to that provided to English and Malay schools (Tan 2002). Overall, the Chinese withdrawal of their support for the Alliance created an environment of fear, as the Chinese sought to gain more political clout in their own right outside of the Alliance (Freedman 2000). Since the 1969 riots, however, the Chinese have struggled to forge the collective political identity necessary to mobilise Chinese support and negotiate Chinese interests.

Conflict and anti-Chinese sentiment

In Indonesia towards the end of the Sukarno period, the ethnic Chinese, whose political loyalties were seen to lie elsewhere, were perceived as a serious threat to national security (see Bertrand 2004). The failed coup attempt of 1965 gave rise to an unfavourable and threatening environment for the ethnic Chinese living in Indonesia. Even before 1965, the ethnic Chinese had faced a powerful army that was steadily gaining control of domestic politics in Indonesia (see Crouch 1978). Towards the end of the Sukarno period, the army asserted its anti-communist and anti-Partai Komunis Indonesia (PKI, Indonesian Communist Party) stance more vigorously. While President Sukarno often praised the PKI and established an informal alliance with the People's Republic of China, the army and other anti-communist forces felt threatened by the PKI's ideology and by Indonesia's close relations with China. In particular, the army felt that the close relationship between the PKI and China had made Indonesia vulnerable to the interference of China in domestic affairs, to the extent that it was perceived that the government was serving the interests of China and not those of the Indonesian people (Sukma 1999: 45–46).

In 1965, with the economy on the verge of collapse as inflation reached a peak and foreign aid became difficult to attract, there were violent clashes between peasants and landowners in the countryside (Liu 2011). During the last three months of 1965 the army arrested those it suspected as being involved in the coup attempt and crushed its main political opponent, the PKI. Following the attempted coup and the collapse of the PKI, Indonesia adopted an anti-China attitude, both in its foreign policy and in its domestic relations between Indonesians and ethnic Chinese in Indonesia (Sukma 1999). In 1966 everything that suggested Chinese ethnicity was banned. The Chinese were required to change their names to Indonesian-sounding names and Chinese religion, beliefs and traditions, including the use of Chinese script, were banned. Participation in ethnic-based organisations was also not allowed and the only path to involvement in politics was through the three main parties – Golkar, the Partai Demokrasi Indonesia (PDI, Indonesian Democratic Party), and the Partai Persatuan Pembangunan (PPP, United Development Party). The success of ethnic Chinese in business continued to be widely resented among the Indonesians in urban slums and rural areas who believed that economic development served only the interests of the military and their foreign and Chinese business partners. On 5 August 1973 rioting anti-Chinese mobs rampaged through Bandung damaging shops and houses. According to Crouch (1978: 300–312), the army did not offer assistance and the ethnic Sundanese officers encouraged the rioters as a means of protest against the government's practice of favouring Chinese and foreign enterprises rather than indigenous enterprises.

Anti-Chinese riots continued and escalated during the 1990s, becoming a regular occurrence by early 1998 (Sidel 2006: 1). In every riot, crowds or mobs attacked shops, supermarkets, department stores and any property owned by Chinese Indonesians. Violence against ethnic Chinese escalated further following the Asian financial crisis and peaked in the weeks before the fall of Suharto's New Order regime in May 1998, when major riots occurred in Jakarta and Solo and in Medan and Palembang. Chinese business were destroyed and more than 1,000 people were killed (Sidel 2006), and there were many reports of the rape of Chinese women being widespread. Van Klinken (2007) observes ethnic violence has tended to peak at times when the President of Indonesia has lacked any real authority, and the above-mentioned peak just before Suharto's downfall supports that observation. During the Suharto years the social and political environment had been threatening for ethnic Chinese; the political and economic chaos after the fall of the New Order regime did little to mitigate this threat and outbreaks of violence against the Chinese persisted.

The ethnic Chinese were not the only victims during the period of political instability before and after the Asian financial crisis of 1997. Ethnic violence in Indonesia also flared between new immigrant communities and those that were longer established. For instance, persistent violence between immigrant and established communities occurred in West Kalimantan, which has a large immigrant Chinese population, estimated to be as high as 11 or 12 per cent of the total population of 3.5 million people (Collins 2004: 169). There are smaller transmigrant communities of Madurese (2 per cent of the population), Javanese (3 per cent) and Bugis (5 per cent). The largest groups at the time were the Malays (39 per cent) and Dayaks (41 percent), which together comprised 80 per cent of the West Kalimantan population (Collins 2004: 169). A few months before the financial crisis in 1997, and again in outbreaks in 1999 and 2001, Dayak and Malay violence against the immigrant Madurese broke out as a result of long-held Dayak resentment towards the immigrant Madurese. The 1997 riots left 500 dead and internally displaced 20,000 Madurese migrants. The death toll after the 1999 riots was lower, but the number of people internally displaced was greater – 35,000 people (van Klinken 2007: 54). Most districts of West Kalimantan became pure Malay or pure Dayak areas as a result of the displacements (Sidel 2006). Altogether, it is estimated that approximately19,000 people have been killed in various kinds of violence, with more than half of them perishing 'as a result of large-scale communal conflict' (van Klinken 2007: 138).

After Malaysia's independence, as we mentioned earlier, the special rights given to Malays engendered ethnic conflict that culminated in bloodshed in the riots of 1969 following the implementation of the NEP. The National Operations Council (NOC), the emergency administrative body established to restore law and order to Malaysia after the riots, linked the riots to three causal factors: the lack of progress in the implementation of Malay as the national language; non-Malays challenging the privileged position of Malays; and the high unemployment rate among Malay and non-Malay youths (Ho 2002: 140). A state of emergency was declared following the 1969 riots and the Malay special rights provisions of the Constitution were given greater legitimacy (Munro-Kua 1996). Solutions to these problems were to be found in the NEP, launched by UMNO in 1971, which it was hoped would achieve national unity. The NEP was intended to eradicate poverty and raise income and employment opportunities for poor Malays and non-Malays living in rural areas. Most of the benefits of the affirmative action schemes were, however, directed towards the Malays and other indigenous communities, collectively known as the *bumiputera* (Arakaki 2009: 81). Among the Malays, the policy was largely viewed as a success in terms of reducing poverty. Between 1970 and 1992, poverty levels among all ethnic groups in Malaysia dropped from nearly 50 per cent to 15 per cent (Crouch 1996). Central to the NEP was an attempt to expand Malay participation in secondary and tertiary education. Scholarships were provided for Malay students and quotas were introduced to restrict the admission of non-Malays to universities. Between 1970 and 1988 the number of Malays studying at Malaysian universities increased from 3,000 to 30,000 and a further 14,000 studied at overseas universities during this time-span (Crouch 1996).

While there is no doubt that the NEP improved the lives of Malays, there are mixed views about the benefits of the NEP for non-Malays, particularly for the ethnic Chinese. Nevertheless, since the restructuring of Malaysian society along the lines of the NEP from 1971 to 1990, ethnic tension in Malaysia has not erupted into violence and bloodshed such as that which has occurred in neighbouring Indonesia. Some have argued that the emergence of Malay business and middle classes in particular has helped to explain the diffusion of ethnic tension since the 1969 riots (Loh 2001; Khoo 2004). But a number of other measures in the 1990s have been taken to reduce ethnic tensions. For example, English replaced Malay as the medium of instruction in some subjects in Malaysian universities, in an adjustment of the 1971 policy that mandated the use of Malay as the only medium of instruction. The Education Act of 1996 also empowered the Education Minister to exempt the use of Malay as the medium of instruction in special circumstances. The celebration of non-Malay cultures in Malaysia was also endorsed by the Ministry of Culture, Arts and Tourism, mainly in order to attract tourism and foreign investment (see Loh 2001). The guarded optimism with which ethnic Chinese have viewed these measures does not dispel the concern they have long shared with other non-Muslim communities about the rise of the discourse related to notions such as *ketuanan Melayu* or *ketuanan Islam* (see Chapter 5), about which these groups can do little. In an effort to avoid the escalation of tension throughout most of the 1990s, non-Malay leaders tended to steer away from public discussion of the role of Islam in Malaysian society. In general, in the 1990s, Malays and non-Malays avoided discussion of ethnic issues in favour of a focus on political and economic stability and put their faith in the ability of the multi-ethnic Barisan Nasional (BN), successor of the Alliance since 1973, to govern (Loh 2001). However, since the mid-1990s, support for the BN has declined as the Chinese have transferred their support to a coalition of opposition parties.

It is worth reiterating that the ethnic paradigm in Malaysia was not only promoted by the colonial government but also motivated by a postcolonial 'ethnic' nationalism (Shamsul 2001: 207). As part of this, in the postcolonial period the Malaysian government has focused on a nation-building project that has stimulated debate on national language, education, culture and religion. Shamsul (2001) observes, however, that contemporary politics has moved away from the colonial-inherited categories of race, ethnicity and religion to more interest-based concerns. Others are more sceptical about the decline of ethnicity and religion as important social cleavages in Malaysia, especially as the interest groups behind interest-based concerns are often crosscut by deep ethno-religious divides. Hefner (2001), for instance, observes that economic expansion in both Indonesia and Malaysia has not diminished the pre-occupation of their peoples with ethno-religious divisions, but has raised new questions concerning justice and participation. Hefner questions whether one ethnic or religious group is disproportionately benefiting from the fruits of economic growth. Given Malaysia's Malay-centric policies, it is difficult to argue that the Malays are not benefiting, but the question of whether their gains are disproportionate to the gains of the rest of Malaysia's population is

still up for debate. In the next chapter we look at civic and political participation of different ethnic groups to see whether ethnicity has continued to
structure power relations following the years of major social and economic
change in Malaysian society wrought by the NEP and its successor, the NDP,
during the last three decades of the twentieth century.

Conclusion

We began this chapter by tracing the development of ethnic relations in
Indonesia and Malaysia, with a particular focus on the experience of the
peranakan Chinese under colonial governments. During this time the political
and economic status of the Chinese varied, depending on their identity as
peranakan, totok, Straits Chinese, *baba, nonya, sinkhek* and so on. Most
importantly, they were not seen as *pribumi* or *bumiputera*, despite the fact that
many were from families that had been in the Indo-Malay world for centuries.
The labeling became less appropriate following the Second World War as
notions of Chinese identity became more fluid and some ethnic Chinese chose
to assimilate to the national culture and ideology while others chose to adopt
a uniquely Chinese identity.

In post-independence Indonesia and Malaysia, the Chinese have contributed
significantly to nation-building and economic growth, particularly in recent
decades in combination with the rising middle classes of the Indonesian *pribumi*
and Malaysian *bumiputera*. Gains made in the economic sphere, however,
have not automatically led to increased political influence for the Chinese.
Ethnic and religious tensions persist beneath the surface in both countries and
simmering resentment flares up from time to time, especially at times of
significant political change. Pluralism is not in itself a source of conflict, as is
demonstrated in many societies where cultures, religions and ethnicities coexist.
What history shows is that conflict between major ethnicities often occurs after
the adoption of state policies that tend to shape, for better or worse, the politicisation and mobilisation of ethnic identities and elite interests. Although this
model has occurred in Indonesia to some extent, it has become the dominant
social and political narrative of contemporary Malaysia, with no sign of resolution. As long as the Chinese minority remains a large minority in Malaysia,
the government's Malay-centric policies will persist. The concomitant politicisation and mobilisation of ethnic identities and elite interests will also persist
and feed ongoing racial tension. While we revealed a snapshot of the
general nature of these tensions in the previous chapter, in this chapter we
have sought to analyse the possible causes and effects in more depth. The end
conclusions, however, are the same.

Finally, through its focus on the experience of the *peranakan* Chinese in the
history of colonial and postcolonial Indonesia and Malaysia, this chapter has
shown that interethnic tensions tend to emerge because of the different statuses
of ethnic groups, systematic discrimination, and exclusion from or differentiated
access to political representation or economic resources. In both Indonesia

and Malaysia, the political identities of the *peranakan* Chinese and the ethnic Chinese during the postcolonial period have been denied for the purposes of political stability. Although there has been little ethnic violence in Malaysia since the 1969 riots, this cannot be seen as an indication that contemporary Malaysia is free from ethnic tension and the occasional race-related incident. This book has already addressed representations of interracial relations in contemporary Malaysia and, if the independent films of Yasmin Ahmad can stand as evidence, it would appear that interracial tension is a permanent fixture of contemporary society, despite the utopian visions of some film-makers and intellectuals (see Chapter 5). Because it is such a salient element of contemporary Malaysian society and politics, in the next chapter we engage once more with ethnic relations, but in a different context – that of Indonesian migrant workers in Malaysia. In the first of two chapters on labour migration, we will suggest that one way to investigate the questions of ethnic relations and access to political representation and economic resources in Malaysia is through examining notions of citizenship. As we have already argued, in Malaysia debates about citizenship, the role of Islam, the political representation of ethnic groups, and the level of access to economic and political resources are continuous themes in public discourse. The debates become more frequent before and after elections when groups mobilise to assert their collective interests through formal and informal channels of political participation. We will argue that a salient, but perhaps underappreciated, element of these debates is the question of Indonesian migrant workers, euphemistically referred to in the Malaysian media as '*pekerja asing*' (foreign workers).

7 Citizenship

In previous chapters, we have tried to preserve a balance between the Indonesian and Malaysian sides of the story. In this chapter the Malaysian narrative will dominate. In Malaysia the potentially negative and divisive ethnic fault lines, based on very significant differences in religion, language, dress and diet, are becoming increasingly pronounced and most commentators recognise the fragility of Malaysia's ethnic harmony. As we have already discussed, contestations between the different ethnic groups continue to occur and are occasionally expressed in street demonstrations or protests. The May 1969 race riots in Kuala Lumpur, the subject of a great deal of research and writing, were both a watershed in Malaysian history and a deeply traumatising event, to the extent that, according to Shamsul (2008: 12), 'in the aftermath of May 1969, Malaysians have clearly stated that they prefer "tongue wagging not *parang* (machete) wielding"'. Some Malays, primarily artists and the like, have been more vocal than others in expressing their frustrations with the present state of affairs, but as we have seen they are subjected to disapprobation. Many other artists and intellectuals, especially those of Chinese or Indian background, however, have simply remained silent or have been deliberately marginalised (see Antoinette 2009), despite the government's endorsement of non-Malay cultural expression. Malaysia's reliance on immigration and migrant labour has only served to exacerbate the sense of unease. It is in this context that the growing public discourse on ethnic differences needs to consider the question of citizenship, a question that is increasing in importance, because, although Malaysia has long opened its borders to immigrants and to migrant workers in particular, the boundaries of citizenship impose a degree of closure to the outside. But the discourse of civil and human rights undermines the state's capacity to maintain the exclusivity of citizenship and to exclude foreigners from participating in society and enjoying at least some of the rights and benefits that are afforded to citizens. Nevertheless, for temporary workers in Malaysia, there is no sense of entitlement to social, welfare and eventually residence rights, and the relationship between economics, citizenship and rights is both complex and increasingly relevant.

In postcolonial societies throughout the world, the importance of transnational migration and the emergence of multiculturalism are undeniable. In Malaysia, the social issues associated with the productive and harmonious integration of immigrants have always been in the spotlight, especially as new arrivals have tended to bring with them different religious, ethnic and cultural backgrounds. Even if the migrants come from a similar religious, ethnic or cultural background, which enables some convergence of a settler's individual and collective identity and the Muslim–Malay value system dominating Malaysian society, the assimilation process, insofar as one exists, is still complex, mainly because of economic disparities. Migration to Malaysia has usually been explained in economic terms and, as we mentioned in the previous chapter, some race-related incidents have also been explained in terms of economics. On the one hand, Malaysia's continuous economic growth in the past three decades has led to severe labour shortages and has generated a demand for immigration to fill the gaps in the labour market. On the other hand, there is economic disparity between Malaysia and the migrants' countries of origin, which ensures that the work available in Malaysia, especially that in the manufacturing and construction sectors, is keenly sought by migrants, especially in sectors such as manufacturing and construction. Indonesian labourers, who speak the same language, enjoy geographic proximity and will accept lower wages than Malaysian workers, are in particularly high demand. The working conditions and associated human rights of these workers, however, have not been a priority of the Malaysian state. Access to citizenship has also been limited, in disregard of the fact that in pre-colonial times the Indo-Malay Archipelago, with its many geographically proximate islands and numerous shallow, narrow waterways to facilitate the movement of goods and people, was a free and open migration zone (Garcés-Mascareñas 2012: 49). What is now peninsular Malaysia began to be settled by migrants from Sumatra and Sulawesi from the mid-seventeenth century onwards. But it was the colonial encounter that opened the floodgates for organised labour migration from the Indonesian archipelago to peninsular Malaysia. According to Garcés-Mascareñas (2012: 50):

> Although at the end of the nineteenth century colonialism divided the archipelago into two separate territories (British Malaya and the Dutch East Indies), the British coined the category of 'Malay' – 'one who speaks the Malay language, professes Islam and habitually follows Malay customs' (Andaya and Andaya 1982: 302) – which left the doors of migration open to culturally similar Indonesians.

To a large extent this has been the dominant narrative of Indonesian labour migration to Malaysia, where many temporary workers have in fact settled there, eventually earning citizenship. However, despite the continuities between the colonial era and present times, cultural similarity has never automatically guaranteed the right to Malaysian citizenship.

While economic development in Malaysia has made enormous progress in the last few decades, a slower rate of change in the political arena has meant that ethnic minorities, including Indonesian migrant workers and, more conspicuously, Chinese and Indians, have become increasingly dissatisfied with the lack of access to citizenship and of human rights protections. This is also partly because of the failure of Malaysia's political system to respect their civil, political, social and cultural rights. Since the early negotiations for independence took place towards the end of the colonial period, Malaysia has allowed for the expansion of citizens' rights for ethnic minorities, but the Chinese ethnic minority, in particular, has struggled to gain momentum in attaining greater political and cultural rights (see Chapter 6). For significant ethnic minorities living in Malaysia, citizenship has come at a cost; in return, they have been required to accept a socially constructed national identity aimed at preserving Malay social and political superiority. Consequently, many Chinese and Indian citizens, whose families have lived in Malaysia for generations and are, therefore, entangled with the history of the Malaysian nation-state, have to some extent been denied their cultural rights and, more obviously, experienced institutional and social discrimination. Institutional and social discrimination are not uncommon in societies where significant ethnic or religious minorities have had to compete for resources with a majority. There has been considerable research in several different nation-states on the way that ethnic or religious minorities may hold full citizenship yet suffer institutional and social discrimination that prevents them from actualising their equal rights (see Kalir 2010; Ong 1996; Schuck 1987; Soysal 1994). For example, Ahmad (2009: 232–34) refers to the lack of accessibility for Muslim minorities in India to state resources and institutions. Ahmad asserts that the abysmally low presence of Muslim minorities in Indian public life points to a failure of democracy. Can a similar judgement be made about Malaysia, where it is the Muslims who are in the ascendancy in public life?

In order to examine the ethnic minorities' experience of citizenship rights in Malaysia, this chapter first looks at the development of postcolonial Malaysia's model of citizenship. We then draw on findings from a range of local, Malaysian and comparative surveys to examine the experience of Chinese and Indian ethnic minorities in Malaysia in relation to citizenship rights and we look at whether they experience social or institutional discrimination. Importantly, we look at whether ethnic minorities in contemporary Malaysia are confident, overall, that the government can represent their interests equally and fairly. We explore this question in the full knowledge that one of the limitations of survey research is that non-citizens and their experience of citizenship rights are invisible. In the third section, we take a look at the experience of citizenship rights of a new and growing ethnic minority which has largely been ignored in studies of citizenship and national belonging – undocumented Indonesian migrant migrants. Studies of ethnic relations in Malaysia often ignore the experiences of undocumented migrants who contribute in meaningful ways to the nation-state in which they live and, often, wish to belong, and we seek to redress this lacuna in this chapter. Because of their invisibility in national surveys and the risks associated with face-to-face interviews, we rely on secondhand accounts of the experiences of undocumented migrants, some of which are drawn from reports of nongovernment organisations and reports in the mass media. We reveal the experience of citizenship rights of this largely understudied ethnic minority living in Malaysia who, like migrant workers the world over, provide the economy in which they live with flexible and often insecure labour.

Ultimately, using a mixed-method approach, this chapter aims to provide an inclusive account of citizenship rights among Malaysia's ethnic minorities. This incorporates not only those who hold full citizenship, but also those not yet able to attain citizenship. Ironically, in some cases, illegal and undocumented workers with similar cultural backgrounds to the Malays are treated more favourably than minority citizens who, although their residency may stretch back several generations, continue to face institutional and social discrimination. Bourdieu (1977, 1984) discusses the ways in which symbolic capital that may belong to one group has the capacity to reproduce the established social order and conceal relations of domination. In this sense, compared to Chinese and Indian ethnic minorities, it is possible that for many Indonesians – particularly Muslim Indonesians – when they eventually acquire citizenship, they are more able to actualise their citizen rights. According to Kalir, 'the ability of citizens to actualize their rights, and feel themselves at "home", depends partly on their ability to embody and perform a dominant national "culture"' (Kalir 2010: 14). Yet the pathway to citizenship for Indonesians is not without multiple risks and experiences of exploitation. We explore some of this journey, which is not unlike the early experiences of many new Chinese and Indian migrants in colonial times.

Multicultural citizenship in Malaysia

Citizenship has always been an important issue in postcolonial societies, particularly in societies that are heterogeneous and divided along ethnic and religious lines. Malaysia is a case in point, as conflict between ethnic groups and its ongoing threat have played a pivotal role in the development of citizenship rights (Hefner 2001). In cases such as this, citizenship tends to be premised not on universal rights but on 'differentiated citizenship' whereby ethnic group rights are recognised alongside individual rights (Parekh 1991: 192). Extrapolating from this argument, ethnic minorities in Malaysia challenge both the modern notion of the nation-state and ideas about citizenship, belonging and entitlements from the state. In contemporary Malaysia, the Malays and indigenous peoples make up 61.8 per cent of the population. The Chinese are the second largest ethnic group at 22.5 per cent of the population and 6.7 per cent are Indian. Other groups only account for 0.8 per cent of the population. A further 8.1 per cent of the population are non-citizens (Department of Statistics, Malaysia 2010b). While a relatively strong economy has developed in Malaysia, ethnic and religious tensions that stem from the privileged position of Malay citizenship have continued to shape modern day politics in Malaysia.

To understand the nature of contemporary citizenship, we need first to review the constitution and the nature of federalist politics in Malaysia. It has been argued that it was the adoption of the Malaysian Constitution that gave rise to a culture of ethnic nationalism, privileging the Malays. It not only privileged the Malays by guaranteeing the special position of Malays and the Malay language (Article 153) but also through the adoption of Islam as the national religion (Article 3) and a Council of Rulers, composed of ethnic Malay Sultans (Article 38, 181) (Arakaki 2009: 81). The Constitution defines all ethnic Malays as Muslims at birth and states that Islam is the 'religion of the Federation' (Human Rights Foundation Malaysia 2011: 16). In 1998, Article 121 of the Federal Constitution was amended to ensure the recognition of Islamic *sharia* courts and their asso- ciated laws. Thus civil courts often concede jurisdiction to *sharia* courts on cases involving conflict between Muslims and non-Muslims, such as the Lina Joy case (see Chapter 5). Article 153 of the Constitution asserts the special position of the Malays and the indigenous peoples anywhere, including in Sabah and Sarawak, as well as the legitimate interests of other races. But the differentiated nature of citizenship has, according to some, undermined democracy in Malaysia while at the same time bringing millions of Malays out of poverty (Arakaki 2009).

The British originally proposed a citizenship framework that would confer the same citizenship rights to Malays and non-Malays, thus provoking a wide- spread reaction from the Malays, who did not want to give up their privileged position as *bumiputera*. As stated in the *Malaya Tribune* and quoted by Garcés-Mascareñas (2012: 60):

[A]n Indian or Chinese after settling down in Malaya under British colonization and British protection may become a British subject or British protected subject according to the English law, but it is not right to identify such a man as a subject of the Malay rulers, unless he adopts the Malay religion, according to the custom.

After much compromise between the Malays and non-Malays, the rights and privileges of Malays as the indigenous people of Malaysia were to be written into the Constitution. In terms of its political system, the Constitution put in place a democratic framework whereby the government was responsible to the parliament, elections were to be held regularly, and the judiciary was to be constitutionally independent. However, the Constitution also included authoritarian controls that restricted political party competition (Crouch 1996: 5). The existence of these controls meant that the Malaysian govern- ment frequently moved between practices associated with democracy and authoritarianism. Reflecting this, from the very beginning, the Malays, some- what undemocratically, were regarded as the legitimate owners of Malaya and the non-Malays were viewed as immigrants. In addition to this, the British recruited the English-educated Malay elite to the highest levels of the new nation-state's bureaucracy. In this context the Malay-dominated political party, UMNO, was established in 1946 (Crouch 1996).

Before Sabah and Sarawak joined the Federation of Malaya in the formation of Malaysia in 1963, the *bumiputera* and non-Malays were almost evenly divided, each forming approximately 50 per cent of the population. The non-Malay component consisted of 37 per cent Chinese, 11 per cent Indians and 2 per cent others (Mauzy 1993: 107). After 1963, the inclusion of Sabah and Sarawak in the Federation increased the proportion of the *bumiputera* to nearly 60 per cent of the population. The arrival of Indonesian and Filipino migrants in the 1970s further expanded the *bumiputera* population (Crouch 1996: 57). In economic terms, however, non-Malays were still better off than the Malays, who continued to be largely rural-based and involved in agriculture and fishing, whereas the non-Malays, especially the Chinese and Indians, were employed in mining, industry and commerce (Crouch 1996). So while Malaysia's model of citizenship has enjoyed many successes, especially in redressing rural poverty, it has been an imperfect solution.

In the 50 years since the end of colonialism in 1957, Malaysia's political and economic policies have been divisive. Nevertheless, Malaysia's 28 million people have forged a democracy of sorts, with each major ethnic group generally committed to achieving prosperity. As we have mentioned, although the official religion is Islam, other faiths are freely allowed and celebrated. Thus while Malaysian society is not always harmonious, the nation is nonetheless pluralistic, even if most people define themselves first and foremost by race, which is a feature of pluralistic societies throughout the world. The greatest achievement of postcolonial Malaysia has, without doubt, been the reduction of poverty among all ethnic groups. However, the decline in poverty was most notable for the Malays, who have been the main beneficiaries of the government's affirmative action policies. Since 1970 the incidence of poverty among the Malays has declined from 65 per cent of the Malay population in 1970 to only 5 per cent in 2009, but not all Malays and indigenous peoples have benefited equally from the affirmative action policies. When we look at the incidence of poverty according to each state in Malaysia since 2002, Figure 7.1 shows that the non-Malay indigenous peoples in Sabah and Sarawak have been significantly more disadvantaged than the Malays in other states. For example, the incidence of poverty in Sabah in 2002 was as high as 16 per cent and increased further to 19 per cent in 2009. As a consequence, Sabah has the highest proportion of its population living in poverty. In 2009, Perlis, the smallest state in Malaysia, located on the northwest coast of peninsular Malaysia, had the second highest proportion living in poverty (6 per cent of the population); Sarawak had the third highest proportion living in poverty (5 per cent of the population). While the incidence of extreme poverty is below 1 per cent in all other states, in Sabah extreme poverty is experienced by 4.7 per cent of the population (Economic Planning Unit 2011).

The special treatment of Malays and non-Malay indigenous peoples has worked to improve the socioeconomic standing of Malays. However, questions have been asked whether a citizenship model that privileges the Malays is still necessary, given that it has disadvantaged other ethnic groups. For example,

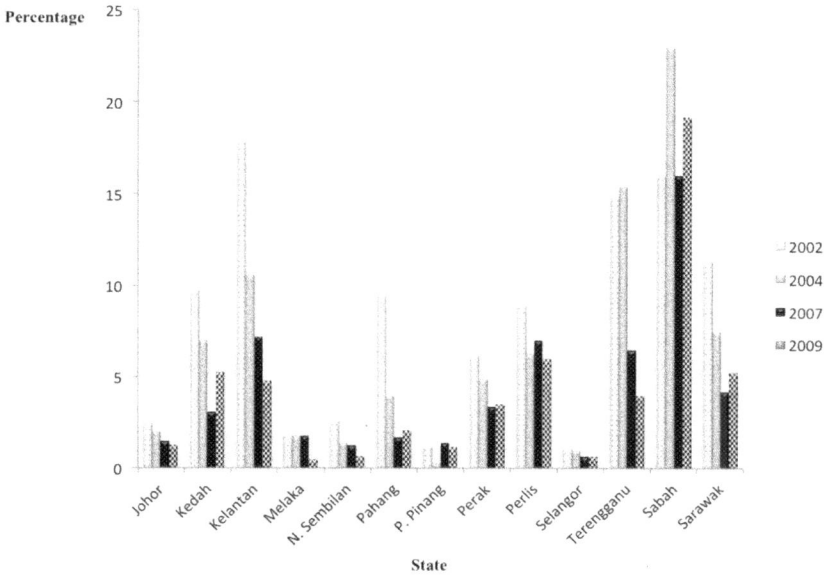

Figure 7.1 Incidence of Poverty in Malaysia by State
Source: Economic Planning Unit 2011.

in a report prepared for briefings at the United States House Committee on Foreign Affairs, the United States Department of State and the Tom Lantos Human Rights Commission, the Human Rights Foundation Malaysia (HRFM) argued that Malaysia's institutions are racially discriminatory (Human Rights Foundation Malaysia 2011). According to the HRFM report, the ethnic structure of Malaysian citizenship has meant that citizens are treated differently within Malaysia's institutions, resulting in systemic and institutional racism. The report argues that the NEP 'was a determined and divisive socio-economic restructuring affirmative action program ... that reduced non-Malays and natives of Peninsula [*sic*] Malaysia in Sabah and Sarawak to the status of second-class citizens' (Human Rights Foundation Malaysia 2011: 3). HRFM asserts that nearly all government projects are given to Malay–Muslim organisations and that Malays are often promoted in the civil service to ensure that the highest policy-making positions will be filled by Malays, regardless of objective performance standards. The findings in Table 7.1 show that in 2005 more than 77 per cent of Malaysia's civil servants were Malay even though Malays only represented 53 per cent of the population. This was an increase of 16 per cent since 1971, indicating that the special position of Malays has slowly but surely become more entrenched in Malaysian institutions.

The disproportionate representation of Malays in administration has reinforced special treatment of Malays in various areas such as scholarships,

Table 7.1 Increase in Representation of Malays in the Civil Service, 1971–2005

	Malay	*Chinese*	*Indian*	*Others*
	%	%	%	%
1971	60.8	20.2	17.4	1.6
2005	77.04	9.37	5.12	8.47

Source: Human Rights Foundation Malaysia 2011: 5

admissions into higher education programmes and pension schemes. As we first described in Chapter 6, government budgetary allocations for education have favoured Malay students at the expense of minority groups. Indian schools are particularly disadvantaged. Up to 371 out of 523 Tamil schools are only partially funded by the government, which only pays for teachers' salaries, leaving the schools to find their own funding for all other expenses (Human Rights Foundation Malaysia 2011: 13). Indian schools tend to be under-funded and under-resourced, which affects the educational outcomes for Indian children. In government universities, more than 80 per cent of university places are reserved for Malay–Muslim students (Human Rights Foundation Malaysia 2011: 15). This is likely to have a flow-on effect in the career opportunities for non-Malays. The findings in Table 7.2 show that even though the Chinese make up 25 per cent of the population, only 9 per cent of Chinese are represented at the top management levels.

With such variation in the experience of poverty among the different ethnic groups in Malaysia, one might expect them to have differing levels of confidence in national institutions. The multivariate findings in Table 7.3 show a significant relationship between ethnicity, religion, education and confidence in national institutions. For example, when all factors are controlled, Chinese ethnicity is associated with less confidence in national institutions. The non-Malay indigenous peoples are also significantly less confident in national institutions than the Malays. Education is also an important determinant of confidence in national institutions. Those with less education are more confident in national institutions than those with a high level of education.

Table 7.2 Representation of Ethnic Groups in the Malaysian Civil Service, 2005

	Top management	*Management and professional*	*Support*	*Total*
Ethnic group	%	%	%	%
Malay	83.95	81.65	75.77	77.03
Chinese	9.25	9.37	9.37	9.37
Indian	5.08	5.12	5.12	5.12
Other *bumiputera*	1.41	3.22	9.01	7.77
Others	0.31	0.63	0.73	0.7
Total	100	100	100	100

Source: Human Rights Foundation Malaysia 2011: 11

Table 7.3 Confidence in Public Institutions among Different Ethnic Groups, 2005–2008

	'A great deal of confidence' (0–10 scale)	
	B	Beta
Ethnicity		
Chinese	−1.237	0.271***
Indian	−0.684	0.099
Non-Malay indigenous peoples (East Malaysian)	−0.774	0.133***
Religion		
Buddhist	1.211	0.247***
Hindu	1.204	0.163*
Christian	0.354	0.058
Background controls		
Age	0.006	0.037
Gender	−0.117	0.030
Income	0.067	0.058*
Education	−0.108	0.102***
Constant	1.174	
Adjusted R-squared	0.137	
N	(1209)	

Note 1. Entries are OLS (ordinary least squares) unstandardised and standardised regression coefficients.
Note 2. *p<0.05, **p<0.01, ***p<0.001.

The Malaysian government is currently implementing an ambitious New Economic Model that hopes to see Malaysia become a developed nation by the year 2020. This economic model has three main goals: high-income economy; inclusiveness; and sustainability. The underlying objective of the economic model is to lift Malaysia's standard of living from its position in the world's bottom 40 per cent, primarily as a critical strategy to ensure cohesion and unity. In response to changing economic conditions, in 2010 the government released the Economic Transformation Programme (ETP), which would rely heavily on private-sector-led growth (Economic Transformation Programme 2010). The ETP is meant to be inclusive by ensuring that all communities benefit equally from the programme's main goals of moving towards a high-income economy. However, survey findings from an independent Malaysian research institute, the Merdeka Centre for Opinion Research, shown in Figure 7.2, shows that the Chinese are far less confident than the Malays and the Indians that this new programme will actually work. Fifty-eight per cent of the Chinese in peninsular Malaysia are not confident in the plan. This compares with only 25 per cent of the Malay citizens and 14 per cent of Indian citizens. Although the plan may be a success in terms of economic development, it makes little reference to political development, which has historically been of greater concern for Chinese and Indian citizens.

There are several explanations for these findings. The first is related to socioeconomic progress. As previously indicated, the non-Malay indigenous

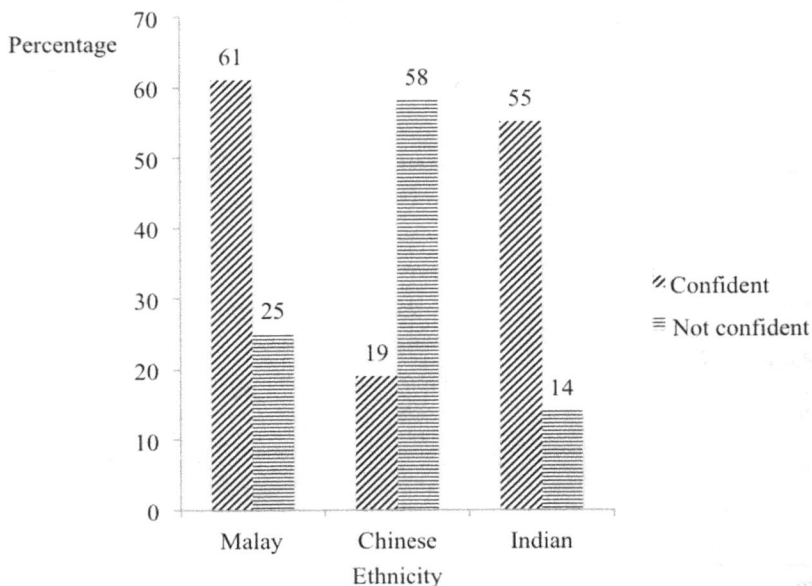

Figure 7.2 Confidence of Ethnic Groups in the Economic Transformation Plan
   Source: From responses to the question 'In your opinion, how strongly are
   you confident or not confident that the Economic Transformation Plan will
   propel Malaysia into becoming a developed nation?' in Peninsular Malaysia
   Voters Opinion Poll, conducted between 30 November and 11 December
   2010 (Economic Transformation Programme 2010).

peoples in Sabah and to a lesser extent Sarawak did not benefit from the pre-
1990s NEP-inspired economic progress to the same extent as the Malays.
Twenty years later, polls provide indicators of persistent dissatisfaction among
these peoples. According to a 2012 poll by the Merdeka Centre, 57 per cent of
all Sabah voters were dissatisfied with Sabah's economic performance and
only 56 per cent 'were satisfied with the state government, a six percentage
point drop from 62 per cent in November 2009' (Darwis 2012). Among non-
Malay voters, this level of dissatisfaction might not be surprising, if we recall
the report produced by the Human Rights Foundation Malaysia, which
asserts that most government contracts are awarded to Malays and that
Malays are also more likely to be promoted to the highest levels in the civil
service and government.
   Another possible explanation is the experience of structural discrimination.
Many highly educated Chinese, for instance, have had greater difficulties gaining
entrance to Malaysian universities compared to Malays. Overall, non-Malays
are significantly under-represented in the education system, the parliament,
the judiciary and the civil service. Whether this arises from choices made by

non-Malays or whether it is related to structural discrimination has not been fully explored. A final explanation is perhaps related to the Islamic resurgence and increasing ethnicisation of the state, which we have discussed in previous chapters. While Malaysia is a secular state under the Constitution, it is generally agreed that over the last 25 years Islam has become more pervasive in Malaysian society (Kortteinen 2008; Ting 2009). Prime Ministers Mahathir Mohamad and Abdullah Badawi both made public statements to the effect that Malaysia is an Islamic state, which sparked widespread consternation among those who do not belong to the Muslim faith, that is, non-Malays (Freedman 2009).

So far in this chapter, we have discussed the experience of citizenship for Chinese and Indian ethnic groups in Malaysia and perceptions of unfair treatment. What is often left out of discussions of Malaysian citizenship is the experience of migrant workers – both documented and undocumented – who are often denied basic rights in Malaysia. Economic development has improved the living conditions of Malays, Chinese and Indian citizens, but as Malaysia has moved up the development ladder it has become heavily dependent on migrant workers, particularly from Indonesia. However, in the context of Malaysia's neo-liberal economic policies, Indonesian migrant workers are susceptible to deteriorating social rights. In the next section, we show that while many are denied basic rights from the state, some are able to gain full citizenship through the assistance of local networks and communities.

Indonesian migrant workers and citizenship

In the British colonial era, when Malaya was becoming more integrated into world commodity and capital markets, new technologies in industrialised Europe created a demand for the tropical products that could be sourced there. The response of the Malay peasants to the possibilities of export production, however, was lukewarm. As Kaur (2005: 5) suggests, 'there were limits to the willingness or ability of the peasants to respond to the opportunities opened by the growing market for tropical commodities'. The colonial authorities thus decided to source labour from outside the country, mainly China and India. A third labour stream flowed from Java, which took advantage of the cultural and historical links within the Malay world. Eventually, the production and export of tin, sugar, coffee and rubber in an increasingly connected world economy was only made possible by the importation of foreign labour which was perceived as cheap, stable and continuing in comparison to local Malay labour. In this regard, the Chinese were initially favoured because they were perceived as a relatively freer workforce, but the early colonial plantations found that Chinese labour was quite well organised and, therefore, expensive. Garcés-Mascareñas (2012: 58) quotes Jackson (1961: 57), who observes that Chinese workers were perceived as 'very closely knit, self-governing communities, homogenous, united in aim, if often mutually antagonistic, and, by virtue of their secret society or guild organization, with strong internal discipline and stability to present a united front to outsiders'. Thus the British were driven to find a cheaper, more docile, more malleable alternative, such as the South Indian Tamils who, unlike Chinese workers, were perceived as 'a peaceable and easily governed race' (Garcés-Mascareñas 2012: 58). In order to counterbalance the growing Chinese presence in Malaya, therefore, the colonial authorities promoted Indian labour. As opposed to Chinese immigration, 'Indian immigration was planned and supervised by the colonial authorities to suit British employers and themselves' (Garcés-Mascareñas 2012: 59).

Given the theme of this chapter, it is important to emphasise that in the colonial era immigration was largely unrestricted until the 1930s, when some quotas on Chinese immigration were introduced. As Kaur (2005: 6) observes, 'these restrictions never attained the importance they did after Malaya gained independence'. Indian migrants were only expected to return home if they were unemployed or had health problems. Otherwise they were allowed to stay in colonial Malaya for as long as they were required. To ensure a stable supply of low-wage labour, the colonial government even encouraged entire Indian families to migrate (Garcés-Mascareñas 2012: 59). While the colonial labour policy in Malaya was focused on 'the acquisition of a plentiful, diversified, and cheap labour supply for colonial undertakings and capitalist enterprise' (Kaur 2005: 6), authorities were also anxious to provide some 'rights', such as a modest amount of freedom of movement and the provision of a limited amount of protection for the workers. The settlement of many Indian and Chinese migrants and their families did not, however, guarantee them an automatic right to citizenship, mainly because the workers were not easily assimilated or readily accepted by the local inhabitants. There were also restrictions on Chinese and Indian agricultural settlement. The British, who in effect ruled the Malay States as colonies from 1870 to 1914, with the imperial process beginning around 1850, played a key role in this state of affairs. According to Kaur (2005: 7):

> The British viewed migrant workers as sojourners, to be repatriated when the demand for their services no longer existed. Nor did they confront the issue of granting full rights to the more settled migrants. This would have been at odds with the stated policy of 'ruling' Malaya for the Malays, and Malay preference.

Significantly, Javanese migrants were viewed and treated by the British authorities quite differently, 'since they were regarded as originating from the same racial stock as the Malays. A pattern of differential treatment was thus established, which was to have implications for labour migration into Malaya after independence in 1957' (Kaur 2005: 7).

Following the outbreak of the Second World War, Chinese immigration to Malaya came to an end. The Immigration Ordinance (IO) legislation of 1953, which introduced stringent border controls and specified which immigrants should be allowed to enter Malaya, ended the migration of unskilled Indians to Malaya (Kaur 2005: 16–17). In the decades since independence, Malaysia's export of manufactured goods within an increasingly globalised world economy has relied on the importation of migrant labour from Indonesia, Bangladesh, the Philippines and other Asian countries. As in the colonial era, at certain times Malaysia has favoured one specific state of origin over another; for example the Hire Indonesians Last policy of 2002 effectively put a stop to the hiring of Indonesian migrants for a period (Kaur 2005: 26–28). In the decade following this brief and ill-fated policy, Malaysia's population of documented migrant workers peaked at approximately two million in 2008 (Chin 2008: 286). According to Chin (2008: 286):

> Migrant workers now constitute one-fifth of the total workforce. Malaysia is one of the world's top receiving countries for undocumented migrants, second only to the US. Estimates of this population range from approximately two to four million people. If added to the number of documented workers, transnational migrants may well constitute nearly one-half of the total labour force in the country.

Cross-border flows of labour migrants are particularly common in areas where Indonesia and Malaysia share land borders. The dynamics of demography and development in Borneo, for instance, have resulted in the two governments co-operating in the establishment of a number of large projects in the Entikong-Tebedu borderland between Sarawak and West Kalimantan (Kaur 2005: 22), leading to an influx of Indonesian workers in the area. Overall, although poverty is not the principal determinant of migration, many Indonesian migrants come from very poor areas such as East Java, Aceh, South Sulawesi, Flores and Lombok (Hugo 2011). They are not, however, the poorest of the poor, as workers must have substantial amounts of money to get to their destinations in Malaysia. All documented workers also have to pay hefty fees in the country they are leaving and on arrival in Malaysia, as well as passport fees, labour recruitment agency fees, insurance fees and bank guarantees.

While it has sustained economic growth, immigration in Malaysia has contributed to a dual labour market, which has, in turn, intensified Malaysia's reliance on migrant labour. Migrant labour is now found not just in export-oriented sectors, but also in all sectors that many Malaysians have come to acknowledge and reject as 'low-status, low-wage work' (Chin 2008: 288), such as construction work. Migrant workers themselves class this kind of labour as the '3Ds', that is, dirty, dangerous and difficult (Lazuardi 2009: 73–119). In periods of economic downturn, or when workers become ill or pregnant and supposedly limit their capacity to work, migrant workers are summarily returned. As one of the workers interviewed by Garcés-Mascareñas put it, 'Malaysia doesn't have migrants, just foreign workers' (Garcés-Mascareñas 2012: 102). In general terms, Garcés-Mascareñas' study outlines the way in which Malaysia uses high numbers of migrant workers to achieve economic growth and development, making next to no effort placed to address concerns about their rights, including the right to citizenship. Given that Malaysia likes to portray itself as a democracy, which by definition means that upholding the human rights of citizens and non-citizens alike is a priority, the Malaysian government could well be somewhat displeased by such a bleak characterisation. Yet Garcés-Mascareñas presents an argument that is very persuasive, and supported by a mountain of evidence demonstrating Malaysia's seemingly ad-hoc efforts to facilitate and regulate migration flows. Strategies put in place have included privatising or commercialising recruitment processes, restricting or immobilising migrant labour in some sectors of the economy, taxing migrant workers as a method of control, and emphasising the temporary nature of the migrant worker arrangement. Malaysia's recurrent regularisation programmes have also served to emphasise the perceived threat of the migrant worker force, which, although much in demand, is disliked and unwanted in the communities they end up in. Narratives of Malaysia being infiltrated by aliens, or uninvited guests, within the territorial borders of the sovereign nation-state are common in Malaysia's government-controlled media and the attitudes embedded in these narratives seem not to disperse with the passage of time (see also Arifianto 2009; Chin 2008). Garcés-Mascareñas (2012) clearly delineates the close relationship between regularisation and mass deportation campaigns, which are often characterised by corruption, abuse and violence. For example, in 2002, the sudden influx of tens of thousands of Indonesian deportees to Nunukan, a small Indonesian island just south of the border with Sabah, caused a severe humanitarian crisis (Ford 2006: 249–50).

The question of citizenship for migrant workers is a sensitive one, as there is a general consensus that migrant workers should only remain in Malaysia temporarily. The temporary nature of migration aims to contain social security costs and prevent the assimilation of migrants into Malaysian society (Kaur 2006). Women are required to take pregnancy tests and they are deported immediately if they are found to be pregnant. Foreign women who marry local men and become pregnant are also deported and, consequently, many migrant women workers choose to terminate their pregnancies (Garcés-Mascareñas 2012). In addition to these policies, temporary workers are only permitted to stay in Malaysia for no longer than five to seven years so that they do not become settled migrants. Many choose to become undocumented migrants to avoid detection and deportation and those who choose this illegal status are particularly vulnerable to exploitation, especially in the construction, plantation and service industries. The work of all migrant workers tends to be insecure, irregular and bound by short-term contracts. They usually have to pay high administrative and agency fees to labour organisations and they cannot stay beyond completion of their contracts. Adding insult to injury, the Malaysian news media, politicians and security forces encourage the notion that low-wage migrants are unwelcome outsiders.

During the 1970s, the phrase '*pendatang haram*' (irregular migrants) was introduced for undocumented workers. Shortly afterwards it changed to the more politically correct '*pendatang tanpa izin*' (migrants without permission). According to Garcés-Mascareñas (2012: 63):

> While at first the terms referred to the Vietnamese refugees ('boat people') arriving in Malaysia in the late 1970s, in less than a decade it would become almost synonymous with illegal Indonesian migrant. This shift came hand in hand with new connotations that associated illegality with contagious diseases, begging, prostitution, 'deviant' religious teaching, urban squatters, criminality and subversive political activities.

Such negative images of migrant workers, matched by the negative terms used to describe them, have only worsened in the following decades. During the 1990s, the preferred phrases were 'illegals' or 'aliens' (*pekerja asing*), which is still in usage. According to Chin (2008: 289), 'The all-encompassing noun of "alien" signifies low-wage migrants (regardless of immigration status) as outsiders who do not have a legitimate place and space within the nation of Malaysia'. Nowadays, the Malay term '*pekerja haram*' (illegal workers) is commonplace. The adjectival '*haram*', with its Arabic roots, has a distinctly Islamic overtone, which is as much suggestive of sinfulness as of illegality. Its use is a particularly galling insult for the many Indonesian migrants who profess the Islamic faith. Synonymous phrases, such as '*migran gelap*' (illegal migrants), are equally problematic. In Indonesian, '*gelap*' means 'dark', thus, for Indonesian migrants, the phrase is imbued, perhaps unintentionally, with a connotation of shady or criminal behaviour. Of course, for the Malaysian media, politicians and immigration authorities, undocumented workers thoroughly deserve such labels. But for so many Indonesian workers, these phrases and their associated connotations are insulting, particularly given the much-vaunted cultural and religious commonalities between Muslim Indonesians and the Malays.

As mentioned earlier, one of the key strategies that the Malaysian government has put in place to control labour migration is the privatisation or commercialisation of the labour recruitment process. Most temporary work in Malaysia is managed by private recruitment agencies that operate both in Indonesia and in Malaysia. In Indonesia, migrant workers are usually recruited at the village level in Indonesia by brokers, referred to locally as '*petugas lapangan*', 'or PL for short, also sometimes called *sponsor*' (Lindquist 2012: 71). As Lindquist describes (2012: 71), since the 1997 Asian economic crisis, the figure of the *petugas lapangan* is 'replacing the *tai kong*, migrant smuggler, who was at the centre of the undocumented labour migration to Malaysia until the 1990s'. The brokers or PL act as important intermediaries between potential migrants living in poor villages and recruitment agencies and handle the recruitment process at the village level before handing potential migrants over to specific agencies. The agencies pay the broker for each potential migrant they deliver to the agency, which organises passports and identity cards and sometimes travels with the migrant workers to transit provinces such as Riau and East and West Kalimantan. Poor villages in rural areas are the main source of migrant labour to Malaysia. Men from very poor areas will often pay up to US$400 before departure for a two-year contract on a Malaysian palm-oil plantation. The increasing role of recruiters in poor villages is part of a much larger trend of documented migration from Indonesia (Ford 2006). Through the facilitating role of brokers, labour migration from Indonesia is more likely to be documented, with the Indonesian government also paying far more attention to the protection of workers. As Lindquist (2012: 73) observes, 'The call for protection has reinforced the regulation of migration in Indonesia, for instance through the creation of special migrant airport terminals, first in Jakarta and later in a number of cities across the country, while leading to an increasing bureaucratization of the migration process'. But while Indonesian temporary labour migration is now more likely to be documented and formalised, this trend has coincided with increasing deregulation of the labour recruitment market, leaving open increased opportunities for exploitation.

At the Malaysian end of the process, migrant workers are handed over to agents who have a reputation in the local media for being unscrupulous people who overcharge the migrants they receive. Some migrant workers are abandoned on their arrival in Malaysia, after they have paid in advance large amounts of money to recruitment agencies in Indonesia. Without proper documentation they then become irregular in status and are denied protections afforded to legal citizens. Employers, nongovernment organisations, trade unions and the government have all openly criticised regular and irregular practices of recruitment agencies, which increase the vulnerability of migrant workers in Malaysia (see Lazuardi 2009; Garcés-Mascareñas 2012; Lindquist 2012).

The exorbitant costs imposed by recruitment agencies are often considered as one of the main reasons for the high level of illegal and undocumented migration. Some migrant workers believe that they have arrived in Malaysia legally, only to find that their passports were forged by unscrupulous private recruitment agencies, rendering them illegal and without any protections at all. As maids or domestic helpers without protections, women are especially vulnerable. This is important because of the growing number of female domestic servants who are able to work for the expanding middle classes in the region (Kaur 2005, 2006; Lindquist 2012). According to Lindquist (2012: 72), 'In 2006, women accounted for 80 per cent of all documented migration from Indonesia, with 88 per cent working in the domestic sector, reflecting the ongoing feminization of labour migration in Southeast Asia'. Between 400,000 and 700,000 migrant workers enter Malaysia every year (Garcés-Mascareñas 2012: 65); many of these workers are domestic helpers or maids. In June 2009, however, Indonesia suspended deployment of domestic helpers to Malaysia after many well-publicised cases of abuse. Eventually, in an attempt to improve Indonesia–Malaysia relations on the issue of migrant workers, the governments of Indonesia and Malaysia signed a Memorandum of Understanding (MoU) on 30 May 2011, which allowed Indonesian domestic helpers to once again travel to Malaysia to work. We shall discuss this move further in the next chapter. While there have been a number of improvements made for low-wage workers, Malaysia has prevaricated on many important issues, such as wages, not least because Malaysia has no minimum wage. As a result, the Indonesian government's demand for a minimum wage for domestic helpers, most of whom earn less than $250 a month, has not been met (Southeast Asia 2011).

In practice, the rights of migrant workers are still not protected in spite of the introduction of the MoU. Workers suffer from not being paid their wages, from working long hours, from living in sub-standard conditions, from having no insurance coverage, from having their travel documents withheld by employers, and from unfair dismissal (Southeast Asia 2011). In addition, migrant workers are still very vulnerable to physical and emotional abuse. An additional stress for many migrant workers is the fact that their visas do not allow any mobility across different sectors, as the visas are linked to a specific economic sector and tied to a particular employer. Their dependence on a particular employer prevents them from leaving an employer when they are abused or exploited. In contrast to legal migrants, illegal migrants are free to move wherever they want, resulting in a much higher job mobility among illegal migrants. In many cases, legal workers leave their employers and become illegal, preferring the relative benefits of illegal but more mobile employment options. According to Devadason (2011), 'The core problem is a lack of a comprehensive migrant worker policy and weak governance structures. The Malaysian case is a classic case of the failure of decentralisation in the recruitment and placement of migrant workers, in addition to lack of enforcement of existing regulations by various stakeholders'. In addition to these factors, Garcés-Mascareñas (2012: 64) observes that 'Most Malaysian scholars have described migration policies as being inconsistent, changing and ad hoc'.

Over the last decade, Malaysian politicians have shifted their treatment of Indonesian migrants from a policy of tolerance to one that considers them a security threat against Malaysian society (Arifianto 2009; Garcés-Mascareñas 2012). Although we discuss this shift in more detail in the next chapter, it is perhaps useful to outline the events of 2002, when the Malaysian government enacted a new Immigration Act, which triggered the mass deportation of undocumented foreign workers and forcibly repatriated almost 400,000 Indonesian workers (Kaur 2005; Ford 2006). Because of a lack of resources, Malaysian authorities recruited civilians and neighbourhood security associations to conduct some of the immigration raids and arrest undocumented workers. Civilians were rewarded with a cash payment for each illegal immigrant they apprehended (Liow 2003: 50). This has been regarded as the beginning of a trend towards the gradual securitisation of illegal migrant workers, which we will discuss in more depth in the next chapter. This policy was introduced at the same time that the previously mentioned Hire Indonesians Last policy was introduced, soon after the September 11 attacks in New York and the Bali bombings of 2002, when there were growing fears that the illegal

Indonesian migrant worker network might provide yet another channel for Islamist terrorism. In general, by 2002, Indonesian workers in Malaysia had become demonised as regular perpetrators of crimes and potential perpetrators of terrorist activity, and were, therefore, according to Malaysian media and public opinion, threats to Malaysian national security (Liow 2003). Amendments were made to the Immigration Act that introduced harsh penalties, such as heavy fines, imprisonment and caning, for undocumented workers (Arifianto 2009). It needs to be acknowledged, however, that these harsh attempts to regulate undocumented migration in Malaysia have generally failed because of corruption, negligence on the part of employers, and the long history of social ties, which facilitate the persistence of undocumented migration.

It is also important to note that not all Indonesian workers have been denied basic human rights. In many cases, nongovernment organisations and local communities actually facilitate their migration and integration into Malaysian society. In Malaysia there are networks of complicity that bend and manipulate state laws to facilitate the entry, settlement, and socioeconomic and political participation of immigrants who are without documentation (Sadiq 2005, 2009). These networks are found in the political leadership, the bureaucracy, the security forces, and the municipal and local administrations. Many immigrants rely on networks of complicity to obtain fake or counterfeit documentation, which gives them access to many of the legal rights enjoyed by citizens. Eventually, through a cumulative process, many are able to acquire the legal documents that are necessary for full membership and citizenship. Sadiq refers to this process as 'documentary citizenship' (Sadiq 2009: 102). The process of acquiring citizenship usually comes about only after a long period of accumulating 'practical national belonging' (Carruthers 2002; Hage 1998). In Sabah, for example, Indonesian migrant workers are regularly provided with citizenship and the right to vote. The Sabah state opposition has alleged that the Barisan Nasional (BN) government in Sabah 'gave out' citizenships to 'foreigners' in exchange for votes to help them stay in power (Darwis 2012). Evidently, in exchange for the issuing of identity cards and the right to vote, the Indonesian immigrants are expected to vote for their benefactor, who is likely to be an UMNO-BN politician. It has also been asserted that the Malaysian government uses illegal immigrants from neighbouring countries to 'Malayize' Malaysia, that is, to increase the numbers of Malay Malaysians (Sadiq 2005: 105). This is especially the case in Sabah where the undocumented Indonesian population has increased dramatically in recent years. The main reason to encourage undocumented Indonesian migration, according to Sadiq, is to use illegal immigrants as voters to assure political control by a Malay-Muslim party such as UMNO (Sadiq 2005). Numerous media reports support this argument and there was, indeed, precedent for this practice in previous decades (Kaur 2005). But while undocumented Indonesian migrants may eventually gain citizenship and political rights, this chapter has shown that there are many risks in the transition from irregular status to full national citizenship. Moreover, in Malaysia, the attainment of citizenship does not necessarily guarantee political inclusion, as the experience of Chinese and Indian citizens attests.

Conclusion

This chapter has shown that, although Malaysia extends citizenship to Chinese and Indian minorities as well as to Malays, perceptions of the rights that citizenship bestows vary markedly among the different ethnic groups. Through our analysis of survey research, we have shown that, even though Malaysia has made substantial economic progress, civil, political and social rights are distributed unevenly, which accentuates Malaysia's differentiated model of citizenship. Chinese and Indians are under-represented in the higher levels of the civil service and in professional management positions. The Chinese, in particular, also have very low levels of confidence in national institutions to which they belong on paper but which they do not feel represent their interests. The research leads us to argue that in Malaysia, the Chinese and Indians are provided with civil and political rights, but feel inadequately represented in civil society.

The reality of citizenship in Malaysia becomes even more contentious when we include the experiences of Indonesian migrant workers, a new underclass now making substantial contributions to Malaysia's economic success. As Chin observes (2008: 288), since the 1980s, the Malaysian state has entered into a number of bilateral agreements with the migrants' countries of origin, it has clarified recruitment and employment criteria, and it has shortened application and approval processes. At the same time, it has put in place measures that ensure that low-wage transnational migrants remain temporary or guest workers, reinforcing the adage that there is nothing as permanent as the temporary nature of migrant labour. Immigration policies also prohibit the entry of migrant dependents, marriage to Malaysian citizens and applications for permanent residency. Migrant workers who fall pregnant also have little chance of continuing their employment in Malaysia. The intent of these regulations, according to Chin (2008: 288), 'is to maintain a strict insider-outsider distinction: the stipulations render such outsiders simply ineligible for citizenship'. Regularisation programmes, as well as the enforcement of identity cards with electronic microchips, allow the state to easily verify migrant identities and pursue deportation if necessary. Overall, this chapter has demonstrated that many Indonesian migrant workers are denied basic social and political rights, rights that are necessary to ensure adequate representation and membership in the national community. Even though many Indonesians have acquired documentary citizenship through informal channels, it has been argued that it is still necessary to extend basic social rights to temporary workers in return for their economic and social contribution to Malaysian society.

Finally, this chapter has demonstrated the need for Malaysia to pay attention not only to economic prosperity but also to the extension of full citizenship rights to all ethnic minorities. It is clear that Malaysia's differentiated model of citizenship is no longer meeting the increasing demands of the increasingly vocal and dissatisfied Chinese and Indian communities, quite apart from the marginalised and disenfranchised community of migrant workers, led by Indonesian nationals, but also including increasing numbers of citizens from other nations in the region, such as Bangladesh, Myanmar and the Philippines. Granting more active forms of citizenship can only benefit Malaysian society, especially as it moves into the twenty-first century with an increasingly multicultural and diverse population. But as the next two chapters demonstrate, Malaysia tends to follow its own path, regardless of its neighbours' increasingly vociferous admonitions, and the criticism by its own citizens. Both chapters will assert that democracy has a salient role to play in providing a solution to the migrant labour issue, and the next chapter in particular addresses the impact of regionalism in this regard. The level of democracy can be directly correlated with the desire to secure regional solutions to regional problems, such as the protection of migrant worker rights. As the leading democracy and main source of migrant labour in the region, Indonesia is an interesting case study in this regard. Whether Malaysia can match Indonesia's democratic progress, with its concomitant foreign policy reverberations, remains to be seen.

8 Regionalism

So far, this book has dipped in and out of considering Indonesia's relationship with Malaysia in terms of neighbourly spats, sibling rivalry, domestic politics, bilateral politics and regional identity. We have emphasised the fact that, although the two countries share much in terms of language, culture, religion and ethnicity, other nations also play a salient role in Indonesia–Malaysia relations, including Singapore, the United States and their former colonial rulers, namely the British and the Dutch. We have focused on people-to-people and government-to-government ties while emphasising the many transnational flows. In this regard, we have examined the role of trade and tourism as well as the flow of material cultures represented in forms such as books, films and textiles. In almost every chapter we have mentioned labour migration. While this chapter does not directly address the micro-histories of particular Indonesian migrant workers in Malaysia (see, for instance, Garcés-Mascareñas 2012; Jones 2000; Ford 2006), it will explore a few of the key issues at the macro level that arise when we consider the migrant worker question. One of these is the difference in the way that Indonesia and Malaysia treat the issue of foreign workers, which has an impact not only on their bilateral relationship but also on regional dynamics more widely. In this sense, this chapter considers the Indonesia–Malaysia migrant labour question in terms of the whole Southeast Asian region and its shared colonial history. Ironically, as we argue in this chapter, taking a regional perspective brings into sharper focus a fundamental theme: domestic politics significantly influence regional efforts to improve the human rights and working conditions of migrant workers. The fact that Indonesia and Malaysia are so different in their domestic politics and attitudes assumes, therefore, a much greater level of importance than might otherwise be expected. This has a profound impact on the Southeast Asian region, which is felt as much in the dynamics of regional integration as in Indonesia–Malaysia bilateral politics.

Regional integration theory, which has grown exponentially in recent years, tends to highlight the causal links between democracy and regional integration. Many scholars have examined the impact of regional organisations on democratic transition and the consolidation of new democracies (see, for example, Pevehouse 2005; Schimmelfennig and Sedelmeier 2005; Featherstone and Radaelli 2003).

Much less frequently studied are the democratisation of regional organisations and the impact of democracy on regional integration. Some scholars have identified domestic interest groups and political parties as drivers of regional integration. In the context of European regional integration, Haas (1958) and Moravcsik (1993) have highlighted the role of business associations as major domestic agents spurring regionalism. The broad conclusion is that a pluralistic and democratic political order provides the best conditions for voluntary groups to thrive and influence governmental decisions on regional decision-making. But democracy does not necessarily translate to greater regional integration, especially when nationalism becomes an all-consuming focus. According to Snyder's 'nationalist elite persuasion' hypothesis (Snyder 2000), budding democracies are particularly susceptible to nationalist impulses, which can potentially hamstring or even railroad efforts to enhance deeper regional integration. Two factors can account for this phenomenon – the historical legacy of the colonial experience, and the mode of democratic transition.

Rüland (2009) explores Snyder's approach in the context of Indonesia and the problematic relationship between its democratic consolidation and its regional behaviour. The Indonesian case is particularly illuminating, according to Rüland (2009), as both the colonial experience and the mode of democratic transition have ensured that Indonesia's democracy is susceptible to a strong nationalist rhetoric. As Rüland (2009: 377) observes:

> In countries which, like Indonesia, had to fight a war of independence, and where independence was associated with great human and material loss, nationalist ideology tends to be deeply entrenched in the collective memory. Therefore, any group that exposes itself to doubts about its patriotism, jeopardizes mass support.

Indonesia's strong nationalist orientation has meant that in the postcolonial era all political parties or non-governmental groups have tended to espouse a nationalist rhetoric, even parties representing political Islam (Rüland 2009: 377). In the post-authoritarian era Indonesia's foreign policy is also squarely framed by a strong nationalist rhetoric (Clark 2011; Clark and Pietsch 2012). Subsequently, Indonesia's bilateral relations with its immediate neighbours, such as Malaysia, are often subject to populist appeals and fearmongering amongst competing political elites (Efantino and Arifin 2009; Susilo 2009; Usman and Din 2009a). Yet somewhat ironically, in Indonesia, political players whose agreement is needed to effect change in a democracy – such as the legislature and civil society organisations – may also on occasion publicly support norms that have the potential to promote the deepening of regional integration (Rüland 2009: 378). According to Rüland (2009: 378), 'Indonesian legislators and civil society representatives have been vocal adherents of majority decisions, democracy, and human rights, that is norms with the capacity to markedly transform and deepen ASEAN cooperation'. Consequently, calls for political reform among ASEAN's members are very much a part of a nationalist discourse; calls for Indonesian regional leadership are also part of this discourse (Rüland 2009: 378).

In contrast to Rüland's approach, this chapter downplays the role of the nationalist discourse as a factor in Indonesia's regional behaviour. We argue instead that Indonesian dissatisfaction with ASEAN, and calls for a more democratic ASEAN, are a by-product of Indonesia's embrace of democracy. While there is no doubt that Indonesia's historically entrenched nationalist ideology is a fundamental element of the political environment, we argue that it is the public's support for democracy that is leading to Indonesia's changing regional behaviour, which is characterised by a greater concern for regional leadership and the human rights of Indonesian citizens, especially expatriate migrant workers. Although a broad range of issues will be discussed, the focus of this chapter is on what is arguably one of the key issues underpinning the nexus between democracy, human rights and regionalism in the region – that of migrant labour, and of Indonesian migrant labour in Malaysia in particular.

The first part of this chapter examines the contours of regional integration in Southeast Asia and of its impact on Indonesia–Malaysia relations. The second part examines why Indonesian migrant workers are regarded as a national security threat in the receiving country of Malaysia. The third part will extend this discussion by examining the way in which in Indonesia labour migration problems can be more accurately categorised as a human security issue rather than, as in the case of Malaysia, a national security issue. This is important because Indonesia appears more determined than Malaysia to seek a regional solution to the migrant labour issue. Indonesia's differing attitude to the issue, it will be argued, is to some extent a reflection of Indonesia's successful transition to democracy. The final section suggests that the transformation in Indonesia's regional behaviour has not necessarily triggered a closer relationship with Malaysia; nor has it encouraged a deepening of regional integration.

Regional integration and Indonesia–Malaysia relations

Moves towards developing regional integration, or rather, more formalised intra-regional co-operation, are often limited by the need to reconcile differences in history, culture, religion and politics (Fawn 2009). As a result, understanding domestic cultural and political factors in regionalism, while necessary, is complicated by the reality that these two factors are both a major driving force and an obstacle to regionalism. Democracy – or the lack thereof – is one aspect of the complexity. For example, while ASEAN has been relatively successful in the fields of security and economics, in terms of democratisation, Southeast Asia has long had a reputation of being, to quote Emmerson (1995: 227), the 'most recalcitrant region', resisting democratising processes and their comparative analysis (Case 2009: 255). Although Emmerson (2008) now looks on democracy's advance in Southeast Asia with greater optimism, there is very little agreement within the region on cultural and political issues that underpin processes of democratisation and governance (Dosch 2008; Jetschke and Rüland 2009). Some of these issues include the environment, human rights and labour migration, all of which are important human security concerns (Arifianto 2009; Dosch 2008; Katsumata 2009). Trans-border haze pollution and population movements within Southeast Asia, which can be regarded as regional problems, are among many issues that have an impact on regional integration (Caballero-Anthony 2008; Tay 2008).

An understanding of the link between democracy and the differing political attitudes of member countries of ASEAN, such as Indonesia and Malaysia, is also crucial in understanding the degree of regional integration in the region. Yet domestic politics and domestic political attitudes are often neglected as key elements in understanding Southeast Asian regional dynamics (Dosch 2008: 70). To take just one issue – say, labour migration – the contrasting outlooks and attitudes of Indonesia and Malaysia can to some extent be explained by varying levels of the diffusion of democratic values at the domestic level, which then flow through to the regional level of decision-making. In practice, the more democratic countries in the region, including Indonesia, have been more active in introducing liberal agendas to ASEAN diplomacy, which have included calls for political reform and for the greater involvement of more nongovernment actors in regional decision-making (Katsumata 2009; Sukma 2008, 2009). For Indonesia, the challenge lies in developing regional policies to address the key human security issues, such as the provision of migrants' rights in the sending and receiving countries in the region.

At the height of Indonesia's democratic transition period, between 1998 and 2004, its ASEAN neighbours were becoming increasingly circumspect. Quite apart from regional annoyances such as the perennial smoke rising from Indonesian forest fires spreading to neighbouring countries (Tay 2008), Indonesia's self-styled role as a 'normative power', according to Rüland (2009: 379), 'was regarded by fellow ASEAN members as a dual threat: it nurtures apprehension about Indonesian hegemony in ASEAN and, especially in non-democratic ASEAN member states, fears of an erosion of domestic political stability'. Yet in recent times almost all nations in the region have benefited from Indonesia's transition to democracy, which has to some extent been 'projected' into the region (Sukma 2008, 2009). On the one hand, Indonesia has been relatively frank and robust in its criticisms of ASEAN, urging its members to consider seriously the benefits of political reform, widely regarded as a euphemism for democratisation (see, for instance, Sukma 2008, 2009). On the other hand, Indonesia has rediscovered a strong international orientation above and beyond the immediate Southeast Asian region. The Indonesian government has been at pains to argue that the two foreign policy spheres are not mutually exclusive. Proving the old Indonesian saying that one can whistle while one walks (*bersiul sambil berjalan*), the Indonesian government consistently asserts that its more global foreign policy orientation has not come at any cost to its policy towards its immediate region. Indonesia's support for ASEAN has remained steadfast and, if anything, strengthened, as was manifested particularly during Indonesia's chairing of ASEAN in 2011, when Indonesia enjoyed a number of notable successes, such as its mediation in escalating border tensions between Thailand and Cambodia and, after several years of mentorship, its oversight of Burma's first steps towards democratic reform. Relations between the leaders of Indonesia and Burma are now quite close and the Indonesian media proudly claims that Burma's recent steps towards democratic progress have almost single-handedly arisen through the influence of ASEAN, lit by Indonesia's guiding light (see, for instance, Riady 2012).

Given Indonesia's preeminent role in ASEAN, it is useful to reiterate the importance of examining the testy relationship between Indonesia and Malaysia. It has often been argued by scholars of the international politics of Southeast Asia that Indonesia and Malaysia are cornerstone members of ASEAN and are thus at the very heart of questions of regional security (Liow 2005). Furthermore, it has often been acknowledged along the corridors of power in ASEAN that, together with Singapore, Indonesia and Malaysia form the security core of Southeast Asia. The Indonesia–Malaysia bilateral relationship also reveals a great deal about the domestic politics of each nation. In relation to this it is worth reiterating that the Indonesia–Malaysia bilateral relationship has seldom been harmonious for any extended period of time. In recent years, as we have argued, growing anti-Malaysia resentment amongst the Indonesian population has led to a widespread public outcry against Malaysia, as well as calls to halt the flow of migrant workers from Indonesia to Malaysia temporarily (Efantino and Arifin 2009; Lazuardi 2009; Usman and Din 2009a). As we revealed in Chapter 3, cultural heritage contestations, while peaking in 2008 and 2009, have not helped to improve relations. The tit-for-tat rumours, such as the quite unfounded claim that the melody of the Malaysian national anthem was inspired by the tune of an old Indonesian *keroncong* song, have also been unhelpful. The charge that several Malaysian tourism campaigns incorporated footage of Indonesian cultural forms was also much ado about nothing. In general, 'overblown' is probably the best way to describe the recent testiness between the two countries. For many, the deeper historical roots to the Indonesia–Malaysia enmity lie in the events of 1963–66 when Indonesia launched its anti-Malaysia policy, *Konfrontasi* (Mackie 1974; Jones 2002). Others have highlighted the ongoing border dispute over Ambalat as a major source of conflict (Liow 2005; Efantino and Arifin 2009). Indeed, Rüland (2009: 392) claims that the Ambalat territorial dispute is currently the most vexing problem in Indonesia–Malaysia relations. The Ambalat controversy is certainly vexatious, as are the cultural heritage spats. But the migrant worker issue, more than any other, has negatively affected the relationship between the citizens and governments of Indonesia and Malaysia. It also reveals a great deal about the domestic politics of each country and their regional orientation, and has important implications for the relationship between democracy and regional integration.

The second biggest transnational migration centre: Southeast Asia

Within the last few decades, transnational labour migration has become a contentious political issue in many countries across the globe – nowhere more so than in the United States whose border with Mexico is the busiest transnational migration centre in the world. The second busiest is Southeast Asia, and Malaysia is its epicentre. Migrant workers now constitute a fifth of the total workforce. Moreover, Malaysia is second to the United States on the list of the world's top receiving countries for undocumented migrants (Arifianto 2009). Existing studies on transnational migration in Southeast Asia have tended to view it primarily from the perspective of economics (Jones 2000; Kaur 2005), although there is growing interest in gender and human rights (Ford 2006; Garcés-Mascareñas 2012). There is now a small but growing body of work on labour migration as a security problem between Indonesia and Malaysia, with an emphasis on how Malaysian politicians have shifted their treatment of Indonesian migrants from a policy of tolerance to one that considers them a security threat against Malaysian society (Arifianto 2009; Chin 2008; Liow 2003). This chapter takes a step beyond these few studies analysing labour migration from a security perspective, and suggests that, coupled with differing levels of democracy in the region, the labour migration problem in Southeast Asia has important implications for regional co-operation.

The recent securitisation of Indonesian migrant workers in Malaysia is a bitter pill for many Indonesians to swallow. For much of the last century Indonesian workers were welcomed in Malaysia, mainly because they shared the racial, linguistic and religious background of the Malays (Arifianto 2009; Ford 2006; Raharto 2007). Large-scale migration from Indonesia to Malaysia first occurred in the early twentieth century, when the British colonial government decided to recruit workers from the Dutch East Indies, especially from the island of Java, for plantation work. The rationale behind this decision was that the Javanese would easily assimilate with the local Malay society and become more productive workers because of the cultural and religious traditions they shared with their Malay counterparts. In the decades after independence, the Malaysian government continued to encourage the migration of Indonesian workers to Malaysia. Because Indonesians were perceived as coming from the same ethnic and religious background as the Malays and would, therefore, assimilate easily, many thought that the Malays' electoral strength could be strengthened over that of other ethnic groups in Malaysia, namely the Chinese and Indians.

From the early 1970s, economic factors went hand in hand with the political motivation behind Indonesian migration to Malaysia. As manufacturing grew, Malaysia experienced a wave of urbanisation, which gave rise to labour shortages in the agricultural sector. Overseas workers, mainly from Indonesia, helped fill the labour shortages, first of all in the agricultural sector and then in the manufacturing sector in the late 1970s and 1980s. Since the Asian economic crisis of the late 1990s, Malaysia has experienced an impressive

construction boom, especially in and around Kuala Lumpur, which has generated a demand for labour that Indonesians and other migrant workers have
been essential in meeting. As the numbers of Indonesians entering Malaysia
increased over the years, particularly in the years immediately after the Asian
economic crisis, fears emerged of the potential for the Indonesian migrants to
significantly disturb or even rupture the fabric of Malaysian society. The
Malaysian government and media highlighted the fact that the influx of
Indonesian labour in Malaysia had coincided with an increase in crime rates,
particularly in the late 1990s. Unfortunately, Malaysia's increasing intolerance
of the criminal activities of illegal migrants has given rise to social prejudice
against legal, documented workers as well. In the last decade the Malaysian
media and government have become particularly vitriolic in their attacks on
Indonesian migrant 'troublemakers' (Arifianto 2009; Ford 2006; Raharto
2007). As we described in the previous chapter, there was an unprecedented
change in Malaysian policy towards migrant labour after 2001, which had a
marked anti-Indonesia stance. By 2002, Indonesian workers in Malaysia had
become demonised as regular perpetrators of crimes and potential perpetrators of terrorist activity, and, therefore, as threats to Malaysian national
security (Arifianto 2009). After we had conducted many ad-hoc interviews
with Indonesian migrants and migrant workers in preparation for this book,
it became quite clear to us that Indonesians are to this day treated as inferior
beings in Malaysia and the perception of Indonesians as security threats has
not abated with the passage of time.

Indonesia's desecuritisation of the migrant labour issue

Malaysia's securitisation of the Indonesian migrant problem has been greeted
with dismay in Indonesia. There have been many protest rallies outside the
Malaysian embassy in Jakarta, criticising Malaysia for their degrading treatment
of Indonesian workers. Malaysian flags have been burnt and headlines in
Jakarta newspapers have warned the Malaysian government of the dangers of
a new *Konfrontasi*. In 2009 a large group of *preman* (pseudo-militia) in Jakarta
declared an invasion on Malaysia and conducted sweepings of Malaysian
citizens in Indonesia. Nevertheless, the popular jingoistic imagining of Malaysia as a racist, ungrateful cad has not resulted in Malaysia emerging as a
threat to Indonesia's national security. On the other hand, some politicians
reportedly joined the *gerakan ganyang Malaysia* (movement to crush Malaysia)
as their response to the 2009 Ambalat-related tensions. Others such as Chozin
Chumaidy (PPP), Jeffrey Massie (PDS), Permadi (PDI-P), Yusron Ihza
Mahendra (PBB) and Soeripto (PKS) recommended the use of force should
diplomatic means not lead to solutions acceptable to Indonesia. Others called
for the recall of the Malaysian ambassador. In reference to the 2009 Ambalat
territorial tensions in particular, President Susilo Bambang Yudhoyono
pointedly stated: 'We will not sacrifice our sovereignty, our rights and our
territory' (Rüland 2009: 393), but at the same time he urged restraint, despite

the heated public debate. Both sides subsequently expressed their firm intention to resolve the Ambalat dispute peacefully and in line with established ASEAN norms of conflict resolution. The Indonesian navy took steps to de-escalate the tensions in the area and the foreign ministry stepped up efforts to enter into negotiations with the Malaysians, but in spite of 14 rounds of government negotiations (Rüland 2009: 393), the dispute remains unresolved. Nevertheless, as we have suggested in previous chapters, Indonesia's overblown reaction to Malaysia's alleged provocations is probably little more than an expression of hurt pride, albeit infused with a strong dose of nationalist sentiment. Pride and national sentiment are both emotional tropes, we would suggest, that can position the individual within a broad social order, and can ultimately be traced back to the colonial encounter.

Indonesians are keenly aware of their role in Malaysia's development and industrial success. Consequently, Malaysia's cavalier treatment of migrant workers has not been taken kindly in Indonesian circles, particularly because Indonesia expects some measure of sympathy from their Malay counterparts who, as revealed in Chapter 1, are widely regarded as *bangsa serumpun* (of the one tree or racial stock). As a result, the harmonious *gotong royong* (mutual help) spirit that defined relations between the two countries in the early years after *Konfrontasi* seems to have disappeared (Liow 2005). For many Indonesians, the *persaudaraan* (familial or sibling) relationship often mentioned by politicians from both countries, and the awareness that Malaysia and Indonesia are both members of ASEAN seem not to have ensured any extra effort on Malaysia's part (Arifianto 2009). Considering that the two 'kin states' have long been regarded as 'blood brothers', Indonesia expects Malaysia to show much greater sensitivity and even deference to its much larger and more powerful neighbour (Liow 2005). Although this is patently not forthcoming, it would be wrong to suggest that Indonesia has securitised Malaysia. Instead, if anything, Jakarta has tended to desecuritise the situation by pulling back from foreign-policy brinkmanship and focusing on what many politicians regard as the fundamental issue – the human rights of Indonesian workers in Malaysia. It is for this reason that the heated cultural contestations between the two countries, as well as the ongoing border tensions, have been quite easy for the Indonesian government to ignore.

Instead of escalating the bilateral tensions, the Indonesian government has focused on government-to-government negotiations, developing bilateral agreements and the possibility of enlisting regional intervention. A great deal of tension over the migrant worker issue dissipated after the breakthrough bilateral agreement of 2004, which sought to impose a minimum wage for Indonesian migrant workers, despite the fact that Malaysia has never set a minimum wage (Arifianto 2009). It also put in place procedures to recruit Indonesian migrant workers and requires employers of migrant workers and the brokers taking them to Malaysia to pay for their transportation costs to and from Malaysia. Agreements of this type have been criticised by non-government groups and activists, of course, who argue that they have many shortcomings and leave many issues unaddressed. According to Alex Ong, the Kuala Lumpur-based director of Migrant Care, an independent advocate for the rights of Indonesian migrant workers, these agreements are mere 'token gestures' and Indonesian migrant workers remain as disempowered as ever (Ong 2010). In reporting the problems experienced by Indonesian citizens working in Middle Eastern countries, reference is often made to the fact that little can be done for them through official channels (Bangun 2010), which heightens the sense of inefficacy of Indonesian government measures to protect its citizens abroad. The Indonesian government has argued consistently that a bilateral MoU is needed and its May 2011 MoU with Malaysia, modest as it is, is seen as the best way of addressing Malaysia's poor treatment of migrant workers. While we were conducting fieldwork for this chapter during 2010, the MoU was still in the pipeline. We interviewed Ong at length in Kuala Lumpur before it had been signed and his response was succinct: 'Despite the many shortcomings of such MoU agreements, they are still better than the alternative, which is nothing'.

Other commentators have also pointed out that these forms of agreements, accords and MoUs are not perfect – many workers, particularly undocumented workers, continue to be mistreated, beaten, threatened, extorted and deported on a daily basis – but they are better than nothing (Bangun 2010). Moreover, the Indonesian government has proven that it is prepared to forego considerable remittance earnings from migrant workers, estimated to be US $7.1 billion in 2010, by enforcing moratoria on the sending of migrant workers until their rights and conditions are able to be significantly improved in the receiving country (Hamzirwan 2010). Demonstrating its readiness to take a stand, the Indonesian government enforced a moratorium between June 2009 and April 2010 on Indonesian migrants travelling to work in Malaysia. This was used as an opportunity for the Indonesian government to lobby the Malaysian government for more humane treatment of Indonesian workers, particularly in informal employment sectors such as domestic service. Efforts were also made to formalise the right of Indonesian domestic workers to one day off from work per week, as well as the right to retain possession of their passports, rather than hand them over to their employer. During the same period, plans were reportedly afoot to develop a sort of Indonesian Social Security Program, which would formalise discussions on ensuring that Indonesian workers are met at the airport by their employer, have automatic access to legal assistance, are registered on an online system, have access to counseling and a 24-hour call-centre, as well as automatic insurance (Bangun 2010).

Of equal importance is ASEAN's step towards the enactment of a regional agreement, through the Cebu Declaration on the Protection and Promotion of the Rights of Migrant Workers, adopted in January 2007. It called for ASEAN members to develop a common standard or charter on migrant workers' rights that would apply to all ASEAN members. Basically the goal was to promote the welfare of migrant workers and improve their access to avenues of justice (Arifianto 2009). The Cebu declaration contains a number of limitations, however. The declaration, like many declarations or statements issued by ASEAN, was short on specifics and contained some 'escape clauses' that provided room for member countries to interpret the declaration in their own way (Arifianto 2009: 626). Also, it is phrased in terms of the obligations of sending countries, rather than in terms of the individual rights of migrant workers. Moreover, these obligations are subject to the prevailing laws, regulations and policies of each sending and receiving state. Nevertheless, the commitment of ASEAN to develop a legally binding charter on the protection and promotion of the rights of migrant workers and the adoption of the Declaration itself are significant developments (Cholewinski 2010: 288). It was, after all, the first time ASEAN had developed a common framework for the promotion of migrant workers throughout Southeast Asia. Of course, there is a long road ahead before ASEAN members can fully agree to the terms of a binding agreement and tensions between labour-sending countries such as Indonesia and labour-receiving countries such as Malaysia will no doubt persist.

Ultimately, Indonesia's transition to democracy, accompanied by an increasingly international outlook, appears to be resulting in a more concerted effort to deal with regional human security issues, such as the treatment of migrant labour, using regional governance. Democracy has also ensured that the Indonesian government is much more prepared to incorporate Track II and Track III diplomacy in its regional decision-making. This is a significant development as some grassroots migrant labour nongovernment organisations have worked hard to develop organisations that can speak directly for migrant workers. For example, as described by Ford and Susilo (2010), in addition to the efforts of these migrant workers' groups:

> NGO workers have begun to use the legal system to put pressure on the government to better meet the needs of the country's migrant workers. For example, in 2002 they organised a class action lawsuit against the Indonesian government following the deportation of almost 140,000 undocumented migrant workers from the Malaysian state of Sabah. Up to 70 deported migrant workers died in the border town of Nunukan and thousands more suffered from serious illnesses, including dysentery and malaria because of the simple fact that the Indonesian government was unprepared for their arrival. The court recognised the government's negligence in the first instance before the decision was overturned on appeal. Even though it failed, this initiative set an important precedent for Indonesian public law, with civilians beginning to use the legal system to sue the state for deliberate failures to provide essential public services.

Subsequently, the Indonesian government has actively incorporated the opinions and input of NGO groups and other nongovernment actors in the regional decision-making process (Oratmangun 2009). Indeed, committed as it is to the key principles of democracy, the government has little choice. Moreover, as part of a newly democratic nation, Indonesian citizens are increasingly well informed about Indonesia's regional engagement. Indonesian citizens and nongovernment actors, frustrated by being continuously locked out of the elite talkfests of ASEAN's summit diplomacy, are also increasingly articulate in expressing their desire to be involved in intra-regional political participation (Suryodiningrat 2004; Sukma 2008).

In addition to Indonesia's apparent commitment to democratic public deliberation processes, Jakarta's signing of the Cebu Declaration is an emphatic signal of the government's preparedness to regionalise the labour migration issue. Academics and nongovernment lobbyists have consistently warned the government that the transnational migrant labour issue is now a regional issue, which is unnecessarily straining diplomatic relations between labour-sending and labour-receiving nations in the region, as we have seen in the last decade between Indonesia and Malaysia (Arifianto 2009). The best way to avoid potential conflict between labour-sending and labour-receiving countries, they propose, is to regionalise the issue, so that a common standard can be applied to the recruitment of migrant workers and the protection of their rights from abusive employers and premature deportation. It is also intrinsically important that Indonesia's labour migration problems with Malaysia are generally regarded as a regional human security or human rights issue and not as a national security issue as it is in Malaysia. This is because a human security framework has the potential to raise the issue above and beyond the domestic sphere and thus above the neo-nationalistic vagaries of competing political voices. This change in focus, however, as with the recent transformation of Indonesia's foreign policy orientation, is not necessarily enhancing regional integration. Indonesia's neighbours are simply not ready for it. Despite the previously discussed benefits of Indonesia's more outward-looking foreign policy orientation, other countries in the region continue to raise their eyebrows. On the one hand, middle powers such as Singapore and Malaysia have remained stoically bemused by Indonesia's at times rather painful political transformation. This is in spite of the cold hard truth of the matter, which is that Indonesia, according to the independent watchdog Freedom House, is now Southeast Asia's only truly 'free' and democratic nation. On the other hand, Indonesia's neighbours are fearful of an ASEAN without Indonesia's full participation or engagement, as they have much to lose from a devalued ASEAN.

ASEAN and Indonesia's post-new order regional imaginary

According to some, divisions between ASEAN's member states undermine ASEAN's supposed unity (Sukma 2009). But the truth is, ASEAN has faced many such divisions and their resulting tensions before and, no doubt, will face them in the future as well. The border dispute between Thailand and Cambodia, for instance, virtually derailed the 2011 ASEAN Summit; the 2012 ASEAN and East Asia Summit were dominated by the South China Sea dispute involving Vietnam, the Philippines and China. Long before this dispute and others like it, such as those over Ambalat and the islands of the South China Sea, Colbert (1986), and later Narine (1998) argued that the continued existence of intra-regional territory disputes disqualified Southeast Asia from being a security community. Nevertheless, ASEAN's unity remains intact, despite occasional differences of opinion, sometimes aggressively expressed. According to Kasim (2005: 3), territorial disputes such as Ambalat are actually of little consequence:

> Rizal Sukma, writing in the Jakarta Post, noted how ASEAN has been absent as an institution throughout this troubled period. There has not been any significant effort from ASEAN to help defuse the tension, he said. At the height of the Ambalat dispute, some Indonesian legislators even called for the disbanding of ASEAN. That is surely an extreme position to take. Why disband ASEAN just because Indonesia, the group's largest member, is embroiled in bilateral disputes with its neighbours? It was, after all, Indonesia that paved the way for the creation of ASEAN in 1967 soon after the end of Konfrontasi in 1965. It should now lead the way to take ASEAN into the future, not dismantle it.

Since the initial stages of the Ambalat dispute, the now fully democratic Indonesia has been keen to lead ASEAN in a fresh direction while also hinting that it has bigger fish to fry. Most obviously, while remaining openly critical of ASEAN's many shortcomings, Indonesia has rediscovered a strong international orientation. In a 2010 speech, Susilo Bambang Yudhoyono (SBY), declared that Indonesia is now ready to embrace an 'All Directions' foreign policy where Indonesia can achieve its aim of 'a million friends, zero enemies' (*sejuta kawan, tanpa musuh*) (Yudhoyono 2010). Paving the way for these statements, besides success with the G20 and the United Nations Climate Change Conference of 2009, Indonesia has earned itself great kudos for establishing the Bali Democracy Forum, with its goal of nurturing the practice of democracy and good governance between the countries of the Asia-Pacific region. Also, in March 2010, SBY addressed the parliament of Australia, one of very few foreign leaders ever to do so; his speech was a warmly received speech and broadcast live on national television. The highlight of his speech was his call for Australia and Indonesia to add more depth and nuance to their bilateral ties, in order to have a more 'fair dinkum' relationship (Yudhoyono 2010). This use of a uniquely Australian colloquialism, in particular, struck a chord with the gathered politicians and news media. Few other nations in the region are making positive diplomatic waves in the style of those that Indonesia is currently making and enjoying the benefits of.

In terms of practical initiatives, Indonesia has willingly embraced its role as Southeast Asia's sole representative in the influential G20. Indonesia has also given much greater consideration to its self-perceived global obligations, such as adopting international human rights standards and increasing its contributions to global efforts to mitigate climate change and support more sustainable paths to development. Indonesia is also pressing ahead with its ongoing involvement in the global war on terrorism. Indeed, reflecting on Indonesia's success, in October 2010 the incoming Indonesian ambassador to Washington boasted that Indonesia's counterterrorism efforts to capture and neutralise terrorist networks have been 'an outstanding success' (Sheridan 2010). This is important because according to some international terrorism experts, in the decade after 9/11, Southeast Asia was the second front if not the global epicentre of international terrorism (Thayer 2008). In Thayer's words (2008: 257), 'Islam in contemporary Southeast Asia undoubtedly has been influenced by global Islamic political currents shaped by modern communications and technology'. Of course, we should not forget the role of Indonesia's colonial past; Islamic strains of anti-Westernism have pervaded the region for centuries, indeed ever since the Europeans arrived. The impact of the colonial experience needs to be factored into the equation, especially as, according to the polls conducted by the Pew Research Center over the past few years, anti-Western sentiments are growing rapidly among Muslims all over the world, especially in Southeast Asia (Kivimaki 2008). As a result, radical Islam and political terrorism are often seen as counterforces against globalisation, which is assumed to be a Western-led phenomenon.

Indonesia's counterterrorism effort is also part of a global effort. In the words of Kivimaki (2008: 231), 'international terrorism and international counter-terrorism are two parts of a global battle between two very different coalitions applying global opportunities for the promotion of their goals against each other'. Nevertheless, with specific reference to Southeast Asia, global discourses, such as the American 'global war on terrorism' must be tempered by local specifics. As Fealy and Thayer observe, domestic factors are crucial when evaluating the nexus between international and regional terrorist organisations, as 'a single template cannot be used to view different *jihadist* groups across the many regions of the world' (Fealy and Thayer 2009: 227). Adding an extra layer of complexity to the situation, once again we return to the key argument of this study: the impact of the postcolonial condition also needs to be taken into consideration. Indeed, the much-maligned Huntington 'clash of civilisations' metaphor was useful insofar as it highlighted both the widespread hostility of the Islamic world towards the West as well as the initial wellspring of the Islamic challenge: colonialism. According to O'Hagan (2000: 141), the Islamic hostility to the West is often 'conceived of as embedded in ancient cultural and religious antipathy aggravated by envy of Western success, the legacy of imperialism and the social dynamics of contemporary Islamic societies'. In Indonesia, there are long-standing undercurrents of antipathy and envy towards the West, the roots of which are no doubt the centuries of often-harsh Dutch colonial rule. The various legacies of imperialism are also centuries old, even if many Indonesian old-timers actually look upon the Dutch with nostalgia. The social dynamics of contemporary Indonesian Muslim groups, of course, are complex, and there can be no doubt that a subtle – and sometimes none-too-subtle – strain of anti-Westernism peppers the average Muslim sermon delivered on a typical Friday lunchtime.

Despite the challenge of Indonesia's radical Islamist groups, who are essentially anti-West, the various initiatives described above, it could be argued, are designed to garner the favour of the United States. Indonesians, who are as a nation unabashed admirers of American President Barack Obama (who spent several years of his childhood living in Menteng Dalam, a suburb of Jakarta), were keenly awaiting the on-again off-again 2010 Presidential visit. The visit finally occurred in November 2010 and was universally regarded as a success. Films, novels, art exhibitions, statues, and numerous essays and edited collections devoted to commemorating 'Barry' Obama's Jakarta sojourn have emerged in the last few years. Besides the President's well-known personal reasons for a return to the Indonesian archipelago, the United States is anxious to shore up its previous hegemonic standing in the Pacific and the Southeast Asian region in particular, which fits in neatly with the logic of critics of the supposedly 'imperialist' behaviour of the United States, its military, and its administration. The contemporary discourse of empire, of course, is a phenomenon born out of the Bush era of United States foreign policy, which has stimulated much criticism of the way in which the United States Administration treated its allies and foes.

With Indonesia's increasingly global orientation and self-styled leadership role within ASEAN, other countries in the region have remained circumspect, if not apprehensive (Rüland 2009: 379). Nevertheless, Indonesia is still seen as the key regional power in the international relations of Southeast Asia. Singapore, on the one hand, is increasingly uncomfortable with Indonesia's growing stature on the world stage, seemingly at the cost of an ASEAN focus. On the other hand, for Singapore, an ASEAN without Indonesia – which by implication would mean the death of ASEAN – would be a major calamity, as ASEAN has served Singapore's business and security interests well and has allowed Singapore to play a major strategic role in the region. Likewise, although initially unimpressed by Indonesia's increasingly blatant criticism of Burma's poor human rights record, the Burmese ruling regime has gradually warmed to Indonesia's 'brotherly' advocacy of democracy in Burma. Meanwhile, Thailand, with its important cross-border trading links with Burma and its allies, including Laos, must remain silent in the face of Indonesia's out-spokenness. Malaysia, which, as we know, has a tendency to patronise its much larger and poorer neighbour, throws in Indonesia's direction the occasional barbed comment about the haphazard nature of Indonesia's democratic consolidation. Nevertheless, despite ongoing irritants such as border disputes, forest fire haze and the migrant worker issue, Malaysia is determined to keep Indonesia on side. Regional circumspection notwithstanding, the transfor-mation of Indonesia's domestic political situation is reverberating throughout the region. Whether the reverberation will translate to a shift in attitude towards upholding the human rights of Indonesia's army of migrant workers remains to be seen.

Conclusion

In Southeast Asia, the causal links between democracy and regional integration, and *vice versa*, are not immediately discernible. Democratisation in founding member countries of ASEAN, such as Indonesia, the Philippines and Thailand and, less markedly, Malaysia and Singapore, has not triggered a deepening of regional integration. Key causal factors for this are the political diversity in the Southeast Asia region and the varying levels of democracy in particular. As a consequence, key regional issues such as intra-regional migrant labour flows, epitomised by the large numbers of Indonesian migrant workers in Malaysia, have failed to find a regional solution. Yet Indonesia's successful transition to democracy has led to stronger efforts to seek a regional solution to complex regional human security issues. The human rights of Indonesian migrant workers in the region are now an issue that the Indonesian government, as it becomes more democratic and broadens its regional foreign policy orientation, is more determined to deal with, both domestically and regionally.

Democratic Indonesia's enlightened approach to human rights has been stymied by its neighbour's intransigence. Malaysia, the country that receives most of Indonesia's migrant workers, continues to regard the migrant worker issue as a national security issue rather than a regional human security issue. As a human security issue it is more likely be solved through regional decision-making. As this chapter has outlined, the problem with regarding the migrant worker issue as a national security issue is that, while Malaysia's politics remains dominated by one particular political party, the primacy of national sovereignty and non-interference also remains and deeply held suspicion of concepts connected to human rights persists. Malaysia's fragile ethnic balance also tends to politicise and constrain debate on both migrant labour and immigration. In effect, weak governance structures and a lack of a compre-hensive migrant worker policy will continue to ensure that Malaysian authorities cannot enforce existing labour regulations among the many stakeholders involved in labour migration. In addition to this, Malaysia and other key ASEAN members such as Singapore regard Indonesia's calls for political reform in ASEAN and other examples of regional muscle-flexing with apprehension. This is because changes to the regional status quo could quite easily have a negative impact on the integrity of ASEAN as a whole and on the domestic stability of each ASEAN member.

In general, Indonesia's push for political reform in the region, coupled with its increasingly pro-active foreign policy orientation, has not triggered greater regional integration in Southeast Asia, seemingly giving credence to the old joke that meetings are held to ensure that nothing changes. Similarly, Indonesia's key regional partners, such as Malaysia and Singapore, are becoming increasingly determined to ensure that change in the region, if it occurs, follows the so-called 'ASEAN way' and all it stands for, including consensus decision-making and non-interference in the domestic politics of member countries. Consequently, this chapter endorses Acharya's (2003) prediction that regional co-operation in Southeast Asia will not necessarily be strengthened by the emergence of democracy in the region. This is mainly due, first of all, to the varying levels of democratisation in Southeast Asia and, secondly, to Indonesia's desire to overcome ASEAN's many limitations through a rather unsubtle process of democratic projection, which is undoubtedly a result of its own domestic political change. While Indonesia's vibrant democratic progress has led to Indonesia pushing, at times rather aggressively, its case for democracy in the region, the soft-authoritarian democracies of Malaysia and Singapore, not to mention the democratic backsliders of Thailand and the Philippines, have ensured that democracy has not yet become the golden key that opens all locks. According to Don Emmerson (2008: 81), it is the degree of democracy in the region which is the problem: 'Too few countries are democratic enough for their leaders to exert effective pressure on the association to liberalize its traditional ASEAN Way – decisions by consensus, the sovereignty of states, acquiescence in what they do or fail to do – by incorporating into its agenda the defense of human rights and freedoms and the promotion of democracy in Southeast Asia'. Having examined the key themes in the migrant worker debate, including rights, freedom and citizenship, in the final chapter of this book we explore in more depth what some regard as a solution to the migrant labour stand-off and to a host of other issues – democratisation. Will Indonesia ever be democratic enough to 'rock ASEAN's boat', to borrow Emmerson's phrase (2008: 81), and will Malaysia ever be upgraded by Freedom House from 'partly free' to 'free', as is the case with Indonesia? As we know, the region is not immune to political change, so these scenarios may well evolve, given enough time.

9 Democracy

While much has been said and written about the importance of democracy in Indonesia and Malaysia, not much has been said about support for democracy. This is an important issue, because it is often assumed that the solution to the labour migration quandary, and to other social and political concerns raised in previous chapters, is democratisation. Support for democracy is probably as important, if not more important, than the mere existence of democracy. Democracy in newly democratising countries matters little if citizens do not support their country's democratisation process (Chu *et al.* 2008; Norris 1999, 2011; Rose, Mishler and Haerpfer 1998; Shin 2011). The underlying question of this chapter, therefore, is an important one: What do everyday Indonesians and Malaysians think about democracy? The answer to this question has regional ramifications. As Emmerson (2008) suggests, the key drivers of internal political liberalisation in Southeast Asia are likely to come from within states, and not from external sources such as ASEAN, ASEAN +3, the East Asia Summit or the EU. But democratic regression in countries like Thailand, the Philippines and Cambodia, one-party dominated political systems like Malaysia and Singapore, and closed authoritarian regimes like Vietnam, Laos and Burma suggest the prognosis for political liberalisation is not good. However, if autocracy declines in some states and political pluralism is able to develop in its place – as appears to be occurring in Burma during the last few years – ASEAN will be able to play a larger, albeit still marginal, role in reflecting and facilitating those democratic trends. Indonesia, which has taken on a more proactive role in ASEAN, is leading the charge in this regard, as demonstrated by its willingness to play peacemaker in the Thailand–Cambodia border dispute and its ongoing political mentorship of Burma.

For all the huff and puff expended on the bilateral relationship between Indonesia and Malaysia, the regional space can offer significant leverage, particularly in Malaysia where domestic civil society remains under pressure. As Indonesia consolidates its democracy, the question will be whether Malaysia chooses to embrace democratic progress, stagnation or repression. An Indonesia-led ASEAN may influence this decision, even if internal factors will be the key drivers. Whatever choice Malaysia makes will greatly impact domestic opportunities for nongovernment and civil society organisations to influence the government, particularly in areas sensitive to elite interests and power, like the treatment of migrant workers.

How much support is there for democracy in Malaysia? In answering this question, we would assert that it is useful to compare, once more, the Indonesian and Malaysian case studies. Despite the much-discussed differences, there are many important similarities. As we have already argued, the denial of citizenship rights and basic human rights for minority groups is often the source of simmering tensions within and between the two countries. At times, this has led to communal violence and, in Malaysia in particular, an almost permanent state of religious and racial tension. As we have argued, ethnic tensions in both countries are largely the legacy of colonial policy. In Malaysia, for example, large numbers of Chinese, Indian and Indonesian migrant workers were brought in either directly by the British colonial administrators or by commercial agents as part of colonial plans to exploit the natural resources of the various Malay states during the nineteenth and early twentieth centuries. How these tensions are resolved in the postcolonial context depends to a large extent on how Indonesia and Malaysia navigate their political future in an increasingly interdependent globalised world. For instance, in the future, will a younger generation of Indonesians and Malaysians feel similarly about how best to respect the human rights of non-citizens and provide fair treatment for ethnic and religious minorities? Will they overcome their cultural and political differences to become part of a much more integrated region, enjoying a greater sense of community and collective identity? To answer these questions, we conclude our research by looking at what everyday Indonesians and Malaysians think about their political system and democracy.

Attitudes towards democracy

Freedom of speech, respect for human rights, and equality are just some of the expectations of a liberal democracy. When these fundamental democratic rights are neglected or denied, tension between groups may escalate and surface in unexpected places. We have illustrated how tensions between Indonesia and Malaysia and among groups within Indonesia and Malaysia can bubble away beneath the surface like an active volcano, threatening and yet at the same time maintaining a relative level of stability. As already noted, it is often assumed that the answer to some of the social and political concerns raised in previous chapters, which are common to many postcolonial countries, is democratisation (Diamond 2008; Inglehart and Welzel 2005). In this section, we find out whether democracy – as a set of reforms aimed at addressing social and political issues – actually has the support of different ethnic and religious groups in Indonesia and Malaysia.

As a result of widespread democratic reforms since the fall of Suharto, Indonesia has become the world's third largest democracy and is the only country in Southeast Asia that is considered an electoral democracy by the independent watchdog Freedom House. In contrast, Malaysia is considered as having a 'competitive authoritarian political system' (Diamond 2012). Competitive authoritarian systems tend to combine electoral competition with varying degrees of autocracy (Levitsky and Way 2002). On the surface, these types of political systems seem democratic but they tend to rely on a number of authoritarian controls to ensure the marginalisation of opposition voices and movements. One of the main reasons why political development has been slower in Malaysia than in neighbouring Indonesia is the persistence of support for authoritarian styles of leadership as an answer to managing social and economic concerns. Notwithstanding this, it is possible that a political culture of authoritarianism also exists to a certain extent in Indonesia, where support for strong leadership and a local military presence is still seen by a minority as an answer to combating ethnic and religious tensions.

Since the fall of Suharto, which was followed by widespread communal violence and economic woes, democratisation has not lived up to early expectations, especially in terms of economic performance. This is an important point to consider, because democratic performance is often evaluated in terms of citizen assessments of their economy (Bratton, Mattes and Gyimah-Boadi 2005; Mishler and Rose 1997). Indonesia has actually performed very well on indicators of economic performance. For instance, Indonesia has grown by 6 per cent annually for much of the post-2004 period, and is now on the verge of being a one-trillion-dollar economy. Nevertheless, Indonesia's performance on social indicators lags well behind that of Malaysia. Given the high levels of social and political instability accompanying Indonesia's democratic consolidation, it is not surprising that many Malaysians have looked at their Indonesian brothers and sisters and wondered whether democracy really is the solution for social and political concerns. If the Indonesian case study is their benchmark, it is quite understandable that many Malaysians think that democracy, or at least Indonesia's version of democracy, is not the answer.

The Malaysian government has traditionally viewed economic growth as essential for avoiding social and political instability, which many believe is a problem in neighbouring Indonesia. As we have seen in previous chapters, the Malaysian government prides itself on substantially raising the income of its lower-income earners in order to move towards a high-income nation. It is not always clear whether the Malaysian public views democracy as an obstacle to achieving their government's higher order priorities. Some scholars have argued that public views on democracy in Asia tend to be fairly instrumental, focusing on the ability of a system to deliver economic development rather than on the more abstract ideals associated with democracy (Chu *et al.* 2008, 2009). As Indonesia's media and civil society have opened up, however, minority groups in Malaysia, particularly the Chinese, have called for much greater attention to be paid to the democratic rights of minority groups, which suggests that instrumental views of democracy may be less widespread among minorities traditionally excluded from the political system and major institutions.

To compare attitudes towards democracy among ordinary Indonesians and Malaysians from diverse ethnic and religious backgrounds, we use the 2007 AsiaBarometer Survey, a cross-national public opinion survey that includes Indonesia and Malaysia. The AsiaBarometer surveys enable an exploration of attitudes towards a range of social and political concerns that underpin support for democracy. First, drawing on findings from the 2007 AsiaBarometer survey, we look at what Indonesians and Malaysians think of each other before we have a closer look at attitudes towards democracy. Table 9.1 presents findings derived from responses to the question 'Do you think the following countries have a good influence or a bad influence on your country?' We also include figures that indicate Indonesian and Malaysian attitudes to China and the United States to see whether there is in general a positive leaning towards the West or towards Asia.

Table 9.1 shows that 65 per cent of Indonesians report that Malaysia has a good influence on their country, but only 39 per cent of Malaysians feel the same about Indonesia. Indonesians also express a high level of support for China (46 per cent) but less support for the United States (22 per cent). It appears that the majority of Indonesians are not very confident about the influence of the West, as the negative perceptions of the influence of the United States on Indonesia suggest. Malaysians share a similar distrust of the United States, which could be attributed to their shared history of Western colonialism in addition to more contemporary issues. In contrast to Indonesia, Malaysia has a much higher opinion of China's influence on Malaysia, with 73 per cent of the population stating that China has a good influence on Malaysia. This is perhaps due to the fact that a much higher proportion of the Malaysian population is of Chinese ethnic origin, in comparison to Indonesia, where the Chinese form only a small minority, albeit with a considerable proportion of the nation's wealth. It is the Chinese enjoyment of a disproportionate share of Indonesia's wealth that is perhaps the reason why China is viewed by Indonesians as not having a good influence on their country.

In terms of what Indonesians and Malaysians think of each other, the 2007 AsiaBarometer findings are interesting. It appears that, even though Indonesia has experienced a range of democratic reforms and is well and truly on a democratic path, a significant proportion of Malaysians appear to be still

Table 9.1 Attitudes of Indonesians and Malaysians towards other countries

	Indonesia (%)	(n)	Malaysia (%)	(n)	(Difference)
Malaysia/Indonesia	65	(621)	39	(369)	(-26)
United States	22	(205)	29	(269)	(+7)
China	46	(409)	73	(677)	(+27)

Source: AsiaBarometer Surveys 2007

concerned about Indonesia's negative influence on their country. Some of this could be related to the ongoing cultural disputes, the securitisation of the Indonesian migrant worker issue, the negative effects of Indonesian forest fire haze that intermittently spreads across to Malaysia, and the Ambalat territorial dispute. However, as we may not have emphasised enough in this book, many Indonesians happily live and work in Malaysia and many have also been welcomed as citizens by the local population (see Sadiq 2005, 2009), which suggests that concerns in Malaysia towards Indonesia's influence might have more to do with the broader economic and political differences between the two countries. There may be other considerations, such as the fear of what might happen to Malaysia if it were to embrace a democracy. For instance, are Malaysians concerned that a government run by the people may not be able to effectively deal with crisis? In Malaysia, would the embrace of Indonesia's model of democracy give the Chinese and other minorities more power, thus threatening the Malays and their way of life? Before we try and answer these questions, we look at some of the main priorities for Indonesians and Malaysians that political elites and institutions are required to respond to.

Figure 9.1, which charts responses to the question 'Which, if any, of the following issues cause you great worry?', shows that Indonesians and Malaysians prioritise a number of different social and political concerns. While poverty and unemployment are significant concerns for Indonesians, in Malaysia the findings show that Malaysians are more concerned than Indonesians about a number of security concerns such as crime and illegal drugs, wars and conflict,

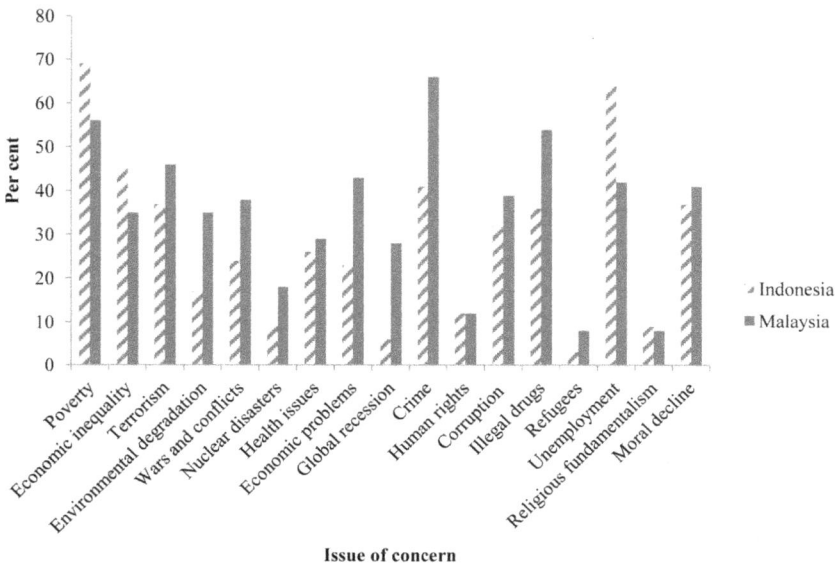

Figure 9.1 Indonesian and Malaysian attitudes towards social and political concerns.

terrorism and environmental degradation. Malaysians are also much more concerned about the state of the economy and a possible global recession.

Post-authoritarian Indonesia, as it has proceeded with the process of democratisation, has experienced a great deal of social and economic turmoil, of which high unemployment and political instability have been a part. By contrast, Malaysia's political system is characterised by very little change, fragmentation or political instability. Among the majority there is widespread public support for Malaysia's developmental approach to democracy where there appears to be no real trade-off between economic growth and democracy. It is possible that Malaysians might prefer a kind of democracy that is tempered by strong authoritarian rule that produces order and stability.

To determine how citizens evaluate the performance of governance and democracy, the AsiaBarometer asked questions that measure attitudes towards two kinds of regime performance: government performance (in terms of managing economic and social concerns) and democratic performance (in terms of satisfaction with democratic rights and freedoms). According to Chu *et al.* (2009), government and democratic performance have positive effects in most East Asian countries on citizens' beliefs about democracy and on their level of authoritarian detachment. In terms of government performance, Malaysians, although living under semi-authoritarian rule, are on the whole more confident in their government's performance in managing social and political concerns. Looking at Table 9.2, we can see that the Malaysian public are generally more confident in their government's capacity to deal with the economy, corruption, human rights, unemployment and ethnic and religious conflict. Only 29 per cent of Indonesian citizens believe that the government is handling the economy well, as opposed to 76 per cent of Malaysians. Malaysians indicate that they are less confident in their government's capacity to

Table 9.2 Citizens' evaluation of government performance

	Indonesia	Malaysia	(Difference)
	(%)	(%)	
Government is handling...well/ not well			
Economy	29	76	(+47)
Corruption	17	35	(+18)
Human rights	58	72	(+14)
Unemployment	10	36	(+26)
Crime	35	31	(-4)
Immigration	67	53	(-14)
Ethnic conflict	55	85	(+30)
Religious conflict	69	87	(+18)
Environmental problems	77	66	(-11)

Source: AsiaBarometer Surveys 2007 (N=2000).Estimates for 'well', combining 'very well' and 'fairly well' in response to the question: 'How well do you think the [Indonesian/ Malaysian] government is dealing with the following issues?'

manage immigration; only 50 per cent of Malaysians reported good management on issues of immigration, compared with 67 per cent of Indonesians. This is no doubt related to the Malaysian government's handling of the Indonesian migrant worker issue, about which many Malaysian citizens, especially those in border-zone states such as Sabah, are dissatisfied (Darwis 2012).

While it appears from our findings that the government of Malaysia garners more confidence from its citizens, one might expect Malaysians, given Malaysia's more authoritarian political system, to have less positive evaluations of the government's performance on liberal democratic rights such as the right to demonstrate and freedom of speech. In Table 9.3 we can see that Malaysians are less satisfied with the current scope of democratic rights than Indonesians, particularly in relation to the right to gather and demonstrate and the freedom of speech. In terms of the right to gather and demonstrate, 76 per cent of Indonesians are satisfied with the government's performance in this area, compared with 53 per cent of Malaysians. This represents a difference of 23 percentage points. Likewise, in terms of freedom of speech, 76 per cent of Indonesians are satisfied with their government's performance, compared with only 62 per cent of Malaysians.

Despite concerns Malaysians might have about Indonesia's democratising influence, one might expect that those who have traditionally felt excluded in Malaysia in terms of their social, cultural and political rights, mainly the ethnic Chinese, are more likely to favour democratisation because of its greater emphasis on free and fair elections, protection of human rights, freedom of speech and equal rights and opportunities for all citizens. Minorities in Malaysia are becoming increasingly vocal about their lack of social, cultural and political rights, as discussed in earlier chapters. The historically dominant position of UMNO in Malaysia has enabled the incumbent government to control the rules of the game continuously and ensure conditions on the electoral playing field favour it. While UMNO controls the electoral playing field and achieves widespread public support, there is little chance of the opposition, a significant proportion of which are Chinese who have abandoned UMNO,

Table 9.3 Citizens' evaluation of democratic performance

	Indonesia	*Malaysia*	*(Difference)*
	(%)	*(%)*	
Satisfied with the right to...			
vote	89	96	(+7)
participate in an organisation	82	88	(+6)
gather and demonstrate	76	53	(-23)
be informed about government	47	62	(+15)
freedom of speech	76	62	(-14)
criticise government	54	52	(-2)

Source: AsiaBarometer Surveys 2007 (N=2000).Estimates for 'satisfied', combining 'very satisfied' and 'satisfied' in response to the question: 'How satisfied are you with the current scope of the following rights in [YOUR COUNTRY]?'

gaining traction in a system supported by a constitution that has always favoured the Malays and their interests over the concerns of minorities.

Although UMNO is part of a multiethnic political coalition, Barisan Nasional (BN), in which the Malaysian Chinese Association (MCA) and the Malaysian Indian Congress (MIC) represent the Chinese and Indian communities, it has always, according to Freedman (2006), championed Malay supremacy. The electoral system is structured so that UMNO has traditionally enjoyed a more favourable outcome than any other party in general elections. The number of voters per elected office holder is far lower in rural Malay strongholds than in urban districts (Freedman 2006). However, even with an electoral system that favoured it, the BN secured only 140 seats in the 2008 parliamentary general election, considered by many as a disastrous result for the BN coalition, which is accustomed to securing a two-thirds majority in the Malaysian parliament. Many have argued that the BN's decline in electoral support is due to the cumulative effects of the politicisation of ethnicity and religion, which, as discussed in previous chapters, have favoured Malay Muslims over minority groups (see Scarpello 2010).

In a closer consideration of whether attitudes towards democracy are structured along religious and ethnic lines, we will now examine the survey findings, presented in Table 9.4, of citizen evaluations of government performance

Table 9.4 Satisfaction of Muslims and non-Muslims with democracy

	Muslims	Non-Muslims	(Difference)
	(%)	(%)	
Satisfied with...			
the democratic system	83	62	(−21)
the right to vote	97	95	(−2)
the right to participate in an organisation	91	84	(−7)
the right to gather and demonstrate	54	50	(−4)
the right to be informed about government	67	53	(−14)
the right to freedom of speech	65	56	(−9)
criticise government	56	45	(−11)
Trust in...to operate in best interests of the country			
central government	93	74	(−19)
the army	93	72	(−21)
the legal system	87	72	(−15)
the police	79	54	(−25)

Source: Asia Barometer Survey 2007 (N=2000). Estimates for 'satisfied', combining 'very satisfied' and 'satisfied' in response to the question, 'How satisfied are you with the current scope of the following rights in [YOUR COUNTRY]?' and estimates for 'trust', combining 'trust a lot' and 'trust a little' in response to the request, 'Please indicate to what extent you trust the following institutions to operate in the best interests of society.'

in terms of democratic rights and trust in government. The AsiaBarometer survey did not include an indicator of ethnicity so we relied on religion as a way of looking at differences between the predominantly Muslim Malays and predominantly non-Muslim non-Malays. In doing so, we recognise that there are some Chinese and Indian Malaysians and indigenous peoples who are Muslim and the occasional Malay who is not Muslim (see Chapter 5). In terms of general satisfaction with democracy, Muslims in Malaysia are 21 per cent more satisfied with the level of democracy in their country than non-Muslims. Muslims are also significantly more likely to feel satisfied with their government's current performance on other rights, such as the right to demonstrate, the right to be informed, the right to freedom of speech and the right to criticise government. In the second half of the table we can also see that Muslims also have more trust in the government and other major institutions, including the army, the police force and the legal system.

One of the main reasons why non-Muslims are more dissatisfied with the scope of democratic rights in their country is because of perceptions of an unfair electoral system and constitutional restrictions on freedom of speech, which tend to work in UMNO's favour. While parliamentary democracy implies a system of representation, the makeup of the Dewan Rekyat (House of Representatives) shows an inequitable representation between states in Malaysia. Up until 2008, the government held the two-thirds majority that was necessary for constitutional reform. The fact that UMNO has historically dominated parliament by repeatedly retaining a majority suggests that UMNO is deciding the 'rules of the game' (Ong 1987). An example of UMNO's use of its majority is seen in alterations to Malaysia's majority electoral system whereby the government has maintained a great deal of influence over the delimitation of constituencies. The Constitution (Amendment) Act of 1962 gave the Malaysian parliament the power to appoint the members of the Electoral Commission, thus ensuring high levels of influence of the party that held a majority in government. Rural constituencies have been given increased weighting in the electoral system, which, according to Crouch (1996), is significant because Malays tend to be more concentrated in rural areas and non-Malays more concentrated in urban areas.

Delimitation exercises have continued to undermine public confidence in Malaysia's electoral system, including the periods preceding recent elections, which were structured in a way to strengthen Malay political superiority. In 1993 the government created rural constituencies with much smaller populations than the urban constituencies. The 2003 boundary delimitation plan further strengthened the position of the ruling BN by creating 25 new constituencies in areas that overwhelmingly supported the BN in the 1999 general election (Grace 2011). Opposition critics in Malaysia have become increasingly frustrated with the widespread practice of gerrymandering in each delimitation exercise.

Restrictions on the freedom of speech, which is guaranteed in the Malaysian Constitution, are among other measures taken to undermine democratic rights in Malaysia. Freedom of speech, the right to gather and demonstrate, and the right to criticise government have been denied by two major pieces of legislation: the Internal Security Act (ISA) 1960 and the Sedition Act, originally enacted by the colonial authorities in 1948. The ISA allows governments to detain without trial and has been used primarily as a form of preventative detention for reasons of national security. There is, however, general agreement among political leaders that the ISA is a negation of the principles of democracy and, given its decreasing popularity among opposition critics, Prime Minister Najib Razak announced on 15 September 2011 that his government would repeal the ISA. He said that the parliament would consider replacing the ISA with new anti-terrorism laws that would respect individual rights. The government also announced that it would consider abolishing the requirement for newspaper and magazine publishers and broadcasters to obtain annual licences from the government, which is often viewed as a form of censorship (Callick 2011). Former Prime Minister Abdullah Badawi remained skeptical that the Dewan Rekyat would pass these reforms and argued that Prime Minister Razak would face political pressure from right-wing elements and hardliners within UMNO who would prefer to retain the control necessary to stamp out subversive activities (Najib could face 2011).

The Sedition Act is also used to control non-Malay opposition critics. In 1971 the Sedition Act was amended so that it became a punishable offence to question in public or in parliament sensitive issues, such as the special position of Malays, the use of Malay as the official language, and the citizenship rights of non-Malays. In short, the sensitive issues were removed from discussion in public forums (Lee 1995: 266). The Sedition Act further protects and entrenches Article 153 of the Malaysian Constitution, which safeguards the special position of Malays and indigenous peoples (as discussed in Chapters 5, 6 and 7), as a means to limit freedom of speech. The combined implementation of the ISA and the Sedition Act has meant that the political system has always tended to favour Malays at the expense of non-Malays and their social, political and cultural rights.

The lack of attention to democratic rights among minorities in Malaysia had a role in the unraveling of Malaysia's long-held pattern of Malay dominance at the 2008 general elections, when many Chinese chose to leave UMNO and vote for opposition parties. Islamic nationalism was also a concern for the more moderate UMNO, as the Parti Islam Se-Malaysia (PAS: Pan-Malaysian Islamic Party) posed a significant challenge to UMNO's ethnic nationalism paradigm (Arakaki 2009). Since the 2008 general election this challenge has been magnified by the informal coalition of opposition parties comprising the PAS, the Parti Keadilan Rakyat (PKR: People's Justice Party) and the Democratic Action Party (DAP) which have agreed informally not to contest each other. The DAP is predominantly Chinese and PAS predominantly Malay. The informal coalition is often referred to as the Pakatan Rakyat (People's Alliance). In 2011 the Pakatan Rakyat released its political manifesto entitled *Ubah Sekarang, Selamatkan Malaysia* (Change Now, Save Malaysia), which outlines a common policy platform based on four primary goals and principles:

a transparent and true democracy to reflect and empower the supremacy of the *rakyat* [the people]; a dynamic and sustainable economy to provide prosperity and social welfare to all; social justice to ensure the complete development of rights and respect of human dignity; and Federal–State and foreign policies based on principles of fairness and justice.

(Pakatan Rakyat 2011: 1)

The coalescing parties of Pakatan Rakyat aim to uphold a united position and to be bound by the common struggle to end the one party-dominated political system that has ruled for more than five decades, thus paving the way towards a two-party political system (Pakatan Rakyat 2011: 2). In the lead-up to the general election in 2013, it was expected that UMNO would work hard to win back Chinese voters, many of whom lost confidence in the political system and its entrenchment of Malay dominance in government, public education institutions, the civil service and law enforcement.

Whether or not Chinese inclusion in political and administrative institutions will lead to democratisation is unclear. Given our research findings that show non-Muslims, many of whom are Chinese, as preferring a system that is more democratic, one could predict that their political inclusion might lead in this direction. Notwithstanding this optimistic assessment, there are significant challenges to democratisation in Malaysia, including the need to moderate more extreme Islamist elements in PAS and to build confidence in a political system that incorporates good governance in terms of economic growth, national security and respect for minority rights. The biggest challenge facing any group running for office will be overcoming the fears of the Malay population that their economic and political rights will be diminished by any change of regime that introduces major political reform.

In terms of political transformation, Indonesia, in contrast to Malaysia, has made substantial progress in democratic consolidation. Indonesia has witnessed significant political transformation since 1998, with the sudden and unexpected demise of not only Suharto's presidency but also his authoritarian regime. Embracing the spirit of *reformasi*, Suharto's successor as president, B. J. Habibie, lifted constraints on press freedom, which has allowed Indonesia's media market to expand exponentially, in ways and directions that the government has often found impossible to control (Sen and Hill 2000: 218). In the following decade, Indonesia experienced an ever-increasing degree of press freedom, which has been regarded by many working in the media and political spheres as a fundamental element of Indonesia's democratisation process. The right to freedom of speech has been vigorously upheld, which explains Indonesian satisfaction with the right to freedom of speech in Table 9.3. President Habibie also lifted constraints on the rights of Indonesians to form political parties (Liddle 2001). In 1999, genuine democratic elections were held, the first democratic elections since 1955. In addition to these significant reforms, Indonesia began to implement one of the world's largest decentralisation programs (Mietzner and Aspinall 2010). Since 1999, Indonesia has been classified as an 'electoral democracy' by Freedom House but in 2009 was finally classified as a 'liberal democracy' (Freedom House 2012).

In the decade following the fall of Suharto, Indonesia's democratic progress strengthened and improved on a number of fronts. The legislative branch of Indonesia's political system, the Majelis Permusyawaratan Rakyat (MPR: People's Consultative Assembly) approved a number of important constitutional amendments. First, the MPR handed over its right to elect Indonesia's President and Vice President to the people (Malley 2003). The new rules stated that candidates must win not only half the popular vote but also at least 20 per cent of the vote in each of the provinces. If this is not possible, a second election is held. Second, in 2004 all 550 seats in the Dewan Perwakilan Rakyat (DPR: People's Representative Council), the lower house of the bicameral MPR, were for the first time popularly elected. During the same period Indonesia also made significant improvements in party-political competition. In the preceding New Order period, only a handful of parties were allowed to compete, including the pro-government Golkar, the Muslim Partai Persatuan Pembangunan (PPP: United Development Party) and the nationalist Partai Demokrasi Indonesia (PDI: Indonesian Democratic Party), which gave birth to the breakaway Partai Demokrasi Indonesia – Perjuangan (PDI-P: Indonesian Democratic Party – Struggle). The 2009 national elections for the DPR, however, were contested by 38 parties, nine of which reached the 2.5 per cent electoral threshold needed for representation in the DPR (Sukma 2010). Ultimately, among other things, the emergence of institutional reforms helped curb military power and marginalise the hardline Muslim voices of Indonesia's extremist fringe (Mietzner 2009; van Klinken 2007). The gradual decline of military power in Indonesia has also been linked to its loss of legitimacy following revelations of its role in the violence associated with the fall of Suharto, coupled with its closely related inability to continue to secure Western funding or support. On the other count, hardline Muslim groups have certainly received their fair share of national attention, but they have been widely criticised and condemned by Indonesia's secular press and by more liberal Muslims. This trend, it can be argued, is as much a symptom of Indonesia's press freedom as it is an indication of democratic political reforms.

Despite the aforementioned reforms, Indonesians continue to report dissatisfaction with democracy in terms of political performance and the provision of democratic rights (Aspinall and Mietzner 2010; Hadiz 2010). Certainly, there have been many improvements made since the fall of Suharto in 1998, but the findings conveyed in Tables 9.2 and 9.3 point to many areas of the political performance of their government with which Indonesians are similarly dissatisfied, especially in managing ethnic and religious conflict and in the provision of democratic rights such as the right to be informed and the right to criticise government.

Democratisation in Indonesia continues to be challenged by the fact that public support for the military still persists. In Indonesia, the AsiaBarometer surveys indicate support for military rule in its finding that up to 58 per cent of the population state that a regime run by the military would be 'good' or 'fairly good' for the country. Figure 9.2 shows the percentage of respondents who stated that they supported a democratic political system and rejected authoritarian alternatives. Only 24 per cent of Indonesians reported that they both supported a democratic regime and thought that it was bad to have a government run by a powerful leader with no parliament or elections or a military government. In Figure 9.3, even when we remove the count of those

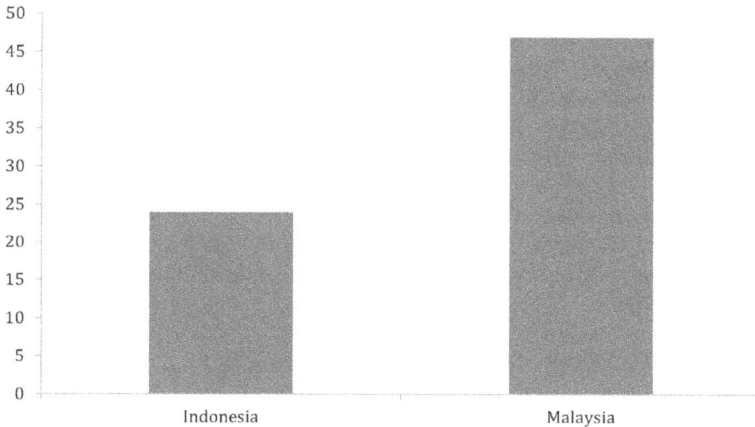

Figure 9.2 Support for a democratic regime and rejection of alternatives
Source: AsiaBarometer Surveys 2007 (N=2000)

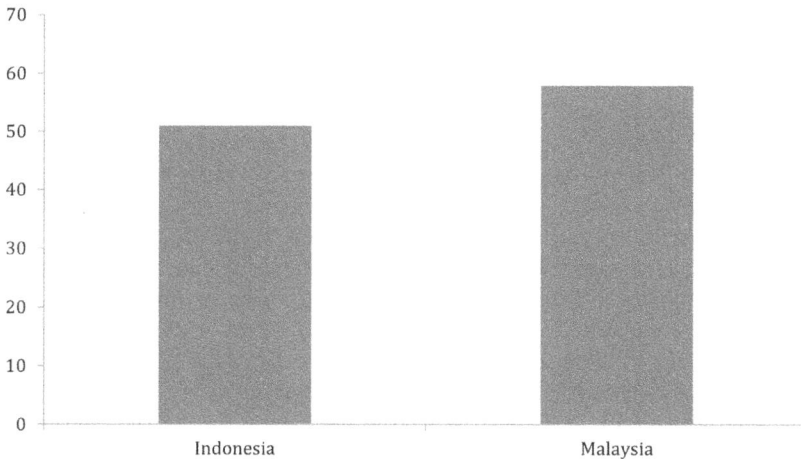

Figure 9.3 Support for a democratic regime, without those who support military regime and reject alternatives
Source: AsiaBarometer Surveys 2007 (N=2000)

who are supportive of a military regime, we find that support for democracy in Indonesia is lower than in Malaysia.

The findings presented in Figures 9.2 and 9.3 are not surprising when viewed with the understanding that post-New Order Indonesia has experienced a great deal of social and economic turmoil, with high unemployment and political instability resulting in outbreaks of ethnic and religious violence in which many people lost their lives (van Klinken 2007). In terms of public support for democracy, the decline of the military in politics has been a double-edged sword. On the one hand, the removal of the military from political affairs is a necessity for democratic consolidation; on the other hand, the military needs to be replaced by an effective police force and strong civil society that can manage ethnic and religious conflict peacefully.

Conclusion

As we conclude this chapter, it is important to note, above all, the significance of Indonesia's emergent democracy, which has not gone unnoticed in Malaysia. The observation of Malaysian commentator and author Karim Raslan (2012) is pertinent:

> When the leader of the world's fourth-most populous nation and Asia's fourth-largest economy (by Purchasing Power Parity) makes a foreign visit, the host nation takes notice – all the more so when that host nation is Malaysia and the visitor is President Susilo Bambang Yudhoyono of Indonesia. While many Indonesians feel that Malaysians refuse to acknowledge (and are blind to) the Republic's dramatic turnaround since Suharto's fall from power in 1998, the truth is quite the opposite. Malaysians – and especially business and political leaders – are all too aware of Indonesia's emergence and its growing might. Indeed, it has become the source of considerable concern and at times, anxiety.

Despite the enormous promise of Indonesia's economic and political transformations, we prefer to remain cautiously optimistic. In terms of economics, Indonesia must contend with poor infrastructure, widespread political corruption, regulatory caprice and bureaucratic inertia. In terms of politics, many Indonesians are frustrated with democracy, matching a pattern common in other countries in Asia, including Malaysia. In a comparative study of East Asia, for example, Chu *et al.* (2009) find that satisfaction with the ruling regime is highest in authoritarian countries. Their findings showed that many East Asians attach themselves to democracy as an ideal but not as a viable political system. Our findings have shown that, despite their differences, in 2007 few people in Indonesia and Malaysia gave democracy unqualified support by indicating overall satisfaction with it. Even though Indonesia has made significant progress at the political level, the attitudes of citizens suggest that it is far from being a consolidated democracy, as a significant proportion of its population displays a mix of democratic and authoritarian political tendencies. In our findings, Indonesians, even though they live in the most democratic country in Southeast Asia, appear to be the most pessimistic about their system's overall performance, and to have low levels of trust in their national institutions. Paradoxically, Malaysians appear to be more supportive of democracy as an ideal and more confident in their regime, but once we looked more closely at the views of the non-Muslim minority in Malaysia, we found evaluations of overall performance on democratic rights to be less positive.

What does this mean for the future of democracy in the Southeast Asian region? It seems that enduring ethnic and religious divisions in Indonesia and Malaysia, which tend to be expressed in persistent socioeconomic disparity, will continue to undermine democratic deepening and may even result in some movement back from democracy in times of political unrest. The ethnic and religious tensions in both countries are not easily resolved through economic redistribution or political restructuring. This chapter, and indeed this book as a whole, has shown that the tensions are a result of centuries of cultural and political differences, resulting in unequal power relations in both colonial and postcolonial settings. We have shown that the legacies of the colonial era and subsequent nation-building efforts in the postcolonial context, in which neo-colonial power structures have been perpetuated under the guise of nationalism, are still raw. This is particularly evident in Malaysia, where negotiations between the British and the Malay rulers resulted in a Constitution that upheld and protected Malay cultural and political superiority, rendering a nation unable to move forward in terms of democratisation without first addressing this fundamental element of the constitution.

Conclusion

It is pertinent to note that as we drafted the final few pages of this book in July 2013 haze from forest fires blanketed significant portions of Indonesia, Malaysia and Singapore. Fires that had been set to clear land for oil palm plantations on Indonesia's island of Sumatra had caused this haze. Haze has become a chronic problem during the dry season from June to September each year, especially on the islands of Sumatra and Borneo. There have been serious forest fires from time to time since the early 1980s, but, as markets for palm oil have developed and grown over the last two decades, slash-and-burn clearing of Indonesian forests has increased the frequency of serious fires. According to official data from Indonesia's forestry ministry, fewer than a thousand fire hotspots were tracked in Riau between 14 and 18 June 2013 (Tampilan peta sebaran hotspot 2013). The number is far lower than the average number of hotspots tracked at other times – 25,000 to 35,000 per month, peaking at 37,938 in August 1997 (Ardiansyah 2013). Nevertheless, the fires of the 2013 dry season were some of the worst to strike Indonesia in more than a decade. In Riau the blazes left two dead, 51 hospitalised and some 16,000 Indonesian citizens suffering from respiratory and skin problems (Lost in the haze 2013). Transboundary haze resulted in extreme air pollution across the region, leading to the declaration of a state of emergency in the southern Malaysian state of Johor. Residents of Muar and Ledang, the worst affected districts of Johor, were advised to stay indoors. The smoke also shrouded neighbouring Singapore, where air quality declined to hazardous levels. Pressured by the public outcry, the government of Singapore launched a strained dialogue with Indonesia about the possible causes and solutions to the problem.

In response to increasing international criticism, Indonesian President Susilo Bambang Yudhoyono apologised to his counterparts in Malaysia and Singapore, stating that his administration was determined to tackle the transboundary haze problem. Indonesia's National Agency for Disaster Management was given an urgent injection of funds to create artificial rain to extinguish the fires, but, as Fitrian Ardiansyah (2013) observes, conventional suppression approaches such as this are only a half-measure: 'Artificial rain, water bombing and firefighting on the ground may tackle the immediate symptoms but not necessarily the causes'. As already noted, the fires are set intentionally to convert rainforest and peat lands into land that can be used for oil palm plantations. They are also used for other types of agriculture and purposes. Among land users there is a common belief that fire is one of the cheapest land preparation methods available (Ardiansyah 2013), even though it often spreads into surrounding forests and plantations.

While smoke-related deaths of Singaporean and Malaysian citizens are widely reported in their respective national media, the human impact at the local level is rarely reported. For instance, very little is known about the tragic deaths of Dulsani and Lamiem Purba, a middle-aged couple caught up in the flames as they protected their modest crop of oil palm in rural Riau, Sumatra. They died in the early days of a blaze that, according to *Jakarta Globe*, later grew to engulf more than 850 hectares of land. The story of Dulsani and Lamiem 'was lost amid the firestorm of news coverage, much of it focused on the ensuing political theater as neighbors with a long-standing history of rocky relations jumped at the chance to lob complaints across the border' (Lost in the haze 2013). Like much of Indonesia's unfettered journalism, the *Globe*'s telling of their story is slightly overblown. Nevertheless, it hints at another aspect of the story, namely the inexplicable impulse to blame the neighbours. Indonesian bloggers insist that the blame for the haze from the forest fires actually lies, in a roundabout way, at the feet of Singapore and Malaysia. There is a common perception that concessions and plantations are owned and financed by Malaysians and Singaporeans, and thus many argue that Indonesia cannot be wholly blamed for the investment patterns leading to deforestation and fires. In this scenario Indonesian smallholders and local farmers are merely the fall guys for Singaporean and Malaysian companies. Given the difficulties of identifying the unethical investors and land-use actors, it is impossible to either prove or disprove this theory. The point to be made here is that transnational issues in maritime Southeast Asia are rarely considered in isolation; each new problem simply reignites the bad faith associated with other problems or with past occurrences of the same problem. The haze from Indonesia's forest fires is one such problem, which seems unlikely to go away in the foreseeable future.

It is our hope that this book is a meaningful contribution to the study of the bilateral relationship between Indonesia and Malaysia and to broader scholarship on cultural heritage, labour migration and the international politics of maritime Southeast Asia. We have questioned assumptions formed in the colonial and postcolonial eras relating to the familial relationship between Indonesia and Malaysia. Although we have highlighted the manner in which similarities in Indonesian and Malaysian culture, language and religion have served to dampen or defuse bilateral tensions in the past, we have also examined the ways in which nowadays this narrative is wearing thin, particularly since the end of the leadership of Suharto and Mahathir. The period since then has been characterised by rapid change for both countries, particularly for Indonesia which has wholeheartedly embraced democracy and all that it stands for, including open and free news media. Thus when a thick blanket of haze from Indonesia's forest fires obscures Kuala Lumpur's iconic Petronas Twin Towers or shrouds swathes of Johor, allusions to a shared kinship tend to fall flat. In fact, given the complex array of transnational issues confronting the post-authoritarian bilateral relationship, previously comforting notions such as *saudara serumpun* are rarely invoked.

The first few chapters of this book set the stage for the rest of the book. The introductory chapter began with a modest exposition of the key bilateral issue dominating the two nations when we began this book, namely the so-called 'Manodrama' of mid 2009. The tale of an Indonesian model fleeing an unhappy marriage with a Malaysian prince captured the imagination of the Indonesian media and the sympathy of Indonesian ultra-nationalist groups such as Laskar Merah Putih (Red and White Force). Characterised by their tendency to wear paramilitary uniforms, Laskar Merah Putih embraced Manohara's cause, and paraded her – dressed in military fatigues – in front of Jakarta's media. Described by some Indonesians as thugs in uniforms, para-military groups have been responsible for intermittent protests at the gates of the Malaysian embassy, public burnings of the Malaysian flag, and even anti-Malaysia sweepings in an effort to remove Malaysian expatriates from Indonesia. As we outlined, these stunts are intended to attract wide coverage in Indonesia's media and have achieved this aim, as was the 'Manodrama', which dominated Indonesia's celebrity news programs for weeks. But what did it all mean and why all the angst over a love affair gone wrong? We were at pains to locate and evaluate the 'Manodrama' within the broader framework of the anxieties associated with Indonesia's attempts to construct and assert a robust national identity. In such a context, any reaction to the supposed mistreatment of an Indonesian model by a Malaysian prince quickly becomes a question of upholding national honour. For some Malaysians such a stance is regarded as an unnecessary distraction, given the long history of human migration within maritime Southeast Asia. The fact of the matter is that many present-day Malaysians are direct descendants of migrants from the Indonesian archipelago.

Early in this book, the postcolonial nature of the Indonesia–Malaysia relationship was emphasised. In doing so we did not intend to convey that Indonesia and Malaysia somehow share a colonial or neo-colonial relationship, but rather that the colonial histories of both nations have encouraged a degree of parochialism. The post-independence experience of both nations has encouraged a significant divergence. Despite the deep links between the people and the cultures of the two countries, and the heavy human and cultural traffic between them, the one thing uniting them in the postcolonial era, para-doxically, is their deep and abiding sense of difference. To this day Indonesia and Malaysia seek to assert their differences as much as their similarities. This is not a difficult task. As most observers would agree, since independence Indonesia and Malaysia have moved in different directions, socially, economically and politically. We described the manner in which the Sukarno-era military confrontation between Indonesia and Malaysia in the early 1960s pushed assertions of difference out into the open, perhaps a bit too forcefully. During the subsequent Suharto and Mahathir eras both nations simply dusted themselves off, patched up their differences, and rolled up their sleeves in order to concentrate on nation building. By all measures both leaders were remarkably successful in this regard, given the significant rupture of the *Konfrontasi* period. By promoting a common sense of kinship and blood brotherhood, in the context of an emergent ASEAN both nations could concentrate on their respective domestic agendas without needing to watch their back. Of course various attempts were made to forge a degree of soft diplomacy between the two neighbours, and this book examines the potentially unifying role of a shared language and cultural understanding. Nonetheless, a common thread through this book is that the greater the sense of cultural affinity, the greater the sense that the two nations seem destined to remain apart. Nowhere is this revealed than in the bitter contestations over disputed territory and shared forms of cultural heritage in the post-Mahathir and post-Suharto era, as this book reveals. There is nothing unusual about such contestations, of course. Australia and New Zealand, for instance, seem forever determined to emphasise their differences, despite the fact that there is a great deal of cultural overlap between the two – albeit a bit too one-sided for Kiwi liking. Likewise, the USA and Canada share obvious similarities, yet their fundamental differences generate a good deal of discussion. Similar narratives of rivalry, often good-natured but sometimes not, occur between Norway and Sweden, England and Scotland, Portugal and Spain, India and Pakistan, Iran and Iraq, Brazil and Argentina, and so on.

In many chapters of this book we took a deliberate step back from the surface tension of the Indonesia–Malaysia bilateral relationship. We aimed to reveal something of the substance underpinning the obvious differences between the two countries. Thus we scratched beneath the surface of the politics of heritage so beloved of the Indonesian media. Evidently Indonesia and Malaysia have vastly different approaches and practices relating to preserving their history and heritage. In Indonesia history has little honour, whereas in Malaysia cultural heritage plays a key role in the government's ongoing efforts to create a stable, unified, prosperous and socially cohesive nation. Providing nuance to this argument, this book examined Islamic popular culture in Indonesia and Malaysia. We believe this discussion is important for several reasons. First, for many, Islam is the most obvious unifier between Indonesia and Malaysia. Some have argued that the recent resurgence of political Islam in the two countries is a possible conduit towards closer bilateral relations. Second, popular Islam allows Muslims in Indonesia and Malaysia to make sense of their everyday lives. There is a pop Islam boom in Indonesia, and Islamic popular culture is pervasive in Malaysia, perhaps even more so than in Indonesia. Third, popular Islamic culture is closely related to the changing social and political landscape of contemporary Indonesia and Malaysia. Thus, on the one hand, we highlighted in the Indonesian context the close links between the demise of the New Order regime and the subsequent embrace of democratisation, which has given many Islamic political parties and institutions the opportunity to shape public discourse. On the other hand, we argued that Muslim culture in Malaysia is much more closely aligned with ethnicity and with the Malay ethnic group in particular, which is overwhelmingly Muslim.

This book is premised on the need to delineate and understand the post-colonial divergence between Indonesia and Malaysia. In particular, our argument is that the colonial experience, which differed fundamentally in each country, is a salient element of the differing attitudes and public policies towards race and ethnicity. Thus we have addressed the thorny issues of citizenship and labour migration in a discussion that is important because the issue of Indonesian migrant workers dominates so much of the discourse relating to the bilateral relationship, despite the fact that it is, at best, secondary. For instance, in terms of Indonesia–Malaysia trade, security cooperation and tourism, there is much to celebrate. The revenue earned from labour migration to Malaysia, which is almost impossible to determine because the migration is inherently informal, no doubt pales in comparison to these achievements. Yet, as we have explained in this book, it seems that the migrant worker issue is a source of perennial discomfort for both nations, for different reasons. Nevertheless, many Indonesian families greatly appreciate the higher wages on offer in Malaysia, and there is a widely held view that if Malaysia were to somehow deport all of its foreign workers, the nation would come to an immediate standstill. The chapters addressing this issue examine the manner in which Malaysia's model of citizenship has failed to properly take into account the conditions and rights of the new underclass of Indonesian foreign workers in Malaysian society.

In order to provide an extra dimension to this analysis, we bit the bullet and examined the state of democracy in both nations, which is what we believe to be at the heart of the citizenship and labour migration dilemma. Ultimately, the different levels of democracy in Indonesia and Malaysia have led to contrasting attitudes towards numerous issues, including questions of citizenship and human rights. The contrast in attitudes has direct relevance to one of the biggest thorns in the side of the bilateral relationship – Malaysia's cavalier treatment of Indonesian migrant workers. Finally, this book's penultimate chapter suggests that in terms of understanding trends in regional integration and cooperation, the findings of this book are relevant. It appears that ASEAN is unlikely to become a driver of internal political liberalisation in Southeast Asia any time soon. Political change in this region, if it comes, is likely to come from within states rather than from external sources. It is for this reason that this book has important ramifications for understanding not just the Indonesia–Malaysia relationship, but also the Southeast Asian region as a whole. By revealing the causes and nature of the dominant social, cultural and political trends in Indonesia and Malaysia, this book helps us better understand the region. Our final conclusion is that, while Indonesia's democratic consolidation proceeds without question, Malaysia's commitment to a more deliberative, open and democratic system is still on trial.

Bibliography

Abdullah, A.K. (2006) 'Kesusastraan Indonesia–Malaysia Mutakhir; Antara sensitiviti dan imaginasi', *Susastra*, 2/3: 64–88.

Acharya, A. (2003) 'Democratisation and the prospects for participatory regionalism in Southeast Asia', *Third World Quarterly*, 24(2): 375–90.

——(2009) 'The strong in the world of the weak: Southeast Asia in Asia's regional architecture', in M.J. Green and B. Gill (eds) *Asia's New Multilateralism: Cooperation, Competition, and the Search for Community*, New York: Columbia University Press.

——and Stubbs, R. (2006) 'Theorising Southeast Asian relations: an introduction', *Pacific Review*, 19(2): 125–34.

Adams, K.M. (2003) 'Museum/city/nation: negotiating identities in urban museums in Indonesia and Singapore', in R.B.H. Goh and B.S.A. Yeoh (eds) *Theorizing the Southeast Asian City as Text: Urban Landscapes, Cultural Documents and Interpretive Experiences*, Singapore: World Scientific Publishing.

——(2006) *Art as Politics: Re-Crafting Identities, Tourism, and Power in Tana Toraja, Indonesia*, Honolulu: University of Hawai'i Press.

——(2010) 'The politics of heritage in Tana Toraja, Indonesia: interplaying the local and the global', *Indonesia and the Malay World*, 31(89): 91–107.

'again, that Hate Malingsia group in facebook, they will never learn now, wont they' (2009) *lowyat.net*, 15 June. Available: http://forum.lowyat.net/topic/1064295/all (accessed 15 January 2013).

Ahmad, I. (2009) *Islamism and Democracy in India: The Transformation of Jamaat-e-Islami*, Princeton, NJ, and Oxford: Princeton University Press.

Andaya, B. and Andaya, L. (2001) *A History of Malaysia*, 2nd edn, Basingstoke: Palgrave MacMillan.

Andaya, L.Y. (2010) *Leaves of the Same Tree: Trade and Ethnicity in the Straits of Malacca*, Singapore: NUS Press.

Anderson, B. (1991) *Imagined Communities: Reflections on the Origin and Spread of Nationalism*, London and New York: Verso.

Anis, M.N. and Krishnamoorthy, M. (2008) 'Thursday is Batik Day', *The Star*, 16 January. Online. Available: http://thestar.com.my/news/story.asp?file=/2008/1/16/nation/20020158&sec=nation (accessed 24 January 2013).

Antoinette, M. (2009) 'The art of race: rethinking Malaysian identity through the art of Wong Hoy Cheong', in D.P.S. Goh, M. Gabrielpillai, P. Holden and G.C. Khoo (eds) *Race and Multiculturalism in Malaysia and Singapore*, Abingdon and New York: Routledge.

Anwar, D.F. (2008) 'Indonesia and the Bandung conference: then and now', in S.S. Tan and A. Acharya (eds) *Bandung Revisited: The Legacy of the 1955 Asian-African Conference for International Order*, Singapore: NUS Press.

Arakaki, R. (2009) '2008 Malaysian election: the end of Malaysia's ethnic nationalism?', *Asian Politics and Policy*, 1(1): 79–96.

Ardiansyah, F. (2013) 'Indonesia's fires: a hazy challenge for Southeast Asia', *East Asia Forum*, 8 July. Online. Available: www.eastasiaforum.org/2013/07/08/indone sias-fires-a-hazy-challenge-for-southeast-asia/ (accessed 10 July 2013).

Arifianto, A. (2009) 'The securitization of transnational labor migration: the case of Malaysia and Indonesia', *Asian Politics and Policy*, 4(1): 613–30.

'Armoured vehicles escort for security reasons' (2011) *The Star*, 17 November: 68.

Asaat (1970) 'The Chinese grip on our economy, 1956', in H. Feith and L. Castles (eds) *Indonesian Political Thinking: 1945–1965*, Ithaca, NY, and London: Cornell University Press.

AsiaBarometer Surveys 2007 (2007) Tokyo: University of Niigata Prefecture. Online. Available: www.asiabarometer.org/en/surveys/2007 (accessed 19 February 2013).

Aspinall, E. and Mietzner, M. (eds) (2010) *Problems of Democratisation in Indonesia: Elections, Institutions and Society*, Singapore: Institute of Southeast Asian Studies.

Aswadi, A. and Osman, N. (2009) 'SBY Says He Raised Concerns About Manohara', *Jakarta Globe*, 3 June. Online. Available: www.thejakartaglobe.com/national/sby-says-he-raised-concerns-about-manohara/278891 (accessed 22 January 2013).

Aveling, H. (1969) 'The thorny rose: the avoidance of passion in modern Indonesian literature', *Indonesia*, 7: 67–76.

'AWAS!!!! Malayria KL' (2008) *Topix Malaysia Forum*, 25 March. Online. Available: www.topix.com/forum/world/malaysia/TCDP1JV0LQJH2NBSH (accessed 15 January 2013).

Ba, A.D. (2009) *(Re)Negotiating East and Southeast Asia: Region, Regionalism, and the Association of Southeast Asian Nations*, Stanford, CA: Stanford University Press.

Bahari, R. (2003) 'Remembering history, w/righting history: piecing the past in Pramoedya Ananta Toer's Buru tetralogy', *Indonesia*, 75: 61–90.

——(2007) *Pramoedya Postcolonially: (Re-)viewing History, Gender and Identity in the Buru tetralogy*, Bali: Pustaka Larasan.

Baird, R. (2012) 'Transnational security issues in the Asian maritime environment: responding to maritime piracy', *Australian Journal of International Affairs*, 66(5): 501–13.

Bangun, A.K. (2010) 'MoU Tak Jamin TKI Terlindungi', *Kompas*, 20 November. Online. Available: http://bisniskeuangan.kompas.com/read/2010/11/20/08194277/MoU.Tak.Jamin.TKI.Terlindungi (accessed 4 February 2013).

Bayuni, E.M. (2010) 'Malaysia's arrogance versus Indonesia's envy', *The Jakarta Post*, 4 September. Online. Available: www.thejakartapost.com/news/2010/09/04/commen tary-malaysia%E2%80%99s-arrogance-versus-indonesia%E2%80%99s-envy.html (accessed 16 January 2013).

Beeson, M. (2009) *Institutions of the Asia-Pacific: ASEAN, APEC and Beyond*, London: Routledge.

Behr, E. (1990) *Indonesia: A Voyage Through the Archipelago*, Paris: Millet Weldon Owen Ltd.

Bertrand, J. (2004) 'Nationalism and ethnic conflicts in Indonesia', in J.A.C. Mackie (ed.) *The Chinese in Indonesia*, Melbourne: Thomas Nelson.

Bharucha, R. (2000) 'Beyond the box: problematising the new Asia museum', *Third Text*, 52: 11–19.

Blackburn, S. (2004) *Women and the State in Modern Indonesia*, Cambridge: Cambridge University Press.

Blackwood, E. (2005) 'Transnational sexualities in one place: Indonesian readings', *Gender & Society*, 19(2): 221–42.

Bodden, M. and Hellwig, T. (2007) 'Introduction', *Review of Indonesian and Malaysian Affairs*, 41(2): 1–24.

Bourdieu, P. (1977) *Outline of a Theory of Practice*, Cambridge: Cambridge University Press.

——(1984) *Distinction: A Social Critique of the Judgement of Taste*, Cambridge, MA: Harvard University Press.

Brackman, A.C. (1966) *Southeast Asia's Second Front: The Power Struggle in the Malay Archipelago*, London: Pall Mall.

Bratton, M., Mattes, R. and Gyimah-Boadi, E. (2005) *Public Opinion, Democracy, and Market Reform in Africa*, Cambridge: Cambridge University Press.

Brenner, S. (2007) 'Democracy, polygamy and women in post-*reformasi* Indonesia', in T. Day (ed.) *Identifying with Freedom: Indonesia after Suharto*, New York: Bergahn Books.

Budianto, L. (2009) 'RI demands KL explain ban on anxious mother', *The Jakarta Post*, 24 April. Online. Available: www.thejakartapost.com/news/2009/04/24/ri-demands-kl-explain-ban-on-anxious-mother.html (accessed 15 March 2012).

Budiawan (2012) 'Sibling tension and negotiation: Malay(sian) writer-political activists: links and orientation to Indonesia', in J. Lindsay and M.H.T. Liem (eds) *Heirs to World Culture: Being Indonesian 1950–1965*, Leiden: KITLV Press.

Burarrwanga, L.L. (2012) 'Memories of my Makassan family', *Macassan History and Heritage: Building Understandings of Journeys, Encounters and Influences*, Australian National University, 8–9 February, unpublished paper.

Caballero-Anthony, M. (2008) 'Challenging change: nontraditional security, democracy, and regionalism', in D.K. Emmerson (ed.) *Hard Choices: Security, Democracy, and Regionalism in Southeast Asia*, Stanford, CA: Walter H. Shorenstein Asia-Pacific Research Center.

Callick, R. (2011) 'Malaysian PM Najib Razak says he'll repeal detention laws', *The Australian*, 17 September. Online. Available: www.theaustralian.com.au/news/world/malaysian-pm-najib-razak-says-hell-repeal-detention-laws/story-e6frg6so-1226139335618 (accessed 19 February 2013).

Carruthers, A. (2002) 'The accumulation of national belonging in transnational fields: ways of being at home in Vietnam', *Identities: Global Studies in Culture and Power*, 9(4): 423–44.

Case, W. (2009) 'Low-quality democracy and varied authoritarianism: elites and regimes in Southeast Asia today', *Pacific Review*, 22(3): 255–69.

'Case Concerning Sovereignty over Pulau Ligitan and Pulau Sipadan (Indonesia *v.* Malaysia) (Merits)' (2002) Judgement in the International Court of Justice, 17 December. Online. Available: www.icj-cij.org/docket/files/102/10570.pdf (accessed 17 January 2013).

Chin, C.B.N. (2008) '"Diversification" and "privatisation": securing insecurities in the receiving country of Malaysia', *The Asia Pacific Journal of Anthropology*, 9(4): 285–303.

Chok, S.L. (2011) 'Champs are made, not born' *New Straits Times*, 24 November: 22, 25.

Cholewinski, R. (2010) 'Labour migration and the rights of migrant workers', in A. Edwards and C. Ferstman (eds) *Human Security and Non-Citizens: Law, Policy and International Affairs*, Cambridge: Cambridge University Press.

Chong, J.W. (2012) '"Mine, yours or ours?": The Indonesia–Malaysia disputes over shared cultural heritage', *Sojourn: Journal of Social Issues in Southeast Asia*, 27(1): 1–53.

Choo, P. (2008) 'Population status, fisheries and trade of sea cucumbers in Asia', in V. Toral-Granda, A. Lovotelli and M. Vasconcellos (eds) *Sea Cucumbers: A Global Review of Fisheries and Trade*, Rome: Food and Agriculture Organization of the United Nations.

Chu, Y., Diamond, L., Nathan, A. and Shin, D.C. (eds) (2008) *How East Asians View Democracy*, New York: Columbia University Press.

——(2009) 'Asia's challenged democracies', *The Washington Quarterly*, 32(1): 143–57.

Clark, M. (2001) 'Shadow boxing: Indonesian writers and the Ramayana in the New Order', *Indonesia*, 72: 159–87.

——(2010) *Maskulinitas: Culture, Gender and Politics in Indonesia*, Caulfield: Monash University Press.

——(2011) 'Indonesia's postcolonial regional imaginary: from a "neutralist" to an "all-directions" foreign policy', *Japanese Journal of Political Science*, 11(2): 287–304.

——and Pietsch, J. (2012) 'Democratisation and Indonesia's changing perceptions of ASEAN and its alternatives', in C. Portela and D. Novotny (eds) *EU–ASEAN Relations in the 21st Century: Strategic Partnership in the Making*, Basingstoke: Palgrave MacMillan.

Cohen, M. (2001) 'On the Origin of the *Komedie Stamboel*: Popular Culture, Colonial Society, and the Parsi Theatre', *Bijdragen tot de Taal-, Land-en Volkenkunde*, 157(2): 313–57.

——(2006) *The Komedie Stamboel: Popular Theater in Colonial Indonesia, 1891–1903*, Athens, OH: Centre for International Studies, Ohio University.

Colbert, E. (1986) 'ASEAN as a regional organization: economics, politics and security', in K.D. Jackson, S. Paribatra and S. Djiwandono (eds) *ASEAN in Regional and Global Context*, Berkeley, CA: Institute of East Asian Studies.

Collins, J. (2004) 'Contesting Straits-Malayness: the fact of Borneo', in T. P. Barnard (ed.) *Contesting Malayness: Malay Identity Across Boundaries*, Singapore: Singapore University Press.

Cooke, M. (1987) *Makassar & Northeast Arnhem Land: Missing Links and Living Bridges*, Darwin: The Educational Media Unit, Batchelor College.

Cribb, R.B. and Brown, C. (1995) *Modern Indonesia: A History Since 1945*, London: Longman.

Crouch, H. (1978) *The Army and Politics in Indonesia*, Ithaca, NY, and London: Cornell University Press.

——(1996) *Government and Society in Malaysia*, Ithaca, NY: Cornell University Press.

Darwis, M.F. (2012) 'Sabah's illegal immigrant issue electoral fodder for Pakatan, says Dr M', *The Malaysian Insider*, 9 October. Online. Available: www.themalaysianinsider.com/malaysia/article/sabahs-illegal-immigrant-issue-electoral-fodder-for-pakatan-says-dr-m (accessed 3 February 2013).

Day, T. and Foulcher, K. (eds) (2002) *Clearing a Space: Postcolonial Readings of Modern Indonesian Literature*, Leiden: KITLV Press.

'Defenders doing a good job protecting me, says keeper' (2011) *The Star*, 19 November: 79.

Department of Statistics, Malaysia (2010a) *Population Distribution and Basic Demographic Characteristics*, Kuala Lumpur: Department of Statistics Malaysia.

——(2010b) *Ringkasan Penemuan Summary Findings*. Online. Available: www.statistics. gov.my/portal/images/stories/files/LatestReleases/population/Ringkasan_Penemuan-Summary_Findings_2010–40.pdf (accessed 12 February 2013).

——(2011) *Taburan Penduduk dan Ciri-Ciri Asas Demografi: Population Distribution and Basic Characteristics 2010*. Online. Available: www.statistics.gov.my/portal/download_Population/files/census2010/Taburan_Penduduk_dan_Ciri-ciri_Asas_Demografi.pdf (accessed 2 February 2013).

Derks, W. (1996) '"If not to anything else": some reflections on modern Indonesian Literature', *Bijdragen tot de Taal-, Land-en Volkenkunde*, 152(3): 341–52.

——(2002) '*Sastra pedalaman*: local and regional literary centres in Indonesia', in K. Foulcher and T. Day (eds) *Clearing a Space: Postcolonial Readings of Modern Indonesian Literature*, Leiden: KITLV Press.

Devadason, E. (2011) 'Policy chaos over migrant workers in Malaysia', *East Asia Forum*, 11 January. Online. Available: www.eastasiaforum.org/2011/01/11/policy-chaos-over-migrant-workers-in-malaysia/ (accessed 3 February 2013).

Diamond, L. (2008) *The Spirits of Democracy: The Struggle to Build Free Societies throughout the World*, New York: Henry Holt.

——(2012) 'The coming wave', *Journal of Democracy*, 23(1): 5–13.

Ding, J-A. (2010) 'The impact of polygamy in Malaysia', *The Nut Graph*, 21 July. Online. Available: www.thenutgraph.com/the-impact-of-polygamy-in-malaysia/ (accessed 29 January 2013).

Donita (2011) '*Kehormatan di Balik Kerudung*: keikhlasan dipoligami', *KapanLagi. com*, 27 October. Online. Available: www.kapanlagi.com/film/indonesia/kehormatan-di-balik-kerudung-keikhlasan-dipoligami.html (accessed 29 January 2013).

Dosch, J. (2008) 'Sovereignty rules: human security, civil society, and the limits of liberal reform', in D.K. Emmerson (ed.) *Hard Choices: Security, Democracy and Regionalism in Southeast Asia*, Stanford, CA: Walter H. Shorenstein Asia-Pacific Research Center.

Dresser, N. (2005) *Multicultural Manners: Essential Rules of Etiquette for the 21st Century*, Hoboken, NJ: John Wiley & Sons.

Economic Planning Unit (2011) *Incidence of Poverty by Ethnicity, Strata and State, Malaysia, 1970–2009*, Kuala Lumpur: Prime Minister's Department.

Economic Transformation Programme (2010) *Economic Transformation Programme: A Roadmap for Malaysia*. Online. Available: http://etp.pemandu.gov.my/upload/etp_handbook_chapter_1–4_economic_model.pdf (accessed 12 February 2013).

Efantino, F. and Arifin, S.N. (2009) '*Ganyang Malaysia': Hubungan Indonesia–Malaysia sejak Konfrontasi sampai Konflik Ambalat*, Yogyakarta: Bio Pustaka.

Eickelman, D.F. and Anderson, J.W. (eds) (2003) *New Media in the Muslim World: The Emerging Public Sphere*, 2nd edn, Bloomington, IN: Indiana University Press.

Eickelman, D.F. and Piscatori, J. (1996) *Muslim Politics*, Princeton, NJ: Princeton University Press.

Eilenberg, M. (2012) *At the Edges of States: Dynamics of State Formation in the Indonesian Borderlands*, Leiden: KITLV Press.

Emmerson, D.K. (1995) 'Region and recalcitrance: rethinking democracy through Southeast Asia', *Pacific Review*, 8(2): 223–48.

——(2008) 'ASEAN's "Black Swans"', *Journal of Democracy*, 19(3): 70–84.

Fawn, R. (2009) '"Regions" and their study: wherefrom, what for, and whereto?', in R. Fawn (ed.) *Globalising the Regional: Regionalising the Global*, Cambridge: Cambridge University Press.

Fealy, G. and Thayer, C.A. (2009) 'Problematising "linkages" between Southeast Asian and international terrorism', in W. Tow (ed.) *Security Politics in the Asia-Pacific*, Cambridge: Cambridge University Press.

Featherstone, K. and Radaelli, C. (eds) (2003) *The Politics of Europeanization*, Oxford: Oxford University Press.

Feith, H. (1978) *The Decline of Constitutional Democracy in Indonesia*, Ithaca, NY, and London: Cornell University Press.

Fenton, S. (2003) 'Malaysia and capitalist modernization: plural and multicultural models', *International Journal on Multicultural Societies*, 5(2): 135–47.

Fitzpatrick, S. (2009) 'Sea skirmish and bedroom abuse reignite old spat between Indonesia and Malaysia', *The Australian*, 2 June. Online. Available: www.theaustralian. com.au/news/sea-skirmish-and-bedroom-abuse-reignite-old-spat-between-indonesia-and-malaysia/story-e6frg6t6–1225720019327 (accessed 15 January 2013).

Ford, M. (2006) 'After Nunukan: the regulation of Indonesian migration to Malaysia', in A. Kaur and I. Metcalfe (eds) *Divided We Move: Mobility, Labour Migration and Border Controls in Asia*, New York: Palgrave MacMillan.

——and Susilo, W. (2010) 'Organising for migrant worker rights: non-governmental organisations continue to fill the gap in the absence of viable alternatives', *Inside Indonesia*, 100. Online. Available: www.insideindonesia.org/feature-editions/organising-for-migrant-worker-rights (accessed 4 February 2013).

Foulcher, K. (1995) 'In search of the postcolonial in Indonesian literature', *Sojourn*, 10(2): 147–71.

——(2008) *On a Roll: Pramoedya and the Postcolonial Transition* (Indonesian Studies Working Papers, 4), Sydney: Department of Indonesian Studies, University of Sydney.

Freedman, A. (2000) *Political Participation and Ethnic Minorities: Chinese Overseas in Malaysia, Indonesia and the United States*, New York and London: Routledge.

——(2006) *Political Change and Consolidation: Democracy's Rocky Road in Thailand, Indonesia, South Korea, and Malaysia*, New York: Palgrave MacMillan.

——(2009) 'Political viability, contestation and power: Islam and politics in Indonesia and Malaysia', *Politics and Religion*, 2: 100–27.

Freedom House (2012) *Indonesia: Freedom in the World*. Online. Available: www. freedomhouse.org/report/freedom-world/2012/indonesia (accessed 20 February 2013).

Gagliano, F. (1971) *Communal Violence in Malaysia 1969: The Political Aftermath*, Athens: Centre for International Studies, Ohio University.

Galeri Petronas (2011) *Irresistible Wear*, Kuala Lumpur.

Ganter, R. (2006) *Mixed-Relations: Asian-Aboriginal Contact in North Australia*, Crawley: University of Western Australia Press.

Garcés-Mascareñas, B. (2012) *Labour Migration in Malaysia and Spain: Markets, Citizenship and Rights*, Amsterdam: Amsterdam University Press.

Gomez, E.T. and Jomo, K.S. (1997) *Malaysia's Political Economy: Politics, Patronage and Profits*, New York: Cambridge University Press.

Grace, J. (2011) 'Malaysia: malapportioned districts and over-representation of rural communities', *ACE Project: The Electoral Knowledge Network*. Online. Available: http://aceproject.org/ace-en/topics/bd/bdy/bdy_my (accessed 19 February 2013).

Greenough, P. (1993) 'Nation, economy and tradition displayed: the Indian Crafts Museum, New Delhi', in C.A. Breckenridge (ed.) *Consuming Modernity: Public Culture in a South Asian World*, Minneapolis: University of Minnesota Press.

Haas, E.B. (1958) *The Uniting of Europe: Political, Social and Economical Forces, 1950–1957*, London: Stevens.

Hadiwinata, B.S. (2009) 'International relations in Indonesia: historical legacy, political intrusion, and commercialization', *International Relations of the Asia-Pacific*, 9(1): 55–81.

Hadiz, V. (2010) *Localising Power in Post-Authoritarian Indonesia: A Southeast Asia Perspective*, Stanford, CA: Stanford University Press.

——and Khoo B.T. (2011) 'Approaching Islam and politics from political economy: a comparative study of Indonesia and Malaysia', *Pacific Review*, 24(4): 463–85.

Hage, G. (1998) *White Nation: Fantasies of White Supremacy in a Multicultural Society*, Annandale and West Wickham: Pluto Press.

Hamid, Z.H.A. (2008) 'Wayang cari pengaruh antarabangsa', *Cinema Malaysia*, 5 November. Online. Available: www.cinemamalaysia.com.my/main/clippingnews/Wayang_cari_pengaruh_antarabangsa_1577 (accessed 22 January 2013).

Hamzirwan (2010) 'TKI: Nasib Pahlawan Devisa di Negeri Citra', *Kompas*, 19 November. Online. Available: http://bisniskeuangan.kompas.com/read/2010/11/19/08161095/Nasib.Pahlawan.Devisa.di.Negeri.Citra (accessed 4 February 2013).

Hardt, M. and Negri, A. (2000) *Empire*, London: Harvard University Press.

Haryadi, R. and Pamungkas, W.W. (2008) 'Celaka membawa nikmat', *Gatra*, 23 July: 62–3.

Hasan, N. (2009) 'The making of public Islam: piety, agency, and commodification on the landscape of the Indonesian public sphere', *Contemporary Islam*, 3: 229–50.

Hassan, A. (2012) 'Malaysia never claimed culture "as its own"', *Bikya Masr*, 4 July. Online. Available: www.masress.com/en/bikyamasr/71633 (accessed 17 January 2013).

Hatley, B. (1999) 'New directions in Indonesian women's writing? The novel *Saman*', *Asian Studies Review*, 23(4): 449–60.

——(2002) 'Literature, mythology and regime change: some observations on recent Indonesian women's writing', in K. Robinson and S. Bessell (eds) *Women in Indonesia: Gender, Equity and Development*, Singapore: Institute of Southeast Asian Studies.

Hefner, R.W. (2001) 'Introduction: multiculturalism and citizenship in Malaysia, Singapore, and Indonesia', in R.W. Hefner (ed.) *The Politics of Multiculturalism: Pluralism and Citizenship in Malaysia, Singapore, and Indonesia*, Honolulu: University of Hawai'i Press.

Hellwig, T. (2011) 'Abidah El Khalieqy's novels: challenging patriarchal Islam', *Bijdragen tot de Taal-, Land-en Volkenkunde*, 167(1): 16–30.

Henderson, J. (2005) 'Exhibiting cultures: Singapore's Asian Civilisations Museum', *International Journal of Heritage Studies*, 11(3): 183–95.

Herlinatiens (2003) *Garis Tepi Seorang Lesbian*, Yogyakarta: Galang Press.

Hermawan, A. (2009) 'Embassies "too slow" to protect Indonesians abroad: lawmaker', *Jakarta Post*, 1 June. Online. Available: www.thejakartapost.com/news/2009/06/01/embassies-%E2%80%98too-slow%E2%80%99-protect-indonesians-abroad-lawmaker.html (accessed 15 January 2013).

Heryanto, A. (2008) 'Pop culture and competing identities', in A. Heryanto (ed.) *Popular Culture in Indonesia: Fluid Identities in Post-Authoritarian Politics*, London and New York: Routledge.

——(2011) 'Upgraded piety and pleasure: the new middle class and Islam in Indonesian popular culture', in A.N. Weintraub (ed.) *Islam and Popular Culture in Indonesia and Malaysia*, London: Routledge.

'Hishammuddin hopes Manohara issue will not tarnish M'sia-Indonesia ties' (2009) *The Sun Daily*, 6 June. Online. Available: www.thesundaily.my/node/154863 (accessed 15 January 2013).

Ho, K.L. (2002) 'Bureaucratic participation and political mobilization: comparing pre- and post-1970 Malaysian Chinese political participation', in L. Suryadinata (ed.) *Ethnic Chinese in Singapore and Malaysia*, Singapore: Times Academic Press

Hoesterey, J.B. (2008) 'Marketing morality: the rise, fall and rebranding of AA Gym', in G. Fealy and S. White (eds) *Expressing Islam: Religious Life and Politics in Indonesia*, Singapore: Institute of Southeast Asian Studies.

——and Clark, M. (2012) '*Film Islami*: gender, piety, and pop culture in post-authoritarian Indonesia', *Asian Studies Review*, 32(2): 207–26.

Hoffstaedter, G. (2008) 'Representing culture in Malaysian cultural theme parks: tensions and contradictions', *Anthropological Forum*, 18(2): 139–60.

——(2011) *Modern Muslim Identities: Negotiating Religion and Ethnicity in Malaysia*, Copenhagen: NIAS Press.

Holst, F. (2007) '(Dis-)connected history: the Indonesia–Malaysia relationship', in E. Streifeneder and A. Missbach (eds) *Indonesia – The Presence of the Past*, Berlin: Regiospectra.

'Home fans not sporting' (2011) *The Star*, 17 November: 69.

Hooker, V.M. (2000) *Writing a New Society: Social Change through the Novel in Malay*, St Leonards, NSW: Asian Studies Association of Australia in association with Allen & Unwin.

——(2003) *A Short History of Malaysia: Linking East and West*, St Leonards NSW: Allen & Unwin.

——and Dick, H. (1995) 'Introduction', in Hooker, V.M. (ed.) *Culture and Society in New Order Indonesia*, Kuala Lumpur: Oxford University Press.

Hugo, G. (2011) 'Migration and development in Malaysia', *Asian Population Studies*, 7(3), 219–41.

Human Rights Foundation Malaysia (2011) *Institutional Racism and Religious Freedom in Malaysia*. Online. Available: http://english.cpiasia.net/dmdocuments/Instituti onal%20racism%20&%20Religious%20freedom.pdf (accessed 2 February 2013).

Imanjaya, E. (2009a) 'The curious cases of Salma, Siti, and Ming: representations of Indonesia's polygamous life in *Love for Share*', *Jump Cut: a Review of Contemporary Media*, 51: 1–14. Online. Available: www.ejumpcut.org/archive/jc51.2009/LoveforShare/index.html (accessed 29 January 2013).

Indonesian Manpower Service (2010) 'Pengiriman TKI Sektor Informal Ke Malaysia Akan Dibuka Awal April 2010', *PT Balanta Budi Prima*, 19 March. Online. Available: http://balanta.wordpress.com/2010/03/19/pengiriman-tki-sektor-informal-ke-malaysia-akan-dibuka-awal-april-2010/ (accessed 4 February 2013).

'Indonesian House Speaker OK with Malaysia's use of songket' (2012) *Jakarta Globe*, 21 September. Online. Available: www.thejakartaglobe.com/home/indonesian-house-speaker-ok-with-malaysias-use-of-songket/545691 (accessed 25 January 2013).

'Indonesia's *Verses of Love*' (2008) *IslamOnline*. Available: www.islamwomen.org/EngIw/HomePage/HPDetails8.aspx?id=1263 (accessed 1 March 2010).

Inglehart, R. and Welzel, C. (2005) *Modernization, Cultural Change and Democracy*, New York: Cambridge University Press.

Jackson, J.C. (1961) *Planters and Speculators: Chinese and European Agricultural Enterprise in Malaysia*, Kuala Lumpur: University of Malaya Press.

Jedamski, D. (2009) 'Introduction', in D. Jedamski (ed.) *Chewing Over the West: Occidental Narratives in Non-Western Readings*, Amsterdam: Rodopi.

Jetschke, A. and Rüland, J. (2009) 'Decoupling rhetoric and practice: the cultural limits of ASEAN cooperation', *Pacific Review*, 22(2): 179–203.

Jones, M. (2002) *Conflict and Confrontation in South-East Asia, 1961–1965: Britain, the United States, Indonesia and the Creation of Malaysia*, Cambridge: Cambridge University Press.

Jones, S. (2000) *Making Money Off Migrants: the Indonesian Exodus to Malaysia*, Wollongong, NSW: Capstrans, University of Wollongong.

'Judul filem, pengisian dan mentaliti penonton' (2009) *Cinema Malaysia*, 19 August. Online. Available: http://beritahiburan.blogspot.com/2009/08/judul-filem-pengisian-dan-mentaliti.html (accessed 22 January 2013).

Kahin, G.M. (1964) 'Malaysia and Indonesia', *Pacific Affairs*, 37(3): 253–70.

Kalir, B. (2010) *Latino Migrants in the Jewish State: Undocumented Lives in Israel*, Bloomington and Indianapolis: Indiana University Press.

Kassim, Y.R. (2005) *ASEAN Cohesion: Making Sense of Indonesian Reactions to Bilateral Disputes* (IIDS Commentaries, 15/2005), Singapore: Institute of Defence and Strategic Studies, Nanyang Technological University.

Katsumata, H. (2009) 'ASEAN and human rights: resisting Western pressure or emulating the West?', *Pacific Review*, 22(5): 619–37.

Kaur, A. (2005) 'Indonesian migrant workers in Malaysia', *Review of Indonesian and Malaysian Affairs*, 35(2): 3–30.

——(2006) 'Order (and disorder) at the border: mobility, international labour migration and border controls in Southeast Asia', in A. Kaur and I. Metcalfe (eds) *Mobility, Labour Migration and Border Controls in Asia*, New York: Palgrave MacMillan.

——and Diehl, F. (1996) 'Tin miners and tin mining in Indonesia, 1850–1950', *Asian Studies Review*, 20(2): 95–120.

Katzenstein, P.J. and Checkel, J.T. (2009) 'Preface' in J.T. Checkel and P.J. Katzenstein (eds) *European Identity*, Cambridge: Cambridge University Press.

Khalid, K.M. and Yacob, S. (2012) 'Managing Malaysia-Indonesia relations in the context of democratization: the emergence of non-state actors', *International Relations of the Asia-Pacific*, 12: 355–87.

Khoo, B.T. (2004) *Managing Ethnic Relations in Post-crisis Malaysia and Indonesia*, Geneva: United Nations Research Institute for Social Development.

Khoo, G.C. (2009) 'Reading the films of independent film-maker Yasmin Ahmad', in D.P.S. Goh, M. Gabrielpillai, P. Holden and G.C. Khoo (eds) *Race and Multiculturalism in Malaysia and Singapore*, Abingdon and New York: Routledge.

——(2010) 'Cinema: films made by women screenwriters, directors, and producers: Malaysia', in *Encyclopedia of Women & Islamic Cultures*, Brill Online. Available: http://referenceworks.brillonline.com/entries/encyclopedia-of-women-and-islamic-cultures/cinema-films-made-by-women-screenwriters-directors-and-producers-malaysia-COM_0646 (accessed 20 December 2012).

Khoo, J.E. (1996) *The Straits Chinese: A Cultural History*, Amsterdam and Kuala Lumpur: The Pepin Press.

Kivimaki, T. (2008) 'Competing globalization: the case of economic cooperation with Indonesia against international terrorism', in T. Chong (ed.) *Globalization and Its Counter-forces in Southeast Asia*, Singapore: ISEAS.

Klinken, G. van (2007) *Communal Violence and Democratization in Indonesia*, London and New York: Routledge.

Knaap, G. (2001) 'Manning the fleet: skippers, crews and shipowners in eighteenth-century Makassar', in E. Sedyawati and S. Zuhdi (eds) *Arung Samudra: Persembahan Memperingati Sembilan Windu A. B. Lapian*, Depok: Pusat Penilitian Kemasyarakatan dan Budaya/Lembaga Penelitian Universitas Indonesia.

Kneps, C.F. (2003) *Liberating Culture: Cross-Cultural Perspectives on Museums, Curation and Heritage Preservation*, Abingdon: Routledge.

Kortteinen, T. (2008) 'Islamic resurgence and the ethnicization of the Malaysian state: the case of Lina Joy', *Sojourn: Journal of Social Issues in Southeast Asia*, 23(2): 216–33.

Krismantari, I. (2010) 'Batik Frenzy Not Strictly Traditional', *The Jakarta Post*, 2 July. Online. Available: www.thejakartapost.com/news/2010/07/02/batik-frenzy-not-strictly-traditional.html (accessed 24 January 2013).

Krisna, Y. (2011) 'Mob destroys four wayang statues', *Jakarta Globe*, 19 September. Online. Available: www.thejakartaglobe.com/news/mob-destroys-four-wayang-statues/466195 (accessed 25 January 2013).

Kurnia, N. (2007) 'In the market of films: a conversation with Garin Nugroho', *Metro Magazine*, 154: 60–3.

Kusnanto, A. (2005) 'Geopolitik, pengendalian ruang laga, dan strategi pertahanan Indonesia', in B. Bandoro (ed.) *Perspektif Baru Keamanan Nasional*, Jakarta: Centre for International and Security Studies.

Laffan, M. (2011) *The Makings of Indonesian Islam: Orientalism and the Narration of a Sufi Past*, Princeton, NJ: Princeton University Press.

Lazuardi, G.C. (2009) *Maumu Apa, Malaysia? Konflik Indo-Malay dari Kacamata Seorang WNI di Malaysia*, Jakarta: Gramedia Pustaka Utama.

Lee, G.H. (1995) *Ethnic Conflict and the Development of Citizenship in Malaysia*, Boston, MA: Brandeis University.

Leifer, M. (1983) *Indonesia's Foreign Policy*, London: Royal Institute of International Affairs and Allen & Unwin.

Levitsky, S. and Way, L. (2002) 'The rise of competitive authoritarianism', *Journal of Democracy*, 13(2), 51–65.

Liddle, R.W. (2001) 'Introduction: crafting Indonesian democracy', in R.W. Liddle (ed.) *Crafting Indonesian Democracy*, Bandung: Penerbit Mizan.

Lim, T.H. (2011) 'Journalists having a nightmare in Palembang', *The Star*, 17 November: 69.

Lindquist, J. (2012) 'The elementary school teacher, the thug and his grandmother: informal brokers and transnational migration from Indonesia', *Pacific Affairs*, 85(1): 69–89.

Lindsay, J. (2003) 'Performing across the sound barrier', in J. Lindsay and T.Y. Ying (eds) *Babel or Behemoth: Language Trends in Asia*, Singapore: Asia Research Institute.

——(2010) 'Media and morality: pornography post Suharto', in K. Sen and D.T. Hill (eds) *Politics and the Media in Twenty-First Century Indonesia: Decade of Democracy*, London and New York: Routledge.

——(2012) 'Language boom', *Tempo English*, 21 October: 50–1.

Liow, J.C. (2003) 'Malaysia's illegal Indonesian migrant labour problem: in search of solutions', *Contemporary Southeast Asia*, 25(1): 44–64.

——(2005) *The Politics of Indonesia–Malaysia Relations: One Kin, Two Nations*, Abingdon: New York: Routledge.

Liu, H. (2011) *China and the Shaping of Indonesia, 1949–1965*, Singapore: NUS Press.

Lloyd, K., Suchet-Pearson, S., Wright, S. and Burarrwanga, L. (2010) 'Stories of crossings and connections from Bawaka, North East Arnhem Land, Australia', *Social & Cultural Geography*, 11(7): 701–17.

Loh, F.K.W. (2001) 'Where has (ethnic) politics gone? the case of the BN non-Malay politicians and political parties', in R.W. Hefner (ed.) *The Politics of Multiculturalism: Pluralism and Citizenship in Malaysia, Singapore, and Indonesia*, Honolulu: University of Hawai'i Press.

'Lost in the haze: the story of a couple's tragic death in Riau's blaze' (2013) *Jakarta Globe*, 2 July. Online. Available: www.thejakartaglobe.com/news/lost-in-the-haze-the-story-of-a-couples-tragic-death-in-riaus-blaze/ (accessed 2 July 2013).

Lubis, B., Ramelan, K. and Syahban, J. (1998) 'Rebut Sinta, pulihkan rupiah', *Gatra*, 7 February: 106.

Mackie, J.A.C. (1974) *Konfrontasi: The Indonesian-Malaysian Dispute,1963–1966*, Kuala Lumpur: Oxford University Press.

——(ed.) (1976) *The Chinese in Indonesia: Five Essays*, Melbourne: Nelson.

——and Coppel, C.A. (1976) 'A preliminary survey', in J.A.C. Mackie (ed.) *The Chinese in Indonesia: Five Essays*, Melbourne: Nelson.

MacKinnon, I. (2009) 'Teenage model who married Malaysian prince "flees abusive marriage"', *The Telegraph*, 1 June. Online. Available: www.telegraph.co.uk/news/worldnews/asia/indonesia/5422894/Teenage-model-who-married-Malaysian-prince-flees-abusive-marriage.html (accessed 15 January 2013).

Macknight, C.C. (1976) *The Voyage to Marege': Macassan Trepangers in Northern Australia*, Carlton: Melbourne University Press.

——(2008) 'Harvesting the memory: open beaches in Makassar and Arnhem Land', in P. Veth, P. Sutton and M. Neale (eds) *Strangers on the Shore: Early Coastal Contacts in Australia*, Canberra: National Museum of Australia.

——(2011) 'The view from Marege': Australian knowledge of Makassar and the impact of the trepang industry across two centuries', *Aboriginal History*, 35: 121–43.

Mahayana, M.S. (2001) *Akar Melayu: Sistem Sastra dan Konflik Ideologi di Indonesia dan Malaysia*, Magelang: IndonesiaTera.

Maier, H. (2004) *We Are Playing Relatives: A Survey of Malay Writing*, Leiden: KITLV Press.

'Malaysia celebrates cup success, declares holiday' (2010) *EuroSport.com*. 29 December. Online. Available: http://uk.eurosport.yahoo.com/30122010/2/malaysia-celebrates-cup-success-declares-holiday.html (accessed 17 December 2012).

'Malaysia hits out at Indonesia over boundary controversy' (2011) *Jakarta Globe*, 14 October. Online. Available: www.thejakartaglobe.com/news/malaysia-hits-out-at-indonesia-over-boundary-controversy/471597 (accessed 17 January 2013).

'Malaysia, Indonesia in a dance-off' (2012) *Jakarta Globe*, 18 June. Online. Available: www.thejakartaglobe.com/home/malaysia-indonesia-in-a-dance-off/524895 (accessed 17 January 2013).

'Malaysia to reward polygamous husbands' (2011) *OnIslam*, 30 June. Online. Available: www.onislam.net/english/news/asia-pacific/452855-malaysia-to-reward-polygamous-husbands.html (accessed 29 January 2013).

'Malaysian ambassador asks for more positive coverage' (2009) *The Jakarta Post*, 6 August. Online. Available: www.thejakartapost.com/news/2009/08/06/malaysian-ambassador-asks-more-positive-coverage.html (accessed 15 January 2013).

Malaysian National Commission for UNESCO (2008) *Malaysia: 50 Years of Membership in UNESCO*, Kuala Lumpur: NATCOM.

'Malaysian official: Tor-Tor dance originates in Indonesia, but … ' (2012) *Jakarta Globe*, 20 September. Online. Available: www.thejakartaglobe.com/home/malaysian-official-tor-tor-dance-originates-in-indonesia-but/545496#.UFt8wAb7m34.email (accessed 17 January 2013).

'Malaysian prince wins £1.2 million defamation suit against wife' (2010) *The Telegraph*, 11 March. Online. Available: www.telegraph.co.uk/news/worldnews/asia/malaysia/7420095/Malaysian-Prince-Wins-1.2-million-defamation-suit-against-wife.html (accessed 15 January 2013).

'Malaysian royal denies abuse allegations: lawyer' (2009) *AFP*, 11 June. Online. Available: www.google.com/hostednews/afp/article/ALeqM5hVJn1qTy9r6_UZzNXi3pythredqQ (accessed 15 January 2013).

'Malaysian singer opts for Indonesian pop sensibility' (2007) *MelayuOnline.com*, 24 December. Online. Available: http://melayuonline.com/eng/news/read/2660 (accessed 22 January 2013).

'Malaysian XI vs 100,011: So how? Do they have a chance or not?' (2011) *The Star*, 17 November: 72.

Malik, C. (2009) 'Malaysia anthem furor hits wrong note, says Indonesian expert', *Jakarta Globe*, September 3. Online. Available: www.thejakartaglobe.com/news/malaysia-anthem-furor-hits-wrong-note-says-indonesian-expert/327697 (accessed 21 February 2013).

Malley, W. (2003) 'Indonesia in 2002: the rising cost of inaction', *Asian Survey*, 43: 135–46.

'Manohara dan Fakhry: Sama-sama Lapor Polisi' (2009) *Bintang Indonesia*, June: 8–11.

Mapson, L. (2010) 'Reog Ponorogo: a bilateral spat reignites a unique cultural practice', *Inside Indonesia*, 102. Online. Available: www.insideindonesia.org/weekly-articles/reog-ponorogo (accessed 17 January 2013).

Marching, S.T. (2008) 'Herlinatiens: between lesbianism, Islam and feminism', *Inter-Asia Cultural Studies*, 9(1): 7–26.

Mattangkilang, T. (2012) 'Indonesia–Malaysia border spat lingers', *Jakarta Globe*, 17 December. Online. Available: www.thejakartaglobe.com/news/indonesia-malaysia-border-spat-lingers/562189 (accessed 6 January 2013).

Maulia, E. (2009) 'Batik selected for UNESCO cultural heritage list', *The Jakarta Post*, 8 September. Online. Available: www.thejakartapost.com/news/2009/09/08/batik-selected-unesco-cultural-heritage-list.html (accessed 24 August 2012).

Mauzy, D. (1993) 'Malay political hegemony and "coercive consociationalism"', in J. McGarry (ed.) *Malay Political Hegemony*, New York: Routledge.

McKay, B. (2010) 'Reclaiming history: the politics of memory and trauma in the films of Amir Muhammad', in Y.S. Guan (ed.) *Media, Culture and Society in Malaysia*, London: Routledge.

——(2012) 'Auteur-ing Malaysia: Yasmin Ahmad and dreamed communities', in M.A. Ingawanij and B. McKay (eds) *Glimpses of Freedom: Independent Cinema in Southeast Asia*, Ithaca, NY: Southeast Asia Program, Cornell University.

Me, A. (2011) 'Letter: RI-Malaysia's Cultural Disputes', *The Jakarta Post*, 5 January. Online. Available: www.thejakartapost.com/news/2011/01/05/letter-rimalaysia's-cultural-disputes.html (accessed 23 January 2013).

Mee, W. (2010) 'A traffic in *songket*: Malay translocal identities in Sambas', *Journal of Southeast Asian Studies*, 41(2): 321–39.

Meereboer, M. (1998) 'Fishing for credit: patronage and debt relations in the Spermonde Archipelago, Indonesia', in K. Robinson and M. Paeni (eds) *Living Through Histories: Culture, History and Social Life in South Sulawesi*, Canberra: Department of Anthropology, Research School of Pacific and Asian Studies, the Australian National University.

Merdeka Center for Opinion Research (2010) *Peninsular Malaysia Voters Opinion Poll Quarter 4*. Online. Available: www.scribd.com/doc/45855828/Survey-Release-Dec-2010 (accessed 12 February 2013).

Mietzner, M. (2009) *Military Politics, Islam, and the State in Indonesia: From Turbulent Transition to Democratic Consolidation*, Singapore: Institute of Southeast Asian Studies.

——and Aspinall, E. (2010) 'Problems of democratisation in Indonesia: an overview', in E. Aspinall and M. Mietzner (eds) *Problems of Democratisation in Indonesia: Elections, Instituions and Society*, Singapore: Institute of Southeast Asian Studies.

Miksic, J. and Tranchini, M. (1990) *Borobudur: Golden Tales of the Buddhas*, Boston, MA: Shambala.

Milner, A. (2008) *The Malays*, Chichester: Wiley-Blackwell.

Minnesota Population Center, Statistics Indonesia (2012) *Indonesia Population Census 2010 from the Integrated Public Use Microdata Series*, Minneapolis: University of Minnesota.

Mishler, W. and Rose, R. (1997) 'Trust, distrust, and skepticism: popular evaluation of civil and political institutions in post-Communist societies', *Journal of Politics*, 2: 418–51.

Moehkardi (1983) *Sendratari Ramayana Prambanan: Segi Seni dan Sejarahnya*, Yogyakarta: PT Taman Wisata Candi Bodobudur Prambanan and Ratu Boko.

Mohamad, M.B. (1996) 'Globalization: what it means to small nations', Inaugural Lecture of the Prime Ministers of Malaysia Fellowship Exchange Programme, Kuala Lumpur, 24 July. Online. Available: www.twnside.org.sg/title/small-cn.htm (accessed 16 January 2013).

Moravcsik, A. (1993) 'Preference and power in the European Community: a liberal intergovernmental approach', *Journal of Common Market Studies*, 31(4): 473–524.

Muhammad, A. (2006) 'Why is Lelaki Komunis Terakhir banned in Malaysia?', *Komunis & Kampung*, 9 May. Online. Available: http://lastcommunist.blogspot.com/2006/05/why-is-lelaki-komunis-terakhir-banned.html (accessed 29 January 2013).

——(2009) *Yasmin Ahmad's Films*, Petaling Jaya: Matahari Books.

Munro-Kua, A. (1996) *Authoritarian Populism in Malaysia*, Basingstoke: Palgrave MacMillan.

Murphy, A.M. (2010) 'US rapprochement with Indonesia: from problem state to partner', *Contemporary Southeast Asia*, 32(3): 362–87.

Murty, M. (2011) 'No bad blood with Indonesians', *New Straits Times*, 25 November: 1.

Nair, S. (2009) 'Colonialism, nationalism, ethnicity: constructing identity and difference', in L.T. Ghee, A. Gomes and A. Rahman (eds) *Multiethnic Malaysia: Past, Present and Future*, Petaling Jaya: SIRD.

'Najib could face hardliner resistance to ISA appeal' (2011) *Today Online*, 20 September. Available: http://imcmsimages.mediacorp.sg/CMSFileserver/documents/006/PDF/2011 0920/2009HNP004.pdf (accessed 19 February 2013).

Narine, S. (1998) 'ASEAN and the management of regional security', *Pacific Affairs*, 71(2): 195–214.

Nasir, Z. (2009) 'Agar tak kecewa terhadap Malaysia', *Majalah Tempo Online*, September. Available : http://majalah.tempointeraktif.com/id/arsip/2009/09/14/KL/mbm.200909 14.KL131379.id.html (accessed 14 September 2009).

'No-holds barred encounter: Malaysia up against hostile crowd and a host dying to exact revenge' (2011) *The Star*, 17 November: 68.

Noor, F. (2000) 'From Majapahit to Putrajaya: the *kris* as a symptom of civilizational development and decline', *Journal of Southeast Asia Research*, 8(3): 239–79.

Nor, M.A.M. (2011) 'Eclecticism and syncretic traditions: the making of Malay folk dance', in M.A.M. Nor and S. Burridge (eds) *Sharing Identities: Celebrating Dance in Malaysia*, London: Routledge.

Norris, P. (1999) *Critical Citizens: Global Support for Democratic Governance*, Oxford: Oxford University Press.

——(2011) *Democratic Deficit: Critical Citizens Revisited*, New York: Cambridge University Press.

'Obesity: Malaysia is No. 1 in Southeast Asia' (2011) *The Malaysian Insider*, 14 November. Online. Available: www.themalaysianinsider.com/malaysia/article/obes ity-malaysia-is-no.-1-in-southeast-asia/ (accessed 23 January 2013).

Omar, N. (2011) 'Sexing Islam: religion and contemporary Malaysian cinema', in A.N. Weintraub (ed.) *Islam and Popular Culture in Indonesia and Malaysia*, London and New York: Routledge.

Ong, A. (1996) 'Cultural citizenship as subject-making: immigrants negotiate racial and cultural boundaries in the United States', *Cultural Anthropology*, 37(5): 737–62.

——(2010) 'Token gestures: despite recent government negotiations, Indonesian migrant workers in Malaysia remain disempowered', *Inside Indonesia*, 100. Online. Available: www.insideindonesia.org/feature-editions/token-gestures (accessed 4 February 2013).

Ong, M. (1987) 'Government and opposition in parliament: the rules of the game', in Z.H. Ahmad (ed.) *Government and Politics of Malaysia,* Oxford and New York: Oxford University Press.

Onghoklam (1970) 'The case for assimilation', in H. Feith and L. Castles (eds) *Indonesian Political Thinking 1945–1965*, Ithaca, NY, and London: Cornell University Press.

Oratmangun, D. (2009) 'Working towards a strategic partnership: a perspective from Indonesia on ASEAN–EU relations', unpublished paper presented at *EU-ASEAN Relations in the 21st Century: Towards a 'Strategic Partnership*, 26–27 November 2009, Monash University, Melbourne.

Othman, N. (2012) 'A look at the prevailing (mal)practice of polygamy in Malaysia today', *The Malaysian Insider*, 23 October. Online. Available: www.themalaysianinsid er.com/sideviews/article/a-look-at-the-prevailing-malpractice-of-polygamy-in-malaysia-today-norani-othman (accessed 29 January 2013).

Pakatan Rakyat (2011) *Ubah Sekarang, Selamatkan Malaysia!*. Online. Available: www.pakatanrakyat.info/wp-content/uploads/2010/12/Buku-Jingga-English-Abridged. pdf (accessed 19 February 2013).

Parekh, B. (1991) 'British citizenship and cultural difference', in G. Andrews (ed.) *Citizenship*, London: Lawrence and Wishart.

Pelizzo, R. (2010) 'Antonio Negri, Reflections on *Empire*', *Australian Journal of International Affairs*, 64(2): 248–9.

Pemberton, J. (1994) *On the Subject of 'Java'*, Ithaca, NY, and London: Cornell University Press.

Perlman, M. (1999) 'The traditional Javanese performing arts in the twilight of the New Order', *Indonesia*, 68: 1–37.

Pevehouse, J.C. (2005) *Democracy from Above: Regional Organizations and Democratization*, Cambridge: Cambridge University Press.

Peycam, P. (2012) 'Broadening intercultural dialogue', *The Newsletter*, 62: 3.

Poulgrain, G. (1998) *The Genesis of Konfrontasi: Malaysia, Brunei, Indonesia, 1945–1965*, Bathurst: Crawford House Publishing.

Prathivi, N. and Wardany, I. (2009) 'Protests over presence of Pendet dance in Malaysia's tourism ad continue', *The Jakarta Post*, 23 August. Online. Available: www.thejakartapost.com/news/2009/08/23/protests-over-presence-pendet-dance-malaysia's-tourism-ad-continue.html (accessed 25 January 2013).

Purwanto, W.H. (2010) *Panas Dingin: Hubungan Indonesia–Malaysia*, Jakarta: CMB Press.

'Putra raja Kelantan culik, sekap dan silet model Indonesia!' (2009) *Kompas*, 21 April. Online. Available: http://entertainment.kompas.com/read/2009/04/21/e093505/Putra.Raja.Kelantan.Culik.Sekap.dan.Silet.Model.Indonesia (accessed 15 January 2013).

Raharto, A. (2007) 'Indonesian labour migration: issues and challenges', *International Journal on Multicultural Societies*, 9(2): 219–35.

Rahman, T.A. (1969) *May 13: Before and After*, Kuala Lumpur: Utusan Melayu Press.

Raslan, K. (1996) *Ceritalah: Malaysia in Transition*, Singapore: Times Books International.

——(2010) *Ceritalah Indonesia*, Jakarta: Kepustakaan Populer Gramedia.

——(2012) 'Same but different', *Jakarta Globe*, 20 December. Online. Available: www.thejakartaglobe.com/columns/karim-raslan-same-but-different/562711 (accessed 18 January 2013).

——(2013) 'Restoring values', *Jakarta Globe*, 17 January. Online. Available: www.thejakartaglobe.com/opinion/karim-raslan-restoring-values/565996 (accessed 25 January 2013).

Reid, A. (2000) *Charting the Shape of Early Modern Southeast Asia*, Singapore: ISEAS.

Resink, G.J. (1975) 'From the Old Mahabharata – to the New Ramayana – Order', *Bijdragen tot de Taal-, Land-en Volkenkunden*, 131(2/3): 214–35.

Riady, J. (2012) 'ASEAN engagement with Burma shows power of good neighbors', *Jakarta Globe*, 10 May. Online. Available: www.thejakartaglobe.com/opinion/asean-engagement-with-burma-shows-power-of-good-neighbors/516936 (accessed 4 February 2013).

Ricklefs, M.C., Lockhart, B., Lau, A., Reyes, P. and Aung-Thwin, M. (2010) *A New History of Southeast Asia*, Basingstoke: Palgrave MacMillan.

Riddell, P. (2008) 'Globalisation, Western and Islamic, into the 21st century: perspectives from Southeast Asia and beyond', *Asian Christian Review*, 2 (2/3): 128–52.

——(2009) 'A film window into political struggle in Malaysia', *Indonesia and the Malay World*, 37(109): 397–400.

Rizal, Y. and Rafiq, A. (2009) 'Opera Terang Bulan', *Tempo*, 20 September: 103.

Robinson, K. (2008) *Gender, Islam and Democracy in Indonesia*, London: Routledge.

Roeder, O.G. (1969) *The Smiling General*, Jakarta: Gunung Agung.

Roff, W.R. (1967) *The Origins of Malay Nationalism*, New Haven, CT: Yale University Press.

Rose, R., Mishler, W. and Haerpfer, C. (1998) *Democracy and its Alternatives: Understanding Post-Communist Societies*, Cambridge: Polity Press.

Rüland, J. (2009) 'Deepening ASEAN cooperation through democratization? The Indonesian legislature and foreign policymaking', *International Relations of the Asia-Pacific*, 9(3): 373–402.

Sadiq, K. (2005) 'When states prefer non-citizens over citizens: conflict over illegal immigration into Malaysia', *International Studies Quarterly*, 49(1): 101–22.

——(2009) *Paper Citizens: How Illegal Immigrants Acquire Citizenship in Developing Countries*, Oxford and New York: Oxford University Press.

Saran, M. and Khanna, V.C. (2004) *The Ramayana in Indonesia*, Delhi: Ravi Dayal.

Sastrosatomo, S. (1998) *Politik Dosomuko Rezim Orde Baru: Rapuh dan Sengsarakan Rakyat*, Jakarta: Pusat Dokumentasi Politik 'GUNTUR 49'.

Scarpello, F. (2010) 'God as Politics in Malaysia', *Asia Times*, 16 January. Online. Available: www.atimes.com/atimes/Southeast_Asia/LA16Ae02.html (accessed 19 February 2013).

Schimmelfennig, F. and Sedelmeier, U. (eds) (2005) *The Europeanization of Central and Eastern Europe*, Ithaca, NY: Cornell University Press.

Schuck, P.H. (1987) 'The status and rights of undocumented aliens in the United States', *International Migration*, 25: 125–38.

Sebastian, L.C. and Lanti, I.G. (2009) 'Perceiving Indonesian Approaches to International Relations Theory', in A. Acharya (ed.) *Non-Western International Relations Theory: Perspectives on and Beyond Asia*, London: Routledge.

Sen, K. and Hill, D. (2000) *Media, Culture and Politics in Indonesia*, Oxford: Oxford University Press.

Setiyaji, A. (2009) *Manodrama: Fakta atau Rekayasa*, Yogyakarta: Best Publisher.

Shamsul, A.B. (2001) 'The redefinition of politics and the transformation of Malaysian pluralism', in R. Hefner (ed.) *The Politics of Multiculturalism: Pluralism and Citizenship in Malaysia, Singapore, and Indonesia*, Honolulu: University of Hawai'i Press.

——(2008) *Many Cultures, Many Cultures, One Nation: The Malaysian Experience* (UKM Ethnic Studies Paper Series 2), Selangor: Universiti Kebangsaan Malaysia, Institute of Ethnic Studies.

Sheridan, G. (2010) 'Djalal a friend in Washington', *The Australian*, 23 September: 12.

Shin, D.C. (2011) *Confucianism and Democratization in East Asia*, New York: Cambridge University Press.

Sidel, J.T. (2006) *Riots, Pogroms, Jihad: Religious Violence in Indonesia*, Ithaca, NY: Cornell University Press.

Sindhunata (1983) *Anak Bajang Menggiring Angin*, Jakarta: PT Gramedia Pustaka Utama.

Siregar, A.S. (2011) 'Review: *Kehormatan di Balik Kerudung*', *At the Movies*, 28 October. Online. Available: http://amiratthemovies.wordpress.com/2011/10/28/review-kehor matan-di-balik-kerudung-2011/ (accessed 29 January 2013).

Slimming, J. (1969) *Malaysia: Death of a Democracy*, London and Southampton: Camelot Press.

Snyder, J. (2000) *From Voting to Violence: Democratization and Nationalist Conflict*, New York and London: W.W. Norton.

Somers, M. (1964) *Peranakan Chinese Politics in Indonesia*, Ithaca, NY: Cornell Modern Indonesia Project.

'Southeast Asia' (2011) *Migration News*, 18 (3). Online. Available: http://migration. ucdavis.edu/mn/more.php?id=3700_0_3_0 (accessed 3 February 2013).

Soysal, Y. (1994) 'Limits of citizenship: migrants and postnational membership in Europe and the nation state', in D. Cesarani and M. Fulbrook (eds) *Citizenship, Nationality and Migration in Europe*, London: Routledge.

Stephenson, P. (2007) *The Outsiders Within: Telling Australia's Indigenous-Asian Story*, Sydney: UNSW Press.

Stubbs, R. (2009) 'Meeting the challenges of region-Building in ASEAN', in M. Beeson (ed.) *Contemporary Southeast Asia*, 2nd edn, Basingstoke: Palgrave MacMillan.

Subritzky, J. (1999) *Confronting Sukarno: British, American, Australian and New Zealand Diplomacy in the Malaysian-Indonesian Confrontation, 1961–65*, Basingstoke: Palgrave MacMillan.

Suditomo, K., Pudjiarti, H. and Dimyathi. M. (2009) 'Membatik di negeri jiran', *Tempo*, 20 September: 99–102.

Sukma, R. (1999) *Indonesia and China: the Politics of a Troubled Relationship*, London: Routledge.

——(2008) 'Political development: a democracy agenda for ASEAN?', in D.K. Emmerson (ed.) *Hard Choices: Security, Democracy and Regionalism*, Stanford, CA: Walter H. Shorenstein Asia-Pacific Research Center.

——(2009) *Democracy Building in South East Asia: the ASEAN Security Community and Options for the European Union*, Stockholm: International IDEA.

——(2010) 'Indonesia's elections: defective system, resilient democracy', in E. Aspinall and M. Mietzner (eds.) *Problems of Democratisation in Indonesia: Elections, Institutions and Society*, Singapore: Institute of Southeast Asian Studies.

Suryadi, L. (1981) *Pengakuan Pariyem*, Jakarta: Sinar Harapan.

Suryadinata, L. (ed.) (1999) *Political Thinking of the Indonesian Chinese, 1900–1995*, Singapore: Singapore University Press.

——(2002) 'Peranakan Chinese identities in Singapore and Malaysia: a re-examination', in L. Suryadinata (ed.) *Ethnic Chinese in Singapore and Malaysia*, Singapore: Times Academic Press.

——(2010) 'Peranakan Chinese in Indonesia, Malaysia and Singapore: the socio-political dimension', in L. Suryadinata (ed.) *Peranakan Chinese in Globalizing Southeast Asia*, Singapore: Chinese Heritage Centre.

Suryodiningrat, M. (2004) 'Looking for common values, a community driven ASEAN', *The Jakarta Post*, 9 August. Online. Available: www.thejakartapost.com/news/2004/08/09/looking-common-values-community-driven-asean.html (accessed 4 February 2013).

Susanto, M. (2007) *Semedi Ning Jenar: Panggung Tafsir dan Kearifan Sejarah*, KPG Jakarta: Kepustakaan Popular Gramedia.

Susilo, T.A. (2009) *Indonesia vs Malaysia: Membandingkan Peta Kekuatan Indonesia & Malaysia*, Yogyakarta: Garasi.

Sutherland, H. (2000) 'Trepang and wangkang: the China trade of eighteenth-century Makassar c. 1720s–1840s', in R. Tol, K. van Dijk and G. Acciaioli (eds) *Authority and Enterprise Among the Peoples of South Sulawesi*, Leiden: KITLV Press.

'Tabik penyokong' (2011) *Sinar Harian*, 24 November: 2.

'Tampilan peta sebaran hotspot' (2013) Direktorat Pengendalian Kebakaran Hutan, Direktorat Jenderal Perlindungan Hutan dan Konservasi Alam, Kementerian Kehutanan, 18 June. Online. Available: www.indofire.org/indofire/hotspot (accessed 30 July 2013).

Tan, L.E. (2002) 'Baggage from the past, eyes on the future: Chinese education in Malaysia today', in L. Suryadinata (ed.) *Ethnic Chinese in Singapore and Malaysia*, Singapore: Times Academic Press.

Tarling, N. (2006) *Regionalism in Southeast Asia: To Foster the Political Will*, London: Routledge.

Tay, S.S.C. (2008) 'Blowing smoke: regional cooperation, Indonesian democracy, and the haze', in D.K. Emmerson (ed.) *Hard Choices: Security, Democracy, and Regionalism in Southeast Asia*, Stanford, CA: Walter H. Shorenstein Asia-Pacific Research Center.

Taylor, K. (2009) 'Cultural Landscapes and Asia: Reconciling International and Southeast Asian Regional Values', *Landscape Research*, 34(1): 7–31.

Thayer, C.A. (2008) 'Radical Islam and political terrorism in Southeast Asia', in T. Chong (ed.) *Globalisation and Its Counter-forces in Southeast Asia*, Singapore: ISEAS.

Ting, H. (2009) 'Malaysian history textbooks and the discourse of *Ketuanan Melayu*', in D.P.S. Goh, M. Gabrielpillai, P. Holden and G.C. Khoo (eds) *Race and Multiculturalism in Malaysia and Singapore*, Abingdon and New York: Routledge.

'Two die at Indonesia-Malaysia football match stampede' (2011) *BBC News Asia*, 21 November. Online. Available: www.bbc.co.uk/news/world-asia-15831434 (accessed 23 January 2013).

UNESCO (2009) 'Indonesian Batik'. Online. Available: www.unesco.org/culture/ich/index.php?RL=00170 (accessed 24 January 2013).

UNESCO (2010) 'Indonesian Angklung'. Online. Available: www.unesco.org/culture/ich/index.php?lg=en&pg=00011&rl=00393 (accessed 24 January 2013).

UNESCO (2011) 'Melaka and George Town'. Online. Available: http://whc.unesco.org/en/list/1223 (accessed 25 January 2013).

'Unesco recognizes 'angklung' as intangible cultural heritage' (2011) *The Jakarta Post*, 19 January. Online. Available: www.thejakartapost.com/news/2011/01/19/unesco-recogn izes-%E2%80%98angklung%E2%80%99-intangible-cultural-heritage.html (accessed 24 January 2013).

'Ungracious hosts' (2011) *New Straits Times*, 23 November: 43.

Usman, S. and Din, I. (2009a) *Ancaman Negeri Jiran: Dari 'GANYANG MALAYSIA' Sampai Konflik Ambalat*, Yogyakarta: MedPress.

——(2009b) *Heboh Ambalat: Ternyata Malaysia Ingin Merebut Sumber Minyak Indonesia*, Yogyakarta: Narasi.

Utami, A. (1998) *Saman*, Jakarta: Kepustakaan Populer Gramedia.

Vickers, A. (1997) '"Malay Identity": Modernity, Invented Tradition, and Forms of Knowledge', *Review of Indonesian and Malaysian Affairs*, 31(1): 173–211. Reprinted in T.P. Barnard (ed.) (2004) *Contesting Malayness: Malay Identity Across Boundaries*, Singapore: Singapore University Press.

Visser, L.E. and Adhuri, D.A. (2010) 'Territorialization Re-examined: Transborder Marine Resources Exploitation in Southeast Asia and Australia', in W. de Jong, D. Snelder and N. Ishikara (eds) *Transborder Governance of Forest, Water and Trees*, London: Earthscan.

Voon, P.K. (2007) 'State and nation: an overview and Malaysian perspective', in P.K. Voon (ed.) *Malaysian Chinese and Nation-Building: Before Merdeka and Fifty Years After*, Kuala Lumpur: Centre for Malaysian Studies.

Wang, G. (2010) 'The *peranakan* phenomenon: pre-national, marginal, and transnational', in L. Suryadinata (ed.) *Peranakan Chinese in Globalizing Southeast Asia*, Singapore: Chinese Heritage Centre.

Waterson, R. (2011) *Paths and Rivers: Sa'dan Toraja Society in Transformation.* Leiden: KITLV Press.

Weintraub, A.N. (2011) 'Introduction: the study of Islam and popular culture in Indonesia and Malaysia', in A.N. Weintraub (ed.) *Islam and Popular Culture in Indonesia and Malaysia*, London: Routledge.

Weiss, M.L. (2010) 'Malaysia–Indonesia bilateral relations: sibling rivals in a fraught family', in N. Gamesan and R. Amer (eds) *International Relations in Southeast Asia: Between Bilateralism and Multilateralism*, Singapore: ISEAS Publishing.

Wichelen, S. van (2009) 'Polygamy talk and the politics of feminism: contestations over masculinity in a new Muslim Indonesia', *Journal of International Women's Studies*, 11(1): 173–87.

Widodo, A. (2008) 'Writing for God: piety and consumption in popular Islam', *Inside Indonesia*, 93. Online. Available: www.insideindonesia.org/weekly-articles/writing-for-god (accessed 29 January 2013).

Williams, L. (2007) 'Interview with Garin Nugroho', *Electric Sheep: a Deviant View of Cinema*, 31 August. Online. Available: www.electricsheepmagazine.co.uk/features/2007/08/31/interview-with-garin-nugroho (accessed 22 January 2012).

Willmott, D.E. (1960) *The Chinese of Semarang: A Changing Minority Community in Indonesia*, Ithaca, NY: Cornell University Press.

Wong, D.T.K. (2007) 'The formation of Malaysia: forging a nation-state from the crucible of colonialism', in P.K. Voon (ed.) *Malaysian Chinese and Nation-Building: Before Merdeka and Fifty Years After*, Kuala Lumpur: Centre for Malaysian Studies.

World Values Survey Association (2008) *World Values Survey 2005–2008 wave datasets.* Online. Available: www.worldvaluessurvey.org (accessed 12 February 2013).

Wyvern (2012) Comment posted, 20 June, in response to 'Malaysia, Indonesia in a dance-off'. Online. Available: www.thejakartaglobe.com/home/malaysia-indonesia-in-a-dance-off/524895 (accessed 17 January 2013).

Yoong, S. (2010) 'Indonesians vent on Twitter after loss to Malaysia'. *USA Today*, 27 December. Online. Available: http://usatoday30.usatoday.com/sports/soccer/2010-12-27-3918584383_x.htm (accessed 17 December 2012).

Yudhoyono, S.B. (2010) 'The national speech of the President of the Republic of Indonesia', delivered to The People's Consultative Assembly, Jakarta, 16 August.

Yunus, N.A. (2011) *Malaysian Batik: Reinventing a Tradition*, Singapore: Tuttle Publishing.

Index

Aa Gym 125
Aceh, Islamic orientation 117
AFF Cup final 2010 75–76
Ahmad, Yasmin *see* Yasmin Ahmad
air pollution: Indonesian response 208;
    Southeast Asia 180, 208–9
Al Qaeda 117
Alatas, Ali 19
Alliance government, in Malaysia 149,
    150–51
Ambalat dispute 7, 29, 35, 181, 183–84
Amir Muhammad 135
Anderson, Benedict 43, 94
angklung 42, 88n1; UNESCO cultural
    heritage listing 67, 69, 85
anti-American sentiment 11, 12, 13, 44
anti-China policy, of Indonesia 152
anti-colonial sentiment 21
anti-communist stance, of Indonesian
    army 151
anti-Indonesia sentiment 4
anti-Malaysia sentiment 11, 19–20, 23,
    69, 70–77, 78; in Indonesia 4, 210
anti-pornography legislation 124
anti-US sentiment 196
anti-Western protests 123
anti-Western sentiment 11, 13, 189–90
Anuar Zain 66
Arabic script, promotion of 13
Arnhem Land–Makassar encounter 93,
    98, 100–103, 114
ASA *see* Association of Southeast Asia
Asaat Datuk Mudo 147–48
ASEAN 17, 51; Committee on Culture
    and Information 54; and
    democratisation 193; divisions within
    187–88; founding 26–27, 45, 46; and
    Indonesia 180–81, 188, 190, 191;
    Indonesian dissatisfaction 179; and

labour migration 185–86; non-
    interference principle 55; and the
    Ramayana 52–56
ASEAN Football Federation *see* AFF
ASEAN Way 56, 191, 192; cultural
    underlay 53
Asia Barometer surveys 196–201, 205–6
Asian Civilisations Museum 42, 96
Asian financial crisis 152
aspirational piety 122
assimilation policies, Indonesian 148
Association of Southeast Asia 25, 26
Association of Southeast Asian Nations
    see ASEAN
Australian aborigines 98, 100, 101–3
Australia–Indonesia relationship 188
authoritarianism: in Indonesia 195; in
    Malaysia 92, 195, 198
Ayat-Ayat Cina (film) 127–28
Ayu Utami 123

baba see peranakan Chinese, in Malaysia
Badan Permusjawaratan
    Kewarganegaraan Indonesia *see*
    BAPERKI
Badawi, Abdullah 32
Bahasa Indonesia 48–50
Bahasa Melayu 48–50; as official
    language 151
Balai Pustaka novels 9
Bali Democracy Forum 188
Bandung, as tourist destination 32
Bandung Conference (1955) 24
BAPERKI 147, 148
Baperki University 147
Barisan Nasional 154, 200, 201
batik 38, 39, 43; Terengganu factories
    81; Indonesian artisans in Malaysia
    81–82; industry in Indonesia 85–86;

For Product Safety Concerns and Information please contact our EU
representative GPSR@taylorandfrancis.com
Taylor & Francis Verlag GmbH, Kaufingerstraße 24, 80331 München, Germany